TAP ROOTS

ALSO BY MARK KNOWLES

The Tap Dance Dictionary
(McFarland, 1998)

TAP ROOTS

The Early History of Tap Dancing

by MARK KNOWLES

McFarland & Company, Inc., Publishers
Jefferson, North Carolina, and London

Library of Congress Cataloguing-in-Publication Data

Knowles, Mark, 1954–
Tap roots : the early history of tap dancing / by Mark Knowles.
p. cm.
Includes bibliographical references and index.
ISBN 0-7864-1267-4 (illustrated case binding : 50# alkaline paper) ∞
1. Tap dancing — History. I. Title.
GV1794 .K67 2002   792.7'8 — dc21   2002000751

British Library cataloguing data are available

On the cover: Silhouette of a challenge dance as depicted on
a playbill from Bryant's Minstrels (January 24, 1859).

Manufactured in the United States of America

*McFarland & Company, Inc., Publishers
Box 611, Jefferson, North Carolina 28640
www.mcfarlandpub.com*

For Don Keller, a true friend

Acknowledgments

I received much assistance and encouragement in writing this book.

I would like to thank Carl Rieder and the Newport Harbor Academy of Dentistry for starting me on this project by asking me to give a lecture on the history of tap dancing. I would also like to thank Ron and Gloria Cocking for spurring me on to turn the lecture into a book, and Debbie Roberts of Showstopper American Dance Championships for expressing her enthusiasm about my writing.

I would like to acknowledge the entire faculty and staff of La Salle High School in Pasadena for their encouragement and support, especially Kathleen Peck, who allowed me to take reference books out on loan, Marie Pedersen for the use of the fax machine, and Tina Bonacci and Anne E. Johnston for their advice on how to do the bibliography and notes. I am so lucky to work with my friends.

In addition, I'd like to thank the staff of the American Academy of Dramatic Arts and the librarian, Marci G. Baun, who also lent me reference books. I would especially like to express my deepest gratitude to the chairman of the movement department there, my dear friend, Theresa Hayes, for reading the first few chapters and giving me her insightful feedback and advice, always peppered with those beautiful smiles.

I would like to express my gratitude to the many librarians that helped with my research, including the kind people at Sierra Madre Library and the Pasadena Central Library, and especially Willard Hunter of Pilgrim Place for helping me check out the books at the Claremont Colleges Library. In addition I would like to thank the many friendly people who assisted me in arranging for the illustrations used in the book. I would like to give extra thanks to my brother-in-law, Keith Snell, for opening up his extensive collection of antique sheet music for my use.

I am also deeply indebted to Career Transitions for Dancers for their generous grant which made the writing of this book much easier.

The love of dancing was planted in me by my first dance teacher, Cheryl Cutler. I was introduced to tap dancing by an amazing individual, Louis DaPron. The gifts I was given by these angels was then fostered in my life by many other fine teachers. I thank all of them for giving me such a great treasure. I am a happy man because of them.

Three special people share in my love of dance and their friendship continues to inspire and encourage me: Alex Romero, Bill Bartlett and Debbie Barlett. Thank you.

Psychological and physical support throughout the writing of this book was generously provided by two extraordinary women whom I am blessed to know, Leni Belcher Belshay and Sai-ling Michael.

The proofreading of this book was done by my friends and family, and I was touched that they would take the time and energy to help on this project. Patricia Rye, my dear friend, read the first few chapters and encouraged me all the way. My sister, Trudy Knowles, helped me with the flow and content, and my other sister, Anne Snell, read the final draft and helped with style and grammar. I am deeply grateful for the invaluable advice they both gave me and I admire and respect both of them beyond words. They and the other mem-

bers of my family — my sister Nancy, my brother Rex, my nieces and nephews and in-laws, my incredible father, Rex H. Knowles — and the spirits of my mother and Apollo, all carried me through the entire process of writing this book. My partner, Don Keller, also helped me with proofreading, and with technical advice concerning the computer. His constant encouragement and belief in me is what really made this book possible. I love you all more than tongue can tell.

Mark Knowles
March 2002
Los Angeles

Contents

PART III. OTHER INFLUENCES

List of Illustrations

Preface

In 1996, I was asked to present a program on tap dancing to the Newport Harbor Academy of Dentistry in Newport Beach, California, as part of their cultural enrichment series of lectures. Initially, I was asked to teach the audience a master class on how to tap. I quickly realized that trying to get several dentists tapping, without tap shoes (and on a carpeted floor no less) might be an interesting challenge, but I doubted I would be able to sustain interest for the three hours that had been allotted for the program. I proposed instead doing a lecture-demonstration about the history and development of tap dancing.

During this time, I was completing my book *The Tap Dance Dictionary*. In the process of writing the dictionary, I had found several antique steps and dances and I thought it might be fun to insert some of these into the presentation. I asked two friends of mine, Bill and Debbie Bartlett, both amazing performers, to join me. Together we recreated for the show old clogs, essences, soft shoes and even an authentic number by Bill Robinson.

The presentation was an amazing success, largely due to the superlative dancing of the Bartletts, and afterwards, several audience members commented, "You should write a book about this." And so, the seed was planted.

Then, in the summer of 2000, I was asked to teach some master classes in tap at the Looking Glass Studio of Performing Arts in San Bernardino. The director of the studio, a wonderful teacher, choreographer, and tap dancer, Ron Cocking, asked me if, in addition to teaching, I would also do a tap demonstration. I told him that I had a program on the history and development of tap and could probably condense it for his purposes. I wasn't able to utilize the talents of my friends Bill and Debbie this time; nevertheless, I presented the program, doing a few of the dances myself. Again, I heard from audience members, "You should write a book about this." I started on it the next day.

When I originally began my research, I had learned that tap dancing basically had evolved out of a merging of various components that were found in West African tribal dances, Irish solo step dancing and English clog dancing.

Irish step dancing was done with hard-soled shoes and involved intricate leg movements and fast footwork. English clog dancing was done with wooden shoes that accentuated the rhythm of the feet. Both of these styles of dancing used a minimum of upper-body movement. African secular and religious dances were highly improvisational, utilized gliding, dragging, and shuffling steps, and included wild upper body movement. As the twin heritages of European footwork and African style and rhythm blended, the European dances became more rhythmic and less rigid and the African elements became more formal. The resulting hybrid was tap dancing.

Yet as I deepened my exploration into the history of American tap dance, I found that there were also other important ingredients in its development. Further research led me into the fascinating world of American Shaker dances, Native American dances, Morris dancing, Spanish zapateado, Bavarian schühplattler, and even Indian kathak, all of which contributed to tap.

I found myself intrigued and often troubled by the vitally important role that blackface entertainment, with its degrading and disturbing stereotypes, had played in the development of tap dancing. I discovered that my own grandfather, Roy Otis Knowles, had been a minstrel and that he had worn burnt cork when he worked as an end-man for the original Christy's Minstrels. My own father told me about his father teaching him to play the bones. When I asked my father if my grandfather danced, he replied, "Yeah, but he wasn't very good."

I scoured libraries and used book stores for references to old jig, clog and tap dancers. I knew that many of these performers had stories that deserved to be remembered. I had read about "Daddy" Rice, Daniel Emmett, and John Durang before, but suddenly I was learning about Mike Mitchell, Johnny Dove, Dan Leno, Lotta Crabtree, Dan Bryant, Barney Fagan, and numerous others. The list seemed to go on and on. I came to appreciate anew the vast contribution of William Henry Lane, by many considered to be the first real tap dancer.

I was amazed again and again at the inventiveness and creativity of the dancers in vaudeville, and found myself thinking, Could I dance with a glass of water on my head without spilling a drop, or tap on a tiny square of slate on top of a six foot tall pedestal?

The stories of these performers are fun and fascinating and serve to remind us of the rich legacy that went into creating the art of tap dancing. The Cherokee dancer stomping out a rhythm, the African-American slave doing a pigeon wing at a corn shucking festival, the English mill-worker clogging to keep warm, the vaudeville legomania artist twisting his legs into unbelievable shapes: all need to be acknowledged and celebrated. Their contributions were as vital to the development of tap as Pat Rooney doing a waltz clog or King Rastus Brown inventing the time-step.

This book focuses mainly on the early roots of tap and the personalities that were there at the inception of the art. As interesting as it is to read about the later stars of the stage and screen, I felt that that part of the subject had already been fully explored in such wonderful books as *Tap! The Greatest Tap Dance Stars and Their Stories, 1900–1955,* by my friend Rusty Frank. Also, because of the many books written about such tap legends as Bill Robinson, John Bubbles, and Fred Astaire, I only mention these important contributors to the art form in passing.

I have chosen 1903 as the general cut-off date for my discussion of the history of tap because in the winter of 1902–03, Wayburn created a show called *Ned Wayburn's Minstrel Misses.* In the publicity for his show, Wayburn used the word "tap" to describe the mixture of clog, jig, and buck dancing that his showgirls used — the first official use of the word "tap" in reference to percussive American show dancing. Of course it is impossible to be rigid with time, and in trying to be as thorough as possible in telling the complete stories of the various contributors to tap, I often go well beyond this date as I relate other events in their lives.

As I was writing this book, I came to appreciate the many intricate textures and intriguing colors that went into the cre- ation of American tap dancing. I hope that this book will express my thanks to all the people that contributed to this popular entertainment form, and I hope it will celebrate the look, the feel, and the con- tagious rhythms of tap.

"The music has got into his feet."

—a description of dancing
at Congo Square in New
Orleans

PART I
PRIMARY INFLUENCES

1

Irish Influences

As with most folk dances, Celtic dance forms were originally based in religious ritual. Dances were performed in an attempt to influence the supernatural and, through ritual figures and steps, to win favor and assistance from the deities. The earliest Celtic dances were ring or circle dances, and since the Celts were tree worshippers, the dances often revolved around trees or maypoles. The Celts were also sun worshipers, and their worship took the form of dancing around a fire. The Celtic people danced clockwise in celebration dances; counterclockwise when mourning. Their dances often included stopping in one spot and repeatedly tapping the foot. Called "stepping it out," "tapping it out," or "dancing it out," these types of movements are still seen today in the percussive solo dances called Irish step dance.[1]

Many aspects of more modern Irish dancing can be directly traced to the Gypsies who migrated to the British Isles around the 15th century. These nomadic people brought with them dances that they had assimilated from the various cultures they had encountered in their travels. Many of these dances contained Eastern elements that heavily influenced Irish step dancing. The practice of tapping the foot repeatedly in one spot and the preference for counterclockwise movement are just two of these features. One component of

Celtic music, which has direct links to Eastern influences, is the use of the rising fifth which caused soaring musical passages in otherwise evenly distributed notes. This jump in the melodic line of the music led Irish dancers to start incorporating sudden, high leaps into the otherwise low stepping intricate footwork.[2]

The Jig

Of all the most popular Irish dance forms — the jig, the reel, and the hornpipe — the jig is the oldest. The jig utilized both heel and toe sounds, and while the body stayed erect and virtually motionless with the hands held close to the sides or placed on the waist, the feet and legs executed elaborate and intricate movements.

Dance historian Curt Sachs, in his classic book, *World History of Dance*, suggests that the word "jig"[3] is derived from the French word *giguer*, which means "to leap, gambol, or frolic."[4] A more thorough study of the word's etymology can be found in the *Dictionary of Dance*, which traces the word "jig" to an ancient Indian word, *jagat,* which meant "the moving thing." The word was linked to the name of the Hindu god, Jaga-nath, the Lord of the World. In Eastern India, annual celebrations which featured processions and

"The Last Jig, or Adieu to Old England" by Thomas Rowlandson. From *A History of Dancing: From the Earliest Ages to Our Own Times* by Gaston Vuillier (1898).

dancing were held in honor of Jaga-nath. This Indian word was probably brought to England by the Crusaders through Syria, or perhaps with the Gypsies. It came to represent anything that moved regularly. "Jig" therefore referred to the rhythm and movement of life itself. Many words we use today are also derived from the original, including "juggler," "jiggle," and "jig-saw."[5]

Usually thought of as an Irish dance, the jig was actually common in many countries. Its roots are traceable as far back as the 13th century. The dance was introduced to the European court during the reign of Louis XIV, when it was toned down from some of the wilder country aspects and "Frenchified" to suit the upper classes. At court, it was done as a couple dance and called the *gigue à deux*.

The jig was the forerunner of a dance called the galliard and there are many stylistic similarities between the two dances.

The galliard, which featured hops, leaps, jumps, and foot beats in the air, was a lively, active dance, and allowed men to show off their virtuosity and agility. Called the cinque-pace (the five step), or the sinky-pace in England, the dance was popular in the Elizabethan court.[6] Shakespeare mentioned it in his play, *Much Ado About Nothing*, Act II, scene 1;

> … wooing, wedding, and repenting, is as a Scotch Jig, a measure, and a cinque pace: the first suit is hot and hasty, like a Scotch Jig, and full as fantastical; the wedding, mannerly-modest, as a measure, full of state and anciently; and then comes Repentance and, with his bad legs, falls into the cinque pace faster and faster, till he sinks into his grave.

Jigs were originally done in the British Isles as outdoor country dances, but under Tudor rule in England they became popular with the upper classes who took the

William Kemp dancing the jig during his marathon dance from London to Norwich. Note the bells around his ankles. From *Kemps Nine Daies Wonder* by William Kemp (1600).

dance over for themselves. As these privileged classes became more interested in building and remodeling their manor houses, they changed the patterns of the original country dances to fit the shape of rooms that were being built. Jigs originally done as round dances gave way to squares and longways dances.[7]

Jigs were often named for places or famous personalities. An example of this was "Kemp's Jigge," which was named after the celebrated English comic actor and dancer, William Kemp. Kemp appeared with Shakespeare in his plays and was listed in the company as "head master of Morrice dancers." He was especially known for his comic jigging in the role of Peter in *Romeo and Juliet*, and was famous for always ending every performance with a jig, as was the practice in Elizabethan England.

Kemp himself said he "spent his life in mad Jigges." He became enormously famous for his "Nine Daies Wonder," during which he performed a marathon jig

from London to Norwich. Kemp actually made the journey in 23 days but is reported to have danced at least nine of them. He later published a booklet which documented his journey in detail, and expressed "his gratitude for the favours he had received during his gambols." Always one to take advantage of a little scandalous publicity, Kemp recounted in his book that when he finally reached Norwich, huge crowds received him, but that as he was nearing the finish of his dance, he executed a leap and accidentally landed on the hem of a maiden's skirt, ripping it off and revealing her petticoats.[8]

Dancing Masters

There are references to the jig in two early dance books, Martin's *Irish Hayes, Jiggs and Rondelays* from 1589 and Heywood's *Country Measures, Rounds and Jiggs* from 1603; however, the most important

THE DANCING SCHOOLE.

Early dancing school. From the frontispiece of *The Dancing Master* by John Playford, tenth edition (1698).

dance manual was John Playford's book *The Dancing Master, or Plaine and Easie Rules for the Dancing of Country Dances, with the Tune to Each Dance.*[9] Published in England in 1650, the book contained 104 country dances and was essentially the first guidebook for dance teachers. In early country dances the patterns were often determined by the musician, usually a fiddler, who accompanied the dance. He would pick a favorite tune and choose patterns that they would call out arbitrarily to fit the song. After Playford published his *Dancing Master,* the names of the tunes were transferred to the dances and in this way, certain dance figures were labeled with specific names. This eventually led to more standardization and uniformity among the various dances and contributed to their marketability. As the dances were codified, they found their way from more rural settings into drawing rooms which catered to the wealthy and socially elite. Playford's manual also helped to create large numbers of professional teachers. Many of these dancing masters eventually made their way to Ireland.[10]

The widespread popularity of the dancing master, or *curinky* as he was called in Ireland, brought about the most dra-

matic changes in Irish dancing. Strongly influenced not only by John Playford's manual, but also French style, etiquette and deportment, the Irish dancing masters came into their greatest prominence in the middle of the 18th century when they began creating the steps and patterns for solo dances.

When dancing masters were most in demand, these traveling teachers divided the Irish countryside into areas of about ten square miles, each territory staked out as the exclusive domain of one master. These boundaries were strictly honored; in fact, if a dancing master died, his area was even bequeathed to another. The dance instructor covered his own territory during a six week rotation period. In the book *A Tour of Ireland, 1776–1779*, Arthur Young spoke of this practice.

> Dancing is very general among the poor people.... Dancing masters of their own rank travel through the country from cabbin [house] to cabbin, with a piper or blind fiddler; and the pay is six pence a quarter.[11]

Traditionally, a village paid the dancing master at the end of every three weeks, usually by having a benefit night to raise the funds. The pay scale was quite high for that period in history, often including room and board as well. Despite this, dancing masters sometimes supplemented their teaching income by moonlighting, although their dedication to the dance always came first. There is an old story of a dancing master who also worked as a porter. He was summoned to carry some luggage, but sent a message back that he couldn't because he was "busy teaching a Jig."[12]

Dancing masters from various territories regularly met at social gatherings and fairs to challenge each other and demonstrate their skill. The dancing stages were most regularly a table top, a half-door, or the top of an overturned barrel — the smaller the dancing space, the greater the test of the teacher's ability.

> In fact, dancing in a limited space was viewed as such an important aspect of the style that one of the greatest tributes to be paid to a dancer was to note that they could "dance on top of a plate."[13]

It was believed that a good dancing master only needed an area about six inches square on which to dance.[14] Sometimes the dancing surface would be soaped to add a further challenge. Arthur Flynn, in his book, *Irish Dance*, tells a story of how one jealous dancing master spread oil on top of his opponent's barrel before one match in an attempt to foil his rival. These challenges became so important in determining the skill of a dancer that they were also held when two masters both claimed control of the same territory. The winner would be deeded the contested area with all its potential students.

There were three types of Irish dancing masters. The highest paid and those at the top of their profession taught dance in the "big houses" to upper classes. These claimed to have been trained in France and often took French names.[15] The lowest class of dancing master was called a "jig actor," or the "village hop merchant." They knew only the most basic simple dance steps and often struggled to make a living. The dancing masters in the middle, who taught all classes of students, were most responsible for spreading Irish dance. When faced with slow learners among their country students, dancing masters taught the difference between the left and right foot by tying a bundle of straw on one foot and a bundle of hay on the other. The master then simply told the dancer to use either their "hay foot" or their "straw foot."

When Irish dancing schools were formed, it was not uncommon for the door to be taken off its hinges and placed in the middle of the room, so the dancing master could display his agility by performing his latest steps. The dancing master would "cover the buckle," a phrase derived

> from circumstances that the dancing-master, while teaching, always wore large buckles in his shoes and by the rapidity of motion with which he would make his many twinkling feet perpetually cross, would seem to cover the appendages in question.[16]

Dancing masters created steps according to their pupils' abilities and according to the rhythms of the tunes that were popular to that particular area. Newer, more fashionable dances, imported from Europe, also had an impact upon which steps were adopted and they were varied to suit the teacher's needs. In this way each dancing master invented and then systemized his own set of solo step dances, jealously guarding each new creation. Since eight bar units of music were considered a step, the title "step dancing" came in to common use.

After the potato famine in the 1840s, as the Irish people struggled to survive, interest in culture waned and sessions with the dancing masters stopped. The Irish fled

"Irish Jig." An engraving after Wrightson from the book *Dancing* by Lilly Grove (1901).

to the United States, and the dancing masters joined the exodus, usually settling in New York where they organized classes.[17]

The jig, which came to the United States with these immigrants, began to diverge from its traditional Irish style and become textured with African-American ingredients. Andrew Burnaby, an Englishman visiting Virginia in 1759, observed this change when he spoke of seeing some jig dancers.

> Towards the close of an evening, when the company are pretty well tired with country dances, it is usual to dance Jiggs; a practice originally borrowed, I am informed, from the Negroes. These dances are without any method of regularity; a gentleman and a lady stand up, and dance about the room, one of them retiring, the other pursuing, then perhaps meeting, in an irregular fantastical manner.[18]

The jig continued to be transformed as it was taken over by such immigrant groups as the Dutch, Scandinavians, and Germans, and as it began to be incorporated into Appalachian clogging.

Aspects of Jig Dancing

Traditional Irish step dances were divided into two groups: reels, slip jigs, light jigs, and single jigs called "light shoe dances" which were done with soft shoes; and jigs, hornpipes, treble reels and solo set dances done in hard-soled shoes.[19]

The jig was performed in triple time and involved a crossing of the feet with every other step. Jigs were divided into single or double jigs, depending upon the number of foot beats per bar of music. In single jigs, the floor was struck twice per bar and this movement was called "battering." In the double jig, the floor was struck six times per bar and the action was called "guiding." There was also an older type of jig which was the original form of the double jig called "tatter-the-road." It used four beats for every bar of music.[20] As the art form developed, a good jig dancer could make at least 15 sounds per second.

Excess arm movements and toe-pointing were most often eliminated from Irish dancing because they were considered too effeminate. As dances developed, there was also an attempt to "de–Anglicize" Irish arts and remove from them English influences to create a separate Irish culture, which further added to the stiff, rather formal style of Irish solo step dancing. Wild arm movements were actually popular in the early 19th century and sometimes dancers would incorporate the waving of a shillelagh, but by the 1900s, arm movements had been removed.[21]

There is some debate over why Irish dancers held their arms so tightly by their sides. Some sources say this was simply done so that the focus would go to the feet. Others say that it originally grew out of a political statement in response to British authority. There was a law that required an Irish citizen to raise his hands whenever he was approached by an Englishman to show that he carried no weapons. In defiance of this law, dancers started holding their hands tightly by their sides. Most experts believe that the arms were held by the side by the order of the Church which wanted dancers to practice self control as well as prevent upper body movement which might be too sensual or provocative.

Church authorities often condemned dancing from the pulpit calling it, "lewd, licentious, immoral and unbecoming to its flock."[22] Perhaps the lyric of one popular 17th century tune reveals why — "Pricilla did dance a Jig with Tom/ which made her buttocks shake like a Custard." Many bishops even threatened excommunication to members of the church who disobeyed the "no dancing" edicts.

Interestingly enough, the adversarial political atmosphere of Ireland also had an important effect on the development of step dancing. In the late 17th century, when England imposed the Penal Laws, Catholics were banned from ordaining clergy and teaching their children. The Mass went underground. A child would be placed outside the door of secret religious gatherings to guard against discovery by the authorities. If the British approached, the child signaled danger by tapping out certain rhythms with his feet, a practice continued until the Catholic Emancipation in 1829.

One fascinating aspect of ancient Irish step dancing was the use of intricate floor patterns. These designs have been found to match exactly the ornamentation carved on ancient Celtic monuments and artifacts. Experts believe that Celtic artisans were inspired by the dancers' movements and attempted to capture these patterns in their art. The main feature in these figures is the equal proportion and perfect balance of each line. This flawless distribution is similarly found in Irish dancing, which stresses symmetrical movements. All steps are balanced right and left, up and down, and backwards and forwards.[23]

The Irish Cake Dance

One particular Irish jig that had interesting similarities to the later American dance, the cakewalk, was the Irish cake dance. Seen as early as 1680, the dance was usually performed on Sundays after church services and was generally accompanied by a piper. The piper dug a hole in the ground next to himself to hold the pennies contributed by the dancers for his playing.[24] During the dance, the jig dancers competed for a prize which was placed upon a round board and held aloft on a ten foot pole. The prize was a cake, just as it would be 200 years later at many cakewalk competitions held in the United States. As in

America, the winner was said "to take the cake," or "take the biscuit."

Rhythmical step dancing reached to its highest degree in Ireland. Thomas Hill, a famous Irish step dancer from the first part of the 20th century commented,

> The thing of greatest importance in Irish dancing is the music of the shoes. In the eleven years that I have been dancing, the greatest part of my attention has been spent on the development and control of the variety of tones that can be produced by Taps of heels and soles on the floor and against each other.[25]

This Irish "music of the shoes" became one of the most important components in the creation of American tap dancing.

2

English Influences

Clog Dancing

One of the most important precursors to modern tap is the English step dance known as clog. The etymology of the word "clog" is most likely traced to the word "log," which is of old Saxon origin and means "to lie" or "to be weighty," such as in the phrase "to sleep like a log." Dance historians and older dance texts have mentioned "log steps" in speaking of percussive wooden-shoed dances from various countries.

Linda Carol Forrest, in her article "What Is Clogging?" suggests that the word "clog" is derived from the Gaelic word meaning "time" and refers to the keeping of time by the feet. The *Dictionary of Dance* states that the term is derived from an Old English dance that mimicked the actions of a clock. The clock dance developed from a Roman ritual in which 12 numerals were traced on the ground inside a circle. Stepping dances were then performed within the circle both to represent the passage of time and to use as a memory device in the teaching of time. In England this dance became the clock dance which some believe is the ancestor of the clog.

The routine was danced so that hours were marked out in a succession of rapid taps while the dancers moved in a circle.

Other variations included exhibition dances in which one dancer marked out the hours while another executed the minutes in a tapping counterpoint. The dance was a common part of peasant festivals and was well known by English mill-workers who were exposed to it at these peasant celebrations. It is believed that the name "clock dancing" gradually metamorphosed into "clog dancing."[1]

Lancashire Clog

In the manufacturing cities of Lancashire, England, the local cotton-mill workers suffered under appalling conditions in the late 18th century during the Industrial Revolution. Not only did workers put up with long hours and dire factory conditions, but also with weather that was consistently cold and damp. The mill workers insulated their feet against the chill by wearing shoes that had a sole made of one solid piece of wood. These shoes were called "clogs."

Historians believe that English clog dancing originated among female mill workers who tapped their feet in their wooden-soled clogs to keep time with the rhythms of the shuttles that went back and forth on their looms. As the boredom of sitting at a loom all day set in, these basic

15

Two clog dancers from the late 1870s. From *Clog Dancing Made Easy* by Henry Tucker (1874).

wooden shoes striking the stones or hitting against each other were interpolated into already existing step dances, such as jigs, reels, and Morris dances.[3] Contests were held to see who could produce the most varied rhythms and sounds.[4] This type of competitive dancing later figured prominently in the development of challenges which became a staple of the American tap dance world.

The clogs worn by English mill workers were made from a shaped wooden sole with a leather upper that could be firmly secured to the foot. The footwear allowed for extremely light footwork because the ankle was free, but the actual weight of the shoe helped the dancer to make extra taps, stamps and heel beats.

Sometimes the clogs were embellished with brass jinks, shaped like horseshoes that were added onto the heels. Clog dancing was often performed on a slate floor to emphasize the sound. Since the shoes were fitted with metal pieces, they would actually spark when struck against the stones, further adding to the flash, appeal, and drama of the dancing.

As clog dances developed and the tempos got faster, steps became more intricate and the thick, heavy, wooden-soled shoes proved to be increasingly unwieldy, cumbersome, and hazardous. Lighter, fancier clogs were made and irons on the heels were eliminated. The soles of these newer types of clogs were made out of beech, sycamore, alder, willow, or ash wood, which was the lightest and gave the clearest, crispest sound, but was also the

rhythms began to be embellished with traditional jig, reel, and hornpipe steps. These types of steps, which previously had been done only in soft-soled shoes, changed with the heavier-soled footwear, and soon "soft jig" steps became "hard jig" steps.[2] What was sacrificed in speed was compensated for with noisier, more driving rhythms. This type of dancing became known as "shoe music" or "noisy shoe" because the clogs were used almost as if they were musical instruments. Unlike jig dancing which visually stressed the many crossings of the legs and feet, clog dancing was danced from the knee down and was purely auditory.

During their breaks, the factory workers also danced on the cobblestone pavements outside the mills, probably to keep warm. The percussive rhythms of the least durable. If dancers could afford to replace their dancing shoes regularly though, ash was always chosen because of the clarity it gave the taps.

By the early 1880s, wooden clogs were starting to be replaced by more pliable leather footwear. In a further development, metal was again added to the shoes, this time in the form of copper pennies that were attached to the heels to accentuate the sound during dancing.

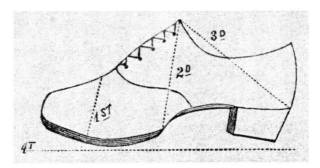

Advertisement for a clog dancing shoe. From *Jig, Clog, and Breakdown Dancing Made Easy* by Ed James (1873).

The Hornpipe

Another type of English dance that was an important source of tap movements was the hornpipe. Part of the rhythmical step-dance tradition, the hornpipe emphasized leg actions, beats, and foot sounds. Although it was sometimes appropriated for use in hard-shoe clog dances, it was most often done in soft-soled shoes.

In her book *Dancing,* Lilly Grove mentions a dancing master who gave the following description of how to dance the hornpipe correctly:

> Slips and shuffle forward, spleet and floorish backwards, Hyland step forwards, heel and toe forwards, slips across forwards, twist round backwards, cross stocks aside and sink forwards, and finally hopp forwards and backwards.[5]

Most of this description is indecipherable to us today, yet it is interesting to see the variety of steps that were suggested.

The etymology of the word "hornpipe," or "hornpype," is traced to the Saxon or Germanic word for horn.[6] The word was generally associated with a bagpipelike instrument that consisted of an inflated sac made out of animal skin and a reed pipe made out of animal horn. It was commonly used among rural shepherds. As the shepherd's hands were occupied playing the pipe, his feet would execute the fancy footwork. There is a theory that the leg and foot movements of the hornpipe developed among shepherds from mountainous regions of Wales and Scotland where the shepherds naturally had strong leg muscles because of their line of work.[7]

Although the first reference to the hornpipe is found during the reign of Henry VIII (1509–1547), the dance didn't move south out of Scotland and Wales until the reigns of Elizabeth I and James I. It was subsequently developed by the English, and as the influence of the ballet tradition grew in England, so the style of hornpipe dancing continually evolved.

It wasn't until 1740, when a man named Yates did a dance called "A Hornpipe in the Character of Jacky Tar" at the Drury Lane Theatre, that hornpipes became associated with sailors.[8] This identification with mariners eventually became so strong that boys training for a naval career were expected to master the dance, and the hornpipe even became part of standard naval training in 19th century Britain. Captain Cook required his sailors to do the hornpipe during ocean voyages to keep them in good health. This practice was later used by slave traders, who forced the slaves to dance in order to keep them healthy.

"Sailor's Hornpipe." From an engraving after F. H. Ramberg, circa 1800, for the book *Dancing* by Lilly Grove (1901).

According to Beth Tolman and Ralph Page's *The Country Dance Book,* there was a legend that the hornpipe was first danced on a boat that was stranded in the south Atlantic near the equator in an area known as the doldrums. Caught in a sudden calm, with no wind for sailing, a Welshman started playing on his hornpipe out of boredom. The sailors began to dance, utilizing movements that they already knew, such as miming the pulling of ropes or looking off into the distance. The hornpipe dance was born and the sailors "came out of the doldrums."

Egg-dances

The hornpipe was just one of several dances that were also performed as egg-dances. Real eggs were placed on the floor around the performing area and blindfolded dancers hopped and danced among the eggs trying not to break them.[9] John Durang, who became well known as the consummate hornpipe dancer in the United States, created a sensation in 1790 when he danced one of his hornpipes while blindfolded on a stage covered with eggs.

The egg-dance originally had a religious significance. It was done with 12 eggs set in the shape of a cross in a pattern called the "twelve apostles," and the dancer, while moving among the eggs, symbolically advanced through the stations of the cross.

In the Netherlands, egg-dances were performed inside a circle drawn in chalk upon the ground. Flowers and greenery were placed inside the circle along with the eggs and, while performing the dance, the dancer tried to maneuver the eggs from among the branches to the outside of the circle. The dancer who did it in the fastest time won a prize, usually a basket of eggs. In one Danish version of the egg-dance, an egg was placed on top of an overturned goblet stuck on top of a pile of sand. The dancer's task was to dislodge the egg from the top of the goblet and then to replace it on top again, dancing all the while.

Sometimes called the hop-egg, the egg-dance can be traced as far back as the Saxons, who brought it to England from Germany as early as the fifth century. The egg-dance and other forms of Saxon dance were spread by traveling minstrels called glee-men. The dances of the glee-men included many variations, but to dance upon one foot was especially respected, and was considered an admirable accomplishment. Women who mastered one-footed dancing, or hopping, were called "hoppesteres," and Saxon dances were often called "hoppings"[10] — the derivation of the American rock-and-roll expression "at the hop." The egg-dance is the ancestor of the children's game hopscotch. In the United States, egg-dancing later became a popular specialty act in vaudeville.[11]

Morris Dances

Another type of English dancing that influenced American tap was the Morris dance or Morisco. Comprised of claps,

"The Egg Dance in Holland." An engraving after Theodor de Bry, 1611, from the book *Dancing* by Lilly Grove (1901).

stamps, leaps, and solo jig steps, as well as other country dance movements and patterns, the term "Morris" is applied to many different forms of male ceremonial dance in England. Most often performed during Lent, Morris dances were associated with tree worship, fertility, and the coming of spring, and often involved symbolic objects like maypoles or garlands. The stamping, pounding and leaping movements in the morris dance were originally done to encourage the crops to grow higher. The circular and serpentine patterns formed by the dancers further demonstrated that the dance was based upon fertility themes.[12]

The name of the Morris dance was derived from the word "Moorish," and was a reference to the Muslim invaders who ruled the Iberian Peninsula from 711 to 1492.[13] In 1149, the dance came to public attention when it was performed at the Spanish court to celebrate the betrothal of Petronilla, Queen of Aragon, to Ramón Berenguer IV of Catalonia. It commemorated the expulsion of the Moors by the Christians in the city of Lérida.[14] Performed as a staged representation of this conflict, the religious dance was called "Moros y Cristianos" and symbolized the victory of good over evil.[15]

During this period in Spanish history, Christian armies pushed the Moors southward on the Iberian Peninsula and the Morris dance followed. It eventually spread throughout Spain, then moved to Italy and France and, with the Spanish conquistadors, across the Atlantic to the New World as well. As Christian military evangelism continued to expand, this symbolic mock combat, which celebrated victory over the infidels, finally made its way to England in the middle of the 15th century where it became known as the Morris dance. By the reign of Henry VIII, the dance was so popular that representations of it were included in the stained glass windows of churches.[16]

Morris dancers wore wild, ragged costumes which had bits of metal and bells attached to them. These costumes added to the noise made by the dancers' feet.[17] The bells, in tandem with the foot taps, caused secondary rhythms and contributed to the rhythmical complexity of the dance. The dancers also carried sticks that symbolized swords which they beat percussively on their bodies and on the soles of their feet.[18]

Traditional Morris dancers disguised themselves by blackening their faces and assuming clownlike characters. The practice of blackening the face originally grew out of pagan rituals which involved the sacred use of masks. Black makeup was used to preserve the anonymity of the performers, and therefore strengthen the magic of the rituals. Some scholars suggest that the practice also represented the dark complexion of the Moors. There is conjecture that in England the black makeup also reflected connections to coal mining. It is impossible not to notice the many striking similarities between these blackface characterizations and American minstrel performers who utilized the same practice later in the United States.[19]

A variation of the traditional Morris dance was done in Lancashire, England.[20] Dancers who performed the Lancashire Morris Dance of Bacup attached small wooden discs, about the size of castanets, to their hands, waist, and knees, and rhythmically struck them. These movements and rhythms were noticeably similar to ones found in ancient Turkish tribal rituals and showed the dance's Moorish origins. Another reference to the Moorish roots of the dance could be found in the name given to the wooden discs. Lancashire Morris dancers commonly called them "coconuts" which hints at their foreign origin.

An interesting sidelight is that the discs also resembled the protective knee and elbow coverings that were used for crawling along narrow areas in the coal mines, and like the tradition of blackening the face, perhaps showed a connection to the local mining industry.[21] The similarities of the Lancashire Morris to African-America's "patting juba," the practice of slapping the body percussively, are undeniable. Perhaps American minstrels of English and Irish descent accepted "patting juba" more readily because they were already so familiar with a version of it from their own culture.

In some Morris dance rituals, one of the dancers was assigned the part of the "wiffler" or the "whipper in." The wiffler preceded the other dancers, cracking a whip or more often, an inflated pig's bladder attached to a stick which they used to hit onlookers who got in the way. This tradition was derived from the ancient practice of using a bull-roarer to drive away evil spirits and warn the uninitiated away from sacred rites.[22]

Morris dancers were also sometimes accompanied by a character called the Cake-and-Sword Bearer, who preceded their procession carrying a sword with a cake impaled upon it. He would distribute pieces of the cake to the crowds for good luck.[23]

One common Morris tradition was the construction of a springtime bower made out of branches, flowers and other greenery, large enough to hold someone inside. This person would prepare and serve drinks to the dancers. The bartender, or Green Man, as he was known, gave host to a wide array of literary and folk personae. At various times he was called by such names as Jack-in-the-Green or Robin-of-the-Wood, better known to us as Robin Hood.[24] Another one of his names was John Barleycorn, the spirit of the corn, symbolized by the last sheaf of corn cut at harvest time.

One of the most common steps in the Morris dance was to jump into the air and land with one foot slightly before the other. Called a double-step, this movement was commonly used in later clog dances in the United States, where it became known as a spring. If the heels were dropped after executing a spring, it resembled what tap dancers now call a cramproll. Other common Morris steps included a wide range of back-steps with such names as hop-back-step, cross-back-step, shuffle-back-step, hockle-back-step, and wide-back-step. These terms seem to indicate a similarity with the irish, the common tap step made up a shuffle, a hop, and a step. Because Morris dancers sewed bells and bits of metal to their costumes, it was common to shiver and shake the free leg to produce sound. Perhaps this movement was the origin of shuffles or nerve taps.

3

African Influences

Almost every aspect of African life was somehow related to dancing. African people danced in celebration and in mourning, during marriage and initiation rites, in preparation for war, to insure a good hunt and a profitable harvest, for healing, and to make social statements. The dance was the "fundamental element of the African aesthetic expression."[1] When African tribesmen encountered a stranger, the stranger was asked, "What do you dance?" because dancing was so prevalent, so complex, so distinctive, and so important among the native peoples of Africa that a person's nationality could be actually be ascertained by the way they danced.[2]

In African cultures, the dance served as an artistic means of communication, and gesture constituted a language. Through the subtlety of their movements, dancers could address social and religious issues, and express gratitude, friendship, or hostility. The dance reflected the community and its social concerns; therefore, if a dance changed, it was "a reflection of new developments in the life-style of the community, not a consciously planned novelty."[3]

The rhythmical nature of most African dances conveyed the rhythms inherent in the various patterns of nature and were often repetitive, just as the cycles of life are. Humanity's kinship with the Earth was a common theme in African dance.

The shuffle, the most common step in African dancing, was an example of this kinship. African dancers kept their feet

Danseuse noire.

Depiction of a female African dancer. Illustration by M. Valvérane, from the book *La Danse* by Raoul Charbonnel (1889).

22

close to the soil in order to stay connected with the power of the Earth deities. The shuffle later became one of the most basic steps in tap dancing.

African dances were sophisticated both rhythmically and stylistically and were guided by drums. "Talking drums" interacted with dancers using different rhythms, as well as communicating messages with pitch and tone. African drummers could actually tune their drums to "speak" linguistically specific sounds so that the drum music itself constituted a sounded text. The musicality of various African words was so precise that they could actually be written as musical notes.[4] Even today, the complexities of primitive African rhythmic structure have yet to be equaled.

In the African cultures, music and dance were inseparably linked and basically constituted one art form. This blending of the physical gestures of dance with audible sound is apparent in tap dance, an art form that is both seen and heard.

Aspects of African Dance

A further investigation of some of the aspects of African dance will help to elucidate how it contributed to the development of tap dancing.[5]

1. African dance was done with bare feet, close to the ground. It was flatfooted, and therefore consisted of gliding, shuffling, and dragging steps. This aspect of African dance is clearly visible in today's tap which often utilizes slides, drags, draws, and chugs.

2. African dance was performed in a crouch, bent at the waist imitating a hunter going in for the kill. This was the opposite of European dances that were performed with an erect spine, imitating riding on horseback. There is a Kongo proverb that says, "Dance with bended knee, lest you be taken for a corpse."[6] The relaxed body attitude which is synonymous with current tap dancing is a direct result of this aspect of African dance.

3. African dance utilized animal mimicry. This practice of was later incorporated in dances that were the early forerunners of tap, such as the pigeon wing and the buzzard lope. Impersonating animal actions and behaviors later became common in several American social dances. Between 1910 and 1920, numerous dances such as the grizzly bear, the turkey trot, the kangaroo dip, the bunny hug, and the buffalo glide were created.

4. African dance was highly improvisational — probably the most important contribution of the art form to Western culture. For the African, dance was an expression of immediate experience. This experience was then interpreted in a stylized, ordered fashion. Within this framework, invention and innovation were encouraged, and individuality and originality greatly admired. The use of improvisation had to do with the African aesthetic of encouraging freedom and exploration. Its purpose was to extend tradition without straying too far. Improvisation in African dance originally functioned as a disruption in the basic rhythmical pattern or beat, which allowed dancers to break out of ordinary consciousness and move into the world of their ancestors by entering a state of possession. The use of breaks were later vitally important in regards to many American social dances such as the Charleston, the big apple, the jitterbug and especially tap.

5. African dance was centrifugal. It moved outward from the pelvis and hips.

> In European social dancing the body is maintained as a single unit of behavior. Integrity is asserted with a strongly unified torso.... The African and African American organization of the body differs most profoundly in locating the

center of gravity at the hips. Movement is initiated from that area and emanates outward…. Thus the flexibility and fluidity in black dancing arises from the division of the body at the pelvis, with the upper body playing against the lower….[7]

Elvis Presley's hip swivels and the 1960s dance the twist can be traced back to African tribal dance.

6. African dance always had a propulsive rhythm. In African dance, body positions were determined rhythmically rather than spatially, and the rhythms conveyed by the drums determined the movement sequences that were used and how they were organized.

7. African dance utilized swinging movements. This type of pendulum action was important because of its relationship to the rhythm. European music usually accented the first and third beats in a bar of music, whereas the swaying motion in African dance tended to cause the accent to fall on the second and fourth beats. This rebounding or bouncy feeling of stressing the offbeat is what led to jazz and swing, and influenced the development of syncopation in American tap.

8. African dance utilized polyrhythmic body movements. In other words, various parts of the body expressed different rhythms at the same time: the hips one; the hands another; the feet a third. Composed and balanced coordination in handling these rhythmical oppositions displayed the performer's adaptability. Therefore, the use of multiple meter in African dance was important because it symbolized a dancer's spiritual ability to deal with duality and to use this duality to create a richer, more vital experience. The juxtaposition of rhythms created a seeming "looseness" in the dance which was later adopted by tap and American social dances. The wild articulation of the knees in the Charleston, the free-moving hips in the black bottom,

and the loose ankles used in tap dancing are all by-products of this aspect of African dance.

9. African dance utilized mockery, derision, and parody. Satire and humor were used to make social commentaries as well as to help preserve traditional values by publicly making fun of those who went outside acceptable societal boundaries. Satire also provided the community with a way to laugh at the irony found in difficult situations. The aspects of mockery and derision were later used in minstrel parodies as well as in corn shucking dances and the cakewalk.

10. Instead of a self-conscious presentation of a dance as something beautiful, the emphasis in African dance was on what was felt. Not concerned with conveying grace or elegance, the dancer's total lack of inhibition created the dance's beauty.

11. In African dance, nonchalance and composure were seen as the most desirable attributes. Although appearing wild and full of sensual abandonment to western eyes, African dance always blended spontaneity with control and stayed firmly inside the norms set by tradition and proper custom. Coolness was all important, and demonstrated how the individual maintained grace under pressure.[8] The African aesthetic of coolness was emphasized by the use of asymmetry as balance. It was believed that balance was achieved by the combination of opposites. This balance is clearly demonstrated in the time-step and break.

> The time step, based on six measures of a repeated rhythmical phrase and two measures of a break in rhythm, is an example of asymmetrical balance found in both African and African-American expression.[9]

This aspect is also apparent in stylistic elements of tap dancing — the feet going wild is juxtaposed with the body maintaining a cool, relaxed attitude. The overall effect is one of equilibrium and control.

The Atlantic Slave Trade

Africans were brought to the Americas as slaves as early as the 16th century. By 1540, 10,000 Africans a year were being transported to the West Indies. By the end of the 16th century, there were already 900,000 black slaves there. During the four centuries of the Atlantic slave trade, an estimated ten million Africans were enslaved.

Africans were often enticed to board slave ships with the promise of rewards for performing their tribal dances for the crew's entertainment. When the dancing was over, they were taken below and given alcohol, only to find themselves at sea when they woke up from their intoxication. These Africans came from a culture that was rich in elaborately ordered tribal ritual, and they had highly developed community celebrations. The slave trade forced them into the restrictive disorder of slave ship holds and threatened them with the dissolution of their cultural traditions.[10]

The death rate from disease, filth, and beatings was usually at least half of the people on board a slave ship.[11] Many Africans tried to commit suicide by jumping overboard or refusing to eat.[12] Often 600 slaves were crammed into ships that were designed to transport only 400. Many actually suffocated in the hold because of the crowed conditions. Disease was rampant and one observer said the slave deck was "so covered in blood and mucus that it resembled a slaughter house."[13] The conditions were so crowded in the hold where the slaves were kept that movement of any kind was virtually impossible. For economic reasons, the slave traders therefore started a practice called "dancing the slaves," believing that if the human cargo were exercised on deck, the slaves would look better and bring a better price at market.[14]

In *An Account of the Slave Trade on the Coast of Africa,* Alexander Falconbridge wrote,

Exercise being deemed necessary for the preservation of their health, they are sometimes obliged to dance, when the weather will permit their coming on deck. If they go about it reluctantly, or do not move with agility, they are flogged; a person standing by them all the time with a cat-o-nine-tails in his hand for the purpose.[15]

In the late 1700s, when testifying for the abolition of slavery in Parliament, James Arnold related the following account:

In order to keep them [the slaves] in good health it was usual to make them dance. It was the business of the chief mate to make the men dance and the second mate danced the women; but this was only done by means of a frequent use of the cat [cat-o-nine-tails]. The men could only jump up and rattle their chains but the women were driven in one among another all the while singing or saying words that had been taught them; — "Messe, messe, mackarida," that is: "Good living or messing well among white men," thereby praising us for letting them live so well.[16]

In his book *Human Livestock,* Edmund D'Auvergne speaks of this practice.

We do all we can, insisted the captains, to promote the happiness of the slaves on board. They were brought up on board for eight hours everyday, while their quarters were being cleaned out, and they were encouraged to dance — in chains. Encouraged, indeed, as other witnesses testified by the application of whips! Those with swollen ankles or

"Dancing the Slaves" on a slave ship. *Courtesy of the Mary Evans Picture Library.*

diseased limbs were not exempt from partaking of this joyous pastime, though the shackles often peeled the skin off their legs.[17]

Because of the shackles the slaves were forced to wear, the dancing they did was really nothing more than frantic hopping. It was accompanied by a drum, or if that was unavailable, the bottom of an overturned washtub. Sometimes the sailors from the crew played the concertina and did jigs themselves. Frequently slaves were forced to mimic the dances of the Irish and English crew, and this could have been one of the first cross-pollinations of European and African cultural styles.

Our blacks were a good-natured set, and jumped to the lash so promptly, that there was not much occasion for scoring their naked flanks. We had tamborines on board, which some of the younger darkies fought for regularly, and every evening we enjoyed the novelty of African war songs and ring dances, fore and aft, with the satisfaction of feeling that these pleasant exercises were keeping our stock in fine condition, and, of course enhancing our prospect of a profitable voyage.[18]

Africans were kidnapped from their homeland and taken to a new environment where they were humiliated, beaten, and dehumanized. Every attempt was made to strip the slaves of their artistic and cultural traditions. Under such adverse and devastating circumstances, it is indeed miraculous that any vestiges of African dance survived at all, considering the magnitude of adjustment necessary for the slaves to exist in such a hostile environment. Yet, the Africans' noble ability to adapt, reinvent, and acculturate themselves allowed for the transformation of traditional forms of African dance into new African-American dance forms, including tap dancing.

4

Dance in the West Indies

When Christopher Columbus landed in Trinidad in 1498, he had one of his sailors play the tambourine, and he ordered some of his crew to perform dances on the deck of his ship, hoping to attract the native Indians. The approaching Indians initially mistook the sailors' capering as a war dance and showered the ship with arrows. When the misunderstanding was finally cleared up, the chief of the Taíno Indians, Guacanagari, arranged for a performance of native dances for Columbus and his crew. With maracas and bones, and snail shells tied around their arms, hips and feet, female dancers pounded out rhythms in celebration of the new friendships they thought were being offered to them by the Spaniards.

Ironically, the celebrations quickly gave way to a gruesome reign of terror as the Spanish conquistadors, in their desire for gold and slaves, subdued, subjugated, and brutally exploited the native peoples.[1] The Spanish invaders were harsh masters. Indian men were sent away to the mines to dig for gold. The work was so physically grueling that at least a third of the men died after laboring for only six months. The women were also forced to do manual labor, usually digging and planting. Bartolome de las Casas, a young priest who accompanied Columbus in his travels, wrote in his book *History of the Indies*,

… husbands and wives were together only once every eight or ten months and when they met they were so exhausted and depressed on both sides … they ceased to procreate. As for the newly born, they died early because their mothers, overworked and famished, had no milk to nurse them, and for this reason, while I was in Cuba, 7,000 children died in three months.[2]

In addition to working the natives to death as slaves, the Spaniards sometimes refused to walk and forced the Indians to carry them on their backs. They often hunted and murdered the native Arawaks for sport, using the dead bodies for dog food. It was not uncommon for the soldiers to slice off body parts of living Indians to test the sharpness of their knives. Those natives that did try to defend themselves were quickly slaughtered, and any that attempted to escape into the hills were hunted down and killed. In sheer desperation, many natives turned to suicide. In 1517, Pedro de Cordoba in a letter to King Ferdinand wrote,

As a result of the sufferings and hard labor they endured, the Indians choose and have chosen suicide. Occasionally a hundred have committed mass suicide. The women, exhausted by labor, have shunned conception and childbirth…. Many, when pregnant, have taken something to abort and have aborted.

27

Others after delivery have killed their children with their own hands, so as not to leave them in such oppressive slavery.[3]

In addition to their terrible treatment of the native peoples of the Caribbean, the Spanish conquistadors also ruined the ecosystem of the islands by forcing the natives to abandon their traditional gardening practices so they could work as slaves in the mines. By introducing livestock such as rabbits, which were not indigenous to the area, further ecological havoc was wreaked.

The Spaniards' colonization of the New World eventually led to the complete depopulation of the native Indian people from the islands. Before Columbus sailed to the New World, the population of Haiti was over eight million. By 1496, only four years after Columbus arrived, five million of these people had been killed by epidemics, slavery and war. By 1516, only 12,000 remained and by 1542, fewer than 200. As of 1650, none of the original Arawak, Carib, Lucayan, Siboney, or Taíno Indians were left.

After this genocide, the Spanish conquerors looked for other means to supply the labor force that was needed to work the mines and raise the crops. They began importing African slaves. By 1660, roughly 20,000 had been imported to Barbados, but the huge labor demand of the sugar industry caused that number to skyrocket, and by 1713 there were 45,000, as compared to only 17,000 whites.

In addition to providing African slaves for the Caribbean islands, it became a common practice among slavers to put the slaves off in the West Indies before they were taken to the American mainland. This practice, called "seasoning the slaves," helped African slaves more quickly become accustomed to their new environment, increasing their survival rate and therefore the profits for the slave traders. A slave "was regarded as seasoned within three or four years and was viewed by mainland planters as much more desirable than the raw Negroes fresh from the wilds of Africa."[4]

By bringing slaves to the West Indies first for "seasoning," authentic African elements within native dances were somewhat preserved. In the Caribbean, there was a general acceptance of African ritual by white slave owners who viewed dance as a non-threatening and therefore viable expression. This toleration allowed the development of a vital, black Caribbean dance culture.

In addition, the West Indies had initially been settled by the Spanish and later, the French, and therefore the islands were predominantly Catholic. The Catholic Church in the West Indies was typically much less hostile and repressive than the Protestant Church on the American mainland. Protestants generally tried to eradicate African rites and rituals when Christianizing the slaves. The Catholic slave owners in the Caribbean, as brutal as they were, did not seem to care if the African slaves retained some of their own customs as long as they converted to Catholicism. Many dances and rituals which had previously been associated with African deities were therefore preserved and merely transferred intact into the worship of Catholic saints. African culture was, in a sense, given a reprieve when slaves were "seasoned" in the West Indies rather than being sent directly to the United States.

The Calenda, the Chica, and the Juba

As in Africa, dance in the West Indies was highly rhythmical, and the movements were usually dictated by drums. The three most popular Caribbean dances were the calenda, the chica, and the juba, the latter being the most important in terms of the development of tap dancing.

The calenda (or calinda) originally came from Guinea and was performed by a couple (or couples) encircled by a ring of other dancers who sang and clapped in accompaniment.[5] The dancers used shuffling and stamping steps, with the movement originating in the hips. The dance included jumps and turns, but the most recognizable trait of the Calenda was the way the man and woman would strike their thighs against each other, sometimes locking arms and spinning and often kissing each other in the middle of the dance. Whites considered these gestures highly suggestive and indecent. In 1694, French monk Jean Baptiste Labat described the dance as dishonest and lascivious, and suggested that slaves should instead be taught minuets "which would satisfy their love of dancing in an innocent way." Despite Labat's denunciation of the dance, blacks continued to dance the calenda; "…the old, the young, and even the children. It seemed as if they had danced it in the wombs of their mother."[6]

The calenda was so popular among black slaves that they would do it for hours at a time. If one of the partners became tired, another dancer would jump in and simply replace them.

By 1724 … the slave owners had banned the Calenda, partly because of its immodesty and partly because they feared uprisings among large gatherings of blacks.[7]

Although the dance was officially prohibited, blacks continued to perform the calenda covertly and it remained one of the most popular slave dances well into the 19th century. The calenda was also known by several other names including, the kalenda, the jo-and-johnny, and the joan-and-johnny. One form of the dance, called the caleinda, involved men only, miming a mock fight with twirling sticks. Elements of the calenda can be seen in many later American social dances such as the black bottom, the Charleston, the fox trot, the shimmy, the American rhumba, and the big apple.

The chica was another couple dance performed inside of a ring. The woman's part was subtle and languid, while the man danced around her wildly and vigorously.

> The main characteristic of the popular Chica was the rotation of the hips, with an immobile upper body. The role played by the woman was apparently coquetry, while the man pursued and enticed.[8]

A couple performing the chica. "Dance from the Island of Jamaica," from an engraving after A. Brunais for the book *Dancing* by Lilly Grove (1901).

The chica was usually accompanied by a drum called the bamboula and eventually the name bamboula was used interchangeably with the name chica, when referring to the dance. Aspects of the chica were later incorporated into the mambo and the rhumba.

The juba (or jumba) was a competition dance in which one dancer challenged the technical skill of another in a series of bravura solos. The dance was derived from an African step dance called the giouba.[9] Although the footwork was similar in some ways to that of the Irish jig, the giouba was done flatfooted, and unlike in the jig, the upper body was also involved in the movement.

The juba was usually performed by two male dancers inside a circle of other performers.[10] The dance started with the outside ring of dancers circling counterclockwise around the two men in the middle using an eccentric shuffling step in which one foot was continually lifted. They followed the shuffling with a step called the dog scratch. Then the two men in the center of the circle began a dance competition. As they performed increasingly difficult and intricate steps, they were accompanied by the others in the circle who clapped, stamped, and slapped their thighs as they kept time and encouraged the competitors in verse and song. Each new step was determined by the shouted and sung commands of the observers in a call-and-response type of format. Some common steps that were called out to the two featured performers included the yaller cat, the jubal jew, blow the candle out, and the pigeon wing. The pigeon wing was later incorporated in many plantation dances, including the buck and wing. It made its way to the minstrel and vaudeville stage, and the flapping arms of this step were later refined as the circular arm movements done during the execution of tap wings.

The use of slapping and clapping as a form of accompaniment was also later used in many dances in the United States. Called patting juba, this method of making music by striking the hands against the body was also incorporated in early tap performances, such as those of America's first real tap dancer, William Henry Lane. Patting juba is discussed more fully in Chapter Six.

In his book *Bahama Songs and Stories,* published in 1895, Charles Edwards mentions the juba, and tells of how "...some expert dancer 'steps off' his specialty in a challenging way."[11] The competitive aspects of the juba were an important contribution in the development of tap dance because they were later incorporated into tap challenges, which in turn fostered experimentation with newer, more intricate footwork.

Other Caribbean Dances

The calenda, the chica, and the juba were only three of the many dances done in the West Indies. Dances performed during holidays and other ceremonial and religious occasions such as weddings and funerals were also prevalent. Funeral dances were especially elaborate because of the position held by ancestors in African religion. According to Albert J. Raboteau,

> Improper or incomplete funeral rites can interfere with or delay the entrance of the deceased into the spiritual world and may cause his soul to linger about, as a restless and malevolent ghost.[12]

On the plantations of St. Croix, one unique dance, known as the masquerade dance, was used to settle disputes. The first dancer presented their complaint in rhymed verse and dance, then the defendant responded with their side of the story, also in song and dance, while a chorus sang the final verdict.

"Negro Dance ōn a Cuban Plantation." From *Harper's Weekly* (1859).

The John Canoe dance, which was performed during Christmas celebrations, was done by male dancers dressed in wild costumes, wearing masks adorned with horns and tusks. The dancers traveled through the town accompanied by crowds of drunken women that were divided into two rival groups; the Reds, dressed in red and led by their queen; and the Blues, dressed in blue and led by their queen. The dancers went from house to house shouting "John Canoe," accompanied by the beating of the gombay drum. Later, in the 19th-century, the headdresses of the men grew into elaborate affairs which looked like dollhouses and actually did contain dolls and puppets.[13] Anthropologist Melville Herkovits suggests that the name of the John Canoe dance is derived from the Ashanti people of Africa and is a reference to the *yankoro* or buzzard. In the United States, the climax of the John Canoe included a buck dance known as the buzzard lope.

Similar to the John Canoe dancers

were the gombay dancers, who also wore elaborate headdresses and performed at Christmas celebrations. The gombay dance involved elaborate footwork and stamping steps similar to those used in Native American war dances, and also included splits, knee slides and pirouettes — in contrast to the John Canoe dancers' more subdued shuffling steps.

Other holiday dances were performed during Mardi Gras and also on St. John's Day, celebrated as San Juan's Day in Cuba on June 24. The Spanish influence was apparent in Cuban dances in which the dancers commonly mixed wild leaping African movements with the more graceful footwork of the traditional Spanish flamenco dance, the zapateado.

People of the Caribbean also danced to celebrate the harvest after the last of the crop was cut and gathered in. These dances were unique in that different races mingled freely during the festivities. Whites as well as blacks danced, sometimes performing native African dances, and at other times, joining together to dance a Scottish reel or English country dance. There are written accounts of European quadrilles being performed by the slaves, transformed with African stylistic elements into rapid shuffling dances and done with hip and shoulder movements and improvisation. The mixture of European steps and African hip and shoulder movements later became the foundation of several jazz steps that are still used today.

Since the islands were originally the conquest of Spain, the black repertoire also included Spanish folk dances. This cross-cultural exchange of dances was extremely important in the development of American tap because the slaves that eventually made their way to the mainland brought with them dances that had facets from each of these traditions, Spanish and African.[14]

Voodoo and Shango

Other Caribbean dances were associated with the religious cults of Voodoo and Shango. The main purpose of dance in the Voodoo ritual was to induce a state of possession in which the dancer was taken over by the god, known in Voodoo ritual as the *loa*. It was believed that the *loa* "mounted" the dancer and made their wishes known by speaking through the person who was possessed. The dancer was called the "horse of the god," since he or she was "ridden" by the god. Each *loa* inspired a different type of dance depending upon the individual characteristics of that particular god. In Haitian Voodoo, the chief *loa* was Damballa, the serpent god. Dancers possessed by Damballa would writhe and wriggle like snakes.[15]

Possession in the Voodoo ritual came about when the chief drummer interrupted the basic rhythm pattern of the other instrumentalists by playing an abrupt counterrhythm. This disruption in the regular beat propelled the dancer into a trance state.[16] In Haitian culture these counterrhythms were called *cassés,* or "breaks," from the French verb *casser,* which means "to shatter" or "to break." The word "break" is of course familiar to tap dancers who also use it to describe a change in the rhythmical pattern, such as in a time-step break. Breaks in percussive dances were later commonly featured in plantation dances in the United States where the word "breakdown"

"Voodoo Dance" by E.W. Kemble. From *Century Magazine* (1886).

came to signify any dance that was so riotously boisterous, that the dancer seemed possessed.

The Shango cult, brought to the Caribbean from Nigeria, was similar to Voodoo in that its main purpose was to induce possession. In Shango, skill and aptitude in dancing were especially valued. During the ritual, dancers circled single file as they bent and straightened their knees rapidly with bouncing steps, becoming more and more animated until they were possessed by the deity.[17] Anthropologists Melville and Frances Herskovits observed one female Shango dancer who danced while balancing water on her head.

> A goblet with a green ribbon about its neck was brought to her, and this she placed on her head and began to dance. Without a headpad to steady it and without spilling any of its contents she danced vigorously for thirty-five minutes.[18]

Balancing water on the head while dancing was a common practice during jig and buck and wing contests in the United States and was often used in minstrel and vaudeville specialty acts to demonstrate a dancer's skill.

Another cult that developed in the West Indies was known as the Shouters or the Spiritual Baptists.[19] Popular in Trinidad, this cult was more accepted by mainstream society than some of the others because the songs used to accompany the dances of possession were hymns taken from the Methodist hymnal. This particular cult was sanctioned by the Protestant Church and the *loa* that possessed the dancer was referred to as the Holy Spirit. Dancers often spoke gibberish which was interpreted as speaking in tongues. "Shouting" was also a familiar practice among Christianized slaves in the United States and it is likely that their services were directly influenced by Africans who were "seasoned" in the West Indies and then brought to the mainland.[20]

Because of the close ties between the West Indies and the United States, Caribbean rhythms and dance styles heavily influenced the development of dance on the mainland. As "seasoned" slaves were shipped to the colonies, they brought with them dances that contained authentic African elements, which were by that time now a step removed from sacred tribal ritual. Dances were also beginning to show certain European stylistic elements. These dances from the West Indies created the foundation upon which American vernacular dance, including tap dance, was built.

5

Dance in New Orleans

New Orleans was founded by the French in 1718, but changed to Spanish rule in 1762. From this date until the 1800s, there was a large influx of Spanish-speaking immigrants from the West Indies. The West Indies had strong commercial ties to the city, and these links to the islands of the Caribbean directly impacted the cultural development of New Orleans. Dance was especially influenced by this intimate relationship. By the time Jefferson transacted the Louisiana Purchase in 1803, buying all of the Louisiana territory from Napoleon (the French had reacquired it in 1800), New Orleans was a melting pot of cultures.[1]

Blacks had been in New Orleans since the city's founding, but in 1803, after the slave insurrection led by Toussaint L'Ouverture in Haiti, the number of blacks living in New Orleans dramatically increased.[2] Many wealthy white planters, trying to escape the uprisings that were taking place throughout the West Indies, immigrated to the United States and made their way to New Orleans, bringing their slaves with them, and establishing a large black community in the area.[3]

These black slaves brought with them the dances that had been popular in the islands, dances such as the chica, the calenda and the juba. They also brought the rituals and religious practices that were commonly practiced there. Because Louisiana was predominantly Roman Catholic, a religion that was more tolerant towards blacks, "...the climate was right ... for the syncretism of Catholic and African beliefs."[4] This allowed the practice of Voodoo to flourish in New Orleans.

Quadroon Balls

When New Orleans was under French rule, the court at Versailles issued an "Edict Concerning the Negro Slaves in Louisiana" in 1724, better known as the *Code Noir*, or Black Code. The *Code Noir* forbade intermarriage between the races and the owning of concubines.[5] Despite this, many white men took black mistresses. The offspring from these extramarital relationships were called mulattos, people who were half white and half black. Because the *Code Noir* forbade mulattos from marrying either whites or blacks, the only alternative for a mulatto woman was to become the mistress of a white man. The child of a white father and a mulatto mother was called a quadroon. Although quadroons contained one quarter black blood, their features and skin color were often virtually indistinguishable from those of whites.[6]

A system called *placage* was developed, whereby dances were set up so that wealthy white men could encounter these women of mixed blood with the specific intention of making them mistresses. The dances were for all intents and purposes, very elaborate, glorified slave markets. No quadroon men were allowed to attend the balls, and the dances were a one-way affair between white males and *femmes de couleur*, or women of color. These dances were called quadroon balls and the women who attended them were called *placées* (placed women).[7]

The *placées* used these balls as an opportunity to further themselves socially. Besides achieving a more comfortable life, many of these women of color were given their freedom. In addition, their children were often protected from slavery. Only the most refined women who had been trained from childhood for this very purpose were presented at the quadroon balls. Proper etiquette and deportment were strictly observed by both parties.

> Mothers brought their thirteen- and fourteen-year-old daughters, dressed in their finery, and paraded them for inspection. Surveying a group of quadroon girls, the "patron" was virtually assured of the young woman's virginity. If he chose to pursue one, he made preliminary arrangements with her mother. After assuring the mother that he could indeed support her daughter in fitting style, and having reached an understanding as to his obligations and duties, the man concluded the negotiations by presenting a gift or a house to the mother. The arrangements would include a financial plan for the girl and any children she might have. The patron was then permitted to call on the girl. After the two principals reached an agreement, a party was given and announcements made to friends. The girl then went to live with her "protector," frequently assuming his name.[8]

The liaison between a quadroon girl and the man that had chosen her often lasted for years or even for life, but most often the relationship was severed when the young man eventually took a white wife.

> ... [W]hen the time comes for the gentleman to take a white wife, the dreadful news reaches his quadroon partner, either by letter entitling her to call the house and furniture her own, or by newspaper which announces the marriage. The quadroon women are rarely known to form a second connection. Many commit suicide; more die broken hearted.[9]

By the 1830s at least three quadroon balls were being given each week in New Orleans. The dances were professionally promoted, admission was charged, and only upper-class white Creole men were invited to attend.[10] The dances became a popular tourist attraction for visiting aristocratic white males and often duels resulted from an out-of-towner giving too much attention to one of the quadroons.[11]

The most popular site for these balls was the *Salle d'Orleans* or the Orleans Ballroom which featured a gambling room on the first floor and the ballroom on the second. The ballroom was elegantly ornate with loges surrounding the dance floor for onlookers. The floor was constructed of triple-layered cypress hardwood and was reputed to be the best dance floor in the world. Food and champagne were served nightly and the orchestra that accompanied the dances was top notch.

Quadroon balls eventually died out during the Civil War, and after their decline, the *Salle d'Orleans* was used as the criminal courtroom of the Parish of New Orleans. The building was eventually purchased by the Catholic Church in 1881 and turned into a convent for the Sisters of the Holy Family, an order of African-American nuns who ran a school and orphanage for black children.[12] The ballroom was converted into a chapel.[13]

At the quadroon balls, emphasis was placed on refinement and elegance, and the dances performed at these gatherings were stately versions of European quadrilles, reels and minuets, far removed from any trace of African influence. Nevertheless, these balls had an important effect upon the development of dance in America because when mulattos and blacks were denied entrance to the gatherings, they organized their own less ritualized black and white dances. Between 1800 and 1850, these less formal mixed dances became common around town in ballrooms as well as in less respectable taverns. They were organized by blacks, although they were often attended by white males who came to the dances with the intention of forming sexual liaisons with the black women. The blacks and mulattos at these dances also emulated the white quadrilles, polkas and minuets of the whites, but in the less formal atmosphere, black stylistic elements found their way into the dances.

Congo Square

In addition to the refined quadroon balls and the mixed black and white dances of New Orleans, there were wild Sunday dances held among the black slaves. By 1786, laws were passed preventing blacks from dancing in public squares until after evening church services had concluded, so slaves started gathering after dinner on the levees and in parks to dance. After the slave revolt in Haiti in 1803, and the huge influx of West Indian blacks, many of them devotees of Voodoo, whites became increasingly paranoid about gatherings of such large number of slaves after dark and the clandestine practice of Voodoo in secret societies around town.[14] In 1817, the city passed laws which limited dancing to the hours before sundown and restricting it to one location. The New Orleans City council passed legislation stating,

Article 6. The assemblies of slaves for the purpose of dancing or other merriment, shall take place only on Sundays, and solely in such open or public places as shall be appointed by the Mayor, and no such assembly shall continue later than sunset, and all slaves, who shall be found assembled together on any other day than Sunday, or who, even on that day, shall continue their dances after sunset, shall be taken up by the officers of police, constables, watchmen, or other white persons, and shall be lodged in the public jail, where they shall receive from 10 to 25 lashes.[15]

The mayor designated a place called Congo Plains, later called Congo Square, or *Place Congo,* as the area where slaves would be allowed to dance, under the careful watch of the white authorities.[16] The park was still reserved exclusively for whites and free persons of color at all other times during the week, but the slaves were allowed to use Congo Plains on Sundays.

The park was an open field northwest of the city limits that had been used by the Native Americans and Creoles as a place for playing the ball game *racquette* and for other sporting events, such as cockfighting and dogfighting.[17] In the summer, tents were set up there for Master Cayetanos' circus and menagerie. Congo Plains attracted thousands of African-Americans who came to meet and dance each Sunday from two in the afternoon until nine at night.

> ... Congo Plains did not gather the house-servants so much as the field hands. These came in troops ... wilder than gypsies; wilder than Moors and Arabs whose strong blood and features one sees at a glance in so many of them; gangs as they were called; gangs and gangs of them, from this and that and yonder direction.[18]

Although drums had been banned in most parts of the United States, they

"Bamboula in Congo Square" by E. W. Kemble. From *Century Magazine* (1886).

re-emerged and were allowed for the dances in Congo Square.[19] Like the quadroon balls, the Sunday dances became a popular tourist attraction.[20] Often frequented by the young gentlemen from the College of Orleans, the gathering also became the hot spot for visitors to the city. Two or three thousand white observers would sit on the surrounding fences to watch the slaves dance.

Visiting the city in 1819, architect B. H. B. Latrobe commented that the dancing was "brutally savage."[21] White Americans, used to erect European dancing with recognizable footwork, were shocked and fascinated by these dances.[22] In an article called "Creole Slave Dances: The Dance in the Place Congo," published in *Century Magazine* in 1886, G. W. Cable wrote that the dancing was "...a sensual, devilish thing tolerated only by Latin-American masters."[23]

After commenting on the "maddening repetition" of the drums, Cable further described the dance:

> And yet there is entertaining variety. Where? In the dance! There was constant, exhilarating novelty, endless invention in the turning, bowing, arm-

swinging, posturing and leaping of the dancers.[24]

Cable's observations are significant because they reveal that not only were the bamboula, the calenda, and the juba regularly danced at Congo Square, but also versions of European dances such as jigs and fandangoes.[25] Because European and African dances were indiscriminately thrown together, a fusion of styles took place and was then disseminated by the thousands of tourists who brought tales of these Sunday dances to the folks back home. Movements that would later become part of such social dances as the twist, the shimmy and the Charleston were frequently described.

Although Sunday dances at Congo Square began to diminish after the Civil War as black dance halls became more popular and African-Americans began to migrate north, their impact was vitally important to the development of tap dancing. In New Orleans, with the popularity of interracial balls, the formal dances of Europe were learned and copied by blacks, and at Congo Square, whites confiscated the driving syncopated rhythms of Africa.[26] This syncretism of styles eventually led to a new form of dance called tap.

6

Dance on the Plantation

The Stono Insurrection

By the time South Carolina became a crown colony in 1721, its population was 18,000 people; almost 12,000 were black slaves, and an additional 1,000 African slaves were being imported each year. White slave owners, who lived in constant fear of the hostile slave majority, created a repressive, punishment-based system that was intended to control the ever-expanding slave population. This system included the establishment of specific "slave laws," the most stringent being the Negro Act of 1740. The development of tap dancing was significantly influenced by this set of laws, enacted in response to the Stono Insurrection, the largest slave rebellion in the United States prior to the Revolutionary War.

Early on Sunday morning, September 9, 1739, about 20 miles west of Charleston at St. Paul's Parish on the Stono River, 20 slaves killed and beheaded two storekeepers at Hutcheson's store and stole arms and ammunition while their masters were at church. Led by an Angolan slave named Jemmy (some say his name was Cato), the slaves escaped towards St. Augustine, Florida, and freedom.[1] Joined by other blacks along the way until their ranks swelled to almost one hundred, they marched to the beating of two drums and

killed all whites that interfered, sparing only one innkeeper at Wallace's Tavern who had been kind to his slaves.

Historical accounts mention that after marching ten miles and killing 25 whites, the escaping slaves

> ... halted in a field, and set to dancing, Singing and beating Drums, to draw more negroes to them, thinking they were now victorious over the whole Province.[2]

By coincidence, Lieutenant Governor Bull and four other men, including a Mr. Golightly, happened to be making their way to Charleston that Sunday morning when they came upon the slaves. Golightly immediately rode to the nearest white settlement at Wilton and warned the settlers who were attending services at a Presbyterian church. The whites formed a militia which caught up with the rebels, secretly encircling them near the ferry crossing of the Edisto River at about four o'clock that afternoon. They fired several rapid volleys into the mob, killing or wounding most of the slaves.[3] A few blacks fled into the surrounding woods but were later rounded up and killed. The planters cut the fugitives' heads off and mounted them on the mile posts along the road.

Whites were aware that slave rebellions were often plotted or scheduled to take place during events that involved dancing, and that the rhythmic cadence of the drums which accompanied dancing could also be used to invite insurrection.[4] Slaves had used drums and dancing prominently during the Stono Insurrection, and in 1730, just a few years before this, they had also hidden their intention to revolt by using the pretense of planning a "dancing bout."[5] The Negro Act of 1740 was a direct result of this understanding. These laws prohibited any African-American from

… beating drums, blowing horns or the like which might on occasion be used to arouse slaves to insurrectionary activity.[6]

Since most states patterned their laws on those of South Carolina or Virginia, the effects of these prohibitions were far-reaching.

When drumming was banned to prevent uprisings, African slaves were deprived of their traditional means of communication. Denied their most prevalent, and indeed sacred means of expression, the slaves substituted the forbidden drums with bone clappers, tambourines, and most importantly, hand and body slaps, and foot beats. The most primitive of all instruments, the human body, became the main source of rhythm and communication.[7]

Using the body percussively in an attempt to mimic the sophisticated rhythms and cadences of drums included elaborate use of heel and toe beats and eventually grew into what we know as tap dance. Even today, when two tap dancers hold a conversation with their feet, they participate in the telegraphing of messages originally done by African drums.

The Use of Dance by Slave Owners

As black slaves were imported to the United States, they were confronted with a society that seemed to them to be devoid of the richness they were accustomed to in their own native lands.[8] African linguist David Dalby stated,

A bitter aspect of the American slave trade is the fact that highly trained musicians and poets from West Africa must frequently have found themselves in the power of slave-owners less cultured and well educated than themselves.[9]

African slaves often found the dances of white colonial Americans inadequate and lacking in creativity.[10] Accustomed to elaborate and complex dance rituals that required improvisational skills, slaves viewed the rigidly codified dances that were learned from European dancing manuals as inhibiting freedom of expression. As they struggled to adapt to their new surroundings, slaves were often forced to accept these European forms. When they did so, however, they infused them with their own rhythms, steps and style. In this way, European dances were Africanized and therefore transformed.

Although the arrival of newly imported slaves helped to perpetuate the African influence upon American dance forms, as early as the beginning of the 18th century, African dances were becoming more and more secularized and less connected to their roots in dance as a form of worship. Ceremonial contexts were dropped although the dance vocabulary drawn from African culture was still used.

In 1807, the international slave trade was banned, and the importation of slaves from Africa became increasingly rare with only a few ships bringing in smuggled slaves. If illegal traders were caught at sea, their cargo, including the human slaves, was usually tossed overboard and destroyed. White slave owners turned to the breeding of slaves for their own use as well as for sale to other plantations. As cultural contact with indigenous Africans decreased, the intercultural blending of the ethnic traditions of those blacks already in America increased. Dances from the multiplicity of different African tribes that had been thrown together on the plantations blended and mutated even more, and a distinct African-American culture began to emerge.

White slave owners believed that the ability to dance added to the financial value

Top: Slaves dancing outside a plantation cabin. "Negro Village on a Southern Plantation," from *Aunt Phyllis' Cabin: or, Southern Life As It Is* by Mary H. Eastman (1852). *Bottom:* Slaves being driven south to be sold, accompanied by the playing of a fiddler. "The Coffle Gang," from *The Suppressed Book About Slavery* by George W. Carleton (1864).

of the slave. Even the auction block was called the "banjo table," because slaves were forced to dance as they were being sold. One slave, named Jolly Old Buck, described watching his friend, Fred, dance while they were waiting to be sold after their first master died.

"Git on de table, Fred," de bossman say.

By-'m-by-Plunk, plunk, plunkety plunk! Dat nigger wid de banjo settin' on de bench waitin' to be sold, he plunk his banjo. Fred 'gin ter shuffle roun' on his big feet.... He slap his big feet on de banjo table, an we all pat wid de banjo music. White man laugh an' clap dey han's. Make him dance some mo'. Wouldn't let de auctioneer start till Fred dance de buck-an'-wing.

De white man what bought Fred say he done paid hundert dollars mo' fo' dat nigger cause he could dance like dat![11]

Slaves were also expected to dance when they were sold to masters in other states. A woman named Jennie Kendricks related how this had happened to her grandmother:

... the slave dealers brought her and a group of other children along much the same as they would a herd of cattle, when they reached a town all of them had to dance through the streets and act lively so that the chances for selling them would be greater.[12]

Amused by the primitive movements that their slaves used while dancing, white slave owners often summoned their slaves to the big house on the plantation. Here, slaves were ordered to perform for the master and his guests, often dancing such dances as the buck dance, the pigeon wing, or the cakewalk.[13]

African-American children entertaining Union soldiers upon the troops' arrival in Baton Rouge during the Civil War. "Contraband Children Dancing the Breakdown," from *Frank Leslie's Illustrated News* (circa 1860s).

The Buck Dance

Any solo dance performed by a man was called a buck dance. The term "buck" is traced to the West Indies where Africans used the words *po' bockorau*, a corruption of the French word *boucanier*, or "buccaneer," to refer to rowdy, noisy, trouble-making sailors. The word, *boucan* was a mispronunciation of the West Indian Tupi word, *mukem*, which was the wooden rack placed over a fire, used for drying and curing meat into jerky. Since early pirates ate jerked meat, the term came to be applied to them as well, and was eventually changed into "buccaneer." The term gradually came to be used to refer to any boisterous behavior. By the 18th century, the label "po buck"

African-Americans dancing inside a plantation cabin. Sheet music cover for "Dancing on De Kitchen Floor" by James A. Bland (circa 1880). *Courtesy of Brown University Library.*

was used to describe the unruly, poor Irish immigrants living in the Carolinas, whose spontaneous jig dancing eventually came to be known as buck. The term was also used to refer to animals that bucked and kicked and danced about, such as horses, goats, or the male deer, which took the name "buck" itself. The dollar was nicknamed a "buck," since a deer skin was worth about a dollar in those days.

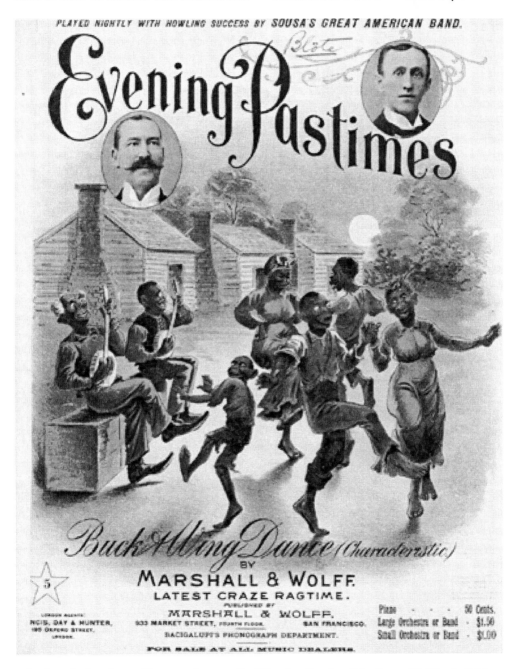

A buck and wing dance. Sheet music cover for "Evening Pastimes" by James H. Marshall (circa 1897).

Old-style buck dancing consisted mainly of stamps and chugs, sometimes embellished with toe bounces. The origins of buck dancing are unclear, but sources indicate that it has many elements in common with the Cherokee stomp dance. There is conjecture that it is also related to ceremonial dances in which Indian braves would put on the antlers and skin of a male deer.

Most authorities believe that the buck dance was the forerunner of the time-step. The connection with the term "wing," as in buck and wing, generally suggests that the wild footwork was accompanied by a flapping of the arms, and that the steps were syncopated. At the turn of the 19th century, buck and wing was used as sort of a catch-all phrase for many forms of percussive dance.

The Pigeon Wing

One of the most popular buck dances among African-American slaves was the pigeon wing, also called the chicken wing. When performing the pigeon wing dancers strutted like a bird and scraped their feet, while the arms, bent at the sides, were flapped like wings. When interviewed for the Virginia Writer's Project, ex-slave Fannie Berry described the pigeon wing thus:

> Dere was cuttin' de pigeons wings — dat was flippin' you' arms an' legs roun' an' holdin' ya' neck stiff like a bird do.[14]

As in the German schühplattler, discussed later, the pigeon wing imitated the courting of birds. The movements, scraping the foot and fluttering the arms, had been part of the juba and survived on their own to become one of the most popular steps among African-Americans. Early minstrels used the dance often and expanded it with more elaborate foot shaking. The

dance's use of animal mimicry can be traced to authentic African elements and a more finessed version of the flapping arms and scraping feet is still used by today's tap dancers when executing wings.[15]

Another popular buck dance was the buzzard lope. Using animal mimicry like the pigeon wing, the buzzard lope included an elaborate pantomime which imitated the walk and pecking motions of a buzzard feeding off carrion.[16] As the dancer performed the buzzard lope, the shoulders were pushed forward and back one at a time so that the body was twisted at the waist. The arms, bent loosely at the elbows, flapped like wings. Many movements from the buzzard lope, later called the eagle wing, were later seen in clog dance styles performed by white dancers. This dance was also important because of its use by Thomas Dartmouth Rice in his famous Jim Crow dance, discussed further in Chapter 13.

The Cakewalk

One of the most lasting plantation dances, which eventually made its way to the minstrel stage, was the cakewalk, sometimes called the chalk line walk, the walkabout or the strut. Based on the grand march at the end of balls and cotillions, this dance started as a parody in which slaves mimicked and mocked their white masters. One slave described the dance thus:

> Sometimes on pleasant evenings, boards would be laid down for an impromptu stage before the verandah so the guests could have a good view of the proceedings and a real shindig would take place with singing and dancing. The Cake Walk, in that section and at that time, was known as the Chalk Line Walk. There was no prancing, just a straight walk on a patch made by turns and so forth, along which the dancers made

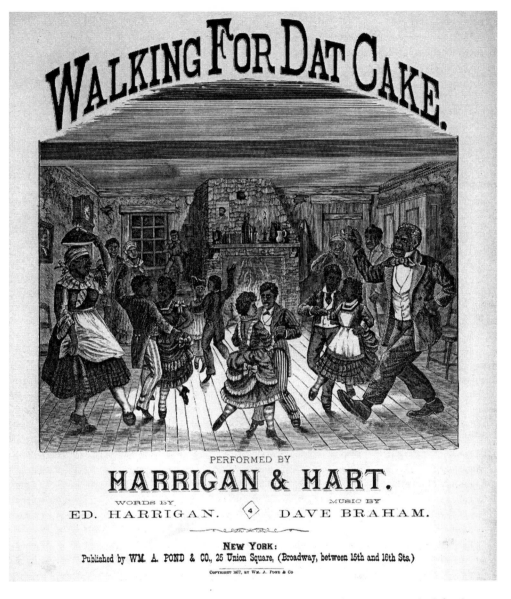

African-Americans dancing the cakewalk inside a cabin. Notice the woman on the left who carries the prize cake on her head. Sheet music cover for "Walking for Dat Cake" by Ed. Harrigan and Dave Braham (circa 1877). *Courtesy of Brown University Library).*

their way with a pail of water on their heads. The couple that was most erect and spilled the least or no water at all was the winner.[17]

Dancers dressed up for the cakewalk in formal attire, donning high hats and long-tailed coats, or white gowns, and par-

odied white society manners. Slave owners seemed to have missed the subtle sarcasm of this satirical pantomime.

Competitions were held with the best dancers winning a huge decorated cake; this is the origin of the expression, "to take the cake." The cakewalk became immensely popular and classes were given in the proper way to perform the dance and to promenade. Cakewalk dancing was affectionately called "peregrination for the pastry," and as the dance's popularity spread north to New York, clubs were formed and champion belts were given out to the best male dancers and diamond rings to the best female dancers. The national championships for cakewalk dancing were held at Madison Square Garden. The competition was usually preceded by a plantation scene with songs and dances. Then the cakewalk parade began led by a drum major. Often 50 or 60 couples participated in the contest, and their dances ranged from buck and wing to dancing on toe. Couples knew that inventiveness paid off. The routines always ended with the high-stepping strut that characterized the dance. The contestants were judged on style, time and execution.

The dance was supposedly first introduced on Broadway in 1885 by Charles Johnson and soon gained worldwide popularity, despite its difficult and strenuous nature.[18] In vaudeville, the cakewalk was sometimes called the prize walk. A later version was the cakewalk wedding, in which the dance mimed all of the various stages of courtship, engagement, marriage and honeymoon.[19]

One of the most popular cakewalk tunes at the end of the 19th-century was a song called "At the Georgia Camp Meeting." It was written in 1897 by Allen Mills, under the nom de plume Kerry Mills, "as a protest against the myriad coon songs of the period, which he said were out of harmony with the true Negro spirit in rhythm and subject."[20] Today, the lyric of the song sounds bigoted and antique, but it does show the way that dancers competed for a prize cake.

When the band of darkies began to play,
Pretty music so gay, hats were then
    thrown away.

Thought them foolish coons their
    necks would break,
When they quit laughing and
    talking,
And went walking for a big chocolate
    cake.[21]

Advice on how to perform the cakewalk was given in a pamphlet entitled *Negro Minstrels; Jokes, Gags, Speeches.* It said.

Cake walks have become such a popular craze during the last few years that society everywhere are introducing them in their many social events, and minstrel performances now seem incomplete without them. While it is a difficult matter to explain everything connected with the many movements, etc., in a cake walk, the author has used his best endeavor to make it plain to the reader. In the first place, to successfully take part in a cake walk, each participant should take great pains in your make-up. The most extreme and flashy suits should be worn, including an endless variety of diamonds or Rhine stones, for jewelry effects. The young lady or young man that takes such part, should wear bright colored dresses. Large hat and high heel slippers and carry a parasol or fan which will show off in excellent taste. The gentleman partner should wear a Prince Albert coat made of red, blue, brown, or green satin, high silk hat of same material, checked trousers, patent leather shoes with white gaiters, a cane with a crooked handle, decorated with ribbons or same colors as his lady's dress. Where more than one couple take part, try and have your costumes, both ladies and gentlemen, different from one another.

Start your walk by taking your partner's hand, elevating it to about the height of your head; step off somewhat in advance of lady, assuming a happy smile; keep step with each time of the music, and be sure to step only on the ball of foot, letting the heel down gently as you touch the other foot to the floor. After passing the audience once in that position let go of hands and continue to walk alone, meeting again at front of audience with bow. Lady will then take your arm and continue walk halfway round when she discovers her shoe untied. Kneeling, place your handkerchief upon knee, and placing lady's foot thereon, proceed to tie it, after which he will arise and accept a kiss which she will offer. The most essential point in a cake walk is to always keep your face towards the audience, not matter if walking directly away from them with your backs turned.

Put in your walks as much different steps or figures as possible, such as imitating an old colored man, a Hebrew, a German, etc. and always bear in mind that the hands, arms, face have much to do with your success as the walking part. A graceful swing of the arms, or if carried out away from the body, is always clever.[22]

Although efforts were made to develop the cakewalk into a regular ballroom dance, it was most commonly and widely used as a stage dance involving stylized strutting with lifted knees and high kicks. Another common feature of the dance was the exaggerated lean of the body backwards from the tip of the extended toe to the top of the head.

Other versions of the cakewalk were called pitchin' hay, corn shuckin', and cuttin' wheat, which indicate that they probably included embellishments which contained common movements from work routines.

The cakewalk in important in the world of American social dance because it was the first African-American dance to achieve wide popularity among white audiences. This, in turn, launched the spread of ballroom dancing and led to the development of many other African-American inspired dances such as the turkey trot, the black bottom and the Charleston. The cakewalk's impact was also felt upon tap, because with the spread of the cakewalk, more and more people began turning to African-American source material.

Patting Juba

As in the West Indies, many plantation dances were accompanied with patting juba, which involved creating polyrhythmical counterpoints by clapping, stamping, or slapping the thighs and other parts of the anatomy. This was sometimes called "body music."

While patting, dancers leaned forward in a crouched position and then struck first their left knee and then their right, and then slapped their two hands together. Variations included using double strokes on the left while continuing with just one hit on the right, and also hitting the shoulders. Solomon Northup, a slave musician described it as

> ... striking the hands on the knees, then striking the hands together, then striking the right shoulder with one hand, the left with the other — all the while keeping time with the feet, and singing....[23]

Patting was also done by hitting rhythms on an instrument, such as a fiddle or banjo. Using the hands, stiff straws, quills, knitting needles, or sticks, people called "beaters" sat at right angles to the instrumentalist and hit the strings between the bridge and the player's left hand. The famous composer W. C. Handy gave a description of this type of patting that was related to him by his grandfather.

> A boy would stand behind the fiddler with a pair of knitting needles in his hand. From this position the youngster

THE JUBA DANCE.

"Dancing the Juba in Colonial America." From *Century Magazine* (1884).

would reach around the fiddler's left shoulder and beat on the strings in the manner of a snare drummer.[24]

Another description was given in an article by David C. Barrow, Jr., written for *Century Magazine* in 1882:

> The performer provides himself with a pair of straws about eighteen inches in length, and stout enough to stand a good smart blow. An experienced straw-beater will be very careful in selecting his straws, which he does from the sedge-broom…. These straws are used after the manner of drum-sticks, that portion of the fiddle-strings between the fiddler's bow and his left hand serving as a drum. One of the first sounds which you hear on approaching the dancing party is the tum tee tum of the straws, and after the dance begins, when the shuffling of feet destroys the other sounds of the fiddle, this noise can still be heard.[25]

These polyrhythms were even more complicated because the fiddler or banjo player also stomped his feet while playing. A gifted fiddler "could stomp the left heel and the right forefoot and alternate this with the right heel and the left forefoot, making four beats to the bar."[26]

In juba beating, or jubilee beating, as it was sometimes called, the performer also improvised rhymes, similar to the way artists do in modern rap music. They accompanied the words with the complex rhythms they beat out on the instrument or on their body. The most familiar lyric for patting juba is still used today in a children's rhyming game:

> Juba dis and Juba dat;
> Juba kill a yaller cat.
> Juba up and Juba down;
> Juba runnin' all aroun'.

There were many variations of this song and lyrics would often conceal satirical jabs at whites which were accented with sharp percussive hits on the instrument or body.[27] The rhythms of patting in this way conveyed covert messages. The word "patting" also came to represent other forms of slave communication.

> The murmured phrase 'patter de pat, patter de pat' ... was used to warn fellow slaves of the presence of patrols in the neighborhood.[28]

When patting juba became popular in the U.S., its rhythms so intrigued the poets Edgar Allan Poe and Sidney Lanier that they experimented with the same complex rhythms in their verses. Lanier wrote,

> Here music is in its rudest form, consisting of rhythm alone ... the most curious noise, yet in such perfect order it furnishes music to dance to ... I have never seen it equaled in my life.[29]

Patting juba also made its way to the professional stage. In 1890, the vaudeville team of Golden and Grayton did a dance move called patting rabbit hash, which was directly related to patting juba.[30] It was

> ... a brisk recitative accompanied by patting and slapping the hands on the knees, hips, elbows, shoulders, and forearms, producing triple time and rolls almost like a snare drum.[31]

Golden and Grayton also patted juba during another one of their dances, the Charleston.[32] The vaudeville team claimed to have been the first to introduce the Charleston to the American stage. Whether or not they were the originators, their patting juba did indeed evolve into a display piece that became part of the wildly popular Charleston. The move, called bees knees, involved the familiar turning in and out of the legs with the hands crossing and

uncrossing on the knees. A later version of patting juba was hambone, and in the 1950s, patting hand rhythms were used in a dance called the charley bop.

The Plantation Stick Dance

The plantation stick dance developed from secret military drills disguised as dance. The dance evolved from the Angolan and Kongolese martial art form of capoeira, and was practiced by young men on plantations to keep their fighting skills honed.[33] Capoeira was a fusion of dance, acrobatics and fighting, and was performed inside a circle. Two combatants danced a simulated fight until one dropped from exhaustion. The observers who surrounded them, clapped and sang rhythmically in a call-and-response format under the direction of a song leader. The songs were repetitive and sung in rhyme as in patting songs. The tempo of the dance was set by a bowed, one-stringed instrument, called a berimbau, which was used because it was quieter than a drum, but was percussive nevertheless.

Because the possession of weapons by any slaves was banned by the white masters, dances such as the plantation stick dance allowed black slaves to practice hand-to-hand combat skills in a covert way. In African warfare, the use of sticks as weapons was valued, as was the skill required in leaping and contorting to avoid body blows or arrows.[34] The dance which utilized such movements camouflaged its true purpose and could be practiced in public before white observers.

In later years, the plantation stick dance became a popular staple of minstrel performers. It was usually performed in the character of an old African-American who tottered on stage with a cane, then proceeded to dance wildly and leap over the cane.

A depiction of the plantation stick dance. "The Old Plantation," watercolor, circa 1800. *Courtesy of Colonial Williamsburg Foundation, Abbey Aldrich Rockefeller Folk Art Collection, Williamsburg, Virginia.*

Jigs and Water Dances

Many different kinds of dances were performed on the plantation, but despite their varying forms, all of these dances had one thing in common — a driving, propulsive rhythm.[35] One name came to be associated with all these forms of syncopated dancing. Although originally used to describe Irish dancing, all forms of African-American dance were eventually grouped into one category by whites and labeled as jigs.[36]

Jigging contests were often arranged by a slave owner between his own slaves, or between his slaves and those of another plantation. The master had a platform built for the contest and invited people from around the area to attend, often with wagers being placed on who would be the best dancer. Sometimes a good dancer was taken from one plantation to the next by

his master and entered into dance contests, while the slave owners bet on the outcome.

Usually a circle was drawn on the floor to delineate a dance area. This practice was called "set de flo'" or setting the floor; the name also came to represent dances performed within the boundaries of drawn lines.[37] These dances contained many elements that later evolved into the cakewalk. For example, the set de flo' couple dances usually began with the woman putting her foot on the knee of her kneeling partner while he tied her shoe. This particular ritual was later commonly found in cakewalk competitions. The dances also always included strutting and often involved competition and, as in the cakewalk, the prize awarded to the best set de flo' dancer was often a cake. As with variations of the cakewalk, other gestures in set de flo' dances mimed work movements such as hoeing corn or swinging a scythe.

Set de flo' dancers tried to remain inside the circle's boundaries while competing with steps called out by the musicians. An added challenge sometimes included dancing with a glass of water balanced on the head as in the early chalk line walk. The winner was the one who could not only stay inside the circle, but also do the most steps without spilling any water.[38]

I must tell you 'bout de best contest we ever had. One nigger on our place was de Jigginest fellow ever was. Everyone round tries to git some body to best him. He could put de glass of water on his head and make his feet go like triphammers and sound like a snare drum. He could whirl round and sich, all de movement from his hips down. Now it gits round a fellow been found to beat Tom and a contest am 'ranged for Saturday evenin'. There was a big crowd and money am bet, but master bets on Tom, of course.

So dey starts Jiggin'. Tom starts easy and a little faster and faster. The other fellow doin' de same. Dey gits faster and faster and dat crowd am a-yellin'. Gosh! There am 'citement. Dey just keep a gwine. It looks like Tom done found his match, but there am one thing yet he ain't done — he ain't made de whirl. Now he does it. Everyone holds his breath, and de other fellow starts to make de whirl and he makes it, but jus' a spoonful of water sloughs out his cup, so Tom am de winner.[39]

Water dances were widespread throughout the South and balancing a bucket or glass of water on the head to determine the winner in a challenge dance was a common element of many plantation dances, especially the cakewalk and buck.

Corn Shuckings

Corn shuckings were another opportunity for slaves to gather as a community and dance in a competitive spirit. Since additional labor was often needed, slaves from neighboring plantations joined in the festivities, providing the chance to reestablish and consolidate the local culture. Usually held at night by the light of burning pine-knot torches, the corn shucking was one of the most important seasonal events of plantation life.[40]

The corn to be shucked was divided into two piles and two teams with two captains were appointed.[41] A prize was awarded to the first group that could shuck all the corn in their pile.[42] An added element included the custom that if anyone participating in the contest found a red ear of corn they either had to be kissed or kiss someone else.

As the group leaders called out instructions, their workers would physically and verbally respond in kind. This type of antiphonal call-and-response had grown out of one of the central elements of African-American dance. The practice stressed social integration, cohesiveness, and communal participation and it acknowledged the leader's role. The caller therefore served to unite the community socially and helped to coordinate the movements that were then deemed acceptable, which helped to establish new standards within each dance.[43] Slaves from the various neighboring plantations then returned home after the shuckings and carried with them these new standards. In addition, call-and-response dancing became increasingly competitive as dancers were urged by the caller to perform harder and harder feats of endurance and virtuosity.

A corn-shucking which is to be considered in light of a finished performance should end with a dance.... These dances take place either in one of the houses, or else out of doors on the ground.... There is a great deal of Jig-dancing in these cotillions, and the man who cannot "cut the pigeon-wing" is considered a sorry dancer indeed.... Endurance is a strong point in the list of accomplishments of the dancer, and other things being equal, that dancer who can hold out the longest is considered the best.[44]

This competitive spirit was extremely important in later tap challenges and dance-offs. Although the role of the caller was sometimes taken over by the audience, the call-and-response format was still in place.

Corn-shucking frolics included plenty of food and always ended with dancing which was a mixture of traditional black African-American plantation dances and white European-based social dances. In his book *He-He Noo: Or Records of a Tourist*, published in Philadelphia in 1850, Charles Lanman described one such corn-shucking dance that he witnessed while traveling in the South.

> The dance is the famous "Virginia Reel," and at least a hundred individuals have formed themselves into the proper places. No sooner do the instruments attain the necessary pitch, than the head couples dash into the arena, now slowly and disdainfully, now

swiftly and ferociously, and now performing the double shuffle or the pigeon-wing. Anon they come to a stand, while the others follow, and go through the same fantastic performances, with the addition perhaps of an occasional leap or whirl.[45]

Before the corn-shucking dances commenced, the master traditionally had a wooden floor built in the yard. Ex-slave Nancy Williams recalled how workers were sent to the local mill to get planks so they could construct a "gra' big platform an' brung it to de house for to dance on."[46] The platform not only raised the dancers so they could be seen but also served to emphasize and amplify the sound of the dancing. In his thorough examination of the corn-shucking ritual, Roger D. Abrahams wrote:

> The slaves did not relish dancing on the ground, in the manner of the American Indians ... the shuffle of the feet, in many instances unshod ... could not be heard as distinctly on the ground as on a plank floor or tight puncheon.[47]

Corn-shucking dances were often satirical in nature, ridiculing the slave owners.[48] Because the whites rarely understood the symbolism of African dances, satirical dancing became a safe means of defiance and expressing disapproval towards slave practices.[49] To white observers the dances merely looked like entertainment.

This dance ritual of deconstruction allowed slaves to assert themselves and to keep the spirit of resistance alive on a personal level....

THE DANCE.

African-American workers celebrate the end of the corn shucking with a dance. "The Dance," from an engraving by W. L. Shepard. From *Century Magazine* (October 1882).

Top: "The Dance After the Husking." Wood engraving by Winslow Homer, *Harper's Weekly,* November 27, 1858. Party scene. *Bottom:* "Lynchburg — Negro Dance." Watercolor by Lewis Miller, 1853. *Courtesy of Colonial Williamsburg Foundation, Abbey Aldrich Rockefeller Folk Art Collection, Williamsburg, Virginia. Gift of Dr. and Mrs. Richard M. Kain.*

The context of enjoyment as well as the lowered defenses provided a situation of maximum camouflage.[50]

Because slaves could not openly criticize whites, dances were a vehicle for self-assertion and an opportunity to affirm their own cultural traditions. African-American dance therefore commingled with resistance. In a lecture at Harvard in 1973, Ralph Ellison said,

> The slaves first sensed it. They sensed it when they looked at the people in the big house dancing their American versions of European social dances. And they first mocked them — and then they decided, coming from dancing cultures, that they could do them better. And then they went on to define what surely is the beginnings of an American choreography.... They had the freedom of experimentation, of trying things out.... And in the doing, they found ways of making the human body move in stylized ways which were different.[51]

Living in the slave quarters, essentially isolated from the outside white world, African-Americans had the opportunity to organize and develop their own cultural values.[52] The gestures of dance, be they ones of derision or celebration, provided a personal language for blacks that functioned to preserve the societal mores of the community. The dance also served as an educational tool for the community, teaching self-control and composure.[53]

The ability to survive under adverse conditions was deeply rooted in the African culture, springing from a ritualization of their lives that allowed them to react creatively and responsively, to have a toughness and resiliency, and to endure. The capacity to disregard outer form while retaining inner values not only helped African-Americans survive, but also fostered the constant transformation and reworking of such cultural expressions as the dance.

7

Slave Religion and the Ring Shout

From the beginnings of the Atlantic slave trade, white Christians justified their actions by convincing themselves that slavery benefited Africans. Their rationale was that because slaves were required by law to be baptized before they were shipped to the New World, their souls were therefore saved.

> ... [F]or though their bodies were now brought into some subjection, that was a small matter in comparison of their souls, which would now possess true freedom for evermore.[1]

To prove that they had complied with the mandatory baptism requirement, slave traders branded each slave with the sign of the cross. Not only physically painful, this branding was also psychologically demeaning, dispiriting, and humiliating because it destroyed the tribesmen's other tattoos, which in African culture represented their status.

The desire to spread Christianity had been one of the motivating factors in the exploration and colonization of the New World, so the education and conversion of African slaves was initially encouraged and fervently practiced. Despite this initial burst of Christian missionary zeal, there eventually developed a reticence among colonial American slave masters to continue the practice of conversion or religious instruction. Arguments against the conversion of slaves ranged from the common belief that blacks were too brutish and ignorant for conversion to be effective, to the fear that if slaves did convert, they would become proud and therefore rebellious.[2] The main fear seemed to lie in the awareness that a Christian slave could claim some sort of equal human worth and upset the master-slave hierarchy. In addition, it was generally believed that according to the laws of England and the canons of the church, a master would be required to free any slave who was baptized.[3]

This belief prompted laws that were carefully worded to deny that baptism would affect a slave's station in life. One such statute that was passed in Virginia, in September, 1667, stated;

> Whereas some doubts have risen whether children that are slaves by birth, and by the charity and piety of their owners made partakers of the blessed sacrament of baptism, should by virtue of their baptism be made free, *it is enacted and declared by this Grand Assembly, and the authority thereof,* that the conferring of baptism does not alter the condition of the person as to his bondage or freedom; that divers masters, freed from this doubt, may more carefully endeavor the propagation of Christianity by permitting children, though slaves, or those of greater growth if capable, to be admitted to that sacrament.[4]

With the legal reassurance that Christianizing their slaves would not affect them economically, slave owners reluctantly began proselytizing slaves, eventually realizing that Christianity could be used to exercise even more control over blacks.[5]

The Great Awakening

The banning of the international slave trade in 1807 coincided with a period of intense religious revivalism in the United States called the Great Awakening. During this period, focus was shifted to the inward experience of conversion and away from the outward trappings of status. Evangelical in nature, revivalism encouraged the conversion of all people which in turn created a revitalized interest in converting slaves among pious whites. Large-scale conversions of blacks took place especially within the Baptist and the Methodist sects.[6] Both of these denominations encouraged experiential forms of worship that were familiar or at least adaptable to African religious rituals, including singing, dancing, and possession.

> The powerful emotionalism, ecstatic behavior, and congregational response of the revival were amenable to the African heritage of the slaves, and forms of African dance and song remained in the shout and spirituals of Afro-American converts to evangelical Protestantism. In addition, the slaves' rich heritage of folk beliefs and folk expression was not destroyed but augmented by conversion.[7]

The Baptists and Methodists stressed eloquence rather than education among their clergy; therefore, blacks who manifested a talent for exhorting were encouraged to preach, even to unconverted whites.[8] These black preachers often chanted sermons in a highly rhythmic style to work the congregation into a frenzy.

A phenomenon that developed during the Great Awakening was the institution of the camp meeting. Camp meetings consisted of religious services that lasted for several days. Often taking place in the woods, small tents were raised to house the participants and a large central tent, called the "tabernacle," was erected for the full congregation to gather under. These services drew thousands of worshipers and usually bordered on hysteria. Worshippers frequently manifested symptoms called "exercises" which early observers classified as dancing, wheeling, laughing, barking, and jerking. Jerking was the most common of these exercises. In his autobiography, published in 1856, Methodist minister Peter Cartwright described the practice.

> A new exercise broke out among us, called the jerks, which was overwhelming in its effects upon the bodies and minds of the people. No matter whether they were saints or sinners, they would be taken under a warm song or sermon, and seized with a convulsive jerking all over, which they could not possibly avoid, and the more they resisted the more they jerked. If they would not strive against it and pray in good earnest, the jerking would usually abate. I have seen more than five hundred persons jerking at one time in my large congregations. Most usually persons taken with the jerks, to obtain relief, as they said, would rise up and dance. Some would run, but could not get away. Some would resist; on such the jerks were generally very severe.[9]

Camp meetings were interracial affairs and often blacks outnumbered whites. Although secular dancing was prohibited by the Protestant Church, many newly converted slaves continued to express themselves through movement within the emotionally charged atmosphere of revival camp meetings. In 1819, John Watson wrote of one such camp meeting.

In the blacks' quarters, the coloured people get together, and sing for hours together, short scraps of disjointed affirmations, pledges, or prayers, lengthened out with long repetitious choruses. These are all sung in the merry chorus-manner of the southern harvest field, or husking-frolic method, of slave blacks; and also very greatly like the Indian dances. With every word so sung, they have a sinking of one or other leg of the body alternately; producing an audible sound of the feet at every step....[10]

As camp meetings were coming to a close, slaves would break down the wooden partitions that separated their camp living quarters from those of the whites and then would have a "grand march round de campment ... accompanied with leaping, shuffling, and dancing, after the order of David before the ark when his wife thought he was crazy."[11] This tradition was called singing and praying bands in the Methodist Church and, as with the ring shout which is described later in this chapter, the participants were discouraged from lifting or crossing their feet.

The Afro-Protestant Church

Many slave owners forced their slaves to attend their own carefully regulated church services in the belief that they might instill in them proper religious and moral lessons. Instead, they often reinforced the reality of their own blatant hypocrisy. One slave reported being given Communion in the morning and being whipped that same afternoon. A slave from Texas named Carey Davenport recalled:

"The Jerking Exercise." Engraving by Lossing-Barrett, circa 1840. *Courtesy of the Library of Congress.*

I'd say old master treated us slaves bad and there was one thing I couldn't understand, 'cause he was 'ligious and every Sunday mornin' everybody had to git ready and go for prayer. I never could understand his 'ligion, 'cause sometimes he git up off his knees and befo' we git out of the house he cuss us out.[12]

Disgust with a hypocritical gospel forced upon them by the masters' preachers led many blacks to begin organizing their own religious meetings. An Afro-Protestant folk church, which took Protestant biblical stories and blended them with

Methodist church service on a cotton plantation near Port Royal, South Carolina. Note the African-American preacher. "Family Worship in a Plantation in South Carolina," from the _Illustrated London News_ (1863).

African cultural characteristics and emphasized the themes of suffering and deliverance, began to flourish in brush arbors or "hush harbors" and secret praise houses that were built away from prying interference of white people. These "hush harbors" provided a place for the expression of community spirit and were a haven from both the harsh routine of slave life and the hypocritical preaching of the white church. Slaves used secret signals and passwords to designate the location of these religious gatherings called "steal aways."[13]

A Virginia slave, Peter Randolph, described these meetings.

Not being allowed to hold meetings on the plantation, the slaves assemble in the swamp, out of reach of the patrols. They have an understanding among themselves as to the time and place.... This

is often done by the first one arriving breaking boughs from trees and bending them in the direction of the selected spot. After arriving and greeting one another, men and women sat in groups together. Then there was preaching ... by the brethren, then praying and singing all around until they generally feel quite happy. The speaker rises and talks slowly, until feeling the spirit, he grows excited, and in a short time there fall to the ground twenty or thirty men and women under its influence.[14]

To avoid discovery, the slaves muffled the sound of the meeting by hanging wetted quilts and rags around the area or speaking into water-filled or overturned pots hoping to drown out the sound. Because these services often culminated in trance possession, fellow members were quick to subdue any worshiper who became

" *The Sabbath among Slaves.*"

"The Sabbath Among the Slaves" from *Narrative of the Life and Adventures of Henry Bibb, American Slave* (1849). *Courtesy of the Library of Congress, Rare Book and Special Collections Division.*

too animated, by putting their hands over his or her mouth.

Fearing these churches to be hotbeds of insurrection, slave masters gave stiff penalties for attending such services without permission, including up to 200 lashes if caught. White slave owners were constantly on guard and remained wary of Christianized slaves, reminding themselves that slave revolts were sometimes ignited by blacks who validated their actions by quoting the scriptures.[15] Laws were passed that required a white person be present whenever the black congregation gathered to worship, a law circumvented by having a white child attend the service.

The Ring Shout

As African-Americans converted to Christianity, they borrowed elements from both African ritual and white Protestant traditions, one of which included the belief that secular dancing was sinful.[16] However, because movement was such an important part of the slaves' cultural heritage, dance evolved as a sacred expression. The ring shout, used during Baptist worship services, grew out of the evangelical Afro-Protestant movement, although its roots can be traced back to African circle dances.[17] It is believed that the dance's origins lay in the BaKongo practice of tracing cosmograms on the ground and dancing over the drawn figures in order to invoke spirits.[18]

Performed in a circle, the ring shout, also called "running sperichils," utilized the whole body and included the tapping of feet, flat-footed shuffles, clapping, waving of the arms, and shouting. Often during the dance, the worshipers lost control and "cut de pigeon wing" as they entered the trance state called "falling out." Poet James Weldon Johnson described this trance inducement when he spoke about a ring shout he attended in Florida as a boy.

The music starts and the ring begins to move. Around it goes, at first slowly, then with quickening pace. Around and around it moves on shuffling feet that do not leave the ground, one foot beating with the heel a decided accent in two-four time. The music is supplemented by the clapping of hands. As the ring goes around it begins to take on signs of frenzy. The music, starting, perhaps with a Spiritual, becomes a wild, monotonous chant. The same musical phrase is repeated over and over, two, three, four, five hours. The words become a repetition of an incoherent cry. The very monotony of the sound and motion produces an ecstatic state. Women, screaming, fall to the ground prone and quivering. Men, exhausted, drop out of the shout. But the ring closes up and moves around and around.[19]

The ring shout utilized the African tradition of antiphonal call-and-response.[20] A song leader, who was called the "songster," called out directions to the dancers as they circled the altar. The dancers were called "shouters."[21] The dance was accompanied by the pounding of a beating stick or broom struck against the floor by the "sticker" or "stick man."[22] A chorus of singers, called "basers," answered the lines called out by the leader, clapping and patting as they sang.

While they clapped, the "basers" feet also moved. The traditional basic footwork was a flat-footed step to one side followed by the second foot touching the floor next to the first with a whole-footed stomp. The stomp was done without shifting the weight, and occurred at the same time the hands were struck together. This movement was called "stepping it down." Although the foot stomp was done with a rather light touch, in tandem with the sound of the hands striking together it caused the rhythmical accent of the clapping accompaniment to fall on the musi-

cal offbeat of the measure on the second and fourth beats. The pattern of the claps was easily changed if double claps were inserted and other rhythmical variations were used. The effect was also enhanced if participants did different variations at the same time, creating polyrhythmic clapping.

The percussive sounds could be further elaborated by varying the tone of the clap, which could be pitched either low or high depending upon how the hands were struck together. There were generally three tonal variations. When clapping a lower bass note the palms were struck at right angles without hitting the fingers together at all, creating a flat sound. Middle or baritone claps were executed with the left palm being struck by the right fingers, which were slightly cupped. Done at right angles, the sound created was a like a sharp pop. Tenor clapping was done in the same basic way that baritone clapping was done, except the fingers were not cupped. The highest tones were possible when the fingers of both hands were relaxed and straight. In most dance accompaniment, the middle tone or baritone clap set the central beat on counts two and four and all other polyrhythmic variations were taken off its lead. The bass was infinitely varied and most often started in a pattern against the baritone clap on the first count of the measure. The tenor claps were used to punctuate the other two types of claps.

The basic footwork of the "shouters" consisted of a step forward on the right foot, and then a closing in with the left.[23] This was repeated with the lead foot always stepping on the downbeat as that beat was pounded out by the "sticker" hitting his rhythm stick against the floor. Sometimes at the end of the verse, the dancer would stop and stamp loudly and then the leading foot would become the left. This movement came to be known as a "ketch-it." The feet only moved forward two or three inches at a time, but with each forward step, the foot was stamped loudly against the floor. The feet also stayed very close to the ground so that the forward progression of the dancer really came from a hitching movement that caused the entire body to shake. The dance was described in the *Nation Magazine*, May 30, 1867.

> All stand up in the middle of the floor, and when the 'sperichil' is struck, begin first walking and by-and-by shuffling around, one after the other, in a ring. The foot is hardly taken from the floor, and the progression is mainly due to a jerking, hitching motion which agitates the entire shouter....[24]

The words of each song that accompanied the ring shout were also acted out, so the dancers changed their arm movements not only with fluctuations in the rhythm, but also as determined by the words of the spiritual that was being sung.[25] Spontaneity and communal participation were essential elements.

> The feet are not supposed to leave the floor or to cross each other, such an act being sinful. The shouting proceeds with a curious shuffling, but controlled step which taps out with the heel a resonant syncopation fascinating in its intricacy and precision.[26]

The close-to-the-floor, dragging, step-together-step, was always performed so that the feet did not cross, which was of critical importance because the Baptists defined dancing as a crossing of the feet.[27]

> If a dancer started to lift his or her feet, a watchful deacon would warn, "Look out Sister (or Brother), how you walk on the Cross, your foot might slip and your soul get lost."[28]

Secular dancing was considered sinful and banned by Methodist, Baptist, and Presbyterian churches. Despite this regulation, African-Americans were able to keep alive their dance traditions under the auspices of the church by developing forms of movement that got around the religious requirement of not having the feet cross. One slave commented:

> Us 'longed to de church, all right, but dancin' ain't sinful iffen de foots ain't crossed. Us danced at de arbor meetin's but us shore didn't have us foots crossed.[29]

This stricture against having the feet cross while dancing was important in the development of tap dancing because it led to the creation of footwork that accented beats without crossing the feet. This style of percussive dance contrasted with Irish jig dancing in which crossing the feet and legs was expected and admired.

Although the main form of the ring shout was a group dance, solo forms developed as well. In his book *A Treasury of Southern Folklore*, Benjamin Botkin described one such Shout.

> One might shout acceptably while standing in one place, the feet either shuffling, or rocking backward and forward, tapping alternately with heel and toe, the knees bending, the body swaying, and the hands clapping.[30]

Botkin also describes a version of the shout in which the dancer lowered herself to the ground while dancing until her head touched the floor. Then as the crowd sang "rise from the mire, higherer [*sic*]" the dancer slowly rose. The dancer took great pride outdoing her companions by performing this feat slowly and steadily; in doing so she affirmed her status as a good church member. This exercise is similar to the turning shuffle dance of the American Shakers which is discussed in Chapter 20.

The origin of the name ring shout is

not what it first may seem. The word "shout" in this context is derived from the Arabic word *saut* which is pronounced like the English word "shout." The word referred to the counterclockwise circling of the sacred stone of Mecca by Muslim pilgrims until they were exhausted. In the Protestant churches in America, the ring shout was done circling the altar; a synthesis of Protestant Christianity with Islamic practices brought to America by captured African Muslim slaves.

The ring shout was probably also influenced by Native American dance rituals. It flourished in areas of contact between blacks and American Indians in the southeastern United States. There are certain similar elements in Native American dance and the ring shouts done along the Georgia coast. For example, the shuffling two-step of the ring shout is characteristic of Seminole corn dances, and both types of dance move counterclockwise.[31]

Although started as a religious dance, the ring shout eventually made its way to the secular stage of minstrel shows in the form of the walk around, the finale of the show during which the entire cast danced, sang and paraded. Because of the wide appeal of minstrel shows, the dance received considerable exposure and eventually influenced other secular dances. It is believed that the cakewalk was in some ways a derivative of the ring shout. Others have recognized shout steps that were later used in the Charleston. Another offshoot of the ring shout was the big apple, with its call-and-response, shuffling steps, and improvisational nature.

8

Dispersion of African-American Dances

White slave owners commonly hired out their slaves when they weren't needed for work on the plantations. Many labored as stevedores on the levees up and down the Mississippi. In his book *Life on the Mississippi,* Mark Twain describes seeing workers on the river in 1840:

Next they got out the fiddle, and one played and another patted juba, and the rest turned themselves loose on a regular old-fashioned keelboat breakdown.[1]

In this waterfront environment, the laborers did dances that they had brought with them from the plantations.

Roustabouts on the rivers between jobs, patted Juba and jumped Jim Crow; they cut the Pigeon's Wing and manipulated the Long Dog Scratch, often devising impromptu parts that later became traditional.[2]

Besides recreating and embellishing traditional African-American plantation dances, the roustabouts created new dances specific to the waterfront environment. A dance called the coonjine evolved from the movements of loading cotton onto the boats. The shuffling movements and swaying shoulders of the dance grew out of workers trying to avoid jarring themselves

AN OLD-FASHIONED BREAK-DOWN.

"An Old-fashioned Break-down." From Mark Twain's *Life on the Mississippi* (1883).

63

"Flatboat Fiddler." From *Frank Leslie's Illustrated Newspaper,* (April 1880).

as they moved on the gangway after depositing the freight on the boat. The rhythmical movements were accompanied with a singing chant:

> Throw me a nickel, throw me a dime
> If you want to see me do the Coonjine.[3]

The coonjine was similar to a dance called the counjaille, which was done in the West Indies at carnival time and was also regularly danced at Congo Square in New Orleans. It is likely that the counjaille was brought to the riverfront by slaves and provided the rhythmical framework for the work movement embellishments which later became known as the coonjine.

After the Civil War, a large number of former slaves left rural areas to find work on the river. More and more honky-tonks and dance halls sprang up in the rough areas around the docks, and black and white roustabouts mingled in these brothels and saloons. The dances done in these clubs became a fusion of white jigs, reels, and cotillions and dances from the Southern plantations and the West Indies. Laf-

cadio Hearn, a reporter who witnessed one of these roustabout dances in 1876, wrote:

> The dancers danced a double quadrille, at first, silently and rapidly ... sometimes the men advancing leap and crossed legs with a double shuffle ... the music changed to an old Virginia Reel ... men patted juba and shouted ... once more the music changed ... to some popular Negro air ... terminating with ... stamping of feet, 'patting juba,' shouting, laughing, reeling.[4]

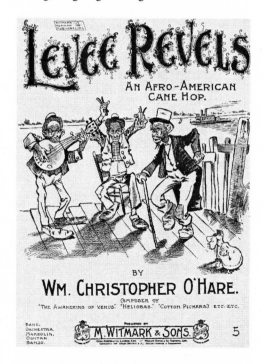

An elderly African-American doing a cane dance on the dock. Sheet music cover of "Levee Revels" by William Christopher O'Hare (1898). *Fron the collection of Keith O. Snell.*

Hearns also gave a description of one particular roustabout named Jem Scott, who was considered one of the best dancers in Cincinnati. He wrote that Scott was "…a marvelous Jig dancer [who could] waltz with a tumbler full of water on his head without spilling a drop."[5] These two descriptions by Hearn, which mention quadrilles with patting juba, and a jig dancer who waltzed while balancing water on his head, reveal how strongly the blending of European and African elements was beginning to take place.

After the Emancipation, many former slaves came to regard mobility as the greatest expression of their newly won freedom. With increasing violence towards blacks in the South during the Reconstruction and with the rise of white mob lynchings, more and more African-Americans fled North, carrying with them their popular dances.[6]

Black Dance in the Northern States

In New York City, the first site of public dancing by African-Americans was a gathering spot that had been popular since the 1700s called the Catherine Market. Located across the East River from Long Island in lower Manhattan, next to the Catherine Slip where boats were tied up, Catherine Market was a bustling area where farmers brought in their produce from New Jersey and Long Island to sell. It was about six blocks away from the Five Points district where hundreds of Irish immigrants and African-Americans lived together in ghetto-like squalor.[7] Here at the market, African-American slaves met after selling their masters' goods, and danced to earn a little extra money for themselves. In 1862, Thomas F. De Voe gave a description of this in his work *The Market Book*.

After the Jersey negroes had disposed of their master's produce at the "Bear Market," which sometimes was early done, and then the advantage of a late tide, they would "shin it" for the Catherine Market to enter the lists with the Long Islanders, and in the end, an equal division of proceeds took place. The success which attended them brought our city negroes down there, who, after a time, even exceeded them both, and if money was not to be had "they would dance for a bunch of eels or fish."[8]

A stiff competition developed between "city slaves" from Manhattan and the "country slaves" from Long Island and New Jersey; dance contests between the various performers were commonplace. One of the most popular dancers who danced for eels at the Catherine Market was a slave by the name of Bob Rowley. He was owned by a Long Island farmer named William Bennett. Mr. Rowley whistled while he danced and called himself "Bobolink Bob."[9]

The most famous dancers were Ned [Francis], "a little wiry Negro slave"; Bob Rawley [Rowley], who called himself "Bobolink Bob", and a chap named Jack, who was referred to as "smart and faithful." The talent displayed by these dancers made one awed observer exclaim that blacks danced as though they "scarcely knew they were in bondage."[10]

Huge crowds gathered to witness the dances and people hired certain performers they especially liked, to dance for them.

So they would be hired by some joking butcher or individual to engage in a Jig or breakdown … and those that could and would dance soon raised a collection; but some of them did more in "turning around and shying off" from the designated spot than keeping to the regular "shakedown," which caused

"Dancing for Eels" at the Catherine Market in New York City. Advertisement depicting a scene from the play "As It Is" at the Chatham Theatre, New York. Drawing by James Brown (circa 1848). *Courtesy of the Library of Congress.*

them all to be confined to a "board," (or shingle, as they called it,) and not allowed off it; on this they must show their skill; and, being several together in parties, each had his particular "shingle" brought with him as part of his stock in trade. This board was usually five to six feet long, of large width, with its particular spring in it, and to keep it in its place while dancing on it, it was held down by one on each end. Their music or time was usually given by one of their party and the noise of the heel.... The large amount collected in this way after a time produced some excellent "dancers;" in fact, it raised a sort of strife for the highest honors, i.e., the most cheering and the most collected in the "hat."[11]

The "shingles," or planks of wood which are synonymous with our present day tap mats, were sometimes placed on top of barrels or balanced between bales of hay and were held down at each corner by four of the dancer's companions. "Music was usually provided by one of their party, who beat a rhythm with his hands on the sides of his legs."[12] Often the patrons called upon the services of two or more performers to engage in a "cutting contest." The term "cutting" in dancing denoted competition, or perhaps breaking away from the group and "showing your stuff" or "making your motion," which meant to improvise. In group dances or more informal competitions, a performer sometimes brought along a friend who led off the dance and provided an example. This person was called a "cutting man" or "cutty." After the dance had started, the real performer then cut in and took over from the "cutty" to demonstrate his ability to surpass what the first dancer had done.

Slave Festivals

Holidays were often a time when African-Americans gathered to dance. One of the most important celebrations for African-American New Englanders was 'Lection Day, or Negro Election Day, which was used by the slaves to honor and celebrate those who had come from royal families in Africa. Slaves were given a few days off by their masters, usually Wednesday to Sunday, and they celebrated the holiday by electing kings and governors. The custom began in Connecticut around 1750 and was still celebrated throughout New England as late as the 1850s. Dancing was always done at these celebrations and one writer described how the slaves "shuffled and tripped" to the fiddles that were played.[13] The most important part of the festivities was a coronation parade with baton twirlers and military drills, followed by an inaugural speech.[14] In his book, *Black Yankees: The Development of an Afro-American Subculture in Eighteenth-Century New England,* William D. Piersen suggests that

> the prototype for the American political parade probably owes more to these black processions in New England than any other corresponding Euro-American institution of the same era.[15]

Negro Election Day was an important way for African-Americans to reconnect with their African roots and honor their ancestors. It unified the black community by reminding slaves that they had come from a culture worthy of remembrance and respect.

In areas heavily settled by the Dutch, such as New York, there was a popular festival called Pinkster Day, celebrated on the first Monday of the Dutch Pentecost. References to the celebration are found as early as 1667, but the holiday wasn't adopted by the African-American community until the second half of the 18th century. As with Negro Election Day, Pinkster festivities were used to pay tribute to ancestors and included the election of a "king."[16] The celebration always involved dancing.

> In New York City, dancing contests between local and Long Island slaves were staged in the streets for entertainment of all, as well as for whatever shillings might be tossed to the contestants. The "jug" [*sic*] and the more difficult "breakdown" were performed to the rhythm of clapping hands and stamping feet.[17]

African-Americans celebrated the holiday by performing authentic African dances which were known to the locals as "double shuffle, heel-and-toe breakdowns." The celebrations always attracted great numbers of white spectators. Writer James Fenimore Cooper called Pinkster Day, "the great Saturnalia of New York blacks."[18] He described it thus:

> ... nine-tenths of the blacks in the city, and of the whole country within thirty or forty miles, indeed, were collected in thousands in those fields, beating banjoes, singing African songs, drinking, and worst of all, laughing in a way that seemed to set their very hearts rattling in their ribs ... some were making music, by beating on skins drawn over the ends of hollow logs, while others were dancing to it, in a manner to show that they felt infinite delight.[19]

Pinkster celebrations were an opportunity for African-Americans to parody whites. Ironically, white minstrel performers used these African-American Pinkster parades as a source for material to create comic burlesques of blacks.

In Philadelphia, before the Revolutionary War, semiannual fairs often reserved the last few days of the festivities for slave dancing. The dances, called slave jubilees, were held in Potter's Field over the graveyard. The African slaves divided into groups according to their various tribes,

> ... the Blacks joyful above, while the sleeping dead reposed below. In that field could be seen at once more than one thousand of both sexes, divided into numerous little squads, dancing and singing, each in his own tongue, after the custom of their several nations in Africa.[20]

After the Civil War, celebrations included parades and dances on Emancipation Day, and Juneteenth, which honored the declaration of emancipation in Texas.

The Emancipation allowed African-Americans to express their culture more openly, a process done in Northern urban areas, by the formation of black community organizations and societies, and churches and schools. Black communities developed "race improvement" organizations which held balls to raise money for educational scholarships or for benevolent causes, such as helping the families of lynch victims. The black social elite that attended these dances usually favored white dances such as quadrilles and waltzes. In subtle ways, these formal dances fostered the refinement of African-American elements, and continued the synthesis between these and European elements.

Jook Joints, Honky-Tonks and After-Hours Joints

As the steady migration of Southern blacks to cities increased, other venues for dancing developed that infused the stagnant Euro-American dance styles with more authentic African elements. Linked to the growing numbers of poor blacks who had moved into urban areas, jook joints, honky-tonks and after-hours joints sprang up, and they reflected the tradition of covert social activity within black culture that had been fostered by the institution of slavery. Related to the worship traditions of hush-harbors and praise houses, the jook joint dances were a secularization of the dances and rituals that had previously been used at clandestine meetings during plantation days. The sacred and the secular truly met in combination in these nightclubs.

The jook joint was generally a small, shoddy, lower-class pleasure house where African-Americans could meet to eat, drink, gamble and dance. Theories suggest that the word "jook" (or "juke") is derived from the west African word *dzugu*, which meant "wicked, disorderly, or violent." In black communities, "to go juking" meant "to go partying."

Music at these establishments was usually furnished by a guitar which in the jook was called a "box." Sometimes if more than one guitar was being played, the first "box" would play the melody as lead, and the second would "fram," or just play chords. If there was a third guitarist, they might execute a tom-tom beat by hitting the lower strings. The resulting music was a polyrhythmical creation.[21] Later when pianos gained popularity as the instrument of choice, this experimentation with rhythm continued. Pianos and player-pianos were eventually replaced by victrolas. The term "boxes" stuck which is how electronic record machines eventually came to be called juke boxes.

Jook joints were important in the development of tap because it was there that the first large-scale syncretism of dances took place. Many dances were created, standardized, fine-tuned, and then spread among the jooks. In addition, dances that were previously performed only in a religious or ritualistic context were reworked into secular dances, and group dances were transformed into solo and couple dances.

> The jook was the only dance arena of its time that successfully accommodated the emerging regional culture among black freedmen. It served as a mixing ground for the remaining strains of African culture and those additional elements that developed during the slave experience. It provided a forum for blending regional and Euro-American cultural elements. It later provided a forum for visitors or travelers to demonstrate new dances or variations, as well as an arena in which whites could observe black culture and dance. And it allowed African-Americans to express aspects of their newly developing national character.[22]

Dances that were popular in jook joints included the Charleston, the black bottom, snake hips, the buzzard lope, the twist, the fish tail, the grind, the funky butt, and the itch, all of which can be traced to African sources. Most were later interpolated into various styles of tap. For example, snake hips was blended with tap in the legomania style, and the itch, a movement that involved vigorous scratching, was performed with eccentric tap footwork. Dances such as the Charleston and the black bottom eventually found their way to the theatrical stage and ended up as huge dance crazes. National exposure to these dances was fostered through the publication of sheet music, meant to accompany each specific dance. Dance songs usually included instructional lyrics which explained how to do the movements, and because this printed material was so widely distributed, these lyrics provided an additional impetus in spreading jook dances throughout the country.

Honky-tonks developed at the same time as jook joints and were similar in nature, differing only in the type of clientele. Jook joints catered more to rural African-Americans; honky-tonks to laborers such as longshoremen, iron workers, railroad workers, and other nonagricultural types. The music tended to be more sophisticated in honky-tonks with more instrumentation and variety. It was in honky-tonks that early ragtime and jazz had its roots.[23]

After-hours joints, the latest to develop in the African-American culture, were even more sophisticated; dances were more refined with less flat-footed steps and a more erect posture. Partner dances here became more popular than group dances.

As a way to get out of poverty and to express and cultivate their talents, many African-Americans ventured into the field of commercial entertainment. Dances that had been developed in jook joints, honky-tonks and after-hours joints began to find their way onto the legitimate stage performed by blacks.

PART II
THEATRICAL INFLUENCES

9

Early Theatrical Developments

The practice of imitating African and African-American dance on the American stage began before the Revolutionary War. In 1767, a magician named Mr. Bayly performed a "Negro Dance, In Character" with another actor named Mr. Tea in Philadelphia. In 1796, in Boston, the first ballerina to win renown in the U.S., Madame Gardie, performed "A Comic Dance, In Character of a Female Negro."[1]

Madame Gardie influenced celebrated American dancer, John Durang, who appeared in blackface on March 20, 1789, in the character role of "Friday" in Robert Brinsley Sheridan's pantomime *Robinson Crusoe, or Harlequin Friday.*[2]

John Durang

Although not a tap dancer, John Durang was an important historical link in the evolution of tap dancing. Born in York, Pennsylvania on January 6, 1768, Durang was the first native-born American to achieve widespread recognition and popularity as a professional dancer. He became interested in performing at the age of 14 after he saw a French hornpipe dancer by the name of Roussel. Durang wrote of the experience in his memoirs:

I saw him dance a hornpipe which charmed my mind. I thought I could

dance as well as any body, but his stile set it off, with his dress. I practised at home and I soon could do all his steps besides many more better hornpipe steps.... The pigeon-wing I never saw done by any other person, and I could not make that out from the front of the house. I contrived to get Mr. Rusell [Roussel] to board at my father's house that I might have the opportunity to dance more correct than I had been used to. I learned the correct stile of dancing a hornpipe in the French stile, an allemande, and steps for a country dance. Except the pigeon was the only difficulty I had to encounter: he could not show me the principle and the anatomy of the figure of the step, nor I never met a dancer since that could have shown it to me. The mystery of the figure occurred to me in bed, for my thoughts were constant on that object. I dream'd that I was at a ball and did the pigeon-wing to the admiration to the whole company; in the morning I rose in the confidence of doing the step. By this strange circumstance on trial, I was master of the step....[3]

At 17, Durang auditioned for a troupe of players in Philadelphia called the Old American Company which presented selections from Shakespeare and patriotic skits celebrating the newly won American independence. These dramas were inter-

73

spersed with songs and dances, and when he was hired as a member of the company, Durang was expected to take part in these musical vignettes. Unfortunately, on his opening night, he developed a severe case of stage fright. To battle his jitters, he decided to make his entrance by jumping from a trampoline in the wings and flying onto the stage to start his hornpipe. The audience responded with wild applause and after he was finished, the theater was in such an uproar, the audience pelted the stage with fruit and other tributes until the curtain was raised again and Durang repeated his dance in its entirety.

Durang's dancing quickly became one of the Old American Company's most popular features. When the troupe relocated to New York in 1785, Durang befriended a German dwarf there named Hoffmaster, who composed a melody to accompany the dance. He entitled the piece "Durang's Hornpipe," and as the catchy tune quickly spread, it helped to cement the dancer's popularity. Several years later in 1855, Durang's son, Charles, published a small booklet on social dancing which included a description of this original hornpipe dance and so helped to preserve it.

A Sailor's Hornpipe — Old Style

1. Glissade round (first part of tune)
2. Double shuffle down, do.
3. Heel and toe back, finish with back shuffle
4. Cut the buckle down, finish the shuffle.
5. Side shuffle right and left, finishing with beats
6. Pigeon wing going round
7. Heel and toe haul in back
8. Steady toes down
9. Changes back, finish with back shuffle and beats
10. Wave step down.
11. Heel and toe obliquely back

12. Whirligig, with beats down.
13. Scissone and entrechats back
14. Running forward on the heels
15. Double Scotch step, with a heel Brand in Plase.
16. Single Scotch step back
17. Parried toes round, or feet in and out
18. The Copper shuffle right and left back
19. Grasshopper step down
20. Terre-a-terre or beating on toes back
21. Jockey crotch down
22. Traverse round, with hornpipe glissade

Bow and finish[4]

The reference to such steps as the "pigeon wing," the "double shuffle," and other such movements clearly indicates the foreshadowing of American tap. It is believed that the "whirligig, with beats down" is similar to a renversé turn such as the kind later done by the tap dancing film star Eleanor Powell.

Durang continued to perform with the Old American Company for over seven years, frequently dancing for the newly elected president, George Washington, at the South Street Theatre in Philadelphia. It was there on November 7, 1790, he introduced a variation of his popular hornpipe, announcing that he would dance "a Hornpipe on 13 eggs, Blindfolded, without breaking one."

In addition to his immensely popular hornpipe, Durang did other styles of dance. In one, called the "Dwarf Dance," he transformed himself from what appeared to be a dancing three-foot dwarf into a dancing six-foot woman. In 1794, he did his hornpipe in *Tammany,* the first American opera to be written about an American subject. On March 20, 1795, he danced the male lead in the New York premiere of *La Forêt Noire, or, Maternal Affection,* the first serious ballet given in the United States. In 1796, Durang joined John B. Ricketts' Circus where he danced on horseback and also on tightrope.[5] Besides performing in the traditional circus venues, Durang starred in several ballets and pantomimes produced by Ricketts. He remained with the circus company until December 1799, when the Philadelphia headquarters of the Ricketts Circus burned to the ground after a drunken carpenter left a lit candle in the adjoining workshop.[6]

Durang had many different talents. He worked as a puppeteer, a clown, a designer, an author, a theatre manager, and even as a pyrotechnic display artist. He often performed with members of his rapidly growing family, all of whom had been trained in dancing. During the war of 1812, he and two of his sons, Charles and Ferdinand, served in the garrison at North Point in Baltimore in the battle that inspired Francis Scott Key to write the words to "The Star Spangled Banner." Durang's son, Ferdinand, was the first to put the poem to its well-known melody and also the first to sing it in public.

John Durang retired from performing in 1819 and died in 1822. He had brought professional dance to a wide American audience and had popularized such dances as the hornpipe, later fused with African rhythms to create American tap.

Changing Theatrical Tastes

After the War of 1812, the desire for some kind of national culture emerged in the United States. Dissatisfied with copying European tastes and concepts, common folks started looking for home-grown symbols that would express American ideals in a uniquely American way. This led to the formation of "a common man's culture that glorified American democracy and the average white man in contrast to European aristocracy and effete gentlemen."[7]

Theatrical riots erupted as ordinary people rebelled against what they considered to be the arrogant, pretentious, European style of theatre. In the name of

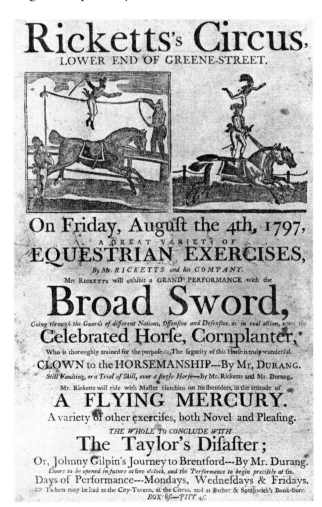

Playbill from John B. Ricketts' Circus featuring John Durang (April 4, 1797).

American nationalism, several famous British actors were pelted with rotten eggs and run off the stage. In New York City a riot involving British tragedian, Charles Macready, actually resulted in the death of 31 rioters.[8]

Against this background of an aggressive, antiaristocratic working class, of frequent riots, and of conflicts over the course of America's cultural development, new forms of entertainment emerged that catered to the tastes, needs, and desires of the common man. Turning to regional folk sources for their material, artists began to include American themes, settings, and folk-based heroes in their presentations. Characters presented on the American stage became rougher and more uneducated, yet often possessed an uncorrupted natural innocence and nobility.[9] The blackface minstrel show was the most important entertainment form to result from this cultural process, becoming the pre-eminent form of American entertainment for the major part of the 19th century. Blackface performers dominated the stage, enjoying the status of national and international celebrities.[10]

In an effort to appear more "authentic" and "exotic," white actors and dancers wore makeup made out of burnt cork. The makeup was made by pouring alcohol over several corks, setting them on fire, and letting them burn down to a crisp. This powder was then mixed with water to make a thick paste. After a cake of cocoa butter had been rubbed over the skin as a base coat, the cork paste was applied evenly. Carmine powder was used for reddening the lips, or an unpainted circle of white skin was left. There was a minstrel superstition that if the makeup around the mouth was done poorly, it would lead to bad luck on stage. Wrinkles used for older black characters were drawn on with India ink. After the makeup was finished, the palms of the hands were wiped cleaned and

a wig, often made out of the filling used in mattresses, completed the masquerade.[11]

Blackface minstrelsy was vitally important in the development of American tap dancing because it was on the minstrel stage that confiscated African-American dances were theatricalized by white performers, a process which cemented the synthesis of black and white styles of dancing. Minstrel shows then presented the mixture in a wildly popular form that resulted in international exposure for this new type of dancing.

George Washington Dixon

Although not a dancer himself, blackface entertainer George Washington Dixon was one of the first American performers to introduce audiences to the type of African-American source material which later became so popular in minstrelsy. Dixon was born in Richmond, Virginia, in 1801 and at 15 joined an itinerant circus company. He toured with assorted circuses and acting companies until, in 1829, he appeared in blackface in three separate New York theatres singing a song called "Coal Black Rose." His fame grew as a result of these three performances, and Dixon started to insert satirical political jabs into his material, a feature which would further increase his popularity and appeal.

On June 19, 1834, at the Arch Street Theatre in Philadelphia, he sang a song called "Zip Coon," to the melody we know of as "Turkey in the Straw."[12] The chorus of "Zip Coon" had the nonsensical words, "O-Zip-a-duden-duden-duden-zip-a-duden-day," and can be recognized in Walt Disney's *Song of the South* in the number "Zip-a-Dee-Doo-Dah." Some scholars suggest that the number was a political statement lampooning Henry Clay and the Whig party following Clay's election to the Senate in 1831. Dixon accompanied the song with a "a rough jig dance"[13] which featured a step called double trouble. This performance brought him national acclaim and guaranteed his place in minstrel history.[14] The character of Zip Coon, sometimes called Jim Dandy, was a dandified city black who became almost as familiar and popular with audiences as Thomas Rice's later character of the shuffling plantation black, Jim Crow.[15]

Despite "Zip Coon's" enormous popularity, not everyone appreciated Dixon's talent. The *Boston Courier* said that Dixon was "...the most miserable apology for a vocalist that ever bored the public ear."[16]

An editor as well as a performer, Dixon printed a scandal sheet that once got him caned, jailed, and even shot at when he libeled a preacher. When the war with Mexico broke out, Dixon rewrote the lyrics to "Zip Coon," adding some updated political references and once again for a short time he returned to the limelight. Later in

George Washington Dixon as a young man. From *Curiosities of the American Stage* by Laurence Hutton (1890).

his life, he tried other careers such as becoming a hypnotist, a spiritualist, and a professional athlete. His athletic specialty was long distance marathon walking. Once he walked "seventy-six hours consecutively without sleep or rest, on a platform fifteen feet long."[17]

Dixon's exploits are relevant to the history of tap dancing because a musician competing with his peers in feats of athleticism is the type of activity that led directly to the popularity of dance-offs and dance challenges. Because of Dixon's high public profile, his participation in such athletic competitions influenced other entertainers to join in the growing trend of contests to determine the best. Music, sport, competition, and minstrelsy became more and more intertwined.

On January 23, 1843, George Washington Dixon gave his last performance at a benefit to honor Daniel Emmett, the man who would later found the Virginia Minstrels. He died in New Orleans in the charity ward on March 2, 1861.

George Washington Dixon in the character of "Zip Coon." From the cover of the sheet music, "Zip Coon" (circa 1835).

10

"Daddy" Rice

Perhaps the most important figure in the development of American blackface minstrelsy was a white actor and hornpipe dancer who became known professionally as "Daddy" Rice. Thomas Dartmouth Rice was born on May 20, 1808, in New York City's Seventh Ward.[1] As a young man, he worked as a carpenter's apprentice for a ship carver named Dodge carving figureheads for ships. In the mid 1820s Rice began appearing in small, comical roles in various New York theatres. There is a story that when he was a young man working as an supernumerary at the Park Theatre, Rice attracted so much attention upstaging the lead actors that they complained to the management and he was fired. Friends described Rice as a "scrambling-looking fellow with a sepulchral falsetto voice."[2]

By 1828, Rice adopted the theatre as a full-time career and joined Noah M. Ludlow's traveling acting troupe which toured the West and was based out of Kentucky. Around the mid to late 1830s, Rice was working at Ludlow and Smith's Southern Theatre in Louisville, Kentucky as a stage carpenter and prop man when he was cast in a small part in Solon Robinson's dramatic play, *The Rifle*.[3] Between the acts of this play, Rice introduced a parody song and dance. Performing in blackface and dancing to a Negro work song, he mimicked the movements of a crippled African-American man named Jim Crow, whom he had seen from his dressing room window. The slave worked in the livery stable behind the theater.[4] Jim Crow's right shoulder was deformed and drawn up high, while his left leg was gnarled with rheumatism, stiff and crooked at the knee.[5] Rice's dance consisted of limping, shuffling, and jigging movements, and ended with a little jump at the end of each refrain, when he "set his heel-a-rickin."[6]

An account of how Rice got his material is given in Noah M. Ludlow's 1880 book, *Dramatic Life as I Found It*:

Thomas Dartmouth Rice as a young man. From *Curiosities of the American Stage* by Laurence Hutton (1890).

One spring season of the Louisville Theatre, on a clear, bright morning, during the rehearsal of some play in which Mr. Rice, had but little to do, as he was standing on the stage, at the back door that looked out upon the rear stable-yard, where a very black, clumsy negro used to clean and rub down horses, he was attracted by the clearness and melody of this negro's voice, and he caught the words, the subject of his song; it was the negro version of "Jump, Jim Crow." He listened with delight to the negro's singing for several days, and finally went to him and paid him to sing the song over to him until he had learned it.... When the piece was produced [Rice] requested Mr. Drake's permission to introduce and sing his newly acquired negro song of "Jim Crow," which Mr. Drake reluctantly consented to. The result was that "Jim Crow" ran the piece to full houses for many nights, when without the song it is highly probable Mr. Drake's drama would have been a "dead duck."[7]

Legend has it that Rice actually bought the stable hand's tattered clothes in order to appear more authentic. He wrote some additional verses to the man's simple song, and when he first introduced the piece, it was a huge hit.[8] Edmon S. Connor, a fellow company member and later a columnist for the *New York Times*, recalled that Louisville audiences "were wild with delight."[9] The dance and accompanying song earned Rice 20 curtain calls that first night and eventually turned him into the highest paid minstrel performer around.[10]

A testament to Rice's enormous appeal and popularity can be found in the story of Leonard Gosling, who hired Rice

Lithograph of Thomas Dartmouth Rice as Jim Crow on the stage of the Bowery Theater for a benefit performance during a production of Shakespeare's *Richard III*, starring Junius Booth. This particular drawing probably shows his closing night on January 8, 1833.

to advertise his boot blacking product, "Gosling's Blacking." When Rice was dancing as Jim Crow, Gosling paid him to sing a jingle praising the product during his act. Soon after Rice sang about the shoe polish, all America had to try the product and Gosling was able to retire shortly afterwards with a considerable fortune.[11]

After conquering the United States, Rice traveled to Europe, presenting his dance there with similar success.[12] Rice's dance became known as Jumping Jim Crow, and eventually was turned into a popular social dance and a major dance craze in the early 1800s. The accompanying lyric was set to an old English Morris dance tune and ended with the refrain:

> First on de heel,
> Den on de toe,
> Ebery time I wheel about
> I jump Jim Crow.
> Wheel about, turn about,
> Do jus' so
> An' ebery time I turn about,
> I jump Jim Crow.

When Rice traveled to London to perform, a review in the *Star* on August 26, 1837, stated,

> ... we shall not be surprised if the youthful Queen [Victoria] herself should send an invitation to Rice to jump Jim Crow for her at the palace.[13]

Rice became an international celebrity. On July 26, 1838, the *Boston Post* stated,

> The two most popular characters in the world at the present time are [Queen] Victoria and Jim Crow.[14]

"Jim Crow" became one of the greatest song hits of the century; it was even translated into Hindi and sung in New Delhi. The dance was so popular that after Rice appeared in London, chimney sweeps and urchins were often seen doing it in the streets.

> From the nobility and gentry, down to the lowest chimney-sweep in Great Britain, and from the member of Congress, down to the youngest apprentice or school-boy in America, it was all: "Turn about and wheel about, and do just so,/ And everytime I turn about I jump Jim Crow." Even the fair sex did not escape the contagion: the tunes were set to music for the piano-forte, and nearly every young lady in the Union, and the United Kingdom, played and sang, if she did not *jump*, "Jim Crow."[15]

Appealing to the upper crust of society in England cemented the dance's popularity because Rice had found most of his success in the United States only by performing to the unsophisticated lower classes. An article in the *Cork Herald* on May 13, 1837, observed:

> ["Jim Crow"] has a feature that belongs to few songs — it is mostly made up of dancing. Half of each verse is a chorus, and then all the chorus is motion.... Mr. Crow's agility in describing the evolutions that the words enjoin — for he addresses himself in the imperative mood "Jump Jim Crow," is truly magnificent. He has all the velocity of a dancing master, with the quaint capers of a cleave-boy — the bewitching grace of Douvernay, in partnership with the sylph-like movement of Taglioni. He varies his jumpings to an infinite extent, starting with different steps, and

Opposite: **Song sheet which lists 150 verses of Thomas Rice's song, "Jump Jim Crow."** *Courtesy of the Library of Congress.*

JIM CROW
COMPLETE
IN
150
VERSES.

One ting tickle me,
To see both brack and white,
For ebery little jig a ma gee,
Day get a patent right.
So I wheel about.
I turn about,
I do just so,
And ebery time I wheel about,
I jump Jim Crow.

In die here city,
Soon as de day peep,
You nebber catch a wink ob sleep,
For de damn patent sweep.
So I wheel about, etc.

Down dare by de park,
To save your shoes from cracking,
Dere's a goose's Greeling,
Wid his patent French Blacking.

One ting puzzle me
I tink it past belief,
Da gib ole Hava a patent right,
For catching ob de tief.

But eb all de patent right,
Massa Crony is de king,
For de president give him one,
For making bese g-s sting.

So when I go to Washington,
I hab you all to know,
I mean to get a patent right,
For jumping ob Jim Crow.

Here om I from ole Kentuck,
As I hab you all to know,
Pe come to learn de Yorkers,
De style to jump Jim Crow;

Oh dat is de plice for niggers,
Dey fatten dem on mush,
But if dey go de bad liger,
Dey make dem cry, OH HUSH?

A lofer gtat is de park,
It is a fact I am told,
A watchman left de gate open,
An do lofer cotcht a cold.

I nebber like New Orleans,
Nor I tink I nebber shall,
Until de white man full am he,
De pretty creole gal.

Den dare is Charleston,
De bragging Nell-Sorn,
He and hab ota uncle Sam,
But uncle made them lorn.

But here dat Baltimore,
Wid a monument obmd,
Erected to de memory,
ob de great massa Washington.

Pre fan here stole,
where de niggra'ies from gummy,
De birth place ob dat great man,
Twas chaer for ol Virginny.

They hanged a tary come,
Ise tree I declare,
Dey found him living in a tree,
Wid an ole brack bear.

Den there is Philadelphia,
Wid dere water on de hill,
But I tink dare whiskey better,
An I tink I cher well.

If you hab got de blue,
And for fun you do luck,
Just go in Division-street,
And buy a Conne Almynack.

Ice cream is bery good,
And so is lemonade.
But I likee better dan dese,
To kiss de pretty maid.

Cuff hoe de bacon,
Sandu drive de plough.
Nobody plays to day,
But our ole sow.

Damn ole sow,
She grunt all de day,
An upsot de swill tub,
When massa gone away.

Oh de Flatbush niggers,
Dey kick up dare heels,
Dey come down to Market,
An dance dare for eils.

Dey taste a mighty deal.
An tink dey make a show.
But I nebber send one of dem,
To shull jump Jim Crow.

Wuen you see tory nigger,
What lob to take about,
You may be berry sartin,
He raised and Walkbout.

I want to go to Canada,
For de only song dey sing,
Is dat darns Brinsey,
An God shave de king.

But we laugh at de Canada,
And de Entish turned our hook on,
For de tune ob Yankee Doodle,
An hurrah for Jackson.

De ole Wirginny nigger,
He knows and is all,
Only for to pull de trigger,
An handle de small owl.

To shoot de turkey buzzard,
I once took a gun,
An when I cocked it at him,
Lord how he run.

Dat was in ole Wirginny,
An I shoot him un de call,
Den I filled my gun wid brandy,
An kicked him wid a tail.

I once want a stiching,
To mend my ole shoe,
As I sat in kitchen,
Wid ole Wirginny Lew.

He took de iron Crobar,
To mend his tarnal boot,
And he had him on he knee,
But he wouldn't no how about.

I shouted de Yankee,
As will do it again,
I pulled him all mad nern stalk,
For de beat suger cane.

Missus sent me to buy oyster,
New vortes I keep,
I gutted dem un road,
For fear dey would'nt keep,
I'm a screamer.
So gib me your daughter.
And you'll find me no un sobown,
Like a sort of pump water.
O I'm a real ladies doctor,
An I got in a hat,
A settler for a rattocnain,
An a cure for chinmw pox.

Ole woman like me,
An tisk me very cute,
Kaze I cure all dere pain,
Wid a little yarb and root.

Do New York doctor,
Sure to go to hell,
When dey send dare potients,
Wid dare debelish Calomel.

Oh I'm a ratler,
An go de hole team,
When I travel round de country,
An cure de folks by steam.

Two Grahamites went to Philadelphia,
For to cut a swell,
But where dey lodged de first night,
I should'nt like to tell.

Dey made excuse ob business,
But dey went more for fun,
When do mayor heard dey wate Yorkers,
Dey had to cut an run.

He fined dem two dollars,
An bid em off to prance,
For being found in Shippen-street,
A learning how to dance,

It took away de cash,
Da paying ob de fine,
So dey glad to get to York,
By de commodities line.

But now dey are back agin,
Dey must do de best dey can,
An make up for lost time,
By de Graham plan.

De way to take a hogcake,
Ole Virginny nebber tice,
Stick de one cake on de foot,
And hold it to de fire.

Ole Sam Patseck,
Stole a side of leather,
Well done Sam.
Can't you teel nuoder.

Dere's neest apon de goare foot,
And marrow on de bone,
Dere's pretty gale in our house,
And mammy's not at home,

I listed in de nay,
As sarve uncle Sam,
Any other servise,
Any when a down.

At New Orleans town,
De Enlish went to teel,
But erres dere see ole stickory,
Dey took to dere heel.

Lord how dey cut dirt,
And did'nt stoo to trifle,
I wont to shif de ole nigger,
Anty's oce de face.
We poured water un he face
See ticking dere wes paint.

And som a nasty figger,
I'm sure was nerver seen,
A face with streaks of red and white,
Dat before looked bery clean.

De song is getting long,
But will no longer tarl,
For I'm fairly tier-dered,
To gib you your fill.

If you want to buy a song,
De one you fine wo'nt meet
In a very purest variety
At 257 Hudson Street.

If I was a regular sweep,
I'd set de town a roaring,
So musical my verses are,
For de ecatntomical singing.

But de nerf fan ob all of,
And de one gib all I don't know
Is to gib de seientcllc touch,
Oh jumping Jim Crow.

I'm a fall blooded niger
Oh de real ore stock.
An wid me head and shoulders,
I smash a horse block.

I smack a Jersey niger,
Is de street de oder day,
As I hone I sober air,
If he did'nt turn gray.

I'm bery much afraid to late,
Dis jumping will no be good,
And not too fond ob de cop,
When oders were getting down,
He'd sure be getting up.

I seen a pretty gal,
Wid a tippet and a muff,
I con't know what her trade is,
But I guess she's un to snuff.

She went in de dry goods store,
And winked at de clerk,
She ca'd him un come to her house,
A little arter dark.

He wait to de tree balls,
All for a painted face,
Which bery soon I see,
Will bring him to disgrace.

I'm for union to a yes,
And dis is a unknown fact
But if I marry and dont like it,
I'll skuffly theart.

I'm sure dere he gale enuff,
To hab a fair chance,
And if I dont mek a good one,
I'll laff it off and dance.

I'm tired of being a single man,
And I'm tormined to get a wife,
For when I hae de knoose,
Is do sweet married life,

It's berry common among de whites,
To marry per gsel of word.
But dat'll do,
Unless I'm really ded.

I tink I see myself un rail road,
Wid a wite sobnow arm,
An to folls up de bubau,
Dare sure none be no harm.

As I caution all white damine,
Not to come lear way,
For as sers sa dey insult me,
Dey'll in de gutter lay.

De One sat street fellos,
When dey carry full sail,
Anand dem water a fussey ting,
Just like a dog's tail.

Whad you hear de name of it,
I sure it cacke you roar,
Way I a'nd on what it was,
And dey said it was a bear.

Wid Jackson et de head
Dey soon de ting may settle
For de Hickory -s a man,
Dat's tarnal full ob mettle.

Should dey get to fighting,
Perhaps de bracks will rise,
For dold with ther freedom
Se sticking in deir eyes.

An if de bracks should get free,
I guess they'll feel some bigger,
As I coule consider it,
A bold crake for de nigger.

I see for freedom,
An for some singuider,
Although I am a brack man,
De white is called my broder.

Wen stuff is a rat mon
To take de deth brock,
I'll poate dat he is white,
By de twinkling of a crack.

For you see blaod broaders,
As ones a fae hab a tail,
I no bees waked deen,
When mking he tore gale.

To go to Hoboak,
'T's fine a ecomodrash,
And aere I aae de pretty girls,
Drinking de lemonade.

Dat soer and dat sweet,
Is berry good by gone,
Bat de best lemonane is
Made by adding rum.

At de Swan Courge,
I so opice I tink,
Wise dey hab dis 'licious
And satisfying drink.

De Firdelphi grog shop,
You can see as you pass,
And dey sell de beed ob licker,
For sxs cents a glass.

Some go to Weehawk,
An some to Brooklyn hites,
But dey better stay at home,
If dey want to see de sizts.

To go to de movents.
I'se were a to der duty,
If for one eyegloss,
Jus to see de sleeping beauty.

And dere's Daddy Lambert,
An a sickten on he justaire,
And Excuses of Broadway's dandy,
In a glass case ob monkies.

Dere was me Sim Fintch,
Who took de ugly keys,
He'd better stay in New-York,
And be a chimney sweep.

And if misded ho rodfescon,
And not too fond ob de cop,
When oders were getting down,
He'd sure be getting up.

O white folks, white folks,
I glad to hear you holler,
But I'll not jump Jim Crow agin,
Unless you hit me with a dollar.

I went to de play house,
Where I hone ebery body go,
Den I saw a jig figure,
Making fun ob Jim Crow.

Of you want to buy a funny song,
I'll tell you where to go,
Find de printer up in Hudson-street,
For he also keeps Jim Crow.

And if you an find him.
There's one I'm sure you'll like,
He lives in Division-street,
Just opposite to Pike.

I hear massa Randolph,
Behaved mighty droll,
De folke dat held ole Andy back,
Was bery big fools.

Best let de ole man fight it out,
Den Randolph's get enuff,
An no fear ob de general,
For de Hickory's hard stuff.

The man declaimin de laws,
To prison ought to go,
Be must be man snsee faller,
Weres dan Jim Crow.

I travel on de Rail Road,
Straight to Amboy,
De car go mighty smooth,
But it got too many bed boys.

And went in de front room,
Two heads fellere fight,
Den de bad fellers keen it up,
Cry hozza, darkie's that's right.

Space in dem cars young ladies
Catch a bad scent,
Before she got to steamboat,
She wish she neber went.

I can to Philadelphia,
Dat very pretty city,
De Indian dress both neat and fine,
Dere beaus are smart and witty,

White folks, white folks,
I bid you all good bye,
Soon as eber hay time come,
Into de country fly.

But may pen and cherry,
Eber be Merican people's fate,
So hurra for industrious Philadelfia,
And N. Y. de great cousus-dal State.

My sister Dinah I see.
Has made a great debut,
But she cannot dance like me,
No more can one ob you.

She's my sista it is true,
But dat is not de ting,
For what in dozen ob wenches,
Trying to jump, dance and sing.

And Cuffeltsna hub got a plan.
Into effect she'll carry,
And dat is to make a match,
And her baby Sambo marry.

But as for poor Dinah,
It's jat as madder and,
She be a berry massy gal,
Dep I saw a jig figure,
She's a tarnal sassy nigger,
As you I guess can see,
O she would'nt make a fuss,
An try to black gaard me,

Now my brodder niggers,
I do not tink it right,
Dat we should look at once,
Who happen to be white,
Kaze is dere misfortune,
And dey cannot enjoy it,
If dey could only be
Gentlemen ob color.

It almost break my heart,
To see dem carry dem,
And from my cool I wish dem,
Full as brack as we.

For I am as tore a niger,
As ever yst was born,
An I am a little freetman,
When I hab a small horn.

For I'm of decate family,
An I'd rader dance dan pray,
For ab de tore gentlemann,
De dancing's de best pay.

As I wast born in a case brack,
An Dinah in a dingit trough
I hope you'll see use difference,
And hustle her off.

Now before I leave you,
One ting I hab to tek,
If de making ob clout rote,
Be not a plag r task.

But if you're not contented,
An tink it is me right,
I'll come up a some oder time,
And dance all night.

Now white folks, white folks,
Don't take offence,
An when I take a bench,
I'll treat to some fence.

670

terminating with different positions in each verse.[16]

Historian Hans Nathan described Rice's dance thus:

How strained, sprawling, and distorted his posture was, and yet how nonchalant — how unusually grotesque with its numerous sharp angles, and yet how natural.... In windmill fashion, he rolled his body lazily from one side to the other, throwing his weight alternately on the heel of one foot and on the toes of the other.... Imaginative though he was, he was undoubtedly inspired by the real Negro.[17]

The references to elements common in African dance in this description, such as asymmetry and nonchalance, are obvious. The bent knees used in the dance were also of African origin.[18] Scholars suggest that the loose arm and shoulder movements came from the African-American shuffle. The hop at the end of the chorus came from the Irish jig. How authentic Rice's imitation of real African-American dance was is anybody's guess. It is important to remember that Rice, in his imitation, was purposely distorting the movements of a physically disabled man, and exaggerating the comedic aspects of that individual, in order to please his audience.

Most of the movements from Jumping Jim Crow have been lost, but it is thought that the dance probably consisted of flat-footed shuffles, mixed with the Irish jig, over-exaggerated upper body movements, pirouettes, and a syncopated hop or jump at the finish of each chorus. One popular song from the period mentions that Rice "cut de pigeon wing."[19] W. T. Lhamon and other scholars have suggested that is highly likely the dance was based upon African animal mimicry and was probably similar to the buzzard lope.[20] This view is supported by one of the verses

that Rice commonly sang while performing his dance:

I kneel to the buzzard.
I bow to the crow,
And eb'ry time I w'eel about
I jump jis' so.

One part of the Jim Crow dance has been preserved however — the swaying of the hips with one arm waving and wagging the finger.[21] This movement later developed into the popular social dance of the 1940s, truckin'.[22]

Because of the dance's enormous popularity, many performers imitated Rice.[23] The stereotypical caricature of the unkempt, ignorant, African-American slave presented by "Daddy" Rice was extremely influential in the way blacks were subsequently seen in future theatre pieces.

Thomas D. Rice himself authored several Ethiopian Operas, musical burlesques that featured African-American characters.

Thomas Dartmouth Rice as the character Jim Crow. From *Curiosities of the American Stage* by Laurence Hutton (1890).

Some of his most famous shows were *Otello, Bone Squash Diavolo, Long Island Juba, Oh, Hush! or, the Virginny Cupids, Ginger Blue, The Virginia Mummy,* and *Jim Crow in London.* Integrating English farce elements with black dance and song, these widely used burlesques were not only imitated, but also extremely influential in shaping the form and the style of all minstrel shows that followed. The comic cliché of the "dancing darky" with the ear-to-ear grin also became a 19th century literary fixture.

In *Raising Cain,* W. T. Lhamon, Jr., describes a fascinating pamphlet which was published first in 1835 and again in 1837 with songs added. Written by Rice, the booklet was called *The Life of Jim Crow.* In it, Rice revealed the history of his famous character and how Jim Crow came to learn his song and dance.

According to the book, when Crow was born he was wrapped in possum skins in order to be presented at the big house. An old crippled white woman suddenly appeared and prophesied,

He [the boy, Jim Crow] will raise to fortune by hopping.

Rice goes on to say that the people who witnessed this event assumed that the baby was the son of a witch because the old white woman disappeared in a cloud of smoke. The Massa, who had been out of town serving in the U.S. Congress, was called back to burn the baby, but when he saw how cute and black the child was, he changed his mind and instead, christened the infant Jim Crow. At the christening, the old white women reappeared and said,

Keep dis slave till he be twenty years of age, an by using him well you shall hab eberry kind of good luck, you family all lib and grow rich; ben he be twenty, you must set him free or your good luck go to de ole Harry.

The old crone "then flew up the chimbly jis like screech owl." The book tells of many other magical incidents that happened in Jim Crow's early life. In one particularly fanciful tale, Rice explains how the famous song "Jump Jim Crow" came into being. When he was 16, the boy wandered through the woods and grew thirsty and a spring of water suddenly poured forth before him. A fairy magically appeared and offered him a drink from a silver cup. After drinking though, Jim Crow's stomach began to hurt so bad he finally threw up. He said,

… ben jis as I got over a fence, up come de intents of my tomach into de road;— guy, I to't it war a gone case wid me, but when I look'd down, it war a big roll of music dat I had heaved up. I looked at him [the fairy], an all at once de tune pat as sugar on de end ob my tongue, ann I rhymed it from dat dey to dis, for twar nothing more or less den de fashionable air ob your humble sarvant to comman, Jim Crow.

After Crow was freed at age 20, as was commanded by the white witch, he wandered the country with a band of strolling players and married Dinah Rumpfizz Quashdiddle, who owned a cake store. After listing a steady string of Crow's successes, the book eventually ends with Jim Crow in Washington where he ate dinner with President Andrew Jackson and met Noah Webster and Davy Crockett.[24]

As the popularity of the Jim Crow character spread throughout the world, other legends and fables about his origins flourished. One biography of the fictitious Crow, called "A Faithful Account of the Life of Jim Crow, The American Negro Poet," suggested that Crow was actually Native American, and that after his father Oulamou died, he was adopted by a merchant who changed his name to Jim Crow.

The worldwide exposure of the Rice

caricature made Jim Crow a household name. Often associated with any person of darker skin, the use of the name "Jim Crow," like the name "Uncle Tom," became a derogatory epithet for African-Americans. The name was eventually attached to the segregation laws that lasted up until the 1960s.[25]

Although Jim Crow was the most lasting and well-loved character created by Thomas D. Rice, he also incorporated other African-American inspired characters into his various acts. One danced to the song "Long Tail Blue" while dressed in striped trousers and blue long-tailed coat,

Thomas Dartmouth Rice singing another one of his hits, "Sich a Getting Up Stairs" (1833).

foreshadowing the character of Uncle Sam.[26] Another source for Rice's material was a black street vendor from New Orleans. Signor Cornmeali, whose nickname was "Old Corn Meal," hawked cornmeal from his cart as he sang and danced. Rice heard him in 1837 on a visit to New Orleans and added a sketch entitled "Corn Meal" to his minstrel act in which he imitated the seller.

He did variations of his beloved Jim Crow as well. One successful number was first presented at the Washington Theatre in 1833 and featured Rice in blackface, entering with a gunny sack slung over his shoulder. He set the sack on the floor and out of the bag crawled a four-year-old child in blackface, named Joseph Jefferson III, who proceeded to mimic Rice's song and dance as his little shadow.[27] Later, Jefferson recalled,

> Of course this fantastic figure had a great influence on me, and I danced Jim Crow from the garret to the cellar. The comedian saw my imitation of him, and insisted that I should appear for his benefit; so on that occasion I was duly blacked up and dressed in a complete miniature likeness of the original. He put me in a bag, which almost smothered me and carried me upon the stage on his shoulders. No word of this Proceeding had been mentioned in the bills, so that, figuratively speaking, the public were as much in the dark as I was. After dancing and singing the first verse he began the second, the following being the two lines which introduced me:
>
> Ladies and gentleman, I'd have
>   you for to know
> That I've got a little darky here to
>   jump Jim Crow;
>
> and turning the bag upside down he emptied me out head first before the eyes of the astonished audience.[28]

At the first performance, after the six-foot Rice and the small child sang and danced to several verses of "Jim Crow," the audience tossed $24 upon the stage which Rice proceeded to hand over to the delighted four-year-old.

On January 10, 1854, Rice appeared at the Bowery Theatre as Uncle Tom in an adaptation of Harriet Beecher Stowe's *Uncle Tom's Cabin.* Appearing in the cast with Rice was the Virginia Minstrel, Billy Whitlock. In the spring of 1854, Rice was succeeded in his role of Uncle Tom by Frank Brower, another founding member of the famous minstrel troupe.

Rice is considered to be the founder of blackface minstrelsy and was celebrated as "the Negro, par exellence."[29] Joseph Jefferson II, well-known actor and father of the four-year-old who Jumped Jim Crow with Rice, called him "the first and best knight of the burnt cork." Although he certainly was not the first to don black face and masquerade as an African-American, he probably was the most successful.

Towards the end of his life, Rice became increasingly eccentric and squandered his fortune, doing such things as using five and ten dollar coins for buttons on his coat and vest, and then giving them out as souvenirs.[30] He had a stroke which left him paralyzed, and although he recovered, his health was severely impaired. He appeared again for six nights in his last performances as Jim Crow on July 28, 1860, at the Canterbury Concert Hall. After suffering a second stroke, he died in New

"Daddy" Rice later in his career. From *Monarchs of Minstrelsy: From "Daddy" Rice to Date* by Edward LeRoy Rice (1911).

York City on Wednesday, September 19, 1860.[31] He was buried next to his wife Charlotte B. Gladstone and his infant children in the Greenwood Cemetery in Brooklyn, New York.

The impact of T. D. Rice's Jim Crow dance and characterization cannot be overstated. His enormous popularity coupled with his innovative use of African-American folk material revolutionized the theatrical world.

11

The King of Diamonds and Master Juba

In the *Morning Herald* on July 18, 1840, there appeared an announcement that Master Diamond would "outdance the nation, [with] 'Heel and Toe Breakdowns' that are a caution to all darkies and no mistake!"[1]

A white man, John (Johnny or Jack) Diamond was considered one of the best percussive dancers ever to grace the American minstrel stage. Born in 1823, he was only 17 years old when he was first brought to the public's attention after winning a $500 prize at a New York City jig contest. After his victory, he was signed by the famous showman P. T. Barnum, and toured the U.S. and Europe as Barnum's protégé. Always one for stretching the truth if it provided better publicity, Barnum listed his dancing prodigy as being only 12 years old.[2]

John Diamond called himself the "King of Diamonds," and was recognized as one of the greatest solo dancers of the period.[3] He was famous for never losing any of the many dancing matches in which he competed from city to city. His drawing power was so great that a host of fake John Diamonds made a good living imitating the young dancer.

Diamond performed such dances as the Negro camptown hornpipe, the ole Virginny breakdown, the Long Island breakdown, the smokehouse dance, and the five mile out of town dance. One of his dances, the rattle snake jig, featured as many as 120 different steps.

As with all minstrel performers of the day, Diamond borrowed heavily from African-American, Irish and English sources. He performed plantation dances as well as the Irish jig and the hornpipe. Diamond's version, like John Durang's famous hornpipe, included the "double shuffle," the "heel and toe," the "pigeon wing" and "running on his heels."

Diamond danced with a relaxed upper body in order to call attention to his feet.

> One of his typical movements was to slink across the stage, looking stiffly sideways, leaning his torso forward with his hands drooping like damp cloths, while treading the ground at once with the heel of one foot and the toe of the other.[4]

"Small of stature, Diamond executed in an extremely neat and slow fashion."[5] He called his dancing "music in his heels." Theatre manager and showman, Noah M. Ludlow, had seen him dance and commented,

He could twist his feet and legs, while dancing, into more fantastic forms than I ever witnessed before or since in any human being.[6]

A playbill from February 24, 1841, read,

Master Diamond, who delineates the Ethiopian character superior to any other white person, hereby challenges any person in the world to trial of skill at Negro dancing, in all its varieties, for a wager of from $200.00–$1,000.00.[7]

The same playbill later stated that Diamond would be "making the greatest display of heel and toe genus [genius] ever witnessed."[8]

John Diamond was often accompanied by the "King of Banjo Players," Billy

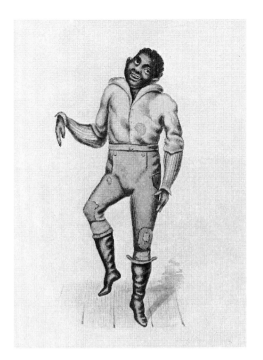

Top: **John Diamond performing a dance in high boots. From *Records of New York,* II, Part 7, by Joseph N. Ireland. *Courtesy of the Harvard Theatre Collection.* Left: Playbill from the New Theatre in Mobile, Alabama, advertising a performance by "Master" John Diamond (February 24, 1841).**

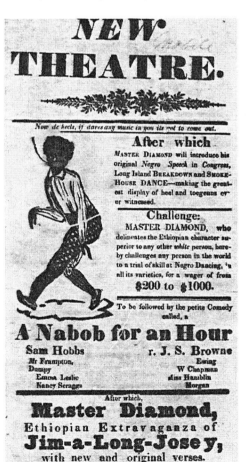

Whitlock. The two became a popular duo and a favorite of audiences in the 1840s. After Whitlock helped found the Virginia Minstrels, he convinced Diamond to dance for the troupe after they had made their debut, hoping that the Diamond's incomparable dancing would add to the appeal of the group.

Although he was often described as one of the greatest dancers of the day, it was said that John Diamond's dancing was "considerably better than his temper and disposition."[9] In February 1841, while working for P. T. Barnum, Diamond suddenly disappeared "after extorting as much money as possible from his manager."[10] He used the misappropriated money for a wild week of nonstop drinking and debauchery. An incensed Barnum circulated a letter among theatre managers, cautioning them about Diamond's character and warning them about hiring him. He also threatened to publish a description of Diamond's conduct and character in the New Orleans newspapers. He wrote:

> [Diamond has] overdrawn the money due him to the amount of $95 and has during the last week expended a hundred dollars in brothels and haunts of dissipation & vice.[11]

Barnum replaced Diamond with another dancer, a young black man named William Henry Lane, who became Barnum's new protégé and was soon featured at Barnum's Museum as one of his most popular attractions. Lane was billed as "Master Juba, the Dancing Wonder of the Age." Thomas Low Nichols, an editor in the early 1840s, wrote of the incident:

> In New York, some years ago, Mr. P.T. Barnum had a clever boy who brought him lots of money as a dancer of negro breakdowns; made up, of course, as a negro minstrel, with his face well blackened, and a wooly wig. One day Master Diamond, thinking he might better himself, danced away into the infinite distance.
> Barnum, full of expedients, explored the dance-houses of the Five Points and found a boy who could dance a better break-down than Master Diamond. It was easy to hire him; but he was a genuine negro; and there was not an audience in America that would not have resented, in very energetic fashion, the insult of being asked to look at the dancing of a real negro. To any man but the originator of Joyce Heth, the venerable nurse of Washington, and the manufacturer of the Fiji Mermaid, this would have been an insuperable obstacle.
> Barnum was equal to the occasion. Son of the State of white oak cheeses and wooden nutmegs, he did not dis-

grace his lineage. He greased the little "nigger's" face and rubbed it over with new blacking of burnt cork, painted his thick lips with vermilion, put on a wooly wig over his tight curled locks, and brought him out as the "champion nigger-dancer of the world." Had it been suspected that the seeming counterfeit was the general [genuine] article, the New York Vauxhall would have blazed with indignation."[12]

William Henry Lane was free-born around 1825 in Providence, Rhode Island, and most likely learned his skills from an African-American jig and reel dancer named "Uncle" Jim Lowe, who performed in saloons and dance halls in New York. At age ten, Lane attracted attention with his dancing in the Five Points district of New York in an area called Paradise Square.[13] The main constituents of the Five Points district were African-Americans and Irish immigrants considered by outsiders as the dregs of society. Forced to live side by side in the filthy, crime-ridden slum, the two cultures intermingled.

Lane lived and worked in this area, successfully blending both African and Irish dance styles into a new form of jig dancing. The young black dancer performed at various saloons around the district, as well as at a popular tourist spot called Dicken's Dance House, where the big attraction was a live elephant.

By the time he was 15 years old, Lane had been "adopted" by a group of white minstrel players who respected his natural-born dance abilities; by the time he was 19, he was viewed by members of the profession as the very best. They said he was

> ... beyond question the very greatest of all dancers. He possessed not only wonderful and unique execution, but also unsurpassed grace and endurance.[14]

Handbills referred to him as "The greatest dancer in the world!"[15] In his show,

Lane, "Master Juba," performed a statue dance and ended with:

> Master Juba's Imitation Dance, in which he will give correct imitation dances of all the principal Ethiopian dancers in the United States. After which he will give an imitation of himself— and then you will see the vast difference between those that have heretofore attempted dancing and this WONDERFUL YOUNG MAN![16]

A challenge dance as depicted on a playbill from Bryant's Minstrels (January 24, 1859).

A feature writer for the New York Herald described Juba's imitation dance performed at Pete Williams' dance hall in New York.

> Those who passed through the long hallway and entered the dance hall … saw this phenomenon, 'Juba,' imitate all the dancers of the day and their special steps. Then Bob Ellington, the interlocutor and master of ceremonies, would say, "Now Master Juba, show your own jig." Whereupon he would go through all his own steps and specialties, with never a resemblance in any of them to those he had just imitated.[17]

The dancers that Juba imitated were Dick Pelham and Frank Brower, both members of the Virginia Minstrels, and other well-known jig dancers of the day such as John Daniel, John Smith, James Sanford and Frank Diamond. The last dancer that Juba imitated was always John Diamond, his only serious rival. A stiff competition developed between these two men, and because their dancing abilities and merit were in question, a series of challenge dances, sometimes called "trial dances," were held to see who was the best.

Traditionally there were three judges at every challenge: one for time, one for style and one for execution.

> The time judge sat on the stage in the first right entrance, the style judge sat in or near the orchestra pit, and the judge of execution sat under the stage. There, with pad and pencil, the execution judge checked the missing taps, defective rolls and heel work, the lagging in the breaks. At the conclusion of the contest the judges compared notes and awarded the prize on points.[18]

On January 28, 1843, the *New York Sporting Whip* stated,

> The favorites now are the dancers, and he who can cut, shuffle, and attitudinize with the greatest facility is reckoned the best fellow and pockets the most money. Match dances are very frequently got up, and seem to give general satisfaction, if we are allowed to judge from the crowds who throng to witness them. We have not had a real, scientific, out-and-out trial of skill since between Dick Pelham and John Diamond at the Chatham; but it appears we are soon to have another of these refined and elevating exhibitions. A match has been made between John Diamond and a little negro called "Juba," by some in the sporting community, and is to come off in the course of a few

weeks. The stake is large, and an un-
paralleled display will be the result.[19]

In 1844, John Diamond and William
Henry Lane held many challenges. On July
8, 1844, an advertisement for one of them
was run in the New York Herald. It read,

GREAT PUBLIC CONTEST

Between the two most renowned
dancers in the world, the Original
JOHN DIAMOND and the colored
boy JUBA, for a Wager of $200, on
MONDAY EVENING July 8th at the
BOWERY AMPHITHEATRE, which
building has been expressly hired from
the Proprietor, Mr. Smith, for this night
only, as its accommodations will afford
all a fair view of each step of these wonderful Dancers. The fame of these Two
Celebrated Breakdown Dancers has already spread over the Union, and the
numerous friends of each claim the
Championship for their
favorite, and who have ...
anxiously wished for a
Public trial between them
and thus know which is
to bear the Title of the
Champion Dancer of the
World. The time to de-
cide that has come, as the
friends of Juba have challenged the world to pro-
duce his superior in the
art for $100. That Chal-
lenge has been accepted
by the friends of Dia-
mond, and on Monday
Evening they meet and
Dance three Jigs, Two
Reels, and the Camptown
Hornpipe. Five Judges
have been selected for
their ability and knowl-
edge of the Art, so that a
fair decision will be made.
   Rule — Each Dancer
will select his own Vio-
lin and the victory will

be decided by the best time and the
greatest number of steps.[20]

In an undated reference to one of the
dance challenges, Diamond is given as the
winner, but in all others, Master Juba is
consistently listed as the victor.[21] The
young black dancer became known as the
"King of All Dancers" and the man who
had bested John Diamond. By 1845, Juba
was so famous he appeared with four white
minstrels in a touring show and received
top billing, unprecedented for a black man
at this point in history.

In the summer of 1848, Juba toured
London with Pell's Ethiopian Minstrels;
his press releases had a description of him
taken from Charles Dickens' *American
Notes*. Dickens had seen Juba dance
six years earlier, in 1842, at the Cow Bay, a
tavern and brothel in Five Points, New
York.

**Pell's Ethiopian Serenaders. William Henry Lane is shown in the
insert on the top right. (circa 1848.) *Courtesy of the Harvard
Theatre Collection.***

Single shuffle, double shuffle, cut, and cross-cut; snapping his fingers, rolling his eyes, turning in his knees, the backs of his legs in front, spinning about on his toes and heels like nothing but the man's fingers on a tambourine; dancing with two left legs; two right legs, two wooden legs, two wire legs, two spring legs — all sorts of legs and no legs — what is this to him?[22]

In addition to the rhythms he created with his feet, Juba interspersed his dancing with vocal sounds. He apparently had an amazing laugh that audiences loved.

There never was such a laugh as the laugh of Juba — there is in it the concentrated laugh of fifty comic pantomimes; it has no relation to the chuckle, and, least of all to the famous horse laugh; not a bit of it — it is a laugh distinct, a laugh apart, a laugh by itself — clear, ringing, echoing, resonant, harmonious, full of rejoicing and mighty mirth, and fervent fun; you may hear it like the continuous humming sound of nature, permeating everywhere; it enters your heart and you laugh sympathetically — it creeps into your ear, and clings to it, and all the subsequent sounds seemed to be endued with the cachinatory quality.... Well, though the laugh of Juba be wondrous, what may be said of Juba's dancing?[23]

While in England, Juba married a white woman. His success and acceptance grew, and he was a huge hit in London, where he was commanded to appear at Buckingham Palace. Reviewers wrote of him with the kind of affection and enthusiasm usually reserved for the stars of the ballet. One critic wrote:

... such a combination of mobility of muscles, such flexibility of joints, such boundings, such slidings, such gyra-

tions, such toe and heelings, such backwardings and forwardings, such posturings, such firmness of foot, such elasticity of tendons, such mutation of movement, such vigor, such variety, such natural grace, such powers of endurance, such potency of pastern [pattern].[24]

Another clipping said,

... the dancing of Juba exceeded anything ever witnessed in Europe. The style as well as the execution is unlike anything ever seen in this country. The manner in which he beats time with his feet, and the extraordinary command he possesses over them, can only be believed by those who have been at this exhibition.[25]

These critics were all familiar with the jigs, clogs, and reels of the British Isles, but what made Juba's dancing different was in "the manner in which he beat[s] time with his feet." His blend of British folk dance and African dance had resulted in a startling new development, one that critics recognized as genuinely original. What these observers had witnessed was the birth of tap dance.

Many scholars say William Henry Lane was the first American tap dancer, and it is appropriate that an African-American is given credit for this art form, because without the vitally important contribution of African syncopation and improvisation, there would be no tap.

William Henry Lane's influence was lasting. The "Gay Negro Boy," as his character was called, was soon a staple on the legitimate stage, as well as in British and American circuses and minstrel shows. Furthermore, Juba's dancing perpetuated the use of authentic African source material by American minstrels. Many white performers maintained Juba's traditions to

William Henry Lane, "Master Juba," dancing at Vauxhall Gardens in London, circa 1849. From the *Illustrated London News* (August 5, 1848).

the letter, both preserving and teaching his repertoire.[26] Historian Marian Hannah Winter said,

Because of the vast influence of one Negro performer, the minstrel show dance retained more integrity as a Negro art form than any other derivative of Negro culture.[27]

She added, that William Henry Lane was

… the most influential single performer of nineteenth century dance. The repertoire of any current tap dancer contains elements which were established theatrically by him.[28]

It is on record that from the age of 16 Juba worked every day, both day and night, from 1839 to 1850—11 years straight without a break. Unfortunately this superhuman schedule proved too much for him, and he died in London at the age of 27.

John Diamond struggled with alcoholism for most of his life and eventually died from it in Philadelphia on October 29, 1857, at age 34. When he died he was penniless; donations had to be raised by Bryant's Minstrels in order to pay for his funeral.

12

The Virginia Minstrels

Daniel Decatur Emmett was born in Mount Vernon, Ohio, on Sunday, October 29, 1815. As a young man, he was described as a "backwoodsman of Irish decent who looked like a Yankee deacon."[1] At 17, he joined the army and while serving in the military, learned drums from John J. Clark, who was nicknamed "Juba." The name "Juba" indicates that Clark was either African-American or that he taught African-style drumming. Emmett had already been exposed to African-American music during his youth in Ohio, but studying with "Juba" Clark solidified his knowledge of black-inspired syncopated rhythms.[2] Emmett was discharged from military service after the discovery that he had falsified his age.

In his article "'Dixie' and Its Author," published in *The Century Magazine* in 1895, Robert Sheerin wrote;

> Mr. Emmett says it was a fashion in those days among young people to try their skill at making verses, and sing them to some popular tune. Jim Crow was a favorite, and the boys and girls found great delight in fitting words to that tune. In this way he formed a taste for verse-making and singing, which later led him to negro minstrelsy.[3]

Emmett learned to play the fiddle by ear in 1828 and soon after, traveled with Sam Stickney's one-ring wagon circus as a blackface entertainer and musician. He then joined Miller's Caravan as a drummer learning to play the fife and piccolo. Though respected as a musician, Emmett's chief duty with Miller's Caravan was to sing "darky songs" and dance.

He eventually ended up in the Cincinnati Circus Company as a drummer, and while there, learned to play the banjo. Traveling with the company, Emmett became friends with Francis (Frank) Marion Brower.

Engraving of Daniel Emmett as a young man. From *Curiosities of the American Stage* by Laurence Hutton (1890).

93

Brower, born November 20, 1823, made his dancing debut at age 13 in Philadelphia at Dick Meyer's Third and Chestnut Streets Museum. He said that he had learned his dances directly from African-Americans. In the spring of 1841, Emmett began accompanying Brower's dances with his banjo. The two became a popular team, with Brower soon gaining the reputation as one of the best blackface dancers around. He started a new trend in minstrel dancing by introducing to the stage the kind of leaps and jumps that had previously been done only by black slaves.[4]

Brower was one of the first to introduce the playing of bones on the minstrel stage. Bones were used to provide percussive accompaniment to instrumental music and to augment the rhythms of dancing feet. Originally made from two bones, they were held between the fingers and clicked and trilled like castanets. As the use of bones became more common, manufacturers carved them out of two pieces of ivory or wood.

In November 1842, Emmett and Brower left the circus and moved to New York where they appeared in small variety theatres around the city. In January 1843, when America was suffering under a financial depression, they joined forces with the famous banjoist, William (Bill) Whitlock, and the dancer, Richard (Dick) Ward Pelham.

Whitlock was born in New York City in 1813. As a youth he had worked as a typesetter at the *New York Herald*. He made his stage debut in Thomas D. Rice's Ethiopian Opera, *Oh, Hush! or, the Virginny Cupids* and eventually toured as a singer with Whipple's Circus. During the tour, he was taught the banjo by Joe Sweeney.[5] He eventually performed as a solo act in New York in 1838 and then established his reputation in P. T. Barnum's shows, accompanying the famous jig dancer John Diamond. After Diamond was fired by Barnum, Whitlock continued the act with the "second John Diamond," Frank Lynch. Although best known as a musician, Whitlock also danced. A playbill from the National Theatre in Boston on June 5, 1840, stated:

Dis very partic'lar nigger [Whitlock in blackface] will jump, dance, and knock his heels in a way dat Madamoiselle Fanny Essler neber did, neber can, and neber will do.[6]

Dick Pelham was born in New York City on February 13, 1815. He made his stage debut at the Bowery Theatre in 1835, appearing with Thomas D. Rice in Rice's show *Oh Hush! or, The Virginny Cupids*. On his 25th birthday, he was so confident in his dancing abilities, he entered a challenge match with the great John Diamond, considered one of the best dancers of the day. Pelham lost.

Hoping to pull themselves out of their individual financial problems, Emmett, Brower, Whitlock, and Pelham, with Emmett as their leader, decided to form a troupe which exclusively presented blackface characterizations.[7] They met in Emmett's room in Mrs. Brooke's boarding house at 37 Catherine Street to rehearse. They called themselves the Virginia Minstrels.[8] Dan Emmett's account of the founding of the group was recorded in the *New York Clipper* on May 19, 1877.

All four were one day [in the winter of 1842–43] sitting in the North American Hotel, in the Bowery, when one of them proposed that with their instruments they should cross over to the Bowery Circus and give one of the proprietors (Uncle Nate Howes) a "charivari" as he sat by the stove in the hall entrance. Bringing forth his banjo for Whitlock to play on, Emmett took the violin, Pelham the tambourine, and Brower the bones. Without any rehearsal, with hardly the ghost of an idea as to what was to follow, they crossed the street and proceeded to "browbeat" Uncle Nate Howes into giving them an engagement, the calculation being that he would succumb in preference to standing the horrible noise. After standing it for a while, Uncle Nate said: "Boys you've got a good thing. Can't you sing us a song?" Thereupon Emmett, accompanying himself on his violin, began to sing "Old Dan Tucker," the others joining in on the chorus. The four minstrels were as much surprised as Uncle Nate. After singing some more songs for him, they returned to the North American, where they resumed their "horrible noise" in the reading room, which was quickly filled with spectators.[9]

The four men introduced their new act to the general public on February 17, 1843, at the Bowery Amphitheatre in New York City.[10] Dressed in outfits designed by Emmett, the four men appeared in white pants, striped calico shirts, and blue tail coats. During the show, the troupe sat in a semicircle on stage with Emmett on fiddle, Whitlock on banjo, Brower on bones and Pelham on tambourine.

Seated on the ends of the semicircle with instruments that were easy to handle, Pelham and Brower were usually the ones who jumped up in the middle of a number and burst into wild dance breakdowns, establishing a form that would later dictate that the two end-men were the best dancers.[11] Audiences loved Pelham and Brower because they interspersed their breakdown dancing with vocals. It was common for them to suddenly shout out such phrases as "Dars musick in dem ole heels," or "Dem ole legs is hung on a swibbel," or perhaps, "O gosh, I kick like an old warginny hoss wid four shoes on one foot."[12]

Although Brower and Pelham were the featured dancers at the debut of the Virginia Minstrels, all four performers danced either solo or in double acts.[13] All four also danced the Lucy Long walk around and the essence of old Virginny at the end of the show, a finale that became the traditional closing for the first part of all later minstrel shows.

The Virginia Minstrels performing in costume. From left to right: Dick Pelham on tambourine; Dan Emmett on fiddle; Billy Whitlock on banjo; and Frank Brower on bones. As depicted on the sheet music cover of "The Celebrated Negro Melodies" (1843).

After their performance at the Bowery Theatre, the Virginia Minstrels became instantaneously famous and immensely popular. The group's influence was far-reaching and led to three important changes to minstrel performing. First, the group initiated the move from theatre to concert hall, refining the variety act and making it marketable to a more respectable audience. A review in the *New York Herald* had even commented that the Virginia Minstrels' show was "entirely exempt from vulgarities and other objectionable features which have hitherto characterized Negro extravaganzas."[14] Second, the Virginia Minstrels attempted to educate their audience as well as entertain them, by presenting Southern African-American life as exotic and idealized. Third, the group hired an agent to represent the act and packaged their performance, thus creating the "show" in the modern sense of the word.[15]

In April 1843, the "Big Four," as the troupe was affectionately called, sailed to England to present their "…oddities, peculiarities, eccentricities, and comicalities of the Sable Genus of Humanity."[16] Unfortunately, the group met with only modest success although certain aspects of their show were appreciated by European audiences and critics. English broadsides advertised R. W. Pelham as the "neatest and best dancer living," and described how Pelham would

… show de science ob de heel to de music ob de banjo, making a grand display ob de heel-and-toe caperbilities … when de right leg, de leff leg, de hind leg, and ole de odder legs will be brought to bear on dat 'ticular 'casion.[17]

The *London Times*, on June 26, 1843, mentioned the "unconquerable jigs by Brower and Pelham."[18] The group was summoned to Windsor Castle for a command performance for Queen Victoria, but the Virginia Minstrels aroused little public interest during their tour of Great Britain and the four men became virtually stranded abroad. On July 14, 1843, the men finally split up in Glasgow, Scotland, because of personal differences.[19] Pelham married and stayed in England permanently, eventually forming his own minstrel company which featured the black dancer Master Juba. Juba danced with Pelham's troupe until his death two years later. Emmett and Brower returned to the United States on October 7, 1844, and formed their own new minstrel band.

In 1858, Daniel Emmett joined Bryant's Minstrels and composed tunes for walk arounds, or horrays, which were the group presentation dances at the end of the minstrel show. The walk around had started in the 1840s as a solo dance, but by the 1850s it included either an ensemble of dancers or the entire cast.[20] The dance was a

Minstrel performers doing the concluding dance of a walk around. From a Bryant's Minstrels playbill (December 19, 1859).

secular parody of the religious dance, the ring shout, and was performed in a circle with the ensemble providing percussive background accompaniment for the soloists by clapping and patting.

The following is a description of a typical minstrel walk around.

At a chord from the orchestra, the company rose to its feet. As the orchestra began a lively tune in 2/4 time, one of the company would step down stage from the semicircle, walk around for sixteen bars of the music and do one step of a reel, finish with a break, then resume his place in the semicircle as another stepped out and repeated the performance, varying [it], though[,] with a different step. This would continue until six or more dancers had appeared. Then all the dancers came down stage and danced together while the rest of the company patted time and shuffled.[21]

Daniel Emmett achieved lasting fame as the composer of one walk around song in particular—"I Wish I Was in Dixie's Land," better known as "Dixie."[22] This famous song was first presented on April 4, 1859, at the Mechanics' Hall in New York City.[23] Although some have contested his authorship, most scholars credit Emmett with writing the song.[24]

"Dixie" became one of the most well-known songs in America. It was played by the Republicans during Abraham Lincoln's campaign for President in 1860 and at the inauguration of Jefferson Davis as President of the Confederate States of America, in Montgomery, Alabama, on February 18, 1861. It eventually became the official anthem of the Confederacy.[25] General Pickett ordered the song played at the charge at Gettysburg. On the day Lee surrendered to Grant at Appomattox, a huge crowd gathered outside the White House in Washington to hear Lincoln give a victory speech. After a few brief remarks, Lincoln

Playbill from the first performance of "Dixie's Land" at Mechanics' Hall in New York. Note that it is advertised as a "Plantation Song and Dance." Also note Richard Sands' presentation of a "Wooden Shoe Dance" (April 4, 1859).

told the crowd, "I propose closing this interview by the band performing a particular tune. I have always thought 'Dixie' one of the best tunes I have ever heard."

Emmett also wrote such well-loved tunes as "De Blue Tail Fly" and "Old Dan Tucker." Affectionately known as "Uncle Dan" in his older years, Emmett worked as a chicken farmer and lived on his pension from the Actors Fund. Despite his huge successes both as a performer and as a composer, he died penniless at the age of 88 on June 28, 1904, at his home in Mt. Vernon.[26] The band played "Dixie" as his coffin was lowered into the grave.

Although remembered mainly as the composer of "Dixie," Daniel Decatur Emmett was an important link in the development of American tap dance. Because of his involvement in the creation of the Virginia Minstrels, he helped set the standard for all minstrel shows that followed and further fostered the use of African-American source material. In addition, when Emmett put aside his fiddle or banjo and danced himself, he consciously combined the Irish dances of his youth with African-American slave dances, and in doing so created steps that are still used today. Some credit him with popularizing the well-known tap step, the Irish. The Irish, as well as his other steps, showed the influence of the Lancashire clog which he is said to have learned on his visit to England in 1843.

After retiring from show business, Billy Whitlock worked for four years in the U.S. Customs office in New Jersey. In 1862, he became paralyzed and was an invalid until he died on March 29, 1878, in Long Branch, New Jersey. Dick Pelham died of cancer in Liverpool, England on October 8, 1856. The original "Brudder Bones," Frank Brower, called "Uncle Frank" in his later years, retired in 1867 and opened a saloon. He died in Philadelphia at age 50 on June 4, 1874. These three men, along with Dan Emmett, originated the first totally American theatrical format; their creation, the minstrel show, influenced all future musical theatre presentations.

As interest in slave culture grew, minstrels became avid "collectors," wishing to acquire authentic black music, dance, and folklore material for the stage. It became more and more fashionable for minstrels to proclaim that they were not only the best, but also the most authentic delineators of the Ethiopian culture.

BILLY WHITLOCK   DICK PELHAM
DAN. EMMETT   FRANK BROWER
The above four performers gave in New York City, February 6, 1843, the first minstrel performance ever given; they were known as the Virginia Minstrels.

Photograph of the "Big Four." Clockwise from top left: Billy Whitlock, Dick Pelham, Frank Brower and Dan Emmett. From *Monarchs of Minstrelsy: From "Daddy" Rice to Date* by Edward LeRoy Rice (1911).

These theatrical impersonations were rarely sympathetic and, even though white minstrels advertised their renditions of blacks as authentic, African-Americans were usually portrayed as exotic curiosities and comic oddities.

Those minstrels that did try to create believable characters often fooled their gullible audiences. Unsophisticated Northern audiences who were unfamiliar with theatrical license often mistook the blackface performers for real African-Americans. After the Civil War, when blacks began to perform as minstrels, audiences were astonished when they appeared without blackface makeup because their faces showed a diversity and variety of skin tones.

A well-known actress of that period, Fanny Kemble, wrote in her memoirs:

> ... all the contortions, and springs, and flings, and kicks, and capers you have been beguiled in accepting as indicative of ... [the African-American] are spurious, faint, feeble, impotent — in a word, pale Northern reproductions of the ineffable black conception.[27]

Wishing to please simple, lower-class, white audiences who wanted to be reminded of their superiority to the enslaved Africans, minstrel performers used stereotypical formulas, couching their representations of blacks in terms that were non-threatening and humorous.

> ... [U]nlike the improvised ecstatic dances of the slaves, minstrel dances were consciously worked out, for the stage demanded planned variety and it encouraged showmanship. The dancer was expected to excel in precision, speed, near-acrobatic flexibility, and endurance, and to stress jolliness and clownishness for their own sake.[28]

The question remains, did minstrel performers help to preserve African dances through this cultural appropriation, or were the portrayals of blacks so overblown and stereotypical that the purity of the steps was lost?

Minstrel performers, mostly Irish immigrants who rarely, if ever, visited the South, first co-opted African dance movements, and then counterfeited them. There may have been a germ of authenticity in the reproductions, but the movements were reinvented out of the social misconceptions about African-Americans of that time, and were presented in overstated, burlesque parody with show business in mind.

Nevertheless, by giving African slave dance steps their own interpretive twists, a new style of dancing took shape which was not only a mixture of the African and Anglo-Celtic cultures, but also a distortion and a heightening of the various elements within each. This stylized organization and control within minstrel dances, with emphasis on the showy, albeit racist, elements led to an urbanized style of dancing. The cultural appropriation of African rhythms and movements, which were then heightened and varied, provided the secret ingredient that changed Irish jigs and English clogs into American tap.

13

The Development of the Minstrel Show

After the success of Daniel Emmett's Virginia Minstrels, Ethiopian delineators dominated the American stage, and many minstrel troupes were formed to cash in on the new art form. The minstrel show, which began as a temporary alliance of solo performers who realized that by working together they could make a little extra money, became established, and these alliances expanded into well-organized business partnerships. The shows also grew in scale; soon large minstrel troupes crisscrossed the country under the leadership of managers, one of the most influential of whom was E. P. Christy.

When Edwin P. (Ned) Christy was a child in the 1820s, he worked as an office boy in a law firm and later he became a traveling shoe salesman. During his youth, he also worked as a banjo and tambourine player in barrooms. At one point, Christy supervised slaves on a ropewalk in New Orleans where he first became interested in learning African-American dances and songs. As a frequent visitor to Congo Square in New Orleans, he was further exposed to the dances of the African-American population. After Christy settled in Buffalo, New York, around 1830, he continued to seek out African-American source material, finding one primary source in a black church singer named One-legged Harrison.

In the late 1830s, Christy began working as a minstrel, drawing heavily on the African-American material he had picked up earlier. In 1842 or 1843 he started his own minstrel troupe from the money he had saved from selling shoes. He called his group the Virginia Minstrels, the same name as Dan Emmett's group. A running

Engraving of Edwin P. (Ned) Christy, the man responsible for codifying the minstrel show format. From *Curiosities of the American Stage* by Laurence Hutton (1890).

feud quickly developed between Christy and Emmett, both of whom laid claim to the name and adamantly declared that they were responsible for the creation of the very first minstrel troupe. Christy eventually sued Emmett, saying he had preceded Emmett's Virginia Minstrels by several months. Whether or not he was in fact the first to create the minstrel format, he did win the claim in the New York Supreme Court. Following this episode, E. P. Christy joined with three other performers and changed the name of his troupe to Christy's Minstrels.

In 1847, Christy's Minstrels opened at Mechanics' Hall on Broadway and played to packed house for almost ten straight years, making Christy the unchallenged top man in the minstrel world. Within 12 years, he was so wealthy, he was able to retire. The name Christy became synonymous with the minstrel phenomenon. In England, all blackface performers were called "Christys."

Originally the various parts in the minstrel show were interchangeable and the chairs were put in a semicircle merely by accident. All four men danced, played instruments, did jokes, and sang. Later under Christy's direction, the traditional minstrel show format consisting of four parts became set.

During the first part of a minstrel show, the interlocutor[1] presided over a presentation of songs, jokes, and instrumental solos. The second part was called the olio — a word derived from the Spanish word for mixture, *olla* — which was made up of a mixture of assorted solos, monologues, and sketches. The olio usually ended with a hoedown in which every member of the cast danced solo while encircled by the other performers who clapped and sang in support. The third part consisted of a song or dance skit organized around a loosely knit plot, often set in a plantation locale. The fourth section, the finale, was done as a walk around during which the entire company was featured in a lively cakewalk dance.

In her book, *Black Dance: From 1619 to Today*, Lynne Fauley Emery suggests that the form of the minstrel show was based upon African ring dances.

"The Ethiopian Serenaders," five minstrel players as they appeared in London in the middle of the 19th century. From the *Illustrated London News* (circa 1843–44).

These shows were basically a development of the primitive tradition of circle and hand clapping dances. For theatrical purposes, the entertainers were seated in a semi-circular line of chairs on the stage. Here the ringleader of the dance became, in transition, the "interlocutor" or master of ceremonies. Those who sang the melody for the dance were transposed into the Chorus, some becoming "end" men, one on either "end" or side of the circle. The rest of the chorus performed the same functions as did the line in Africa — they clapped their hands or shook tambourines. Every man in the chorus had the opportunity for a solo bit of some sort, just as had the Negro in many of his primitive African ceremonies.[2]

E. P. Christy was responsible for codifying the format of the minstrel show around 1850 and popularizing such familiar aspects as the interlocutor's famous command, "Gentlemen, be seated." Christy also helped to spread the popularity of songwriter, Stephen Foster. Foster sold many songs to Christy such as "Old Folks at Home," and "Massa's in the Cold Ground," and Christy himself was one of the first to perform such songs as "My Old Kentucky Home" and "Old Black Joe."[3] After E. P. Christy retired, his stepson, George Christy, took over the leadership of the company. As he grew older Christy suffered from melancholia and delusions. He committed suicide on May 21, 1862, by jumping out of a second story window.

E. P. Christy's step-son was born George Harrington in Palmyra, New York. He started as a jig dancer in Christy's shows, and when E. P. married George's mother, Harrington took his stepfather's last name. He then became known professionally as George Christy.

George Christy was well known for his female impersonations and his "negro wench" character. His most famous number was "Lucy Long." After he took over for E. P. Christy, George Christy became a wealthy man. He died in 1868 from inflammation of the brain.

Minstrel Dancers

As the popularity of the minstrel show grew, new mixtures of African-American and European styles were disseminated throughout the country by performers who specialized in this unique and innovative form of dancing.[4] Most of the names and stories of the many minstrel dancers have faded into obscurity. Those stories that have been saved demonstrate the influential lives these men and women had upon the art of show dancing. Although it is impossible to list them all, many of these talented and influential performers deserve mention.

Solo Acts

Dick Sliter was considered one of the world's greatest jig dancers. He was listed in the *Ohio State Journal* in 1850 as "the most brilliant dancer of the day." His dances included "A Fancy Hornpipe" and "A Championship Jig." He started dancing in the 1830s and eventually formed his own minstrels troupe called Booker and Sliter's Minstrels. When Sliter died in 1861, his spot in the minstrel troupe was filled by jig dancer Ben Brown (1846–1910). Ben Brown later won a jig championship against the "English" Tommy Peel and dancers Johnny Boyd and Alex Ross. His prize was a diamond studded cross containing 11 stones. One of Brown's feats was to dance with a tumbler of water on his head and never spill a drop. There are accounts that he later danced with a plow balanced on his head!

Otto Burbank was a minstrel fancy

dancer and was also considered one of the best jig dancers around. He performed with Christy's Minstrels and eventually toured California where reviewers called him the best dancer in the state. Jim Sanford, another of minstrelsy's earliest jig dancers, appeared with companies as early as 1843. He traveled with John Diamond and was known for his fastidiousness in dress.

Joe Brown was another world-class jig dancer. After he appeared with Christy's Minstrels in London, he sailed to South Africa to perform. On the way, the boat was wrecked, and although Brown survived, he lost everything, including the silver belt he had won competing against Dick Sliter in 1856.

Johnny Dove's act was called the "Dancing Burglar." The story goes that as a young man, Dove was asked by his father what he'd like to do for a living. Dove replied that he'd like to become either a dancer or a burglar. One night, after everyone in the house had gone to bed, young Johnny Dove slipped out and went into town where he entered a dance contest in which the first prize was a 24-piece silver service. Dove won the contest. Back home, he placed the service on the dining table and went to bed. When his father woke up the next morning, he found the silver on the table and concluded that his son had decided to become a burglar. So, Johnny Dove became known as the "Dancing Burglar."

David Reed (1830–1906) had learned his style from black dock workers when he danced on the steamboat *Banjo,* which sailed up and down the Mississippi. His dancing was described as "a certain comical and characteristic movement of the hands, by placing the elbows near his hips and extending the rest of his arms at right angles to his body, with the palms of his hands down"[5] These moves were directly derived from the African buzzard lope and ring shout. Reed also developed a stiff-legged dance that he had learned from a

JOHNNY DOVE

Johnny Dove, the "Dancing Burglar." From *Monarchs of Minstrelsy: From "Daddy" Rice to Date* by Edward LeRoy Rice (1911).

one-legged performer who had a peg leg. Part of Bryant's Minstrels, Dave Reed was identified with the song and dance "Shoo Fly" which he popularized along with Dan Bryant. He later appeared with his wife and four children in a vaudeville act entitled the "Reed Birds."

Mike Mitchell (1830–1862), who, in 1854, the *Cincinnati Gazette* called "the never-was-outdone dancer of the present age," was a popular minstrel jig dancer on the West Coast. His specialty was a song called "The Laughing Darkie," to which he danced his famous rendition of the plantation rattlesnake jig. In the 1850s he had his own minstrel company which toured the West Coast and eventually Hawaii. He left the engagements there without paying his bills and three years later, died in Portland on January 11, 1862, at age 32.[6] The *Oregonian* printed this obituary three days later:

Top: Minstrel dancer Dave Reed. From the sheet music cover of "Sally Come Up" by Fredrick Buckley (circa 1862). *Courtesy of Brown University.* **Right:** Engraving of Fred Wilson, believed by some to have been the first performer to introduce clog dancing in a minstrel show. Sheet music cover for "Queen at the Ball in New Orleans" by Fred Wilson (1873). *Courtesy of the Library of Congress, Music Division.*

At an early hour yesterday morning, Mike Mitchell, the minstrel and well known as the best Jig dancer ever on this coast was found in the yard of a house where he had been lodging—laying [sic] in the snow, and life nearly extinct. A physician was called in, and restoratives applied, but without avail, and he expired shortly after being taken into the house. An inquest was held, and the verdict was that the deceased came to his death by freezing, while under the influence of liquor. It appears that on Saturday night Mitchell, while drunk, abused some of his fellow lodgers and on Sunday night, when he asked ad-

mittance, the inmates, thinking that his admission would be followed by still further abuse, denied him and being stupified with liquor, he sank down on the spot and froze to death. Mitchell was a gentleman when sober, and possessed of many fine qualities, and was well liked by his comrades but his love of strong drink over-came him, and like it does thousands of others—dragged him to an early grave. And thus died the wandering minstrel. It will be along time his like is seen again in this country.[7]

It has been said that Fred Wilson introduced clog dancing to the minstrel show. Born in Boston on November 9, 1827, his first stage appearance was in 1843. In 1848, he joined Thayer's Minstrels. He danced with Bryant's Minstrels in the fall of 1858 and later was part of several other reputable companies. He traveled to China in the early 1860s for the U.S. government, but later gave up his post because he didn't like Chinese food. He sailed back to the States, returned to performing, and eventually formed his own minstrel troupe. He later worked in the business end of several

minstrel companies and as a promoter for various attractions. Wilson had a long career and was the first American clog dancer to tour England. In 1911 he earned the title of "the oldest living minstrel."

Dick Sands (George R. Sands) was considered one of the best cloggers in the country. Born in England in 1840, he was the first clog dancer of note to perform on the West Coast. He achieved fame in P.T. Barnum's "Old Woman in the Shoe," and was associated with Bryant's Minstrels, Haverly's Minstrels, Morris Brothers Minstrels, and many other topnotch companies. He sometimes billed himself as "Sands! The Best Clog Dancer Living!"

John "Johnny" Tuers was a trapeze artist as well as a champion clog dancer. He once leapt 125 feet from a trapeze, from the dress circle to the back of the stage. His dance specialty was the essence of old Virginia. He was purported to be the best flatfoot dancer on the West Coast. In 1869 Tuers accidentally killed a man.

Frank Lynch was called, "the best representative of Ethiopian break-downs." He traveled with P.T. Barnum's shows and was billed as "John Diamond," after the real Johnny Diamond was fired for being a troublemaker. He was considered by many as one of early minstrelsy's greatest dancers. After gaining weight, he was unable to dance and began directing shows on a showboat called the "Floating Circus Palace," teaching such young performers as Ralph Keeler.

Barney Fagan (Bernard J. Fagan, 1850–1937) learned dancing on the streets of Boston, where he was born, and by the age of five he was already considered something of an expert at doing the Lancashire clog. He made his professional debut at age ten and later gained fame for doing a number called the "Heifer Dance." Sometimes Fagan had the lights turned out in the theatre and he would then dance on a metal

BARNEY FAGAN

Barney Fagan added syncopation to the Irish jig and was the first white tap dancer. From *Monarchs of Minstrelsy: From "Daddy" Rice to Date* **by Edward LeRoy Rice (1911).**

plate which sparked as he struck it with his feet. He was part of Billy Sweatnam, Billy Rice, and Barney Fagan's Minstrels, which was one of the premier minstrel troupes in the 1880s. The troupe comprised 110 performers, two bands, a group of sax players, two drum corps, mounted buglers and two drum majors. Fagan was recognized as one of the world's greatest all-around dancers of his day. He is sometimes called the "Father of Tap" and is credited with being one of the first real tap dancers because he added syncopation to his Irish jig dancing. Harland Dixon, a famous clog dancer himself, and part of the team of Dixon and Doyle, said of Fagan,

> He [Fagan] was a great technician and one of the first to syncopate the Clog, but his steps were so intricate that the audience and even other dancers couldn't follow what he was doing.[8]

Even in his eighties Fagan was still dancing. Few dancers could compete with his longevity or popularity.

Ralph Olmstead Keeler was born on a farm in Ohio on August 29, 1840. After his parents died when he was eight, he was sent to Buffalo, New York, to live with his uncle, but because of the continual beatings he received there, he finally ran away. In his article "Three Years as a Negro Minstrel," Keeler wrote,

> Meantime I bought a banjo, and had pennies screwed on the heels of my boots, and practiced "Jordon" on the former, and the "Juba" dance with the latter, till my boarding-house keeper gave me warning.[9]

Keeler said he learned his dancing by studying the "complicated shuffles of Juba [William Henry Lane]."[10] At age 11 in Toledo, Ohio, he was discovered by a minstrel actor named Johnny Booker while performing in saloons. He was asked to join the minstrel shows and became known as something of an infant prodigy. He befriended the company's black baggage handler, Ephriam, from whom he learned African-American dances. Keeler started at five dollars a week dancing the juba, and sand jig to a song entitled "The Lucy Long."[11] He toured with various minstrel companies, and while still a young boy, tried to organize his own minstrel troupe. The boys practiced in a room he had rented over a saloon. When they danced during rehearsals, the ceiling plaster showered down on the drinkers below.

> On certain occasions, when I executed my Juba dance, or in company with others performed the Virginia Walk-around, these honest Germans would leave their beer, and sometimes, their hats and pipes, behind them in terror, and rush precipitately into the middle of the street.[12]

While touring with the Booker Troupe, Keeler stopped at state prisons along the way and entertained the inmates with his dancing. At one point, he joined a group called "The Mitchells," headed by the famous clog dancer Mike Mitchell. His last job was dancing jigs and juba on a showboat called the "Floating Circus Palace." The main part of his act on the showboat, though, consisted of female impersonations and wench dancing. He had learned this from a Parisian ballet dancer.

> Madame Lowe had taught him all the posturings and pirouettes of the Paris ballet girls, insisting on using her little whip whenever he "stepped out of the line of beauty."[13]

The "Floating Circus Palace" minstrel shows were directed by Frank Lynch, who

Engraving of Ralph Olmstead Keeler, who learned dancing by studying the "complicated shuffles of Juba." From *Curiosities of the American Stage* by Laurence Hutton (1890).

was so overweight he could no longer dance himself; nevertheless, he taught Keeler many new steps. Keeler said of himself,

> ... for dancing I had, I am confident, such a remarkable gift as few have ever had. Up to this day, I do not think I have ever seen a step done by man or woman that I could not do as soon as I saw it.[14]

At age 16, Keeler entered college and eventually became a journalist. He published several articles for various papers and magazines as well as a novel and his autobiography. A close friend of Mark Twain, he often accompanied the legendary author on his lecture tours. In 1873, he was sent by the *New York Tribune* to cover unrest in Cuba. Returning on the night of December 17th, he either fell or was thrown overboard and was lost at sea.

William W. Newcomb (1823–77) is credited with inventing the original essence of old Virginia, forerunner of the soft shoe, while a member of Fellow's Minstrels in 1851.[15] He originally did the dance at a rather fast tempo, and his style was called "quintessence." Newcomb started dancing in the circus and later formed a group called the Rumsey and Newcomb Minstrels that toured the country, as well as Europe and the British Isles, with great success. He eventually retired in 1868 in ill health.

Dan Bryant (1833–75), born Daniel Webster O'Brien, was the most famous essence dancer and considered one of the greatest minstrel performers of all. Unlike Newcomb, he performed the essence of old Virginia very slowly. He played in many minstrel companies across the country, including in California.

In 1857, Dan and his brothers Neil and Jerry, formed Bryant's Minstrels. One of their most famous numbers was a parody of the anvil chorus in which the entire company tapped out rhythms on huge

DAN. BRYANT

Dan Bryant in blackface. His specialty was the essence of old Virginia. From *Monarchs of Minstrelsy: From "Daddy" Rice to Date* by Edward LeRoy Rice (1911).

anvils with little hammers. Bryant's Minstrels are also remembered for their genuine characterizations of African-Americans. Later in his life, Daniel Emmett joined this troupe and composed walk arounds for the shows, including "Dixie." Bryant is credited with making many technical advances in the art of clog dancing.

Bryant did a famous song and dance

to "Shoo Fly" "shaking up a grotesque essence."[16] But his real fame came from the essence of old Virginia. The dance developed from another dance called the Negro shuffle which was basically a waltz clog slowed down and with the meter changed. The lifted knees and high steps of the popular Irish jig were replaced with the sliding motions of the African shuffle. The heels and toes rocked without much changing of the position of the legs, so that the dancer appeared to be gliding. The essence became the first popular dance for professionals that was totally of African-American origin. Essence dancing developed rapidly and often dancers were so smooth that it almost looked as if they were ice skating. The essence was performed in many different ways; the more elegant and graceful parts of it, when done with taste and refinement, became known as "picture dancing," because it was considered as pretty as a picture.

GEO. H. PRIMROSE

George Primrose, considered to be the best soft shoe dancer ever. From *Monarchs of Minstrelsy: From "Daddy" Rice to Date* by Edward LeRoy Rice (1911).

Essence dancing was eventually transformed into a dance called the soft shoe shuffle. As opposed to the clogs and jigs which incorporated African-American influences while utilizing an erect stance in the upper body, the soft shoe shuffle employed the crouched, casual body position of African-American plantation dances. This allowed more freedom in the arms, spine, and pelvis, which in turn led to the development of more character and comic dances, and even the use of instruments that could be played while dancing. Elaborate footwork was still important, but as tempos were slowed down, style became even more important. George F. Moore created a completely noiseless essence around 1875 that further became associated with the soft shoe type of dancing.

The honor of being the best soft shoe dancer ever is still given to a man named George Primrose, the Fred Astaire of his day. He was sometimes called the "Adonis of Step Dancing" and was considered one of the greatest stylists of them all. Dancer Billy Maxey said, "Everybody was influenced by Primrose."[17] Primrose, whose real name was George Delaney, was born in Canada on November 12, 1852. He started his career in Detroit as a juvenile clog dancer in 1867 with McFarland's Minstrels, and was billed as "Master Georgie, the infant Clog dancer." He went on to become the greatest purveyor of soft shoe in the world. A coworker described him thus:

He was of medium height, weighed a little over one hundred and ten, and could wear clothes like Fred Astaire; he smoked cigars but he didn't drink; I never heard him raise his voice or swear; I never saw him practice a step and yet I never saw him perspire — even during the minstrel street parades on the hottest summer days. He wore a high, stiff collar and looked up over the audience as he danced; he had a flat stomach, beautiful legs, and fine hips and shoulders — and just the way he walked was poetry.[18]

Despite the fact that Primrose was white, he influenced many black dancers and often performed with black minstrels and on the same bill as black vaudeville acts, which was highly unusual for this time in history.[19] Because of his brilliant style and technique, Primrose was regularly imitated; he, in turn, would also imitate. He would take a black dance, give it sophisticated polish, and then hand it back to its black originators.

Primrose started as a minstrel and formed the famous troupe, Primrose and West, with William W. West. The group, which lasted for 30 years, was viewed as "the ne plus ultra of song and dance." Primrose and West refined the minstrel show and often had the cast perform without blackface. Their specialty was large production numbers. They were so successful, they were called the "Millionaires of Minstrelsy." They so changed the basic ingredient of the minstrel show that it was virtually indistinguishable from other forms of entertainment. Lew Dockstader, another great minstrel promoter, said, "They have refined all the fun out of it." Interestingly enough, Primrose was later associated with Dockstader.

Primrose's career stretched from minstrel shows at the turn of the century well into vaudeville. He died at age 66 in 1919 in San Diego, California.

Eddie Girard, another essence dancer, was later considered one of the greatest legomania artists in vaudeville.

When Girard danced the essence, "it had a slow tempo, made up of old-fashioned darkey steps, a kind of bastard Clog danced to Southern tunes."[20] Girard also did buck and wing and pointed-toe dancing. Having never had training, he developed his own buck and wing steps while working for the railroad as a boy. He entertained the railroad crews and station attendants until he won a dancing match and quit the trains. He teamed up with the dancer he had beaten in the match, Willie Mahoney, and together they started doing the essence of old Virginia. They wore overalls because they couldn't afford costumes, until a theatre manager took them under his wing, built up the act and bought the boys clog dance shoes and garish dancing costumes. The manager directed Willie Mahoney to change his name to Girard and the boys were billed as a brother act.

The Girard Brothers toured successfully until a smallpox epidemic stranded them in Vermont. Girard used the time in quarantine to work out new clogs in 3/4 time and to figure out some sand jigs. The boys eventually ended up in New York working for three years for Tony Pastor in his new vaudeville venue. At one point in their careers, the Girard Brothers formed a quartette with another double act called

EDDIE GIRARD   (GIRARD BROS.)   WILLIE GIRARD

Eddie Girard (left) and Willie Mahoney (Willie Girard.) From *Monarchs of Minstrelsy: From "Daddy" Rice to Date* by Edward LeRoy Rice (1911).

Seamon and Somers. The four dancers were considered one of the greatest four-person acts around. They called themselves the "Grotesque Four." Later Eddie formed a vaudeville act with his wife and they performed as "Girard and Gardner."

Lotta Mignon Crabtree was the Shirley Temple of the 1800s. Born in New York City on November 7, 1847, the child left for California with her family when she was only four. At the age of six she began dancing in mining camps during the California Gold Rush; the miners tossed coins and gold nuggets on the stage to the little girl. She became the most successful of the Fairy Stars. Fairy Stars, the name given to singing and dancing child stars of the period, were most popular in the West, and infant prodigies were a part of almost every circus and minstrel show.[21]

By the time Lotta was eight, her mother had a habit of sweeping the coins and nuggets off the stage and putting them in a satchel which she carried until it grew too heavy. She then bought real estate in the cities where they were touring and started over again filling the satchel, eventually turning her daughter into a multimillionaire.

Lotta first started dance lessons in Grass Valley, California in 1853 with a man named Bowers, who ran a small dancing school. Bowers once "kidnapped" Lotta without her mother's knowledge and took her to another town to demonstrate and sell his system of teaching dance to children. He used Lotta to show his talent as a teacher by perching the little child on an anvil in the local blacksmith's shop and having her do steps to the accompaniment of clapping hands.

Lotta's real training came from the Irish-born Countess of Landsfeld, better known as Lola Montez, who took an interest in the youngster's career. Lola Montez was best know for her scandalous spider dance. While doing a combination of

Lotta Crabtree in the character of the "Marchioness." From *A History of the Theatre in America*, vol. 2., by Arthur Hornblow (1919).

polka, waltz, mazurka and jig, Lola would shake whalebone and rubber spiders out of her costume thus revealing glimpses of her skin. Lola taught Lotta ballet, fandangos, and Highland flings; she also taught her how to smoke cigars.

Mart Taylor, a local Italian tavern keeper, added to Lotta's repertoire of steps. In the 1850s, half of California's population was Irish, and Taylor made sure that his young pupil excelled at the jig.

For her first real public appearance, Lotta's mother made her a green long-tailed coat with knee breeches. She danced an Irish jig and reel, constantly laughing and giggling while she danced, which only added to her appeal. During one early performance, Lotta kept putting her hands in the pockets of her little breeches. Because this was considered unladylike behavior, her mother sewed them up. During the next show Lotta tried to put her hands in the pockets; when she couldn't, she burst into tears and left the stage. She refused to return to her dance until her mother ripped out the stitching. When Lotta finally returned with red nose and watery eyes, the audience cheered and clapped even more loudly. A notice in one mining town paper said "The singing and dancing of little Lotta was admirable, and took our hearts by storm."[22]

When touring the mining camps, Lotta was introduced to an African-American dancer who taught her breakdowns, soft shoes and buck and wing dances. One of her popular songs included the lyric;

Trike de toe and heel, cut de pigeon wing,
Scratch gravel, slap de foot, dat's jus' de ting.[23]

Lotta Crabtree's chief competition were the three Worrell sisters, Irene, Sophie, and Jennie. A running battle existed between Lotta and the "Juvenile Graces," as the sisters were known. Lotta was outnumbered, but then it was discovered that Jennie Worrell's clog dancing shoes had trick heels. They had been hollowed out and had tin-lined boxes placed inside them which held two bullets to make it sound as if she was dancing faster than she really was.

Lotta had bright red hair which she sprinkled with cayenne pepper to heighten the redness. In addition to dancing, she sang, played the banjo and became quite a popular actress. When she performed in regular plays, she would often break into jigs or reels to the audience's delight. In one performance of *The Dumb Belle* she was supposed to walk across the stage and place

Lotta Crabtree. From *The Marie Burroughs Art Portfolio of Stage Celebrities: A Collection of Photographs of the Leaders of Dramatic and Lyric Art* (1894).

a bottle on a table. She walked across the stage with overexaggerated dignity, added a jig as she set the bottle down, and exited with a cartwheel. As much as the other actors in the play hated being upstaged, the audience loved the precocious little child, cheering and pelting the stage with money.

In her later years Lotta Crabtree became the toast of Broadway. The *New York Clipper* said,

She can dance a regular breakdown in true burnt cork style and gives an Irish Jig as well as we have ever seen it done.[24]

Although she never married, Lotta was always surrounded by men; admirers included Grand Duke Alexis of Russia and Brigham Young. She stopped performing at age 44, and even in old age, it was reported she always looked half her years. An ardent animal activist, late in life she

JOHNNY THOMPSON   FRANK KERNS

(Thompson & Kerns were the original double song and dance team; 1862.)

Johnny Thompson (left) and Frank Kerns. From *Monarchs of Minstrelsy: From "Daddy" Rice to Date by* Edward LeRoy Rice (1911).

for his whistling solos as well as dancing. Wally Thomas was a drummer in addition to being a highly respected jig and clog dancer. Jimmy Clark was one of the best jig dancers of the day. He also played the banjo. Later in his life, after giving up performing, he manufactured banjos. Henry E. Dixey was the most famous pedestal dancer. He put whitewash on his body and started his act frozen like a statue of Apollo or the Discus Thrower. Other solo dance performers included Barney Williams the first top Irish clog dancer, Willis Pickert, Tommy Hyde, Frank McNish, Tommy Peel, Tommy Gettings, "Hank, the Mason," Bert Sexton, Sam Hague, Rolland Howard, Ben Cotton, and John Hodges, better known as

wandered the streets of Boston and put hats on horses to protect them from the sun. There is a story that, as a very old woman, she once slipped on the street and called out "Prima donna in the gutter!" Lotta Crabtree died in 1924 at the age of 76.

Other minstrel dancers included Luke West (William Sheppard) who gained fame

JOHN QUEEN   R. M. ("DICK") CARROLL

Johnny Queen (left), who teamed with R.M. Carroll (right) in the first double clog act, and later with William West.

WM. H. WEST

William H. West, who also teamed with George Primrose and founded one of the premiere minstrel companies. From *Monarchs of Minstrelsy: From "Daddy" Rice to Date* by Edward LeRoy Rice (1911).

Cool White, who was a favorite among audiences and most famous for his Shakespearean burlesques. White (1821–91) helped organize the Virginia Serenaders, and in 1846 he and his brother formed a troupe called White's Serenaders that included the famous black dancer Master Juba. Billy Emerson was called "one of the most graceful men on stage."[25] Around 1890, Emerson supposedly became the first to use the word "hoofer" when referring to a tap dancer.[26]

Double Acts

Probably the first double song and dance act done in blackface was Johnny Thompson and Frank Kerns, who first appeared together in Washington, D.C., in 1861. They were followed by many talented dancing duos.

A Vermont native, Johnny Queen (1843–84) moved to Boston and at age 19 joined the Morris Brothers Minstrels. Here he appeared with Richard M. (Dick) Carroll in the first double clog act. The two men continued working together for two years as Carroll and Queen, sometimes supplementing their income by giving dance lessons.[27] While in Boston with the Morris Brothers Minstrel troupe, Queen also sometimes danced on stage with his wife, another professional clog dancer.

In 1868, Johnny Queen formed a partnership with William West, considered one of the best clog dancers of his day. The two men became one of the most popular dance teams to ever appear on the minstrel stage. In the 1880s, when Queen and West were on a tour to England, Queen was suspected of trickery because of his incredibly fast dancing. There is a story of how he made his entrance in slippers, with shoes in hand, proceeding to pass his dancing shoes around through the audience to prove he used no "clappers or other Yankee gadgets."[28]

William H. West (Flynn) had started in circuses. He played the banjo, did comedy, and was considered one of the great clog dancers. His first appearance was in Buffalo at age 17; the next year he joined Skiff and Gaylord's Minstrels where he met the great soft shoe dancer, George Primrose. They also did an act together and eventually the two men formed the premiere minstrel troupe Primrose and West Minstrels. West was married three times. His first wife was the famous actress Fay Templeton. He died February 15, 1902.

Perhaps the most famous dancing team was McIntyre and Heath. James McIntyre, born in Kenosha, Wisconsin, on August 8, 1857, and Thomas K. Heath, born in Philadelphia on August 11, 1852, joined forces in the spring of 1874 in San Antonio, Texas.[29] Both men continued to

JAS.—McINTYRE & HEATH—THOS. K.
(1874)

James McIntyre (left) and Thomas Heath, the first team to introduce the syncopated buck and wing, and the first to dance to ragtime on the legitimate stage. From *Monarchs of Minstrelsy: From "Daddy" Rice to Date* by Edward LeRoy Rice (1911).

perform together throughout their careers, moving from circuses to minstrel shows, eventually working for Primrose and West Minstrels, and famous minstrel impresario, Lew Docstader.

In the 1880s, McIntyre claimed that he and his partner, Heath, were the first to introduce the syncopated buck and wing. McIntyre told a reporter that he had learned it by "watching Negroes in the South soon after the Civil War." The dance was done to a tune called "Rabbit" and the team introduced the number at Tony Pastor's Theatre in New York in 1879. McIntyre also claimed that this was the first time ragtime had been presented on the legitimate stage.

During the 1890s a full-time understudy was hired to cover McIntyre, who had a drinking problem. Although the understudy frequently went on, audiences never knew because he was disguised by blackface makeup.

McIntyre and Heath were widely respected for their authentic, faithful portrayals of African-Americans. They continued dancing in vaudeville and became one of the oldest two-man acts in the business. They retired in 1924; however, the team rejoined to do one last performance in 1929 on the radio with Rudy Valee. There were rumors that the two men had not spoken to each other for 25 years. Joe Laurie, Jr., in his book *Vaudeville: From Honky-Tonks to the Palace*, stated,

> They very seldom spoke to each other, except for business reasons. They lived in different hotels when possible. One was a bottle man and the other liked champagne.[30]

Many sources substantiate this claim although some state that the men remained close friends throughout their lives. McIntyre died in Noyack, Long Island, on August 18, 1937. Exactly one year to the day, on August 18, 1938, Heath died in Setauket, Long Island.

Another famous minstrel team, Delahanty and Hengler, decorated their dancing shoes and advertised that they danced in silver clogs. This team was the first to do a "neat" Irish song and dance and were one of "the most sought after dancing act[s] of their time."[31] Rhett Krauss, in his article "Step Dancing on the Boston Stage: 1841–69," relates a story of how the dancing talents of the team were so valued that when one minstrel troupe in New York City contracted the team away from another minstrel troupe in Boston, the managers of the two rival companies ended up in a gunfight in the middle of Broadway. One person was killed and another seriously wounded in the melee.

William H. Delehanty premiered at age 14 and went on to become a successful composer as well as a dancer. Irish born T.M. Hengler (Slattery) premiered at age 12. The clog dancing team made their first appearance in 1866 in New York and stayed together until 1875. Hengler split with Delehanty in 1875 and did a single act for one year billing himself as the "Merry Minstrel." In 1876 he rejoined his partner and the two performed together until 1880 when Delehanty died. Hengler was so distraught, he gave up performing; he died eight years later. The team's most famous song was called "Pickanniny Nig," and their style of dancing became known as in vaudeville as the "pickaninny," which was of "the slide, skip, and slap technique, covering a lot of the stage."[32]

Sheridan and Mack (John F. Sheridan and James H. Mack) were another top dancing team. They danced with the Morris Brother Minstrels in Boston, one of the premiere troupes that regularly featured the top dancers. Sheridan and Mack have the distinction of being the first blackface team to later perform without blackface.

The Impact of Minstrel Shows

Minstrel shows were the vehicle through which white Northern audiences dealt with the issues of slavery and abolition. Before the mid–1850s, blacks were depicted as predominantly happy and contented on the plantation, images that were juxtaposed in the same shows with con-

WM. H. DELEHANTY — THOS. M. HENGLER
(DELEHANTY & HENGLER.)

William Delehanty (left) and Thomas Hengler, "the most sought after dancing act of their time." From *Monarchs of Minstrelsy: From "Daddy" Rice to Date* by Edward LeRoy Rice (1911).

demnations of the brutality and inhumanity of the slave system. These condemnations disappeared however in the early 1850s as the country began to grapple with the issue of slavery and the Union was being threatened. The lampooning of cruel slave owners was removed from minstrel shows; all that was left were caricatures of happy plantation blacks like Jim Crow or unhappy Northern free blacks. This allowed Northern audiences to deny the cruelty of slavery, rationalize the racial caste system, and to ignore the prospect of social change, further perpetuating negative stereotypes of African-Americans. Especially insidious in these portrayals was the attitude of benevolent paternalism, which cloaked prejudice in humor and masked the propaganda of racial subordination.

The popularity of minstrel shows declined for a number of reasons. With stiffer competition between numerous companies, rising production costs, and the flourishing of other forms of entertainment, it became increasingly harder for minstrel shows to make money. The best minstrel performers began to be lured away by the higher salaries available in musical comedy or vaudeville. After the huge success of the musical, *The Black Crook*, in 1866, audiences began to demand different kinds of entertainment. In an effort to compete, minstrel shows became larger and more extravagant and the simple, unsophisticated flavor was lost. Shows began to degenerate and productions became gaudier and more risqué. Critics and audiences alike complained about the loss of simplicity and genuineness, and the rise of vulgarity and stereotyping.

In addition, minstrel shows had traditionally been an all-male domain. When musical comedies and varieties began to feature women, the minstrel form seemed stale, monotonous and limited in comparison. In an effort to increase the public's interest, minstrel shows increased their advertising with larger, flashier posters and handbills. They had drawings for door prizes and giveaways featuring such gifts as watches, toys and sewing machines. When these did not prove effective, they began incorporating elements from other forms of entertainment, the most common of which was the inclusion of "freaks." Midgets, dwarfs, giants and strongmen were frequently featured. One of the most famous was Ebenezer Nicholson who adopted the stage name "Little Mac," after the popular Civil War figure, General McClellan. "Little Mac" who was three feet tall, did essence dancing and the big shoe dance. Charles S. Stratton better known as General Tom Thumb, probably one of the most famous celebrities of the period, danced the Lucy Long and "wirginny breakdowns" as well as the Highland fling.

Any gimmick was used to attract crowds. The famous showman P. T. Barnum presented dancers in armor dancing the "Silver Combat Clog." One minstrel company featured performers who posed as statues. Another advertised a "company of Dancing Turkeys and Singing Cats."

Minstrel shows also began promising a glimpse of female limbs, and started including women clad in revealing tights. In San Francisco, one all-female minstrel show that mixed traditional minstrel songs and comedy with the cancan, was received with wild enthusiasm.

14

Black Minstrelsy and Musical Theatre

Black entertainers were typically banned from performing in minstrel shows until after the Civil War. There were rare exceptions: William Henry Lane, "Master Juba," was the most famous; another was a dancer named Horace (or Howard) Weston. Weston was born in Derby, Connecticut in 1825. His father was an African-American dancing master and teacher of music. In 1855, Weston began teaching dance like his father and also learned to play the banjo. After fighting in the Civil War, he joined Buckley's Minstrels, and in 1867 toured England with the Georgia Colored Minstrels. When he returned to the U.S., he took up teaching again and began to work for P. T. Barnum. He later played on a showboat called the "Plymouth Rock." In late 1878, Horace Weston returned to England with an enormously successful production of *Uncle Tom's Cabin*. He stayed in Europe for a while, touring Germany, Austria, and France. He eventually returned to the United States, embarking on a successful coast-to-coast tour. Before his death in June 1890, Horace Weston became one of the most respected African-American performers of his time.

Another African-American dancer who worked on the professional stage before the Civil War was Thomas Dilward (or Dilworth). Dilward's height was listed as somewhere between 23 and 36 inches. He played the violin and was considered a fine singer and dancer. He was popularly known as "Japanese Tommy," and because he was considered an oddity, he was permitted to perform in white minstrel shows performing with such famous troupes as Christy's Minstrels and Bryant's Minstrels.

Black Minstrel Troupes

Black minstrel troupes made their appearance around the mid–1850s, although no permanent troupes were established until after the Civil War. These early black minstrels advertised themselves as "genuine" and "real," but often continued to use burnt cork to cover their faces, following the tradition of white minstrels. Black entertainers were restricted in how much they could modify the white-created stereotypes they had inherited, which had the odd effect of legitimizing minstrelsy's black caricatures. As African-American performers struggled to redefine their own identities, these stereotypes slowly began to change, and blacks pioneered new ways to present valid depictions of African-American life. When they first appeared without blackface, their audiences were astonished at the variety of skin colors. Noticing the effect that this diversity of skin tones had on audiences, black minstrels often heightened the effect by having the end men still use cork.[1]

As more and more African-American performers took to the stage, old dances that were minstrel favorites were reintroduced and stripped of some of the more grotesque and unrealistic qualities. An authenticity and integrity was brought therefore to the presentation of genuine indigenous material. New dances such as stop-time tapping, and sand dances also found their way to the stage. As it was with white minstrels, the essence was probably the most popular dance performed by African-American performers.

Billy Kersands

Perhaps the most famous essence dancer was Billy Kersands, who many credit with creating both the Virginia essence and the buck and wing.[2] Born in 1842 in Baton Rouge, Louisiana, Kersands began performing around the time of the Civil War and rose to fame shortly afterwards in the late 1870s. He played heavily exaggerated, slow-witted, black caricatures. Despite weighing over 200 pounds, his dancing was agile and graceful, and he also tumbled. His popularity grew out of his comedic approach to performing and the outrageous facial contortions he made while dancing.

W. C. Handy said Kersands was "a man who could make a mule laugh."[3] He swore that he had seen Kersands fit an entire cup and saucer inside his mouth. Kersands used to dance the essence while stripping off a dozen or so vests or with his mouth full of billiard balls. One quote about him stated,

Kersands did the Virginia Essence perfectly, so much so that when he did it before Queen Victoria, he had her laughing heartily over it.[4]

Kersands himself is reputed to had said to Queen Victoria, "If God ever wanted my mouth any bigger, he would have to move my ears."[5]

During his heyday, it was said, "A minstrel show without Billy Kersands was like a circus without elephants."[6] At the height of his career, Kersands was not only the most popular black minstrel, but also the highest-paid.

On the Lowe's Circuit in 1911, he put five large soda crackers and a regulation size cup and saucer in his mouth while he danced. He performed in blackface using his traditional stereotypical caricature throughout his life, and danced up until two years before his death in 1915. He died

Billy Kersands as pictured on a poster for Callender's Georgia Minstrels. *Courtesy of the Harvard Theatre Collection.*

suddenly from heart disease at the age of 73 when he was performing in Artesia, New Mexico. He had just finished the last performance of a very successful season, when on June 29, 1915, he returned to his private railroad car to talk with friends. He sat down to chat and fell over dead. After his death, his friend Sam Lucas wrote about him in an article in the *New York Age* (August 15, 1915):

> His main specialty was his dance, "The Essence of Old Virginia." In that dance he would lie flat on his stomach and beat first his head and then his toes against the stage to keep time with the orchestra. He would look at his feet to see how they were keeping time, and then looking out at the audience he would say, "Ain't this nice? I get seventy-five dollars a week for doing this!"[7]

Ernest Hogan

Dancer-comedian Ernest Hogan started in minstrel shows and later was a favorite in vaudeville. Born in Bowling Green, Kentucky around 1859, his given name was Ernest Reuben Crowders, but he changed it to Hogan when he went into show business because Irish performers were in vogue at the time. As a minstrel, with his troupe, the Georgia Graduates, he introduced a comedy dance step called the pasmala, which consisted of a walk forward with three hops back. A song called "La Pas Ma La" accompanied the dance and was published in 1895. The lyrics of the chorus were:

> Hand upon yo' head, let your mind
>   roll far,
> Back, back, back and look at the stars,
> Stand up rightly, dance it brightly,
> That's the Pas Ma La.

Other dance steps were introduced in the song as well, such as the Saint — a Louis pass and the Chicago salute, which were both references to the World's Fairs held in those cities. One verse mentioned the bumbishay (known by some as the fanny bump). The bumbishay, or as we know it, the bombershay, is still commonly used in tap routines today. The song also mentioned the turkey trot at least 15 years before it attained national popularity.

Hogan also wrote and published the hit song "All Coons Look Alike But Me," which started a craze in what was called "coon-songs." When the word "coon" became an epithet for an African-American, Hogan was heavily criticized for writing the immensely popular song. Composer E. B. Marks wrote,

> Hogan died haunted by the awful crime he had unwittingly committed against the race.[8]

Ernesst Hogan in blackface. From an insert on the sheet music cover of "Ma Gal's de Town Talk" by Ernest Hogan. *Courtesy of Brown University Library.*

Hogan was considered one of the most talented performers in the business and one of the best dancing comedians of his day. He toured with Black Patti's Troubadours, billed as the "Unbleached American," and also appeared in the road show *The Smart Set.* When he was cast in the black musical *Clorindy — The Origin of the Cakewalk* he achieved stardom. In 1907, Hogan joined the cast of *The Oyster Man,* but became ill from overwork and retired to a small home in Lakewood, New Jersey. He died there in 1909.

Other African-American Minstrels

The Bohee Brothers, James and George, were among the first song and dance acts in black minstrel shows. They were superb soft shoers who did the dance while accompanying themselves on banjo. They toured internationally with their double act and while in London they even gave banjo lessons to members of the royal family.

Wilton Crawly not only danced, but also played the clarinet and juggled while balancing a lighted lamp on his head. William Allen performed a pedestal clog on a 15-inch square on top of a post that was four feet high. Joseph Holcomb was another well-respected pedestal dancer. Mr. Benjamin Franklin, a black minstrel performer around 1879, danced with a pail of water on his head while simultaneously playing the French horn. Other African-American dancers of note included Billy Wilson, William Goss, Billy Banks, the Hunn Brothers, and the Hyers Sisters. An African-American dancer named Billy Farrel introduced the cakewalk into vaudeville in Brooklyn in 1886 at the Grand Opera House, and was also the first to present the dance in England a few years later at the Alhambra Theatre in London.

Black minstrels often met with less than welcoming receptions while touring. Life on the road was uncertain and even dangerous, as these performers faced racial discrimination. There are stories of a train engineer, transporting one black minstrel troupe from town to town, who purposely jerked the train every morning so the minstrel's coffee would spill on them. In one Texas town, the local doctor denied treatment and suggested an entire black minstrel troupe be lynched after one of its members contracted smallpox. The disease spread to 14 members of the company when the troupe was denied food, water, and sanitation facilities. In desperation, the performers finally put on a show to create a diversion and smuggled the sick men out by disguising them as women.

Because performers sometimes were shot at or lynched, private railroad cars were constructed which had special secret compartments to hide the performers if things got out of hand. W. C. Handy recalled using this type of compartment once when he stopped a white man from killing one of the black minstrels in his troupe. A lynch mob came after Handy and he escaped by hiding in the train's secret compartment. Despite these kinds of difficulties, many African-Americans continued to pursue careers in the minstrel field, realizing that it offered them one of the few opportunities to attain some semblance of financial freedom.

"Tom" and "Plant" Shows

The two most popular types of indoor shows were "Tom shows," productions of some version of *Uncle Tom's Cabin,* and "Plant shows," productions which featured representations of plantation life. "Plant shows" were also known as "Tab," or tabloid shows because they were often shortened versions of the vaudeville show.

A few African-Americans appeared in productions of Harriet Beecher Stowe's *Uncle Tom's Cabin* in the middle of the 19th century, and by the end of the 1800s, as their involvement grew, black dancers were often hired to perform cakewalks, breakdowns, the buck and wing, the Virginia essence, and the knockabout song and dance, all which were interpolated into the play. By the 1890s, large troupes performing *Uncle Tom's Cabin* even inserted military drills and animal acts into it.[9]

In 1891 (or 1893?), *The South Before the War*, a romanticized depiction of black plantation life, opened.[10] Besides such dances as the traditional Virginia essence, new dances were often introduced in this production, including Billy Williams' possum-ma-la, which made its appearance in 1895. The musical featured many great tap dancers, including a woman named Katie Carter, billed as "the Queen of the Female buck and wing dancers." She was largely responsible for establishing Buck and Wing dancing as a popular attraction in black shows. One 12-year-old member of the general chorus of *The South Before the War* was to become one of the greatest tap dancers of all times — Bill "Bojangles" Robinson.

In the summer of 1895, plantation shows reached their zenith with the presentation of *Black America* which was done at Ambrose Park in South Brooklyn, New York. The show had over 500 performers in it, including numerous singers, dancers, and extras. It featured a living tableau of plantation life, complete with full-size log cabins, livestock, and live cotton plants, 63 vocal quartets, sports exhibitions, and military maneuvers performed by members of the U.S. Ninth Cavalry. The show included a cakewalk, with the winners being decided by the cheers of the audience. It ended with a buck and wing contest in which the dancers literally danced until they dropped. *Black America* also utilized

the talents of such well-known African-American artists as the cakewalking team of Charles Johnson and Dora Dean. The review in the *New York Times* mentioned that the show had "the best dancers obtainable."[11] The scale and fantasy of *Black America* brought about a transition that eventually led to black musical theatre.

Besides the typical "Tom" and "Plant" shows, there were three other important touring shows: *In Old Kentucky, The Smart Set,* and *Black Patti's Troubadours. In Old Kentucky* opened in St. Paul, Minnesota, in 1892; it utilized white performers but also featured black dancers. One of the star attractions of the show was a dancer named Harry Swinton, who did a phenomenal sand dance. Eubie Blake remembered: "[Swinton] did more just spreading the sand than other dancers could do with their whole act."[12]

In Old Kentucky was important because it featured an amateur dance contest every Friday night. The only musical accompaniment for these contests was a stop-time banjo. As in the old tap challenges, judges were placed under the stage, in the wings, and out in front. As the show had many incarnations and toured extensively, its regular contests introduced many talented young tap dancers, including Willie Covan, who won the contest in Chicago in 1915. Covan related that most dancers began their dance with the traditional time-step to set the beat, which actually shortened the time they had to do the rest of their routines. "So I came jumping out with a Wing, a Grab Off, and a Roll, and managed to get in a lot of new stuff before my time ran out."[13] Covan easily won the contest; the audience rushed him backstage and carried him out on their shoulders, ensuring Covan's fame from then on. Bill Robinson also won a contest sponsored by *In Old Kentucky* when the show played the Bijou Theatre in Brooklyn. He beat Harry Swinton, but there were rumors that

Swinton had actually allowed Robinson to win. Eubie Blake stated that "When you mentioned Swinton's name, Bill Robinson shut up."[14]

The Smart Set revolved around a flimsy plot about horse racing interspersed with songs and dances. The show also featured dance contests. Buck and wing challenges were held every Wednesday night. *The Smart Set* featured great performers like Ernest Hogan, and was known as the "Ebony Ziegfeld Follies" because of its line of beautiful chorus girls.

Black Patti's Troubadours showcased many African-American performers, but the production was centered around Matilda Sissieretta Joyner Jones, an accomplished opera singer who was nicknamed by the press, "Black Patti," after Italian opera star Adelina Patti. When she toured the U.S. beginning in 1896, her show featured a buck dancing contest at the end of act one, and a cakewalk contest at the end of act two. Her legendary show attracted many great dancers such as King Rastus Brown, the man who popularized the time-step.

Black Musicals

As the popularity of minstrel shows declined, African-American entertainers began to move into the theatre. In 1889, an all-black show called *The Creole Show* opened in New York and set the trend for African-American artists on the legitimate musical stage. It was one of the first productions to abandon blackface makeup. The show was done in a standard minstrel show format with the performers seated in a semicircle, but only the endmen were male; the interlocutor was a male impersonator named Florence Hines and the rest of the lineup were female. The show also featured an additional chorus of 16 women, an important innovation at the time.

Poster advertising the buck dancing contest held by Black Patti's Troubadours (circa 1897).

The addition of women to the cast of *The Creole Show* fostered a new emphasis on couple dancing. One such dance was the cakewalk, performed by Charles Johnson and Dora Dean. Johnson and Dean changed the cakewalk from a simple plantation walk into a high-stepping strut, with the body inclined backwards and the knees lifted, a style that was later copied in both music hall and vaudeville. The first African-American team to play Broadway (1897), Charles and Dora Dean Johnson, were also the first to wear evening clothes on stage. They were considered the best-dressed team on the American stage. Dora's gowns frequently cost more than $1,000 each and were copied by Sarah Bernhardt, Lillian Russell and other white stars of the period. When they performed overseas, the German artist, Ernest von Heilmann, was so anxious to paint Dean, he bought out her contract so she would be free to pose for him. The picture was unveiled at

Top: **Photograph of Charles Johnson and Dora Dean. From a small insert on the sheet music cover of "I Want to Play Hamlet" by Paul West and John W. Bratton (circa 1903).** *Left:* **Photograph of Dora Dean. From an insert on the sheet music cover of "Don't You Think You'd Like to Fondle Me" by Hughie Cannon (circa 1900).** *Both courtesy of Brown University Library.*

the coronation of King Edward VII in 1902.

Johnson and Dean's dance act not only included their famous version of the cakewalk, but also soft shoe and wing dancing. At the height of their fame in 1910, the couple divorced, breaking up their act. Both formed new acts which comprised four men and four women each and toured for a while. In 1934, the couple got back together and revived their old routines, but because of the growing popularity of motion pictures and the fading popularity of vaudeville, the act was short-lived. They retired together to Minneapolis and lived quietly until their deaths.

Other all-black shows included *The Octoroons* in 1895, a musical farce which featured as its finale "a cakewalk jubilee, a military drill, and a 'chorus-march-finale,'"[15] and *Oriental America*, which made its debut the following year. *Oriental America* held the distinction of being the first show to open on Broadway with an all-black cast; it was innovative because it replaced the cakewalk and military drill finale with opera selections. Both *The Octoroons* and *Oriental America* retained the basic format of the minstrel show.

A Trip to Coontown in 1898 marked an important change in the black musical. This production was the first to completely depart from the minstrel show format; instead it used a progressive storyline. The first African-American musical comedy, it was also the first to be produced, directed, managed and performed entirely by blacks. Independence from white managers who had controlled previous shows and tours was an important step for black artists.[16]

Will Marion Cook's *Clorindy—The Origin of the Cake Walk* opened at about the same time as *A Trip to Coontown*. Cook had written the show for Bert Williams and George Walker, but because they were out of town, he enlisted the talents of the popular African-American minstrel performer, Ernest Hogan.[17] Cook first pitched the show to producer Isidore Witmark who told him he was "crazy to believe that any Broadway audience would listen to Negroes singing Negro opera."[18] Cook then approached producer Ed Rice. He went to his office for 30 straight days trying to get an interview. He failed, but overheard Rice mention that he was auditioning another act the following Monday at the theatre. Cook lied to his performers, telling them they had a booking to get them to the theater. He then took the baton from the theatre's English conductor and launched into the opening number from the show. Halfway through it, Rice stormed into the theatre, saw Cook in the pit conducting the orchestra and screamed, "No nigger can conduct my orchestra on Broadway!" The

English conductor looked at Rice and said, "Go back to your little cubby-hole and keep quiet! That boy's a genius and has something great."[19] Rice booked the show to open on the rooftop of his theatre. Their opening night was canceled because of rain, but the show was an enormous success when it opened the following week; the audience stood and cheered for ten minutes straight at the end. Cook recalled,

> My chorus sang like Russians, dancing meanwhile like Negroes, and cake-walking like angels, black angels![20]

Clorindy—The Origin of the Cake Walk was important for two major reasons: first, it showed that performers could dance vigorously and sing at the same time, in contrast to the gentle movements of the choruses in English light operas. More importantly, it was the first musical to feature the syncopated rhythms of ragtime music.[21]

Williams and Walker

On February 18, 1903, *In Dahomey*, the first black musical to appear in Times Square, opened at the New York Theatre. It starred Bert Williams and George Walker remained one of their greatest hits. During the San Francisco Winter Fair, Williams and Walker witnessed authentic Dahomean dancers. They were so impressed with the performance they tried to add authentic African tribal material into the musical.

> However, after three or four centuries the manners and customs of the American Negro had become so far removed from those of West Africa and had been so overlaid with indigenous — if frequently fallacious — characteristics, that the elements of Dahomean culture had

to be distorted in order to be incorporated in a way that audiences understood.[22]

In Dahomey toured to London in 1903 and Williams and Walker gave a command performance for the Prince of Wales's ninth birthday. A persistent rumor existed that Williams taught the young Edward VIII how to shoot craps.

Acceptance by British royalty meant little back in the States. Bert Williams once ordered a gin at a New York bar. The bartender looked him in the eye and said in a controlled voice, "That will be one hundred dollars." Williams quickly responded, "Then I'll have ten," and calmly pulled a thousand-dollar bill out of his vest pocket.[23]

Born Egbert Austin Williams in New Providence, Nassau, Bermuda, Bert Williams (1874–1922) was the grandson of the Dutch consul and probably fifteen-sixteenths white. When he was a young man, his family moved to San Pedro, California. He graduated from high school and intended to study engineering at Stanford University but couldn't afford the tuition; instead, he began singing and playing the banjo along the Barbary Coast. He first performed with a Hawaiian song and dance group, then with a black minstrel company that played lumber camps.

He met George Walker in 1893 in San Francisco when they were still in their teens. Walker was from Lawrence, Kansas, and had been working as a performer in medicine shows. Williams convinced Walker to leave his song and dance act to join him in Seig's Mastadon Minstrels. The two young men performed in small run-down variety houses around San Francisco. At one time they were hired to imitate "real savages from Africa" at an exhibit in Golden Gate Park. Hoping to move on, Williams and Walker worked their way across the country with a small medicine show. In El Paso, Texas, a group of white rowdies attacked them for being dressed well, stripped them, and forced them to put on burlap sacks. They survived the attack, but when the owner of the medicine wagon laughed at them, Williams and Walker quit the show and went to Chicago to audition for *The Octoroons*. They got the job but were fired at the end of one week. Hoping to improve their act, they began a tour of the Midwest, billing themselves as the "Two Real Coons," with Walker playing the Jim Dandy stereotype and Williams doing the slow-witted Sambo caricature. "It was so foreign to Williams he had to observe, study and master it, as well as take off his elegant clothes and put on rags and blackface every night."[24] The adoption of these stereotypical minstrel characters brought Williams and Walker instant success. Eventually the duo returned to New York to work the top vaudeville houses.[25] They toured again, this time with the major companies, sometimes appearing in the top white vaudeville houses around the country.

Williams and Walker were famous for their cakewalk which they performed to ragtime music; they were responsible for the ultimate theatrical development of the dance which remained a popular ingredient in all their shows. One fellow dancer commented, "George 'Bon-Bon' Walker was the greatest of the strutters, and the way he promenaded and pranced was something to see."[26] When the cakewalk became popular among the social elite of New York, the two black performers challenged William K. Vanderbilt to a cakewalk contest for the title of world champion and prize money totaling 50 dollars.

Walker became ill in 1909, and Williams continued to perform briefly in vaudeville with Walker's wife, Ada Overton. When Walker died in 1911, Williams

Bert Williams and George Walker. Sheet music cover for "I'm a Jonah Man" by Alex. Rogers (circa 1903). *Courtesy of Brown University Library.*

Before I got through with "Nobody" I could have wished that both the author of the words and the assembler of the tune had been strangled or drowned or talked to death. For seven whole years I had to sing it. Month after month I tried to drop it and sing something new, but I could get nothing to replace it, and the audiences seemed to want nothing else.[27]

After Williams left the *Follies*, he signed with the Shuberts. A heavy chain smoker and drinker, he developed heart problems and battled with depression in the later years of his life. While touring with a Shubert show in Detroit, Williams caught a cold which developed into pneumonia, but he refused to cancel his show. On February 21, 1922, he collapsed on the stage of the Shubert-Garrick. He was taken home to New York where he died on March 4, at the age of 49. Williams once told his friend Eddie Cantor about his hurt and anger at being forced to take freight elevators when he stayed at hotels with his fellow white performers. "It wouldn't be so bad, Eddie, if I didn't still hear the applause ringing in my ears."[28]

embarked on a solo career. He was asked to star in the *Ziegfeld Follies* with the contractual stipulation that he would never appear on stage at the same time as any white female cast members. Williams became a staple at the *Follies* and performed there for ten years from 1910 to 1919, missing only two of the editions. It was in the *Follies* that he introduced his famous song, "Nobody." Williams said,

15

Other Forms of Entertainment

There were many forms of popular entertainment in the late 19th and early 20th centuries. Besides the minstrel show, there were showboats that played up and down the Mississippi and Ohio Rivers, medicine shows that featured specialty acts which accompanied the hawking of potions and wares, and tent shows, such as gillies, carnivals, and circuses. As in minstrel shows, blackface entertainment dominated these forms of entertainment. Other venues included museums, honky-tonks and concert saloons.

Showboats

Civilization along the Mississippi and Ohio Rivers flourished during the first few decades of the 19th century. As the populations in such thriving cities as New Orleans, St. Louis, Natchez, and Cincinnati exploded, the desire for entertainment increased. Traveling players made their way into these booming cities hoping to capitalize on the new demand for theatrical entertainment. One troupe of actors, led by theatre manager Noah Ludlow, traveled from Albany, New York, down the river to Pittsburgh in a flatboat. After playing there for three months, they continued to Limestone, Kentucky, with the intention of traveling overland to entertain the legislature in

Frankfort, Kentucky. Their reception at the capitol was less than enthusiastic, so they continued touring overland through Kentucky and then into Tennessee. In Nashville, Ludlow purchased a keelboat he christened "Noah's Ark," and the itinerant actors again took to the rivers, this time heading for New Orleans. Ludlow's troupe reached Natchez-under-the-Hill on December 10, 1817, two years after they had left Albany. Five days later, Ludlow sold the keelboat and the actors booked passage on a steamboat to New Orleans. Noah Ludlow's keelboat "Noah's Ark" is believed by many to have been the first showboat. The long tradition of floating entertainment that followed became a training ground and performing opportunity for many dancers.[1]

Entertainment along the rivers of the Midwest began as medicine and whiskey boats plied their trade up and down the river using dance and music to attract customers.[2] Western audiences were entertainment-hungry and because river travel was the only real means of transportation, the showboat became the inevitable outgrowth of an Eastern theatrical institution adapted for the Western frontier.

The first boat constructed solely as a floating theatre was built by William Chapman a decade after Ludlow's "Noah's Ark" in 1831. Called Chapman's "Floating

Theatre," it played the lower Mississippi and the Ohio River. The players comprised of Chapman and eight other members of his family, who mainly performed selections from Shakespeare.[3] In his book, *Dramatic Life as I Found It*, Noah Ludlow described Chapman's "Floating Theatre":

> I beheld a large flat-boat, with a rude kind of house built upon it having a ridge-roof, above which projected a staff with a flag attached, upon which was plainly visible the word "Theatre." This singular object attracted my attention as it was lying tied up at the landing in Cincinnati, and on my making inquiries in regard to it, I learned that it was used for a theatrical company, under the management of a Mr. Chapman.[4]

Ten years later, Chapman began construction of a larger showboat, but he died unexpectedly. After his death, his wife completed the ship and ran it for five years under the name "Chapman's Floating Palace." In 1847, she sold the vessel to theatre producer, Sol Smith. The day after it was purchased, Smith and his troupe of performers set out with new costumes and stage scenery, but after only a short time on the river, the ship collided with a steamboat, split in half, and sank.

The success of William Chapman's venture spawned many imitators. As new showboats were built, the popularity of river entertainment increased; the format expanded, moving away from Shakespearean dramas towards song and dance varieties such as minstrel shows. One of the principal showboats on the upper Mississippi specializing in this type of entertainment was a steamer called the "Banjo" which was in operation for ten years and featured some of the top blackface minstrels of the day.

Other floating theatres featured full circuses. These were sometimes called boatshows to distinguish them from the earlier showboats, although eventually the terms became interchangeable. The largest circus boat was Spaulding and Rogers' "Floating Circus Palace." It was twice the size of the St. James Theatre in New Orleans which at that date in 1851, was the largest building in the city. The boat had two decks. The main deck, called the dress circle, held 1,000 seats. The family circle held 1,500 settees. Nine hundred seats were set aside for African-Americans, and there was an area for standing room. In addition to the circus ring, the boat had a museum containing over 100,000 oddities and curiosities.[5]

The "Floating Circus Palace" was towed by a vessel called the "James Raymond" which also featured entertainment. The two boats were so brilliantly lit with gas lamps that they were visible at great

Chapman's Floating Theatre, the first vessel built specifically to be a showboat. From *A History of the Theatre in America*, vol. 2, by Arthur Hornblow (1919).

distances from the banks of the river. The shows on the "James Raymond" were directed by Frank Lynch, the dancer who had replaced John Diamond at P.T. Barnum's museum. These shows featured some of the top dancers of the period including Dave Reed, Johnny Booker, and Ralph Keeler, the most popular dancer on the bill. The "Floating Circus Palace" operated until 1862 when it was confiscated by the Confederate army and converted into a hospital ship.

"Spaulding & Rogers' Floating Circus Palace." From *Gleason's Pictorial Drawing-Room Companion* (1852).

Medicine Shows

Medicine shows were a great training ground for many dancers, especially African-Americans, who used these small shows as an opportunity to develop their craft in the hope of breaking into minstrel shows or vaudeville. The most important tool used by medicine shows to hold an audience's interest and excite people into buying the products was dancing. Dancing was also used to demonstrate the health benefits attained by taking certain tonics which were bought by gullible audiences when the dancers drank the medicines themselves, and suddenly burst into athletic, energetic dances.

One group of traveling salesmen, called the "Quaker Healers," tried to capitalize on the reputation for honesty among the Quaker sect by dressing in conservative Quaker garb and assuming a pious attitude when hawking their tonics. Despite their pious approach, however, these men were well known for suddenly bursting into wild clog dances in the middle of their sales pitch.

Medicine show dancing was a blend of many African-American dances, including shuffles, buck and wings, breakdowns, jigs, struts and flat-footed buck. The emphasis was usually on eccentric moves that could capture an audience's attention. Medicine show performers had to be extremely versatile because the company depended upon repeat business. They were often expected to change their act every performance. One company is reputed to have changed the bill every night for 40 straight days in a row. As a result, dancers were constantly expanding and improving their repertoire.

Dance acts drifted back and forth between medicine shows and other tent shows, such as carnivals and circuses, hoping to move eventually into vaudeville, legitimate theatre or the moving pictures. Black dancer, Dewey "Pigmeat" Markham explained it thus:

In the old days show business for a colored dancer was like going through school. You started in a medicine show — that was kindergarten — where they could use a few steps if they could cut them, but almost anything would do. Then you went on up to the gilly

show, which was like grade school—
they wanted dancers. If you had something on the ball, you graduated to a
carnival—that was high school—and
you sure had to be able to dance. College level was a colored minstrel show,
and as they faded out, a vaudeville circuit or even a Broadway show. Vaudeville and Broadway sometimes had the
best, although a lot of great dancers
never got out from under the rag, never
left the tent shows.[6]

Legendary performers such as George
Walker and Slow Kid Thompson began as
dancers in medicine shows. Composer
Eubie Blake also worked as a buck dancer
for a short time with Dr. Frazier's Medicine
Show.

Medicine show dances were usually
presented in blackface and most often done
in the racially stereotyped characters of the
plantation black, Jim Crow, or the city
dandy, Zip Coon. Despite this, African-
American tent show dancers were able to
use these shows as a springboard to further
their dance careers, which eventually fostered greater social acceptance of black
artists in general. The shows also helped
to further disseminate the vocabulary of
African-American dance steps. As this material was adopted by white culture and
white entertainers began to exploit
African-American culture for its own use,
stylistic elements within the dances were
refined even further.

Gillies

Gillies were a step up from medicine
shows for dance performers because they
allowed dancers the opportunity to develop
material and begin to build careers. Similar to small fairs, sometimes the shows employed as many as 50 people. Gillies got
their name from the wagon, called a gilly,
that transported such equipment as me-

chanical rides, sideshow tents and shooting
galleries. Often the gilly also carried a small
stage for dancers. Dances were used as a
preshow teaser to entice the crowd to enter
the tent which was called the "jig top."
Barkers tried to entice the customers to buy
tickets for the show. If they shouted "Bally,
everybody!" the dancers had to rush outside to the platform to give prospective
ticket buyers a taste of what was waiting inside. Slow Kid Thompson recalled, "A
dancer cut his craziest capers at that
point."[7] If the barkers were enthusiastic in
their work, the dancers had to be just as
enthusiastic in theirs, or more so. Dancer
Leonard Reed remembered a Fourth of July
when the dancers of one gilly did 48 shows
in a row.

Inside the "jig top," a rope was
stretched across the tent to divide the white
customers from the African-Americans.
The program usually consisted of a fast-
talking comedian who inserted bursts of
eccentric dancing into the opening mono-
logue. This act was followed by specialty
song and dance acts, and the show usually
ended with a skit utilizing the entire cast,
often the popular "Eph and Dinah."

"Eph and Dinah" varied from company to company but usually the skit told
the story of Uncle Eph and his wife Dinah,
played by two young dancers disguised as
old folks. The skit culminated in Eph and
Dinah's golden wedding anniversary celebration during which other members of the
cast urged the decrepit couple to dance.
The two hobbled around, and after a short
while, feigned exhaustion.

Suddenly Eph surprised the audience,
switching gears and breaking into the possum walk or some other dance. As the astonished audience applauded the old man's
agility and virtuosity, Uncle Eph progressed to even harder and more athletic
dances. He then grabbed Aunt Dinah and
danced with her in a wild number that included lifts and acrobatic maneuvers. This

skit became the most popular attraction of all the gilly shows.

Carnivals

Carnivals were larger than gillies, although similar in nature. More established and reputable, they often included animal acts as well as the usual rides and sideshow attractions. Carnival performers traveled by rail rather than by wagon. The minstrel show format was used with the traditional semicircle, end-men, and master of ceremonies. Specialty dances were often the highlight of the show, so that dancers had more opportunities to become known as featured performers and were usually guaranteed more pay.

Some of the outstanding African-American dancers who performed in tent shows were Cliff Pettiford, Kid Neal, King Nappy, Kid Sapp, and Peg Lightfoot, one of the first one-legged dancers. Other dancers such as "Peg Leg" Bates, Leonard Reed, and Willie Covan were able to transition from these tent shows to the vaudeville circuits.

Circuses

The golden age of the American circus was from 1870 to the 1920s, although the first record of an African-American circus performer was in 1808. His name is unknown but he was advertised by the Pepin and Breschard Circus as a "young African [who] would dance the hornpipe on the back of a horse traveling at full speed."

During the heyday of the big circuses, African-Americans were usually hired as musicians. Sometimes black dancers were also hired as part of the band, dressed as Hawaiians or in some other exotic costumes. They were used to attract patrons into the freak shows and to provide a little entertainment once the customers went inside. It wasn't until 1899, in Sells Brothers and Forpaugh's Circus at

Traveling circus. "Circus Coming to Town." Engraving by Paul Frenzeny and Jules Tavernier, from *Harper's Weekly* (1873).

Madison Square Garden, that black vaudeville acts were included in the circus.

Museums

Unlike today's museums, those of the 19th century combined entertainment with freak shows. The first was Barnum's Museum in New York which had a little theatre in tandem with the curio hall. Aware of the reputation of theatre in his day, Barnum banned drinking and prostitution from his establishment, hoping to attract a wider audience.

Museum shows were usually 30 to 40 minutes in length and ran continuously from ten o'clock in the morning and throughout the day. The stages were notoriously tiny; presentations consisted mainly of singers, dancers and comics because acrobats needed more space and animal acts were not feasible because of the exhausting

schedules. Nevertheless, many important dancers appeared in museum shows including William Henry Lane.

Honky-Tonks

Honky-tonks, or hurdy-gurdy houses as they were also known, were an outgrowth of saloons. Entertainers in these Western establishments played for money that was tossed at them while they danced or sang. The women on stage often moonlighted as prostitutes. Many were not performers themselves, but were displayed on stage in the opening number nevertheless. Their main job was to entice audience members to purchase drinks. "Wine room girls," as they were called, also had men buy them drinks, but their drinks were usually just colored water or weak tea, costing the management a tiny portion of what the customer was charged. If real alcohol

Children dancing on stage in a museum. "La Petite Angelina and Miss C. Thompson, at the Boston Museum." Wood engraving by Winslow Homer, from *Ballou's Pictorial Drawing-Room Companion* (March 12, 1859).

"DANCE-HOUSE."

Dancing in an Abilene honky-tonk (circa 1878). *Courtesy of the Library of Congress.*

was used, another trick to fleece the men was to pour the girls' drinks into a hidden trough that led back to the bar so the liquor could be recycled and sold again.[8]

Women who performed in honky-tonk shows often missed their stage entrances because they were too busy entertaining cowboys in the hall, so it was a common practice for other actors on stage to improvise at these moments. Similar in nature to the Western honky-tonk was the Eastern concert saloon.

Concert Saloons

There were about 300 concert saloons in New York City. The notorious slums of the Five Points district were especially known for their many dance halls and concert saloons.[9] Condemned by moral reformers because these establishments fostered prostitution, crime and drunkenness, the concert saloons' main attraction was the girls.

The girls were traditionally garbed in short skirts and low cut bodices and wore high boots which had bells attached to them.

The one dance hall that stood out as sumptuous in comparison to its rookery rivals ... was presided over by John Allen. In 1868 his fine brick building stood out like a palace over the other mean dens along Water Street. Allen is said to have been a student in the Union Theological Seminary and was educated for a sacred calling. He had blood relations in the ministry and Bibles and religious papers were often conspicuous through his establishment. The female inmates were uniformed in scarlet and bright-colored dresses, and red-topped boots with ankle bells were part of the uniform.[10]

The waitresses, often younger than 12 years old, were encouraged to drink with the men they served, and perhaps make a date for later. In the less reputable establishments there were curtained booths

Dancing in a concert saloon in New York City. "Interior of a dance house." From *The National Police Gazette* (January 1880).

caused the New York State legislature to pass a law which virtually shut down concert saloons. The law required each establishment to pay for entertainment licenses and prohibited the sale of alcohol which led to the development of alternative forms of entertainment, the most important being vaudeville.

Concert saloons, like so many of the institutions that have influenced American popular culture, flourished on the margins of polite society. They were part of the socially stratified theatre world of mid–nineteenth-century New York, where immigration and industrialization had created audiences divided by race, class, gender, and ethnicity. Vaudeville entrepreneurs attempted to reverse this fragmentation and create a kind of theatre that could appeal to all New Yorkers and gather them together under one roof.[12]

in the balcony where the girls put on private shows for the right price. Wages for the average working girl in a factory, laundry, or store around this time were about $6 a week. A waitress in a concert saloon could earn up to $20 a week if the patrons liked her. If a girl chose to go into prostitution as well, her earnings went even higher.[11]

In April 1862, growing moral outrage about the lewd conduct in these venues

16

Vaudeville

The most important factor contributing to the development of new forms of variety entertainment in the United States occurred before the Civil War when female performers were introduced into the minstrel show format. As more and more women braved the world of show business, the rigid structure of popular minstrelsy crumbled. Audiences expected entertainment with more variety and sex appeal. Seeking ways to satisfy their patrons and to broaden their audience base, theatrical entrepreneurs looked for solutions to the growing discontent with the previously male-dominated minstrel show format. They found their answer in a new concept of family entertainment called vaudeville.

The word "vaudeville," some say, was derived from the French *voix de ville*, which meant "voices of the town." The expression referred to the dances and dance songs of the market place. Other sources suggest that the word came from *val de Vire*, or *vau de Vire*, which meant "the valley of the Vire River," an area in Normandy. Known for its lively drinking songs written by mill owner Olivier Basselin in the 15th century, this area came to be associated with variety entertainment. The first documented use of the word in the United States, in relationship to variety presentations, was John Ransome's use of it to describe a show he put together in the 1880s.[1]

Tony Pastor

Scholars widely hold that American vaudeville was officially started by Tony Pastor on October 24, 1881, in New York at the 14th Street Theatre in Tammany Hall.[2] Pastor presented a family entertainment that consisted of eight acts of comedy, acrobatics, song, dance, and an inoffensive sprinkling of topical humor to a "double audience," of both men and women. "It was the first 'clean' vaudeville show in America and to its bill," as Fred Stone used to say, "a child could take his parents."[3] Up until this point, variety shows were frequented mostly by men.

Tony (Antonio) Pastor was born May 28, 1837, in Greenwich Village, New York.[4] He started performing as a child, singing at Hand-in-Hand Temperance Society meetings. His father disapproved of his theatrical leanings and sent the boy away to work on a farm in upstate New York, but Pastor was shipped back after a short while because his constant clowning distracted the other farm hands. Considered something of a prodigy, Pastor gave his first paid performance at age 10 at P. T. Barnum's Museum; he sang and played the tambourine in blackface. At 14, he became the youngest ringmaster to play the circus tours. He continued as a ringmaster until the outbreak of the Civil War.

..CHASE'S THEATRE..

Washington, D. C.

DEVOTED TO

Mr. Chase's Original Idea,

POLITE VAUDEVILLE.

In the presentation of POLITE VAUDEVILLE in the CHASE THEATRES it is the constant aim of the management to prevent the use of a single word, expression, or situation that will offend the intelligent, refined, and cultured classes.

PROGRAM.

Week of May 20, 1901.

P. B. Chase's Amusement Enterprises:

Chase's Theatre, Washington, D. C.
Polite Vaudeville.

Chase's Theatre, Baltimore, Md.
Percy Haswell Stock Co.

H. WINNIFRED DE WITT.
General Manager.

Daily Matinees,
Entire House, 25c.
Evenings, 25 and 50c.

An advertisement for a "Polite Vaudeville Show" at Chase's Theatre, Washington, D.C. (May 20, 1901). *Courtesy of the Library of Congress, Rare Book and Special Collections Division.*

When Pastor was 24, he opened his first theatre in New York. Over the next several years he ran various theaters until he took over one at 585 Broadway in 1875. He called it "Tony Pastor's New Fourteenth Street Theatre" and opened with a parody of Gilbert and Sullivan's *Pirates of Penzance* which flopped miserably.[5] Then on October 24, 1881, he tried what most called a "daring venture." He opened a clean variety show and invited women to attend. In an effort to make the material suitable for women, Pastor posted a sign backstage that

any performer who used lewd, suggestive jokes or obscene and vulgar gestures would be immediately fired. He also prohibited smoking in the theatre and banned the traditional selling of alcohol.[6]

Pastor's gamble paid off. He continued to cater to female audiences by having what he called "Ladies Matinees" which featured giveaways. During these matinees, Pastor offered door prizes such as hams or sacks of potatoes to the first 25 women who attended the performance. Attendance soared when he offered dress patterns, new hats, and even silk dresses to his feminine patrons. Pastor commented, "That really got 'em. No woman in this world can resist a silk dress for free."[7]

Pastor's New York vaudeville theatre was small but successful, attracting some of the best entertainers in the business. Around the turn of the century, though, the area around it began to decline. Two other vaudeville houses opened, charging less for admission. The Keith Circuit then bought and refurbished a third theatre, and Pastor's audiences began to wane. In addition, performers' salaries had risen sharply; the cost of producing his vaudeville varieties had escalated to ten times what it had been when he had first started. By 1908, Tony Pastor was unable to pay the rent on his tiny theatre and it closed. The showman continued to haunt the empty theatre, going there to sit and read the daily paper. That same summer on August 6, he died.

Tony Pastor began a tradition which produced some of the most inventive and entertaining performers the world has ever seen. Many of these acts featured dancing, and it was during the heyday of vaudeville that tap dance developed into the form we know today.

Dancing in Vaudeville

By the time vaudeville developed, tap dancing was primarily divided into two distinct styles: one in which the dancers wore wooden-soled shoes, generally called buck and wing or clog; and the other in which the dancers wore soft-soled shoes, generally called soft shoe or more commonly, song and dance. Straight jig dancing began to lose its popularity as these other types of dancing gained prominence, although its influence was already well-established.[8]

In the 1880s it became more and more popular to have contests between variety performers, especially clog dancers. Winners won prizes such as silver cups, diamond belts, or medals, but the real advantage of competing was that if a performer won, the time they were booked at the various theatres in the area increased. Clog dancing contests were numerous and varied, including competitions in Lancashire clog, hornpipe clog, American clog, statue and pedestal clog, and trick clog. Some of the most prestigious competitions for clog and buck dancers were sponsored by the *Police Gazette* newspaper which awarded the Fox Medal. Some great wooden-shoe dancers such as Phil Cook, Ida May Chadwick, Maude Kramer, and Lulu Beeson, all won the *Police Gazette* Fox Medal. Traditional clog and buck dancers mixed in other styles of dancing to spice up their act. The first to do an acrobatic clog act were the Poole Brothers in 1877. They eventually combined legomania with acrobatics and clog. Another well-known acrobatic wooden-shoe act was Emma Francis and her Arabs.

Wishing to find a gimmick to set a dance act above the others, vaudeville dancers entered a period of tremendous innovation and creativity. Egg dances became popular. Usually performed by women, a dancer placed about two dozen eggs around the stage in a tight group and proceeded to dance around and over them. After finishing the performance, during the applause, the dancer

Playbill for Tony Pastor and His Traveling Company for Ford's Opera House in Baltimore (April 12, 1875). *Courtesy of the Library of Congress, Rare Book and Special Collections Division.*

purposely broke all the eggs to prove they were real.

Spade dances were performed by a dancer who held on to a spade handle and stood on the blade, rhythmically hopping around the stage as if on a pogo stick. The dance included hopping over objects such as bottles or lit candles. These types of acts were often reminiscent of the old English dance called leap-candle, or candle-rush, in which young dancers leapt forward and backward over a lit candle.[9]

T. F. GRANT.
THE CHAMPION ONE-LEGGED CLOG
DANCER OF THE WORLD, AND HOLDER
OF THE POLICE GAZETTE CHAMPIONSHIP
TROPHY.

T.F. Grant, "the most graceful one-legged clog dancer the world has ever seen," and winner of the Police Gazette Championship Trophy. From *The National Police Gazette* (March 26, 1892).

Transformation dances involved quick costume changes on stage. A dancer appeared wearing several layers of clothes with hidden strings that could be pulled to rip off layers revealing a new costume. Perhaps starting in military garb, a female dancer performed a military style tap, and when the string was pulled, she was instantaneously transformed into a washer-woman who then did a jig. One more pull revealed a child's outfit and the dancer would go into a jump-rope dance. The fourth pull of the string transformed her into a policeman who sang and danced on his beat. In the 1880s and 1890s, the added aspect of female impersonation became popular as men began to do transformation dances masquerading as women. The most well-known were Robert Fulgora who billed himself as "Trebor, the Man of Mystic Changes," and a dancer who called himself, the "Great Layfayette."

Charles Guyer and Nellie O'Neill are credited with creating the first roughhouse dance act, although one of the most famous teams to feature physical violence mixed with dance was Ferguson and Mack who were on the bill that first night at Tony Pastor's Theatre. Ferguson and Mack presented their dance as if it were a fight. Besides dancing, the act consisted of beats and falls, and ended with Mack hitting Ferguson in the head with a hatchet. The hatchet stuck in Ferguson's skull and remained there as they danced off. Unfortunately the act with Mack took its toll and he went deaf from the constant pounding to his head. Although he had won the clog championship in New Orleans in 1868, Ferguson ended up working solo in small-time honky-tonks to support himself.

Another famous roughhouse team was the Three Keatons — Joe and Myra Keaton and their son Buster, the same Buster Keaton who went on to become a silent film star. Young Buster joined the act at age five. Consisting mainly of burlesque dancing and imitations, the routine eventually evolved into a violent knockabout sketch in which Keaton's father tossed his rebellious son about the stage. Dancer Eddie Leonard recalled,

> In the act with his father, Buster was thrown all over the stage — in the footlights, down in the orchestra pit, out in

the front row against the audience — and it looked as though his dad would break his neck.[10]

Rival dances, usually with men, also involved violence. The first man entered and sang and danced and during the dance break at the end of the chorus, went up to a set piece representing a cottage, knocked on the door, and then exited the stage by entering the cottage. As he exited, his partner entered on the other side of the stage, sang and danced, and as with the first man, he also knocked and entered the cottage. Suddenly from inside the cottage there was the sound of fighting and a pistol shot, and the first man came barreling through the cottage door, back into audience view. The second dancer then came flying through the breakaway window of the cottage.

The two men confronted each other about whose girlfriend the "maiden in the cottage" was. After resolving the dilemma, they then proceeded to dance together. The best know rival dance acts were Mackin and Wilson, and Welsh and Rice.[11]

Eccentric and legomania acts were also popular. A legomania act popular in the U.S as well as in English music halls was the Majiltons. Comprising three dancers, two men and a woman, and called "A Study in Points," it was the first act of its kind in the United States. The men wore cutaway coats in which the collars, lapels, and tails were pointed. Their eyebrows, moustaches, and goatees were also pointed as well as the lobes of their ears. All three dancers wore wigs with three sharp pointed spikes of hair. Long pointed dancing shoes completed the costumes. The three dancers made their entrance down a long staircase, the men effortlessly kicking over the head of the woman between them. They then danced a reel with high kicks and splits thrown in.

The elegant sand jig was the forerunner of our modern sand dances. The per-

James Mackin (left) and Francis Wilson, one of the most popular rival dance teams in vaudeville (circa 1875). From *Monarchs of Minstrelsy: From "Daddy" Rice to Date* by Edward LeRoy Rice (1911).

former entered carrying a pint of sand and proceeded to sprinkle it around the stage floor. There were no taps on the shoes and the dancer would shuffle, slide, shift, and dig into the sand to produce the sounds.[12] The first sand jig dancer was purported to be a man named Jimmy Bradley in 1876, although perhaps the most famous sand dancer was a woman named Kitty O'Neill. It wasn't until the time of the Civil War that any women were accepted as popular entertainers in the United States, and O'Neill, who appeared around this time, created a soft-shoe sand dance that turned her into one of the country's first great female entertainers, making her a match for George Primrose and his softshoe dances.

Kitty O'Neill danced for Tony Pastor in his theatre in New York. Two famous double sand jig acts were the Barlow Brothers and the Girard Brothers, who had already gained success in minstrel shows.

Brother dance acts were very popular and included such great teams as the Field Brothers, the Caits Brothers, the Foley Brothers, the Ward Brothers, who won the Fox Medal, King, King and King, the Three Slate Brothers, the Four Small Brothers, the incomparable Ritz Brothers, and the amazing Condos Brothers.

Juvenile performers were all the rage in vaudeville because of the emphasis on family entertainment. Some famous dance

Assorted vaudeville dancers waiting in the wings to go on. Drawing from a Weber and Fields Pictoral Souvenir Program, entitled "Waiting for a Cue." *Courtesy of the Library of Congress, Rare Book and Special Collections Division.*

acts that featured children were the Hengler Sisters, Harry Delf, the "Kid Romero," Elseeta, the "American Dancing Girl," Eva and Harry Puck, and Rae Dooley. When the Geary Society, also known as the American Society for the Prevention of Cruelty to Children, cracked down on working conditions for children, labor laws were created that prevented full-time employment for minors. Many acts got around the laws by lying about the age of the performers or simply moving the act to another city or state.

Eddie Foy created the most famous family act in vaudeville, "Eddie Foy and His Seven Little Foys."[13] Foy is credited with inventing the hand dance. George M. Cohan, one of the most important men in American theatre, also worked with his family as a vaudeville dancer. His family's act, the "Cohan Mirth Makers," later called the "Four Cohans," became the highest paid variety act of its size in vaudeville.

Vaudeville was a time of spectacular invention within the art form of tap dancing. The Purcella Brothers dressed like convicts and danced with their legs chained together. Harper and Stencil did the first double one-legged act. Harper had only his left leg, and Stencil, his right. Because they both had the same size feet, they only needed to buy one pair of wooden-soled dancing shoes.

Clara Morton danced and played the piano at the same time. Will Mahoney did pratfalls and tap danced on a xylophone. Robert Stickney performed his dance on stilts. Rose and Moon danced back to back, and Dick Henry and Carrie

Adelaide changed costumes while dancing. The Daly Brothers did an act in which they kicked hats, cigar boxes and other inanimate objects. Dancers imitated scarecrows, animals, and drunks falling down stairs.

Billing themselves as Marion and Bell, Dave Marion and his wife did a vaudeville act in which they wore egg-shaped costumes, about 2½ feet in diameter, made out of wicker. The couple did a rather odd dance number with only their heads, feet, and arms protruding from the "eggs."

Tom Patricola was famous for the comic characters he imitated in his dances, and many credit him with furthering the use of character pantomime as a valid source of material for tap routines. Patricola, who played the ukulele while he danced, contributed many original steps still used by dancers today, including one series of moves later named for him, that utilized the suzi-q. Harland Dixon called Tom Patricola "a mop gone crazy."[14]

The dancer Charlie Diamond became a success by doing a soft shoe while playing the harp. Max Ford's specialty was wing dancing, and he created a step most tap dancers use today called the maxiford. Harry Bolger invented slap shoe dancing. Jimmy Monahan was celebrated for Irish jig dancing with a glass of beer on his head. Monahan taught James Cagney the tap dances for his role in the film, *Yankee Doodle Dandy.*

Al Leach did stair dancing in the 1880s before Bill Robinson popularized it, and Harry Pilsar did an acrobatic run up a wall into a flip, just as Donald O'Connor did years later in *Singin' in the Rain.* Another innovator was an Irishman named Eddie Horan, who introduced a waltz clog routine with a cane. The use of a cane while tap dancing soon became standard fare for nearly every song and dance act after that.

Around the turn of the century, white vaudevillians began adding power and flair

EDDIE HORAN

Eddie Horan, the man who introduced the waltz clog with a cane. From *Monarchs of Minstrelsy: From "Daddy" Rice to Date* by Edward LeRoy Rice (1911).

to comedy dancing. Harry Kelly and John T. Kennedy were credited with introducing lightning-fast staccato tap steps, a routine later improved by the famous Condos Brothers who were the first to master the five tap wing, a difficult step that made the brothers legendary among their fellow dancers.

Lew Randall is credited with being the first dancer to introduce buck and wing to vaudeville in 1888, and from that day, the vaudeville stage was filled with legions of talented, innovative dancers.[15]

Other great hoofers in vaudeville included Sammy Lee, Harry Evans, Lou Lockett and Jack Waldron, Boyle and Brazil, the Lovenberg Sisters, Charles O'-Conner, Ben Ryan and George White, Bisset and Scott, and the brother-sister act of Johnny and Brenda Gleason. The Gleasons traveled with their own accompanist to insure correct tempos and were the first to carry their own portable tap mat. One of the greatest tap dancers was Johnny Boyle, who was well respected among his peers but never achieved star status in vaudeville because he lacked real showmanship.

Eddie Leonard

Eddie Leonard, whose real name was Lemuel Gordon Toney was perhaps one of the best soft shoe dancers in vaudeville. Born in Richmond, Virginia on October 18, 1875, he made his stage debut at age 12 and was known by the nickname of "Dots." He auditioned as a baseball player for the Baltimore Orioles but after not making the team, joined Primrose's Minstrels instead. He changed his named to Eddie Leonard and appeared in many productions, including a show in 1893 called *The South Before the War,* the show in which Bill Robinson made his stage debut.

Leonard had great success in minstrel shows and was affectionately known the "Grand Old Man of Minstrelsy," but he is mainly remembered for his work in vaudeville. Not considered a great technician, his dancing was, nevertheless, widely imitated by other dancers. His specialty was the Virginia essence. According to dancer Harland Dixon, "He had a nice backward-shuffle exit, but he was more of a singer and personality."[16] One of his most famous numbers was "Ida, Sweet as Apple Cider," a song which Leonard composed himself. Leonard was notorious for milking applause from an audience and taking bow after bow. He was once hired to do one show but the theatre wanted to limit his act to ten minutes. His manager replied to this request by telling them, "My God! It takes Eddie Leonard ten minutes just to bow!"[17]

As vaudeville waned in popularity, Eddie Leonard's career ended. He appeared briefly with Bing Crosby in a film called *If I Had My Way* and later performed his

blackface act one last time in Billy Rose's Diamond Horseshoe cabaret revue called "Nights of Gladness," choreographed by Gene Kelly. Eddie Leonard died of natural causes in New York on July 29, 1941.

Pat Rooney

Pat Rooney, Jr., was born in New York City on the Fourth of July, 1880. Son of performers, he started dancing when he was ten years old. He first went on the stage in a act with his sister Mattie. They billed themselves as the "Premier Eccentric Dancing Act of the Business — Bar None." He once told of how as a child he practiced his tap steps:

> When I was a kid in Baltimore, I'd go down to the corner grocery where they had one of those wooden cellar floors. On that I would practice my tap dancing. It was fun because the floor had a nice hollow sound and, besides, I could attract a lot of attention before the grocer got fed up and chased me.[18]

After performing in vaudeville and nightclubs, Rooney did a melodrama called *Daughters of the Poor*, in which he met his wife Marion Bent. They formed an act and toured the United States, becoming one of vaudeville's best-loved couples. In 1919, Rooney introduced a dance to the tune of "The Daughter of Rosie O'Grady," called a waltz clog. He performed the dance with his hands stuffed in his pockets while hitching up his pants. The dance became his trademark. He was also well known for his bell-kicks that sailed into the air to amazing heights. Frederick James Smith of the *New York Dramatic Mirror* (May 20, 1916) described Pat Rooney, Jr., as "a sort of electrified hairpin."[19]

In 1950, Rooney appeared in the original *Guys and Dolls* on Broadway, creating the role of Arvide Abernathy. He was originally slated to do his famous waltz clog in the production, but because it was out of character, he never performed the dance. Instead, Rooney introduced the song "More I Cannot Wish You," which became a classic. A tireless performer, Rooney also appeared in many small films and on television.

Rooney's wife, Marion, died in 1940 and Rooney declared bankruptcy in 1941. In 1942, he married the divorced wife of his son. She died in 1943 and he remarried again in 1944.

Along with his famous waltz clog, Rooney is credited with popularizing two of tap dancing's most famous steps, the shuffle off to Buffalo, and falling off the log. Rooney's dancing, always classy and graceful, helped change the way the Irish were viewed by showing a softer, more decent attitude in his act as opposed to the popular caricature of the rough and tumble, hard-drinking Irishman. W. C. Fields once remarked, "If you didn't hear the Taps you would think he was floating over the stage."[20] Pat Rooney, Jr., died in New York on September 9, 1962. A tradition still exists that, in honor of Pat Rooney, who was left-handed, all waltz clog dances should start on the left foot.

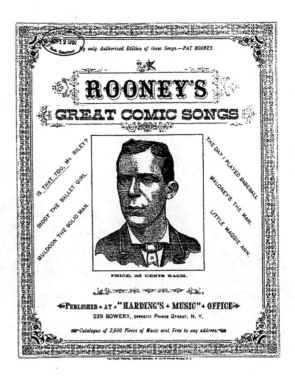

Drawing of Pat Rooney. From the sheet music cover of "Is That You, Mr. Reilly?" by Pat Rooney (1883). *Courtesy of the Library of Congress, Music Division.*

Harland Dixon

Born in Toronto, Canada, in 1885, Harland Dixon performed in minstrel shows, vaudeville, and on Broadway. His Scotch-Irish parents were deeply religious and preached constantly to their son, threatening him with the fires of hell. He first experimented with tap when he was 12 years old while attending gym classes at the local Y.M.C.A. During a jogging exercise the boy in front of him accidentally did a flap with his foot; Dixon was intrigued and imitated him.

As he related the story,

> The kid in front of me was making a slap with his foot, a sound I remembered later when I saw my first tap dancer. I imitated the kid. After a while I got so good I could do it with one foot, then the other, finally was able to do a roll. Before long I could do it with both feet, also could hop with the right foot, rattle with the left."[21]

Shortly after this, Dixon started learning tap steps from a newsboy he had met. They began to meet on the street corner to dance together. He was frequently fired from the odd jobs he had because he was always disturbing the other workers with the rhythms he pounded out with his feet.

He eventually started dancing with a boy named Jimmy Malone who worked at the drugstore. Malone later became Dixon's first partner. At age 15, Dixon went to the theatre for the first time and saw his first professional dancing. The performers he saw were Johnny Ford and a woman named Mamie Gerhue. Ford had won the Fox medal for buck dancing offered by the *Police Gazette,* and was part of a popular act with his brothers, the "Four Dancing Fords." After seeing him dance, Dixon worked hard to recreate Ford's routine. His next exposure to professional tapping was when he saw Johnny's brother Maxie. Maxie Ford was credited with creating one particular tap step that was later named after him, the maxiford.

Dixon entered a dance contest sponsored by a traveling production of *In Old Kentucky.* He won second prize and three dollars. He was beaten by Georgie White, the man who later produced the famous *George White Scandals.*[22]

Dixon's conservative parents were not happy with their son's career choice, and they frequently warned him about the evils of show business. Even after Dixon had achieved enormous success as a dancer, his mother refused to use the ticket he sent her when he was performing in his hometown of Toronto. She was finally coaxed into sneaking into the theatre from the back and watching her son dance from the wings. She told him later, "It would be terrible if the neighbors heard about this. They'd never get done talking about my sinfulness."[23]

Dixon's first professional job was when he and his first partner, Jimmy Malone, were hired by George Primrose to dance in his minstrel show. While the two boys were preparing for their first performance, Primrose sent them to be coached by Jimmy O'Connor, who was responsible for staging the chorus numbers in the show. O'Connor taught them buck dancing, Lancashire clog, toe and heel, soft shoe and the Virginia essence. When opening day finally arrived — a Sunday — Dixon preached to his fellow minstrels about how sinful it would be to do the show and how God would strike them all dead with bolts of lightning. However, when he saw his boss, Primrose, standing in the doorway, Dixon closed his mouth and proceeded to do the show.

Primrose became a great influence in Dixon's life and upon his style of dancing. Dixon tried hard to imitate the master, but whenever he tried the results tended to be comical. Dixon recalled,

> I was copying Primrose, but it came out different; while he was all grace and elegance, I was more stiff and angular — in a humorous way.[24]

One of Dixon's idiosyncrasies was to hold his arms stiffly by his sides and twist his shoulders back and forth, a signature gesture of his that was later widely imitated.

Dixon split up with Malone, and in 1907 left Primrose to work with Lew Dockstadter's troupe. One theatre manager in Denver told Dixon, after seeing his solo dance, "Dixon, you are the best dancer I ever had on the stage of this theatre."[25]

Harland Dixon was considered a master at mimicking others and was well-respected for his ability to capture anyone's style while he danced.[26] As did others in vaudeville, he observed fellow dancers and added to his repertoire by stealing steps. He once said,

> The good ones all had an effect upon my work, because I copied them. But you want to do something original. So you experiment, take a step and try it,

forwards and backwards and sideways, then you put the middle in the front, the front at the end, keep shifting and experimenting, and after a while you have an original step.[27]

Dixon then met Jimmy Doyle in New York at an actor's club. These two men would form one of the most well-respected dance acts in vaudeville and on the musical theatre stage. They first appeared together in a show called *Let George Do It.* Later, around 1912, they did a regular gig at the Winter Garden, and because of their success there, were instantly in demand as character dancers for Broadway shows. Their routines were elegant and inventive, mixing in a bit of story with each number. One featured Dixon as a man waiting in a dentist's office writhing in agony from a toothache.

Harland Dixon was a conservative man who didn't smoke, drink or gamble. He married his childhood sweetheart and stayed with her until his death in 1969. His partner, Jimmy Doyle, spent every spare minute at the racetrack or with a new woman. Dixon rehearsed constantly and Doyle never did. He just watched the routine that Dixon had created one or two times and then he'd have it down pat.

They danced together for nine years. The act broke up when they were rehearsing for a musical in 1921. The producer, Charles Dillingham, discovered that Doyle wasn't there because he had sneaked out of rehearsal to go to the racetrack to gamble. Dixon tried to cover for his partner, but Dillingham fired Doyle on the spot and demanded that Dixon go on as a solo act, which he did with great success. While Dixon continued performing in his single act, his former partner Doyle had trouble finding work and eventually opened a dance school but it failed. After that he disappeared from sight and was not heard from again.

Dancer Jack Donahue said of Harland Dixon, "As a creator of eccentric [dance] with the greatest variety of steps, in my opinion Harland Dixon stands alone."[28] Nick Castle added, "And he used a cane better than anyone in the world."[29] Dixon could imitate anyone and anything. He was a pioneer of character dancing and his longevity attested to his amazing ability.

In his eighties, Dixon had trouble with his legs and walked with a cane, but he kept dancing. He would sit in a chair and while seated, tap wildly.

James Barton

James Barton was born in 1890 in New Jersey. His father was a member of Primrose and West's Minstrel Show and his mother was a ballet dancer. He was part of the act by the time he was four years old. He traveled with his family in their vaudeville act from 1898 to 1902 doing roughhouse comedy dance, and then on his own in various vaudeville and burlesque houses until 1919. His first part on Broadway was in *The Passing Show of 1919,* when he replaced Ed Wynn during an Actors' Equity strike. After glowing reviews in the show, he became a huge success. Wherever he appeared, he stopped the show with his energetic, eccentric dancing. When Bert Williams died while rehearsing for *Dew Drop Inn,* Barton stepped in and, appearing in blackface, literally stopped the show ten separate times with his dancing. When he did his act at the Palace, the management had to break an iron-clad rule of not raising the curtain again once it had come down at the end of an act. After Barton danced, the audience so wildly demanded his return that the management was afraid they might destroy the theatre, so they raised the curtain again. Reviewers and audiences alike loved the dancing of James Barton. Alexander Woollcott wrote of him,

Such exploits as his should not be described in terms of the ordinary hoofers of the two-a-day. When you talk of Barton as a dancer and a pantomimist, you should mention him in the great company of Nijinski and Charles Chaplin.[30]

Another critic added, "When he dances, he reduces to absurdity all the philosophical schools in the world."[31]

When he performed, Barton carried his own portable six- by six-foot tap floor with him. He often started his routines with a single, then a double, and then a triple time-step. He then launched into his other steps without ever repeating himself. A master mimic, he could imitate any step he saw and change it into his own. Many young dancers stole his steps. Barton once commented,

When I played the Palace the boys would turn up in the audience and then disappear in the men's room after my act to practice my steps.[32]

For five years from 1934 to 1939, Barton gave up dancing to star in the Broadway production of *Tobacco Road*. He died at age 71 in 1962.

He was an original who, aided by an Irish background of jigs and reels, absorbed the rhythms and movements of Negro dancers early in his career and added earthy, uninhibited genius for satirical pantomime. Sidetracked into legitimate theater, Barton nevertheless remains on of the great pioneers who brought a new and shamelessly vital blend of vernacular dance to the notice of Broadway critics and thence to the rest of the country.[33]

T.O.B.A.

Because of segregation, African-American entertainers were severely limited in the number of venues in which they could perform. As a result, a man named Sherman Dudley in the second decade of the 20th century leased and bought theatres which featured black performers exclusively. In addition, he formed a partnership with various white and black theatre owners throughout the South to book these acts on what was called the "Toby" circuit, which was a corruption of T.O.B.A. or the Theatre Owners Booking Association. Because of the humiliations and problems that these performers regularly suffered, T.O.B.A. was more commonly known as "Tough on Black Actors." Although most of the artists on the T.O.B.A. circuit performed after the cutoff date of this book, it is worthwhile to mention a few.

As in white vaudeville, all styles of tap dancing talent abounded on the Toby circuit. "Rubberneck" Holmes did eccentric tap, better known as rubber legs. Ollie Burgoyne and Usher Watts did wonderful tap in an act they called "Duo Éclatant." The Brittons became famous for asking the audience after each step, "How's that?" Ulysses "Slow Kid" Thompson was the master of the slow-motion dance. Born in Prescott, Arizona, Thompson ran away from home at age 14 and started to work in the medicine shows touring Louisiana. He danced on a small platform in front of the tent to the accompaniment of clapping and patting. He moved into carnivals and eventually did an act for the Keith circuit which included his wife, the famous Florence Mills. His tap dancing and acrobatic skills were said to be spectacular.

Florence Mills was born January 25, 1895, in Washington, D.C. Her first appearance was at the Bijou Theatre at age four and she eventually went on to become one of the most popular stars on Broadway in shows such as *A Trip to Coontown* and *Shuffle Along*. Mills also held the distinction of being the first black woman to headline at Keith's Palace.

Born in Orange, New Jersey, on December 12, in the late 1890s, Eddie Rector's first professional job was at age 15 as a "pick" in Mayme Remington's act. (Picks, or pickaninnies, were black children hired by a female headliner to assure a successful show and a big finale.) He teamed with Toots Davis and toured in T.O.B.A.; later he toured with his wife, Grace, and after that with Ralph Cooper. He eventually replaced Bill Robinson in the international tour of *Blackbirds*. When he returned to the U.S., he danced at the Cotton Club with Duke Ellington. It was here that he developed his famous act of tapping on a big drum.

Eddie Rector was well known for his elegance and grace, setting the style and standard for what came to be known as the class act. He also moved around the entire stage instead of staying stationary and concentrating on footwork. As a result, Rector's style was influential in the development of American tap dancing.

In 1913, Eddie Rector appeared with his former vaudeville partner, Toots Davis,[34] in the groundbreaking black musical the *Darktown Follies*.[35] He died in 1962.

Flash Acts

Because of the enormous popularity of the cakewalk at the turn of the century, circuses and carnivals often hired African-Americans to do the dance during shows. These black entertainers were thrown together with trained circus performers and as a result, began to learn acrobatics and tumbling. Dancers added somersaults, flips, splits and other acrobatic elements to the popular cakewalk in a desire to top other acts, and a new type of tap dancing developed, called the flash act. It quickly became a popular staple of the vaudeville stage.

Increasing rivalry and competition quickly compelled dancers to try more and more intricate, dangerous, and taxing routines. Some of these acts also incorporated singing although generally the dancers were too out of breath to do much of that. Most flash acts included clowning and were reminiscent of the old Eph and Dinah skits that had been popular in tent shows.

One of the first famous flash acts was a group called the "Crackerjacks." It had grown out of another act called the "Watermelon Trust" and originally comprised of four dancers: the acrobatic dancer, Sherman Coates, his wife, Lulu, and a comedy dancer called Grundy and his wife. When the act broke up in 1913, Lulu Coates formed another act with three young male dancers, and later, when Coates retired, two of those young men joined up with two others and continued to bill themselves as the "Crackerjacks." The size and makeup of the group varied but the troupe stayed under the same name until 1952. This group which utilized comedy, singing, acrobatics and lots of tap dancing, set the standard for many flash acts that followed such as the Three Little Words, the Berry Brothers, the Step Brothers and the amazing Nicholas Brothers.

The Whitman Sisters

The Whitman Sisters, who were considered the royalty of African-American vaudeville, earned the distinction of being the highest paid performers on the T.O.B.A. circuit. From 1900 to 1943, their show consistently featured the finest dancers; it was probably the most important avenue for developing African-American dance talent. Many hundreds of black dancers got their first break while dancing with the Whitman Sisters.

Daughters of a Methodist minister, the four sisters who comprised the act were

Mabel ("May"), Essie, Alberta ("Bert") and Alice, who joined the troupe in 1909 when the girls' mother passed away. Their father had taught them to do the double shuffle when they were young and the girls frequently entertained at church socials and benefits.[36]

The Whitman Sisters were black with light skin and blonde hair, so when producer Arthur Hammerstein hired them to perform in his theatre, he made them wear blackface and wigs. At the finale, they took off the wigs; when their blonde hair fell free, the audience was puzzled but quickly began laughing with amazement. May managed the troupe and soon retired from performing to arrange bookings and take care of the business side of things. Essie designed and made the costumes, and did comedy and sang. Alberta did an enormously successful male impersonation which included flash dancing, and the youngest sister, Alice, was billed as the "Queen of Taps." She was described by dancer Jeni Le Gon as such.

> She was the best there was. She was tops. She was better than Ann Miller and Eleanor Powell and me and anybody else you wanted to put her to! I mean she did it all.[37]

Once, when about to do their act at the Regal Theatre in Chicago, the management decided to pay them less than the agreed-upon amount. The Whitman Sisters went across the street to the Metropolitan Theatre, which didn't even have a stage, had a stage built, and opened their act there, ruining the Regal's business for two weeks.

Many black and white female headliners in vaudeville used pickaninnies in their acts. (Even though the term pickaninny now has negative connotations, the word probably came from the Portuguese word for "little one," *pequeno*.) Every star from Sophie Tucker to Blossom Seeley carried juvenile pickaninny troupes with them. Most of the greatest tap dancers started out as picks. Being both black and children, these young dancers were often mistreated and taken advantage of. The one troupe that treated their picks fairly, if with a stern maternal hand, was the Whitman Sisters.

May trained the young dancers with a fair but iron fist. Her sister Essie recalled,

> "Get those feet up there," May would order during rehearsals. "What the hell do you think you're doing? Get those feet moving!"[38]

One youngster who started as a pick was Leonard Reed. He went on to have a very successful act of his own with partner Willie Bryant, and is credited with inventing the shim sham shimmy.[39]

Another pick who danced in the Whitman Sisters' show was Aaron Palmer who eventually married Alice Whitman. Their son Albert, or "Pops" as he was nicknamed, became a dancer and appeared in the family act at the age of four. He was one of the first dancers to include acrobatics in his tap dancing routine. Throughout his career, Aaron Palmer was teamed with many talented dancers.

The Whitmans were always discovering new talent, and in the 1920s one of their most popular acts featured a little person known as "Princess Wee Wee." Willie Bryant remembers dancing with her when he was 16. "She'd sing in a cute, high-pitched voice and then she'd dance around and between my legs."[40]

The Whitman Sisters' show continued until 1943.

King Rastus Brown

One man who was influential in the development of tap and who played the T.O.B.A. circuit was a dancer named King

Rastus Brown. Brown's dancing talents became known in the New York area around 1903 and although his early history is sketchy, there were reports that he won a buck dancing contest at Madison Square Garden in 1910. Some sources say he was born in Louisville, Kentucky; others say Boston. He was thin, about five foot nine inches tall, and he always danced wearing spats and a derby hat. He smoked cigars, and when he danced he always had a bottle of corn whisky or gin nearby. Dewey "Pigmeat" Markham recalled a time he saw Brown dance in Cincinnati.

> A saloon was located across the street from the theatre, and the King danced all over the stage, down the aisle, across the street, where they had a drink waiting for him, and then tapped back to the theater, up the aisle, and onto the stage, while the audience cheered.[41]

This tap dance legend was one of the many regulars at the Hoofers Club in Harlem.[42] When he walked in the room, such was the respect and adoration he commanded that all other dancers stopped to see what the "King" was about to do. Brown always turned to the piano player and requested what was known as "The Buck Dancer's Lament," a simple tune that could be played with one finger. King Rastus would start with his own version of the time-step and during the break in the music throw in some improvisation.[43]

King Rastus Brown was rarely seen by white audiences and so never enjoyed the same exposure and appreciation as Bill Robinson. He tapped with what was basically a buck dancing style. Dancing with his body bent forward, he interspersed the many stomps with intermittent clogging. He tapped up on his toes but his dancing style was more flat-footed than Bill Robinson's and he seldom bounced in the animated up-on-the-toes way that Robinson did.[44]

It was said that Brown could imitate anything and that he could dance for an hour straight while standing up, then continue to tap for another hour while seated, never repeating a single step. He was very versatile in other styles of tap and well-respected for his sand dances, cakewalks, and cane dances. He was also known to dance an excellent Irish jig. Dancer Willie Covan said, "He could do everything and keep it up forever."[45]

King Rastus Brown was considered the very best ever at the buck style of tap. He took the form to its very heights and was always coming up with new steps. Many credit him with creating the time-step which grew out of the standardization of some of the simpler elements of buck dancing.

17

English Music Hall

In England, the variety arts were developing in music halls at the same time vaudeville was developing in the United States. Music hall variety shows grew out of small presentations that were initially given in saloons, pubs, supper clubs, and other eateries to amuse the patrons while they ate and drank. The Theatre Regulation Act of 1843 banned the consumption of alcohol in legitimate theatres but allowed it in what was referred to as "music halls." In an attempt to take advantage of this new law and provide entertainment for their drinking customers, bar owners renovated their saloons and set up minimal stages to accommodate dancers, singers and comedians. As this new form of entertainment became increasingly popular, the music hall began to develop as a separate entity outside of the tavern. The first establishment to charge an extra fee for the entertainment alone was the New Canterbury in London, which was opened by Charles Morton in 1854 and is considered the birthplace of the pure English music hall.

Music halls were divided into two categories — small, intimate halls, closely connected to saloons, and large halls built specifically to present more extravagant entertainments. The latter were instrumental in the development of the spectacular which featured huge casts, opulent scenery, and eye-catching stage effects.

Most music halls had rather shallow stages, so singing rather that dancing was emphasized, although larger venues, such as the Alhambra Palace of Varieties in London, did introduce full "ballets" so male patrons could ogle the tight-clad legs of female dancers.[1]

Unlike American entertainments — which were divided into vaudeville and burlesque, with "clean" vaudeville catering to mixed male and female audiences and cruder "dirty" burlesque catering to the male clientele — English music halls were able to present naughty elements covertly in a way that eventually became a unique form of entertainment. Double entendre and innuendo became the hallmarks of English music hall.[2]

Music Hall Performers

Comedian Dan Leno (1860–1904), became one of the most celebrated entertainers and pantomime artists on the English music hall stage. He was born in London with the given name George Galvin, and started dancing for pennies at age four outside public houses. Shortly afterwards, he began appearing on the stage billed as "Little George, the Infant Wonder, Contortionist and Posturer." After his father died, his mother remarried a man named

English music hall performer. "Serio-comique song and dance artiste at 'the Middlesex.'" From *Harper's Magazine* (January 1891).

William Grant, a music hall performer who worked under the stage name Leno. Little George took his stepfather's stage name, calling himself Dan Leno. He began dancing with his brother and by the time he was nine years old, he was earning his own living. In 1883, at age 20, Leno entered a dance contest at the Princess's Music Hall in Leeds and won the gold and silver belt as the "Champion Clog-Dancer of the World."

Leno made his first appearance as a solo act in 1885 at Forester's Music Hall in London and was billed as "Irish comedian, vocalist, and pantomimist, the first and only champion dancer of the world — Dan Leno." He continued to feature clog dancing in his act for the next five years. When he appeared in London, though, his dancing was not appreciated by the cockney audiences who were not as familiar with the rural art of clogging, so eventually Leno dropped most of the dancing from his act:

> … he no longer danced, although he could casually take a stride of six feet or slap the sole of his shoe on the stage with a report like a pistol shot.[3]

In 1896, Leno toured with a clog dance troupe called "John W. Jackson's Eight Lancashire Lads." The troupe had a nine-year-old clog dancer named Charlie Chaplin, who was popular with audiences for a step he did called the "cellar flap." "John W. Jackson's Eight Lancashire Lads" retained its popularity well into the 1930s and eventually changed from performing clog to doing tap numbers.

Both Chaplin and Leno worked in a pantomime troupe called "Fred Karno's Speechless Comedians."[4] It was during this time that Leno's work and movement style had its greatest effect upon the young Chaplin, eventually influencing the creation of Chaplin's famous "Little Tramp" character. Stan Laurel, who understudied Chaplin, was also greatly influenced by Leno, borrowing from his stage act certain mannerisms which later became identified with him after he became a comic in early films.

From 1883 to 1903, Leno frequently appeared at the Drury Lane Theatre.[5] He became famous for his many outrageous and grotesque comic portrayals and was especially beloved for his "dame" characters, such as Mother Goose. In 1901, Leno did a command performance for King Edward VII and was thereafter known as the "King's Jester." He remained one of the most well-loved performers ever to grace the English music hall stage. In 1903, Leno suffered a breakdown, and died insane in October of the next year. His death was viewed as a national tragedy in England

The dancer Little Tich was called the "World's Greatest Wonder." His real name was Harry Relph, but he took the stage name Little Tich as a comic reference to the Tichborne claimant trial, one of the hottest subjects of discussion in England in the 1860s. The trial involved a butcher's son, named Arthur Orton, who claimed that he was Roger Tichborne, heir to an English baronetcy and believed to have been lost at sea. After a long-drawn-out trial, the impersonation was uncovered, and Orton was sentenced to 14 years of penal servitude. Upon his release, he toured the music halls of England as a freak attraction, telling his story and recalling his life in prison. Harry Relph, hoping to capitalize on Orton's fame, took the name Little Tich, contrasting his four foot height to Orton's large size.[6] The word "tich" has since come to be a generic term for a small person.

Tich was born in 1868, the 16th son of

an innkeeper. He started his career whistling for pennies outside the music halls of London, then made his professional debut in 1884 performing in blackface. He went on to become world famous for his big boot dance, in which he wore shoes that were 28 inches long, over half his height. During his famous dance, he would spring into the air and balance on the tips of his toes, or sometimes lean forward at a 45 degree angle.[7] The ballet star Vaslav Nijinsky was a great admirer of Little Tich and once commented, "C'est un grand artiste." Little Tich made one film that featured his big boot dance, and Jacques Tati, the great French comedian, called it the "foundation for everything that has been realized in comedy on screen."[8]

Little Tich also traveled to the U.S. and performed for Tony Pastor in vaudeville for three seasons. His last performance was at the Alhambra Theatre in London in 1927. He died at his home the following year on February 10, 1928.

Other dancers gained celebrity status in English music halls. Mrs. E. Bawn, better known as "My Fancy," appeared at the London Pavilion in 1894 and the Oxford Music Hall in 1894 and was billed as the "Finest Sand Dancer in the World." Wilson, Keppel, and Betty had a well-known dance act on the music hall stage which featured an Egyptian sand dance. G.H. Elliot and Eugene Stratton appeared in blackface and did softshoe or "light dancing" in leather shoes.

Tommy Royal and Walter Munro both did top boot dancing, which was clog done in tall boots that had bells attached to them. Tom Leamore was a proponent of soft shoe and schottische clog. Jim Cosgrove did a pedestal dance while balancing on a two inch thick piece of slate. Cosgrove had trained with Dan Leno and came in second in the World Clog Dance Championship. Jim Parkinson did trick clog, nimbly dancing on a piece of glass without breaking it. Veronica Lyon at age seven trained with both Cosgrove and Parkinson and performed a waltz clog which she called Dutch dance. Her shoes were made to look like Dutch clogs. Other female clog dancers included Molly Chappell and Hylda Baker.

Another well-known female clog dancer was Lottie Collins (1866–1910). Collins began her career as a chorus girl and skip rope dancer. In 1891 at the Gaiety Theatre, she premiered a song she had picked up in the United States doing vaudeville for Tony Pastor. Collins had rewritten the simple song for her English audiences. Wearing a huge hat and a bright red dress she timidly sang the verse and then burst into a wild chorus. The song was "Ta-ra-ra-boom-de-ay" which became for many "the symbol of the new spirit of freedom that emerged in the 1890s."[9] Collins' version of the song included an energetic dance in which she whirled her skirts, giving the audience a glimpse of her stockings.

Skirt Dancing

As Victorian morals began to relax and it became more acceptable for females to show their legs, solo performers looked for new ways to satisfy the male audience's demand for a titillating peek at feminine flesh. On the music hall stage and later in American vaudeville, this took the form of the skirt dance, also called the leg dance or the fancy dance.[10] The movements of a typical skirt dancer consisted of a hodgepodge of swirling turns, simple ballet steps, clog dancing, and minimal gymnastic tricks. Although the main purpose of the dance was to show a glimpse of the leg to the primarily male audience members, the art form did develop into something more.[11] In his book *A History of Dancing*, Thomas Reginald St. Johnson wrote,

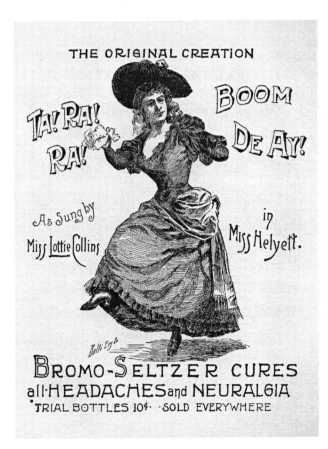

Lottie Collins performing her famous song and dance "Ta-Ra-Ra Boom-De-Ay!" Notice the music hall tradition of advertising medicine on sheet music. Sheet music cover of a song credited to Henry J. Sayers (1891). *Courtesy of the Keith O. Snell collection.*

And this skirt-dancing, what is it?

A vision of laughing eyes and twinkling feet, a swift rushing of floating draperies through the air, a twirl, a whirl, now here, now there, yet all with a certainty and a precision whose very apparent absence declares its art; then, as the music slows down, a delicate fluttering, like a butterfly hovering among the flowers, and lastly, as a soft falling snow-flake, silently she sinks to the ground. Is not this something worth living for, to be able to dance it, to be able to see it?[12]

Dainty Katie Seymour from London was supposedly the first skirt dancer, but the dance was popularized by Kate Vaughan in English music halls. Other well-known skirt dancers included Mabel Love, Alice Lethbridge, Sylvia Grey, Florence Levy and Topsy Sinden. According to Thomas Reginald St. Johnson, Sinden's version included "occasional bursts of step-dancing, almost

Three skirt dancers who were popular on the English music hall stage: Kate Vaughn (*left*), Mabel Love (*top right*) and Topsy Sinden (*above*). From *A History of Dancing: From the Earliest Ages to Our Own Times* by Gaston Vuillier, photographs by the London Stereoscopic Company (1898).

of clog-dancing, and at times a slight suggestion of high-kicking, both of which are fatal to the artistic effect."[13]

The skirt dance was also a popular staple of the American vaudeville stage. It was supposedly introduced to American audiences by the London Gaiety Girls who did a number in accordion-pleated skirts while touring the U.S. in the late 1800s.

Modern dance pioneers Loie Fuller and Ruth St. Denis both began their careers as skirt dancers in vaudeville. Fuller took the art of skirt dancing to unusual heights. She experimented with colors and effects in stage lighting as they played against the voluminous folds of her costumes. Known as the "magician in light," Fuller considered herself more of a scientist than a dancer.[14] Her experiments with

lighting effects and luminescence led not only to many lasting innovations in the art of stage lighting, but also to important changes in costuming and cinematic techniques.

Ruth St. Denis saw Fuller perform between 1900 and 1902 and then created her own style of skirt dancing. St. Denis eventually transitioned into other forms of modern dance as her interest in Oriental and Indian dances grew. She believed that behind each physical gesture lay an emotional or spiritual motivation, and this belief led her to become one of the leading exponents of a spiritual approach to dancing. The charismatic St. Denis was instrumental in the growth of the modern dance movement, and is sometimes called the "Mother of Modern Dance.[15]

18

Women on the Stage

As early as 1847, scantily dressed women appeared on the New York stage, posing in classical tableaux as living statues. Huge audiences flocked to see the women who represented such subjects as "Venus Rising from the Sea," or "Psyche Going to the Bath." Theatres advertised themselves as art centers, portraying the beauty of the classics, but the male patrons went to catch a glimpse of feminine flesh, and the theatres were frequently raided and closed down by the police.

> From the 1840's on, women's bodies remained standard features of show business. But before the Civil War, women in revealing union-suit-like tights were on display only in disreputable variety halls and saloons or as alluring but minor decorations in semi-respectable theaters.[1]

In the 1850s, one woman in particular attracted international attention with her risqué flaunting of traditional Victorian standards. Adah Isaacs Menken (1835–1868), sometimes called the "Mother of the Girlie Show," was a captivating, controversial figure in her day. She spoke six languages, was a poet and literary critic, friends with Mark Twain, Bret Harte, Walt Whitman, Charles Dickens, George Sand, and Henry Wadsworth Longfellow, and the mistress of two famous authors, A.C. Swinburne and Alexandre Dumas.[2]

Menken was born in Louisiana to a Creole mother and a black father.[3] Orphaned at 13, she began dancing in the New Orleans French Opera House. She acted in minor roles in various productions around the country until 1861, when she was offered the lead role in a stage adaptation of Lord Byron's poem "Mazeppa," a part previously played only by men. In the climax of the play, the script called for the lead character to be stripped and tied to the back of a horse. Traditionally, a stuffed dummy was used, but Menken insisted on performing the stunt herself. When the production first opened in New York, audiences saw Menken stripped down to a small shift, which resembled a leotard and trunks, and then tied to the back of a live horse which proceeded to gallop up a ramp at the back of the stage as it exited. Audience members were not only astonished that a woman could perform such a dangerous feat, but also scandalized that she would appear in such a skimpy outfit.

> She wore "baggy trunks ... enough for three bathing suits" and a wide sash covering her breasts, but her arms, shoulders, and legs appeared naked to the audience which had never seen "fleshings." Although modestly dressed by modern standards, she gained fame and notoriety as the Naked Lady.[4]

Top: Adah Isaacs Menken tied to the back of a horse as depicted on a theatrical poster for "Mazeppa." From *Specimens of Show Printing: Being Facsimiles of Poster Cuts* (circa 1870). *Left:* Adah Isaacs Menken. From *A History of the Theatre in America*, vol. 2, by Arthur Hornblow (1919).

fatally ill.[6] Hours before her death she wrote, "When all is said and done, have I not at my age tasted more of life that most women who live to be a hundred?"[7] Menken died on August 10, 1868, at the young age of 33. Eight days after her death her book of poetry, *Infelicia*, was published. Adah Isaacs Menken's daring theatrical accomplishments and bohemian lifestyle made her an international celebrity. Her success exploiting her sexuality led to many imitators and helped foster the general acceptance of women clad in tights on stage.

The Black Crook

Mazeppa toured successfully across the United States and then Europe.[5] Menken gave her last performance in London in May 1868. She went to Paris and tried to get a book of her poetry published, but fell

Women wearing tights on the stage were finally accepted by the general public with the advent of one particular show. In May 1866, a spectacle from Europe called *La Biche au Bois* was scheduled to go into the Academy of Music in New York City. Before the production was mounted, though, a fire broke out in the theatre and destroyed the interior of the building causing the cancellation of the production. In desperation, the theatrical managers who had imported the show sold the scenery and costumes, as well as the contracts of the dancers, to the proprietor of Niblo's Garden, William Wheatley. Wheatley utilized his purchase by fitting the various pieces into the framework of a poorly written, 5½ hour melodrama called *The Black Crook*. The show created a sensation and made theatrical history, not because of the great book or the brilliant score, but rather because the chorus girls on stage appeared in tights.[8]

When *The Black Crook* opened at Niblo's Garden on September 12, 1866, the beefy chorines who appeared on stage in flesh-colored tights actually had nothing to do with the plot of the musical, but persistent rumors that they were appearing almost in the nude fueled publicity and created a public outcry that insured a flurry of ticket sales.[9] One New York critic wrote, "Nothing fires the masculine bosom like the anticipation of a ravishing prospect of calf."[10]

Men flocked to the theatre and even curious women attended the

Playbill for the "Black Crook." Presented at Niblo's Garden Theatre in New York (March 5, 1879). *Courtesy of the Library of Congress, Rare Book and Special Collections Division.*

Niblo's Garden

THEATRE.

EDWARD F. STARIN.............................PROPRIETOR AND MANAGER
Wm. A. Mulford, Jr....Business Manager | John Hammond Assistant Stage Manager
Prof. Charles Puerner..Leader of Orchestra | Clifford G. Reeve............Treasurer

Commencing Wednesday, March 5, '79
EVERY EVENING AT 8 P. M.
GRAND FAMILY MATINEES WEDNESDAY AND SATURDAY AT 2 P. M.
UPON A SCALE OF UNEXCELLED MAGNIFICENCE,

KIRALFY BROS.
Grand Spectacular Production of the

BLACK CROOK

With entirely new and gorgeous scenery, painted by ED. SIMMONS, WM. WOEFFLIN, HARLEY MERRY, H. TRYON, THOMPSON and others. Brilliant Armers and Jewels, by GRANGER, of Paris, and KENNEDY, of London. Beautiful Costumes by MISS FISHER, of London, and LORRAINE, of New York. Marvelous Mechanical Effects, by JOHN LEO. Accessories by CHAS. HALLE, of Paris.

GRAND BALLETS
Led by the GREATEST STAR PREMIERS DANSEUSES OF THE WORLD,
WITH THE FOLLOWING CAREFULLY SELECTED CAST:

MORTALS.
Rudolph, a poor artist..............................Mr. Wm. A. Sands
Count Wolfenstein.................................Mr. Harry S. Duffield
Hertzog, surnamed the Black Crook..............Mr. J. F. Peters
Greppo, his servant...............................Mr. John Ward
Von Puffengrants, the Count's steward............Mr. Wm. H. Collings
Bruno, a ruffian.................................Mr. Chas. Livingstone
Wolfgar, a ruffian...............................Mr. John Hammond
Caspar, a peasant................................Mr. Peter Toole
Armena, betrothed to Rudolph.....................Miss Annie W. Tiffany
Carlina, Armena's maid...........................Miss Marion Fiske
Dame Barbara, Armena's foster mother.............Mrs. Harry Jourdan
Rosetta, a peasant...............................Miss Lillie Pearson
Ladies, Lords, Villagers, Peasants and Pages

IMMORTALS.
Stalacta, Queen of the Golden Realms..............Miss Belle Howitt
Dragonfin, her faithful sprite...................Mr. August Seagrist
Zamiel, the arch fiend...........................Mr. Chas. Mason
Skuidawelp, familiar to Hertzog..................Mr. S. C. Clifford
Fairies, Water Sprites, Demons, Skeletons and Spectres.

STAGE ARCHITECTURE.......................by.....................JOHN LEO
ILLUMINATIONS............................by.................EMMET DAVIDSON
PROPERTIES..............................by.....................M. BOUGARD
CALCIUM EFFECTS.........................by..........N. Y. CALCIUM LIGHT CO.

SYNOPSIS OF SCENES AND INCIDENTS.
ACT I.—Scene 1. **VILLAGE.—View of Castle Wolfenstein**, by Merry. Village Festive Dance and Chorus by Coryphees of the Ballet Scene 2.—A WOODY PASS, HARTZ MOUNTAINS, by Merry. Scene 3.—A Hall in Castle Wolfenstein, by Thompson. WALTZ SONG, by CARLINA. **Scene 4.—Laboratory of the Crook**, designed by Sig. Ferario, of Milan, painted by Merry. Scene 5.—Wild Cross Path in a Glen of the Brocken, designed by J. Kiralfy, painted by Merry. Beautiful Cascade of Real Water. The Demon Fight. The Walking Skeleton. The Incantations. Grand Tableaux Infernale.
ACT II.—Scene 1.—Subterranean Vaults, from model of Ferario, painted by Ed. Simmons. View of the Count and Armena. Scene 2.—Gothic Chamber, by Simmons. **The Grotto of Stalacta**, by Voegtlin. Song by Stalacta.

GRAND BALLET DES DEMONS
Composed and arranged by Mons. Kiralfy. New Music by JACQUES OFFENBACH.
1. Entree Diabolataire, by Ladies of the Ballet. 2. Entree Diabolataire, by Coryphees. 3. Les Salamanders, by Danseuse Secondas. 4. GRAND ENTHEMS BY THE PREMIERE DANSKUSES ASSOLUTAS. 5. Grand Adagio. 6. Entermede Brillante, by Coryphees. 7. VARIATIONS D'ART, by the PREMIERS. 8. Finale Ensemble Infernale, by the Entire Corps de Ballet.
ACT III.—THE PALACE OF LACE, designed and modeled by Mons. Fromont, of Paris, painted by Simmons. Tableaux of Armena's Bridal Festival. The Leotard Brothers, in their marvelous acrobatic act. The 3 Lorellas, the eccentric dancers of the age. The Miranda Sisters, beautiful aerial feats.

——KIRALFY'S CELEBRATED GRAND BALLET OF ALL NATIONS.——
1. Entree, Tartars, Italic and Austria, Corps De Ballet. 2. La Flora, D'Espagne, by Danseuse Secondas. 3. Ensemble et Hongroise, by Coryphees. 4. L'ITALIE, by Mlle PAGALERI. 5. Dance De Normandie, by Ladies of the Ballet. 6. South American Dance, by Corps De Ballet. 7. L'AMERIQUE, by Mlle De ROSA. 8. Great Britain, by Danseuse Secondas. 9. Grand Finale, China, Japan and all Nations by the Entire Ballet Corps.
Scene 2.—A Hall in the Castle, **The Ulm Sisters**, in their charming Trois. LES FRERES LANGLOIS, Marvels of the 19th Century. Duet by Carlina and Greppo. Scene 3.—Grand Staircase of the Illuminated Terrace, designed from Models of Imra Kiralfy, painted by Merry.

Grand Maneuvre D'Amazon, by 120 Ladies of the Ballet,
Led by STALACTA, Queen of the Fairies.

The Combat! Thrilling Tableaux!
ACT IV.—Scene 1.—Gothic Hall, by Thompson. Scene 2.—Rocky Pass, by Merry. Scene 3.—Burning Forest, by Merry. Scene 4.—Wood, by Merry. Scene 5.—Pandemonium, by Merry. Scene 6.—Rocky Pass, by Merry.
Scene 7.—Grand Transformation Scene, Representing

THE ENCHANTED HOME OF THE FAIRIES!
Models of ROBECHI of GRAND OPERA HOUSE, Paris, painted by H. Tryon.

OPERA GLASSES AND BOUQUETS TO BE HAD IN THE LOBBY.
Curtain Rises at 8 P. M., Doors open at 7 P. M. Seats Secured Two weeks in advance.

——POPULAR PRICES——
The above Spectacle Produced   at a Cost of $75,000.

The Patrons of this Theatre are Particularly Requested Not to Purchase their Tickets from SPECULATORS.

Metropolitan Job Print, 26 Ann Street, N. Y.

show wearing long veils to conceal their true identities. *The Black Crook* was an instant success and ran for 16 straight months in New York, making almost a million dollars. Two years later, another production of it opened in the city. There were also mountings of it in 1871, 1873, 1879, 1881, 1884, 1889, and 1903. The musical also toured continuously for several years until 1929. It became the prototype for future musical theatre extravaganzas and set the stage for American music hall, vaudeville and burlesque. It also spawned several other shows which directly mimicked it,

including *The White Crook, The Red Crook, The Golden Crook,* and *The Black Crook, Jr.* Many famous dancers appeared in various productions of the show including one young dancer named Agnes de Mille in 1929.

The main dancing in *The Black Crook* was ballet, but productions frequently featured clog, minstrel dances, and other novelties. Loüret de Ducale did a pedestal clog dance in the first production. During the run of the show, new specialty acts were regularly inserted to keep the audience's interest. Military drills were added to the first version, as was a "baby ballet," a production number with 150 children. Another version created a sensation by presenting the first roller-skater ever seen on the American stage.

The original production of *The Black Crook* starred an Italian ballet dancer by the name of Marie Bonfanti, a student of the great Italian dancing master, Carlo Blasis. Although it was said she didn't excel at jumps and beats, she was reputed to be exquisitely graceful. After leaving the show she taught dance in New York. Isadora Duncan and Ruth St. Denis both studied with her.[11]

A group of "Black Crook" chorus girls surrounding Marie Bonfanti. Sheet music cover for "Black Crook Waltzes" (1867).

Other "Tights Shows"

In 1868, hoping to take advantage of the scandal created by *The*

Lydia Thompson. From *A History of the Theatre in America*, vol. 1, by Arthur Hornblow (1919).

Black Crook, P. T. Barnum created a show called *Ixion* with English actress, Lydia Thompson.[12] Thompson (1838–1908) had started at age 14 as a child pantomime star in England, and three years later in 1855 she toured Europe creating a huge sensation, especially in Germany and Russia, where she wowed audiences with her flings and hornpipes.[13] When Thompson came to America, Barnum billed her and the chorus girls as "Lydia Thompson and her Imported English Blondes." The show was so successful that Thompson spent the next twenty years entertaining American audiences with glimpses of her legs.

When *Ixion* opened in New York on September 28, 1868, it was a smash hit. The show's finale included a bevy of beautiful chorus girls standing across the stage, punctuating the last song with high cancan kicks, a tradition that later became popular with such groups as the Rockettes.[14]

In a letter to the *New York Times* in the late 1860s, a woman named Olive Logan wrote that Miss Thompson and her Blondes were "brazen-faced, clog-dancing creatures with dyed yellow hair and padded limbs" who had made the American stage no place for an "honorable self-respecting" woman.[15] Critics and audiences alike attacked the production, calling the chorus girls immoral. The New York critic E. F. House accused the show of "driving legitimate drama off the stage."[16] When the show played Chicago, the editor of the *Chicago Times*, Wilbur S. Story, lambasted the performance and hinted that the girls were immoral offstage. Incensed by the editor's comments, Lydia Thompson waited for Story outside his office and "literally horse-whipped him for impugning her honor."[17] Story took Thompson to court where the judge fined the performer $100, "a cheap price for the national publicity that she and the troupe received from the incident."[18]

The "Blondes" toured the United States in various shows for at least 20 years, making Lydia Thompson a national celebrity. Because of her earlier tours, she was also immensely popular in Russia and Eastern Europe. In the Baltic, it was said that her picture was "given equal prominence with the Czar's — one on either side of the stove, in every house in Riga."[19] A member of the Russian dragoons, hoping to prove his love for the actress, placed some flowers and one of Thompson's gloves on his chest and shot himself through the heart.

Cashing in on the success of this popular new form of entertainment, producer Mike Leavitt created another "tights show." His was based on the minstrel format and was called "Madame Rentz's Female Minstrels."

Female minstrels. From *Specimens of Show Printing: Being Facsimiles of Poster Cuts* (circa 1870).

The troupe proved so popular that within a year there were at least eleven female minstrel companies, one of which directly acknowledged its debt to Lydia Thompson by wearing blonde wigs.[20]

Led by Mabel Santley, America's first native-born burlesque star, the show became the model for future American burlesque entertainments.[21]

The rising popularity of "tights shows" and the use of large choruses of untrained dancers who were put on the stage merely to show their legs, caused the technical side of dancing, including early forms of tap, to deteriorate. Eventually economic factors led to the reduction of the size of the chorus, which in turn reversed the trend and began raising the level of technical skill. As technical expertise improved, Broadway revues began to utilize lines of chorus girls that frequently featured synchronized tapping.

Revues

As early as the late 1860s, the Gaiety Girls in England, who were legendary for their beauty, perpetuated the appreciation of the feminine form on the legitimate stage by appearing in the sophisticated revue show. These chorus girls were not classically trained in dance but were required only to move well and wear expensive costumes with poise. Similar American groups included the Floradora Girls in 1900 and the Yama-yama Girls in 1905.

Precision chorus line dancing reached its height around 1910 in England, when a wealthy manufacturer named John Tiller had his Tiller Girls performing in the music halls of London. Tiller opened a dance school and developed a "Tiller system" of intensive training for his precision troupes.[22] Several of these troupes were imported to the U.S. by well-known producers such as Oscar Hammerstein I, George White, and Florenz Ziegfeld. Although the dancers did many styles of dancing, their specialty was tap with lots of high kicks. Tiller's companies were admired for the exactitude and precise uniformity of their dancing.

From 1907 to 1931, the beautiful girls of the *Ziegfeld Follies* set the standard for the American revue. The shows were the brain-child of impresario Florenz Ziegfeld (1869–1932).[23]

> [Ziegfeld's] early revues were overtly erotic, but thereafter they emphasized elegance, and moments of nudity were brief, meeting the American demand for implied rather than revealed sensuality. Ziegfeld had a genuine pride in his unspoken equation between wealth, elegance and sex. His aim was to "Glorify the American girl," and to this end he treated his theatres like colleges of femininity, demanding that his charges should be equally lady-like offstage as on, and insisting that the conspicuous glamour which his audiences flocked to worship should be authentic: his stars wore real silk, while for a stage "banquet" gourmet food was provided, along with gold utensils and sumptuous napery.[24]

When the Great Depression came, Florenz Ziegfeld refused to accept any restrictions on his production budgets and continued to lavish money on his shows which American audiences were finding increasingly irrelevant. He died in 1932, leaving his wife, Billie Burke, with a million-dollar debt.

Ziegfeld's influence on tap was threefold. First, he featured tap in his shows; the first *Ziegfeld Follies* actually had 50 tap-dancing girls. Second, he produced many shows which starred some of the top dancers to ever grace the stage, including Fred and Adele Astaire (*Smiles*), James Barton (*No Foolin'*, also called the *Ziegfeld*

American Revue of 1926), Ford Lee Washington and John S. Sublett, better known as Buck and Bubbles[25] (*1931 Follies*), Ann Pennington[26] (*1913–16, 1918, 1923, 1924 Follies* and *Miss 1917*) and Bert Williams (*1910–19 Follies*). Finally, Ziegfeld utilized the talents of dance directors and choreographers who trained tap dancers and regularly featured tap in their routines, thus refining the art and spreading the popularity of tap in general.

Ned Wayburn

The most successful dance director was Ned Wayburn, born Edward Claudius Weyburn, with an "e," on March 30, 1874, in Pittsburgh, Pennsylvania. As a dance director and choreographer, he staged more than 200 vaudeville acts, as well as 300 musical spectacles for such producers as Oscar and William Hammerstein, the Shubert Brothers, Lew Fields, and Florenz Ziegfeld. His New York school of dance, which promised "Health, Beauty, Fame, Popu-larity, Independence," trained many of the top performers including Fred and Adele Astaire.[27] It was Ned Wayburn who supposedly convinced Fred Astaire to give up ballet and become a tap dancer. Astaire's later style was based on the training he had first gotten under Wayburn's tutelage.

> On one occasion Wayburn brushed aside several assistants and personally demonstrated some steps to young Astaire, who was impressed because Wayburn looked more like a preacher than a dancer.[28]

Wayburn also influenced many other entertainers. Richard Kislan, in his book *Hoofing on Broadway*, wrote:

> Ned Wayburn allegedly guided and inspired Eddie Cantor, Al Jolsen, W. C.

Ned Wayburn's Minstrel Misses in blackface. Insert from the sheet music cover for "My Dixie Land Daisy" by Max Hoffmann (circa 1903). *Courtesy of Brown University Library.*

Fields, Marilyn Miller, Marion Davies, Ann Pennington, Will Rogers, Vivienne Segal, and no fewer that 122 other stars.[29]

Like John Tiller, Wayburn's style stressed precision and exact execution. When he devised a special stylized walk for the Ziegfeld girls so they could negotiate the many staircases used in the staging of the *Follies,* he created what became known as the "Ziegfeld Walk" which was used in all of the other Follies shows and is still used by showgirls today.[30] Wayburn's use of geometric patterns best seen from overhead was also instrumental in the development of later movie musical dance sequences

Although the majority of Ned Wayburn's work happened after the dates covered in this book, the words he used to describe the dances in one particular show became the deciding factor for the cutoff date itself. In the winter of 1902–03, Wayburn created a show called "Ned Wayburn's Minstrel Misses." The act consisted of:

... a chorus of sixteen women [who] marched onstage wearing "the long coats of fantastic design and collar and high hats of a Minstrel parade." Then, "in full view of the audience," the dancers made themselves up in blackface at tables set at the rear of the stage. The sequence took ninety seconds to perform, but made the reputation of the act, which ran for eleven months on tour.[31]

"Ned Wayburn's Minstrel Misses" combined African-American inspired minstrel movements with feminine gestures. They wore light clogs with split wooden soles.

To describe this new hybrid form, Wayburn coined the phrase "Tap and step dancing." This was the first time that the term "Tap dancing" had been publicly and professionally used.[32]

So, with Ned Wayburn's chorus line of 16 girls, percussive show dancing was officially dubbed "tap dancing."

PART III

OTHER INFLUENCES

19

Indian, Gypsy, and Spanish Influences

Indian Dance

Indian dance is one of the oldest known dance traditions in the civilized world; there are references to dancing before 1500 B.C. in the sacred Hindu writings. Although it took many forms, Indian dance arose within the context of religious ritual and "the Indian dancer [used] the body to suggest an abstract, universal form."[1] The nuance of each gesture and the statuelike poses were carefully orchestrated to create movement which evoked a sense of the sacred in the audience.

The Indian dancer's preoccupation is not so much with space as with time, and the dancer is constantly trying to achieve the perfect pose which will convey a sense of timelessness.[2]

Dancing was especially important within Indian culture because it was thought to be the main activity of Shiva, one of the most powerful Hindu deities and the central god in the Indian trinity. Known as the Lord of the Dance, Shiva created heaven and earth when he did his Dance of Creation. Explaining the significance of Shiva's dance, Projesh Banerji wrote:

The essential significance of Shiva's dance is threefold: First, it is the image of his rhythmic play as the source of all movement within the cosmos; … secondly, the purpose of His dance is to release the countless souls of men from the snare of illusion; thirdly, the place of the dance … the centre of the Universe, is within the heart.[3]

Indian dance is made up of three components: the dramatic quality, called *natya*, the expressive quality, or *nritya*, and the rhythmic quality, called *nritta*. A particular type of classical dance from northern India that is almost totally based upon the rhythmic elements of *nrittya* is a dance called kathak, the most relevant in terms of the development of tap.

Kathak is derived from the word *kathakar*, which means traditional storyteller. The word refers to wandering holy men who imparted moral instruction and religious teachings through their singing and dancing. These minstrel bards gathered students as they wandered, and eventually these pupils in turn became teachers of the story dances. In this way, essential qualities of Hindu dance were preserved and passed down from generation to generation. Many of the gestures of the kathak were initially based upon the movements of martial arts, and the training of dancers originally grew out of military exercises. Dancers were often drawn from the military caste. Kathak eventually developed into a sacred dance performed only by Brahmin priests.

When India was invaded by the Muslims around the tenth century, sacred Indian dance made its way into the courts of the Muslim rulers, who were looking for new forms of entertainment. The interaction of the two religions, Hinduism and Islam, impacted the style of ancient Indian dance. Hindu dance was originally done with wide turn out in deep plié, with the hips and head cocked to the side. With the influence of the Muslims, came a more erect stance and an increased importance of rhythm and intricate patterns. The Muslims also brought the influence of the Sufi dervishes, and turns were incorporated into the dance. Kathak was unique in that it completely combined Hindu and Muslim elements. As these elements mixed, the religious aspects of kathak became secularized and the style of the dance came to include many rhythmic variations, dazzling footwork, and numerous turns.[4]

Kathak performances included a series of dances; the concluding dance usually consisted of rhythms tapped out in a display of elaborate footwork. The hands remained still so that the emphasis remained on the feet as the dancer started slowly and then accelerated the tempo. Intricate counterrhythms were used in a call-and-response interplay with the accompanying drummer.

The emphasis in kathak was on demonstrating the technical aspects of timing, or as it was called in Indian dance, *tal*. The dancer executed quicker and more difficult gestures as they kept pace with a particular beat, dividing and subdividing that beat into more and more exacting fractional parts.[5] Dancers displayed unbelievable feats of technical and foot gymnastics. One example of this virtuosity was the ability of dancers wearing bells on their ankles to move their feet with such control that they were able to ring a single bell at a time. The training required for such mastery was comprehensive; dancers usually studied at least 25 years mastering the art of kathak dancing.

With the increase of temple building, in the ninth and tenth centuries, a special class of female dancers emerged who dedicated their lives to Shiva. Called devadassi, derived from two words, *deva* meaning god and *dassi*, meaning slave, a devadassi was literally "a slave of the god." These highly educated women performed devotional dances and acted out in movement texts from the ancient Sanskrit scriptures.

Photograph of Indian Nautch dancers and musicians. From the book *Dancing* by Lilly Grove (1901).

During the decline of the Moghul Empire and the rise of European powers, kathak dancing degenerated and became more secularized giving birth to an offshoot called nautch. Professional female dancers performed nautch dances for the sole purpose of entertainment; thus it was far removed from its ancient spiritual context. With the rising numbers of British Christian missionaries in India, by the end of the 19th century, nautch dancers, called bayadères by the Europeans, were no longer considered respectable and were thought by many to be associated with prostitution.

Nautch dancers. "Dance of Bayadères." An Engraving by Poisson for *A History of Dancing: From the Earliest Ages to Our Own Times* by Gaston Vuillier (1898).

> It was beyond the conception of the Victorian Christian to imagine that faith could be expressed through so immodest and voluptuous a medium as the "nautch dance."[6]

Although it was removed from its religious context, nautch dancing, like kathak, retained many amazing feats of technical prowess and expertise. One dance was executed by first spreading colored sand upon the floor. A nautch dancer then danced on top of the grains to create an intricate design by gradually tapping the sand into place. Sometimes the design was already created on the floor and she danced over the sand without disturbing the pattern. A third variation involved the dancer changing an existing pattern by gently tapping her toes. At one time, the nautch dancing utilized a type of Morse code, and the dancer could communicate encoded messages by tapping out rhythms with her feet.

One type of nautch dance involved the use of eggs and was described by Louis Rousselet who saw it in Bhopal.

After a dance of young men, cathaks, a dancing-girl made her appearance. She was dressed in the costume of women of the people, a bodice and a very short sarri, and bore on her head a large wheel of osiers, placed horizontally on top of her skull. Round the wheel hung strings at equal distances, each terminating in a running knot, kept open by means of a glass bead. The dancer advanced to the spectators, carrying a basket of eggs, which she handed to us that we might satisfy ourselves that they were real.

The musicians struck up a monotonous staccato measure, and the dancer began to whirl round with great rapidity. Seizing an egg, she slipped it into one of the running knots, and, with a sudden jerk, threw it from her in such a manner as to draw the knot tight. By means of centrifugal force produced by the swiftness of her rotations, the string flew out, till the egg stood in a straight line with the corresponding ray of the circumference. One after the other, the eggs were all thrown out on the strings, until at last they formed a horizontal halo round the dancer's head. Hereupon her movements became more and more rapid; we could scarcely distinguish her features. It was a critical moment; the least false step, the slightest pause, and the eggs would have smashed one against the other. How then was she to interrupt her dance, how stop it? There was but one way: to take out the eggs as she had put them in. Though it hardly appears so, this last operation is the more difficult of the two. By a single moment of the utmost neatness and precision, the dancer must catch the egg and draw it to her; it will be readily understood that if she were to put her hand into the circle unskillfully, and touch one of the strings, the general harmony would be at once disturbed. At last all the eggs were safely extricated, the dancer stopped abruptly, and apparently not in the least giddy after her gyrations of some half-hour, she walked firmly towards us and presented the eggs, which were immediately broken into a dish to prove that there had been no deception.[7]

Nautch egg-dance. From *The Dance, Ancient, and Modern*, translated from the French by Arabella E. Moore (1900).

Kathak and nautch dancing from northern India played a significant role in the development of tap. The roots of tap dancing can be directly traced to the percussive footwork and rhythms that were brought to Europe by nomadic Gypsies who had been driven out of India and migrated to Spain, England and Ireland.

Gypsy Dance

There is an old Gypsy legend:

The Gypsies used to live all together at that time in one place, in one beautiful country. The name of that country was Sind (northern India). There was much happiness, much joy there ... but then there was a big war there. The Moslems caused the war. They made ashes and dust of the Gypsy country. All the Gypsies fled together from their own land. They began to wander as poor men in other countries.[8]

Northwest India was attacked at least four times by legendary conquerors: first by Alexander the Great, then by Sultan Mahmud of Gorh, next by Genghis Kahn, and finally by Tamerlane. The last three invasions resulted in the expulsion of huge numbers of Gypsies. The largest numbers left when the area was devastated by Genghis Khan. These refugees left India and traveled to Turkey, and then into Eastern European, finally moving into western Europe and the British Isles.

Commonly called by the name "Tarters," or "Egyptians," Gypsies were often treated with contempt.[9] They were viewed as social outcasts and were forced to live on the fringes of society, forbidden from participating in any national or community events or even from attending schools. In the 14th century, when plague killed over 25 million people, many Europeans feared that the Gypsies had brought the disease with them, and reacted to these wandering bands of people with anger and hatred.

Gypsies were also feared because they were well known for their thievery. The roots of this "thievery" lay within the Gypsy culture which did not focus on owning property. In fact, the Gypsy language did not have a word for the verb "to possess." Therefore, in order to survive, Gypsies were sometimes obligated to steal.

During the period of the Crusades, many Gypsies were accused of being Turkish spies. To justify their harsh persecution, rumors were started that the Gypsies were the ones who had originally cast the nails that were used to crucify Jesus Christ. During the Spanish Inquisition, they were punished as heretics.

Nomadic gypsies had no folk dances of their own but assimilated various dances from the countries in which they traveled. Their pattern was to impose broken and irregular cadences and rhythms upon a country's native dances and in this way, transform them. As Gypsies came from the northwest part of India, they traveled to Persia (Iran) and divided into three tribal

factions, the Gitanos, the Kalderash and the Manush.

Gypsies supposedly reached Paris on August 17, 1427, telling residents there they had come from Egypt where they were driven out because they were Christian. They told the Parisians that they had since visited the pope and received his blessing along with a penance. To atone for their sins, they

Top: A Gypsy woman performing a dance on a table. "A Gipsy dancing the Vito Sevillano" by Gustave Doré. From the book *Dancing* by Lilly Grove (1901). *Left:* A young Gypsy girl dancing. "Gipsy dance." From an engraving after Marie Weigmann for the book *Dancing* by Lilly Grove (1901).

were required to wander the world for seven years and never sleep in a bed.

Gypsies appeared in Great Britain around 1490. They split at this time, one band going to Ireland and the other to Scotland. They were welcomed at first and given alms, but as early as 1530 persecution began against them and by 1541, laws were passed against the Bohemians, as they were called in England. In 1596, 106 Gypsies were accused of being idle persons and condemned to death.

In 1665, Gypsies living in England were banished to the West Indies. Many simply escaped to Ireland. It is believed that Irish step dancing was influenced in some ways by the percussive kathak dance of India which was brought to Ireland by these Gypsies.[10] It is likely that Gypsies also influenced dance in the West Indies, as large numbers were sent there by the English.

Spanish Dance

Flamenco dance was not brought to Spain by the Gypsies, but rather developed by them, using influences brought from India and northern Africa, as well as Moorish elements that were already present in Spanish dance. Among the elements Gypsies added were arm and hand movements and footwork that were common in the kathak dance of the Punjab region of northern India and articulation of the fingers, which was related to Indian mudrás. Delicate use of hands, the curves in the torso, and rhythmic percussive footwork are the most obvious reflections of the Indian influence. The call-and-response between dancer and instrumentalist showed the influence of North African traditions and elements of belly dancing.[11]

When the Moors invaded Spain in 711, Muslim elements began to influence the dances of the region. Between 822 and 852 the arts flourished under the auspices of the Moorish king, Abd al-Rahmân II. The king's court musician Zyriab, also known as the "Black Nightingale," is said to have composed ten thousand songs during this time and to have invented a five-stringed instrument that later became the guitar. The eventual blending of this type of Moorish court music with Gypsy folk songs was an important element in the formation of flamenco style and rhythm. Moorish elements are also apparent in the wailing of the Flamenco singer, reminiscent of an Islamic muezzin's call to prayer. In fact, the use of the word *olé* can be traced to the Muslim word *Allah*.

Flamenco originated in the southern province of Andalusia in Spain. The word "flamenco" was derived from the word *fleme* which meant to "banish or drive away."[12] When Spain conquered the Netherlands in the 15th century, Spaniards began to refer to any foreigners as "Flemish." The word became an epithet for ill-bred, rowdy persons. Therefore the word "flamenco" referred to the wild foreigners, also known as the Gypsies, who performed the dance.

One important part of flamenco dancing was the inducement of a trance state, called *duende* in Spanish.[13] Unlike trance dancing in the African cultures, the performer did not fall to the floor, but instead symbolically fell into a freer state of consciousness in which attention was focused inwards. This usually occurred after 15 minutes of vigorous repetitive, rhythmical footwork. During *duende*, the dancers' lips trembled and sweat poured off their face.

Some Gypsies believe that a spiritual presence inhabits their dancing and that, at that moment, they are "in the flamenco." In his lecture in Cuba, Spanish poet Federico García Lorca called this moment the time when *los sonidos negros* ("the dark sounds") visit the performer's body. The distinction between this world and the next, between mortality and death, join in the body of the performer as he or she becomes totally absorbed by the rhythm (compás).[14]

In 1492, under the Catholic rule of Ferdinand and Isabella, Spain instituted the Spanish Inquisition; flamenco became an important artistic reaction to the severity of the regime. A dozen years before, the rulers of Spain, in 1480, in an effort to suppress rebellion and reunite the country, forced all Gypsies to move into designated areas called *gitanerías*. During this era, Spain was becoming an increasingly important world power, in military, political, and cultural terms. At the same time, dance moved into theatrical venues, and this played an important part in the development of Spanish dancing. One traditional dance, the jota, originally performed for its curative powers, was refined into a dramatic show dance which included flashy footwork. Other Spanish dances began to include heel work in addition to the driving rhythms of castanets.[15]

In the late 1880s, flamenco was generally limited to the Gitano barrios. Around this time, an African-American was brought to a Barcelona music hall where he danced the cakewalk. His dance became wildly and instantly popular among the Spanish people. In response, a young Gitano boy appeared in public and challenged the cakewalker by performing a flamenco dance. The Spanish audience shifted their adoration and applause to flamenco, and Gypsy dances found their way to the public stage.

Various rhythmic forms of flamenco exist. The most dramatic theatrical impact is found in the zapateado. Cervantes referred to it as "the shoe-sole beater." The fiery footwork of the zapateado is an expression of the passion and abandon of Spanish dancing.[16]

The zapateado influenced tap in two ways. First, Spanish dance was taken to the Americas when the Spanish conquered the New World. With the intermarriage of Native Americans and Spanish settlers, certain elements in Spanish dance were transferred to American culture and later

"The Bolero." Illustration by M. Valvérane. From *La Danse: Comment On Dansait, Comment On Danse* by Francis Casadesus and Jules Maugué (1899).

transferred through Native American dances into African-American culture. Intermarriage of Spanish conquerors with Native Americans was urged by Spain and there was even a program in which children of noble Spanish families were exchanged with those of Native American families. The exchange of dance forms traveled both ways. For example, the Spanish fandango, with its fast heel work and close to the floor feel, is traceable to a dance called the reinos de las Indias of the Native Americans.

Second, with the migration of Spanish Gypsies to the British Isles, both Irish jigs and English clogs were directly influenced by their dances. The intercultural sharing is obvious in such dances as the English morris, traceable to Spain.

20

German and Shaker Influences

German Influences

German peasants, like the Irish, suffered from a potato famine in the 1840s. At the same time, the country's intelligentsia and university students called for the overthrow of the monarchy. The German government used repressive measures to stem the political upheaval and after the German Wars of 1847, a steady stream of German immigrants began heading to America. These immigrants brought with them the music, rhythms and dances of their native culture, including the Bavarian schühplattler, the schottische, the polka and the waltz.[1]

The schühplattler was mentioned in Latin writings as early as A.D. 1000. It came from the Tyrolian region in Bavaria and grew out of a distinctive group of folk dances called "shoe clapping" dances. The movements of the schühplattler came from ancient animal dances that mimicked the mating or fighting of the native Bavarian black grouse. There were two basic versions of the dance. In the male-female version, the male dancer imitated a strutting cock and his partner imitated a demure hen. When the dance was performed by two men, it symbolized the fighting of two birds.

In the schühplattler, the body was hit percussively creating highly complex syncopated rhythms. The dancers slapped the thighs, knees, buttocks, feet, and cheeks, and hit the leather shorts they traditionally wore. These movements were called *platteln*. Dancers used every possible part of their anatomy, at times hitting the other dancers, in an effort to create unique sounds. The actions were accompanied by a rhythmic stamping of the feet and the effect was similar to the African practice of patting juba.

The couple dance version of the schühplattler was divided into different sections. In the nachsteigen section, the man hissed, clicked his tongue and clapped his hands as he leaped and somersaulted around his female partner. The style of the dance was exaggerated; the man's body was kept erect so that the knees and feet had to be lifted up high to be hit by the hands. Arms were swung so that they flapped like wings. The section called einlaufer was the most similar to patting juba. In the traditional form, the dancer first hit the right thigh with the right hand, then the left with the left. This was repeated and then followed by hitting either foot with the right hand. Then, the left foot was hit once more with the left hand.

During plattler, the man slapped his body continuously as his female partner spun around. The man was rewarded for his attentions to the woman in the last section

174

of the schühplattler called the landler. The landler is extremely important in dance history because it is the progenitor of the waltz.

The schühplattler dance done by two men had the same stylistic movements as the percussive sections of the male-female version. An added factor was the element of competition. The two dancers echoed each other back and forth with increasingly difficult rhythms and figures, the final challenge step resulting in the victory of one competitor and the defeat of the other.[2]

American minstrel performers and their vaudeville successors, often created caricatures based on foreign immigrants. Ethnic peculiarities were heightened and exaggerated to entertain audiences. Because these ludicrous distortions were represented as accurate portrayals, they embedded vivid stereotypes in an audience's mind. Germans were treated more fairly than other groups. Usually depicted as hefty, hardworking, practical people, they fit into the white American value system and were viewed as model immigrants.

The representation of German dances in minstrel and vaudeville skits introduced German rhythms and styles to the general public. The most significant contribution of German dance and music to tap, was the common use of 3/4 time which was superimposed upon the Irish jig and resulted in the waltz clog. The extensive use of challenge dances in American tap can also be linked to the competitive aspects of the German schühplattler.

The Shakers

Another more subtle influence upon the development of tap was the dances of the United Society of Believers in Christ's Second Appearing, a religious sect more commonly known as the Shakers. Started by an Englishwoman named Ann Lee, this sect of "shaking Quakers" spread rapidly in the United States during the last part of the 18th century and into the 19th, reaching a membership of about 6,000 before the Civil War.

The Shakers practiced ecstatic dancing in their worship services, jumping, stamping, marching and trembling during their devotional "exercises." During early phases of the religion, the structure of the dance was not set, and consisted of convulsive movements that grew out of religious fervor. The ecstatic dancing, called "labouring," was used to shake off "doubts" and to mortify the desires of the flesh. Dancing was originally seen as a sign of spiritual influence and was therefore beyond the worshiper's control. Later, however, Shakers began to formalize movements.

Dancing during worship was justified by the Shakers for four basic reasons. First, they felt it added a greater dimension to prayer. Second, they felt that the spirit was a gift of God and should not be ignored. If the spirit propelled them to dance, this divine prompting should be followed. Third, the Shakers believed that worship should be active and should involve the whole body. Lastly, the use of dance in worship affirmed communalism and equality of the sexes which were both tenets that the Shakers espoused.

When Father Joseph Meacham took over the leadership of the sect after Mother Ann died, he organized the entire social structure of the Shakers communities, including the dances. In 1788, he choreographed the first specific dance to be used in the worship service. Meacham called it the square order shuffle; he said the movements were patterned on angels dancing around the throne of God, and came to him in a vision. The dance consisted of three-step movements forward and back, with turns, and ended with shuffling in place. In the middle was a double step which the Shakers called a "tip tap."

Top: A square-order dance. Note the female figure in the lower left-hand corner representing an audience member from outside the community. Print by A. Imbert (circa 1825–30). *Right:* "The Whirling Gift." Wood-engraving from *Two Year's Experience Among the Shakers* by David R. Lamson (1848). *Courtesy of the Library of Congress.*

A later dance used around 1790 was called the turning shuffle and involved shuffling slowly as the body turned and bent lower and lower until the fingers touched the floor. The dance was used to mortify the flesh; one elder who tried the dance commented, "I scarcely ever felt so distressing a cross as to attempt it."[3]

As Shaker dancing became more refined, movements were simplified into symbolic gestures. The body shaking was toned down to a shaking of the hands, symbolizing "shaking off the sins of the world," and then further refined to an inward movement of the hands with the palms held upwards, to mean "waving love towards oneself." Other religious symbols included walking the "narrow path," and the "whirling gift," which consisted of rapid turns. The patterns within Shaker dancing symbolized the tenets of the religion and reflected the order and control within the Shaker community.

Shaker music was initially improvisational; songs that were received through divine inspiration were learned by rote, and then used to accompany the ecstatic dancing. As the sect grew, melodies and rhythms were borrowed from English, Irish, Scottish and French sources. It is uncertain if the floor patterns of contredanses, jigs, reels, and quadrilles were adopted along with the outside musical sources, although many similarities have been pointed out by dance scholars. One highly animated dance that was created for the younger members of the Shaker community closely resembled the Virginia reel. The acceptance and adoption of American Indians and blacks into Shaker communities also influenced the stylistic elements found within the sect's music and ritual dances.[4]

Around 1807, more animated dances were adopted as the Shakers sought to interest prospective converts. Joseph Meacham's successor, Lucy Wright, who was also inspired by a vision of dancing angels, sped up the tempos and freed the dance from some of the previous restrictions. During the Great Awakening, floor patterns for Shaker dances became more varied. Crosses, diamonds, double squares, and star patterns were all used. Circle dances also became more popular. One ring dance, called the wheel-within-a-wheel dance, was done with three or more concentric circles turning in alternate directions around a group of singers who stood in the center.

In a further attempt to win converts, Shakers opened their Sunday services to the general public. Shaker dances soon became a popular tourist attraction in the 19th-century. The Shakers held rehearsals during the week to insure a polished performance. The reaction to Shaker dancing by the "world's people," which is the name given by the Shakers to outsiders, was mixed. Though many found the dances graceful, inspired, and sincere, others called the dancing Shakers "rheumatic kangaroos," "penguins in procession," and "dogs splashing in water."[5] Evert Duyckinck, a friend of author Herman Melville,[6] wrote,

Yesterday found us at the religious services of the Shakers at Lebanon—a

Wheel-within-a-wheel dance. "The Shakers in Niskeyuna-Religious Exercises." Wood engraving probably drawn by Joseph Becker. From *Leslie's Popular Monthly* (1885).

ghastly scene. A glass eyed preacher was holding forth like an escaped maniac.... The audience was very full of the city fashionables from Columbia Hall and it is said they have had some pretty strong doses lately from these Shaker expounders — The dance was long and protracted striking up afresh with new tunes, to the old saw filing, and some of them were profusely jolly. The hand-shaking accompaniment is ludicrous enough having the appearance of weighing some imaginary groceries in each hand.[7]

Mary Dyer wrote in 1822, in *A Portraiture of Shakerism,*

Their family and church worship is to sing songs of their own composition (no form or appearance of prayer) in adoration to Ann Lee, in the most merry tunes ... with such ridiculous gestures, and motions and dance, and with their appearance so farcical, that it is difficult for spectators to tell whether they are in Church or a Theatre![8]

Around 1845, the belief in possession by departed spirits came to be popular throughout the cult. Channeled spirits, such as George Washington, Napoleon, Lafayette, or Mahomet, frequently made appearances to teach the Shakers about the ways of God. If the spirits were Scottish or Irish, the possessed Shakers danced a fling or a jig. Often the spirits were Native American or African-American and the possessed worshipers then reflected Native American or African-American styles in their ritual dancing. A large body of songs and dances developed based on these types of channeled messages.[9]

An anonymous author who lived with the Shakers for four months in 1842–43 related how one eldress received a direct communication from Mother Ann. The message appeared in the form of two angels who told her that a tribe of Indian

spirits who had died before Columbus wished to be "taken in" at the next meeting. On the following evening during the community meeting, after the usual dances had been performed, the doors to the meeting house were opened and the Indian spirits were invited in. The sister who had received the original message confirmed that the spirits were now inside the room:

The Elder then urged upon the members the duty of 'taking them in.' Whereupon eight or nine sisters became possessed of the spirits of Indian squaws, and about six of the brethren became Indians. Then ensued a regular pow-wow, with whooping and yelling and strange antics, such as would require a Dickens to describe.[10]

The same author went on to write:

It appeared to me, that whenever any of the brethren or sisters wanted to have some fun, they got possessed of spirits, and would go to cutting capers; all of which was tolerated even during the hours of labor, because whatever they chose to do, was attributed to the spirits.[11]

Although the movements of Shaker dance were not directly appropriated by tap, the fascination with the sect by everyday Americans did have an affect upon tap's growth, especially in the world of the professional minstrel performer. Because the material in minstrel shows was often based upon the latest and most popular social issues, American minstrels sometimes presented parodies of Shaker dancing to an audience's delight. A perfect example of this is a number by a minstrel troupe called the Ethiopian Serenaders in a performance on November 6, 1861, entitled "the laughable Black Shakers."

Shakers who had left the sect started performing groups that toured and gave

Oil painting depicting minstrel characterizations of the Shakers. "Minstrel Show" by C. Winter (1850s). *Bequest of Martha C. Karolik for the M. and M. Karolik Collection of American Paintings, 1815–1865 — Courtesy of the Museum of Fine Arts, Boston.*

concerts. A group of Shakers who had defected from the sect appeared at Barnum's American Museum from November 23, 1846, through mid–December. An advertisement from the *New York Daily Tribune*, on September 7, 1846, read,

THE MOST EXTRAORDINARY Exhibition ever known. The celebrated FAMILY SHAKERS BROTHERS AND SISTERS ... will give their second GRAND CONCERT AND LECTURE ... consisting of A complete illustration of the system. Mode of life, manner of worship, peculiarities ... of this singular, and hitherto unknown people; their origins, progress &c; and

their Chaunts, Dances ... with the utmost fidelity and truthfulness of originality.[12]

These apostate Shakers quickly became the subject of ridicule among minstrel groups who created songs and skits that warned of women being tempted to leave their families and become members of a cult.[13] To the general population, Shakers remained an object of intense curiosity, especially during the period of spiritualistic manifestations. By 1842, the sect began to close its Sunday services to the public. Large white crosses were placed outside the meeting houses with inscriptions that read:

Third and Last

ENTERTAINMENT BY THE

Shaking Quakers!

From Canterbury, N. H.,

Who have been giving their Entertainments at New-York for the last six weeks to flowing houses, beg leave most respectfully to announce to the ladies and gentlemen of this vicinity, that they intend giving a Grand Levee

ON SATURDAY, SEPT. 4th, 1847.

AT THE PAVILION FOUNTAIN HOUSE.

Admission 25 cents; children half price.— Two tickets will admit one gentleman and two ladies. Doors open at 7 1-2 o'clock. Performance to commence at 8 o'clock.

September 4, 1847.

Advertisement for a performance by apostate Shakers. *Courtesy of the Library of Congress.*

Enter not within these gates, for this is my Holy Sanctuary saith the Lord. But pass ye by, and disturb not the peace of the quiet, upon my Holy Sabbath.[14]

The Shakers observed strict rules of celibacy and depended upon winning new converts to expand the membership of the sect. After the Civil War, the ranks of the order began steadily to decline. Shaker dancing became more and more sedate, and "worship was in main a mechanical repetition of the old forms."[15]

SONG OF THE
BLACK SHAKERS.

Sung nightly with tremendous applause, by all the Ethiopian Bands in the City.

I went down to Sally's house,
  Sally wasn't home,
So I sat in de corner dar,
  An played on de jaw bone.
    Dancing Chorus.

      Fi-yi-ya, it te oot te doodle dum.

Possum up a gum tree,
  Cooney in de hollar,
Show me de colored man
  Dat stole my dollar.

      Fi-yi-ya, it te oot te doodle dum.

Now shake yourselves, darkies,
  An dance to de fiddle—
Swash shay, hands across—
  All go down de middle.

      Fi-yi-ya, it te oot te doodle dum.

Pompey plays de bango,
  Zezer plays de fiddle—
Obediah skins de eels,
  An' fries 'em on de griddle.

      Fi-yi-ah, it te oot te doodle dum.

Why am de Jim Crow Polka like bitter beer. Bekase dar am so many HOPS in it.

PRICE ONE CENT.

1282

Song sheet of the "Song of the Black Shakers" by Eph Horn. Notice the riddle at the bottom of the sheet: "Why am de Jim Crow Polka like bitter beer. Bekase dar am so many HOPS in it." *Courtesy of the Library of Congress.*

21

Native American Influences

In 1848, Henry R. Schoolcraft wrote,

Dancing is both an amusement and a religious observance among the American Indians and is known to constitute one of the most wide spread traits in their manners and customs.... [Dancing is] interwoven throughout the whole texture of Indian society, so that there is scarcely an event important or trivial, private or public, which is not connected, more or less intimately, with this rite.[1]

One of the first references to Native Americans dancing is found in the writings of the French explorer, Jaques Cartier, in 1534. While on his ship in the St. Lawrence River, Cartier saw seven canoes of

Wilde men, ... all of which approached neere unto our boate, dancing and making signes of joy and mirth, as it were desiring our friendship.... Some of the women who came not over, we might see stand up to their knees in water, singing and dancing.[2]

There are many references to Native American dancing by the early white explorers of the American continent. In the early 1600s, Captain John Smith described a welcome Dance performed by the Native Americans of Virginia.

After they had feasted us, they shewed us, in welcome, their manner of dauncinge, which was in this fashion. One of the Savages, standing in the midst of singing, beating one hand against another; all the rest dauncinge about him, shouting, howling and stamping against the ground, with many Anticke tricks and faces, making noise like so many Wolves or Devils. One thing I observed; when they were in their dance, they kept stroke with their feet just one with another, but their hands, heads, faces and bodies, every one of them had a severall gesture; so they continued for the space of halfe an houre.[3]

Smith continued,

... their dauncinge, which is like our darbysher Hornpipe, a man and then a woman, and so through them all in a round, there is one which stand in the midst with a pipe and rattle, which when he beginns to make a noyse all the rest Gigetts [Jig] about wriing [twisting] their neckes and stamping on ye ground.[4]

Smith's references to the hornpipe and the jig do not necessarily demonstrate that Native Americans had somehow absorbed European dances into their culture at this period in time, but rather that the type of

Native Americans dancing while Captain John Smith is being led away to be killed. Engraving by Robert Vaughan from *General Historie of Virginia* by John Smith (1624). *Courtesy of the Library of Congress.*

Native American Slavery

The slave trade on the American continent not only involved the importation of slaves from Africa but also the buying and selling of Native Americans. As early as the 1500s, with the arrival of Ponce de León and Hernando De Soto, the Spanish acquisition and exportation of Indian slaves to work their mines in the West Indies was flourishing. With the arrival of the English, this practice continued and escalated; the indigenous peoples of the Southeastern United States were considered a commodity to be exploited.

Charleston and Savannah were the commercial centers for this heinous enterprise, shipping out more than 10,000 natives a year to the West Indies as slaves. The English formed partnerships with the coastal Native American nations, arming them and urging them to war against the weaker inland tribes in order to provide a steady stream of slaves. The captive slaves were brought to Charleston, then shipped to the West Indies or to the colonies in New England, or sold to plantation owners around the immediate area. By 1708, Native Americans made up one fourth of all the slaves in the Carolinas. The Cherokee people were especially victimized by the early slave trade, and by the beginning of the 18th century, the buying and selling of Cherokee slaves eclipsed the fur trade as the primary commercial enterprise in the South.

Because of constant warring between tribes to try to satisfy the insatiable demand

footwork that the dancers were using contained hops, stamps and heel-and-toe movements which somehow resembled the step dances that Smith had seen in Europe. The footwork that he witnessed was similar, yet it was also different. The Native American dances he saw were danced flat-footed instead of on the toes. These dances were performed in a crouch with a bouncy feel, and contained wild twistings of the neck and body, unlike the stiff, erect bearing used in the jig and hornpipe. These Native American stylistic elements and steps were eventually incorporated into tap dancing and Appalachian clog dancing.

for slaves of the English, and because of the Native American's susceptibility to imported European diseases, entire peoples were nearly decimated.[5] By the 1750s the slave trade began to transition from an Indian-based to an African-based institution because the few Native Americans who remained were not as suitable for intensive agricultural labor as African slaves, and Indian slaves who were kept in the Carolinas had easier avenues of escape into familiar territories.[6]

During this transition, Native Americans and the newly imported Africans worked together, lived together, and ultimately intermarried.[7] The integration of these two peoples fostered an intertwining of many social and cultural aspects, including handicrafts, folklore, music and dance.

As the African slave trade grew towards the end of the 18th century, more and more African slaves fled into areas settled by indigenous tribes in order to escape bondage. Having once been enslaved by white men themselves, many Native Americans considered it justified revenge against their previous captors to help African slaves who were trying to escape.[8] Blacks who did escape and were made part of native tribes often returned later to their own plantations to help their family members and friends escape.[9] Around this time, a new Indian nation was formed near Gainesville, Florida, made up of the remnants of Yamasee, Lower Creeks, and other tribes that had nearly been destroyed by war and the slave trade. This tribe provided a safe haven for escaping black slaves.[10] The new Indian Nation was called the Seminole, a name derived from a corruption of the Spanish word *cimarron* which meant "run-

away." African slaves brought with them the dances of their native Africa as well as the jigs and reels they had assimilated in captivity. These in turn were infused with new elements absorbed from the Native American cultures.[11]

The Green Corn Ceremony

The most important dance ceremony among the Seminole, Creek, and Cherokee nations of the Southeastern United States was the green corn ceremony. The dance was also known as a busk, a corruption of the Creek word *púskita,* which means "a fast," a reference to the practice of abstaining from eating maize until after the ritual.

When the corn was ripe, tribes gathered together to celebrate and usher in their new year, which was held in July or August. The ceremony usually lasted from four to eight days. A sacred spot was prepared for the dance and the area was strewn with soil that had never been walked upon. This area was carefully

Native Americans performing a circle dance. Drawing entitled "A Religious Dance" by artist John White (1585–1593). *Courtesy of the Library of Congress.*

guarded, and strangers were forbidden to walk within the area until the consecration was complete. Before the ceremony, every fire in the village was extinguished and each hut set in order. A new fire for the year was ignited and placed in the center of the sacred space. Then various dance ceremonies began.[12]

Some of these ceremonies involved the performance of clan dances. Each clan of the tribe was represented by an different animal, and each had a special dance which represented the movements and characteristics of that animal. Typical clan dances included the deer, the bear, the rabbit, the fox, the turkey, the eagle, and the buzzard. Dances other than clan dances were also done, such as the chicken dance, the crazy dance, and the Negro dance. A former slave, Lucinda Davis, described seeing a green corn busk:

> Dat busk was justa little busk. Dey wasn't enough men around to have a good one. But I seen lots of big ones. Ones where dey all had de different kinds of "banga." Dey call all de dances some kind of "banga." De chicken dance is de "Tolosabanga," and de "Istifanibanga" is de one whar dey make lak dey is skeletons and raw heads coming to git you. De "Hadjobanga" is de crazy dance, and dat is a funny one. Dey all dance crazy and make up funny songs to go wid de dance. Everybody think up funny songs to sing and everybody whoop and laugh all de time.[13]

There are similarities between the animal mimicry found in these Native American dances and dances that were popular among African-Americans such as the chicken wing and the buzzard lope. There is possibly a relationship between these native dances and the many animal dances that became popular during the first decade of the 19th century, such as the fox trot, the turkey trot, and the grizzly bear.

Other similarities between Native American corn dances and African-American dances include the practices of not crossing the feet and of speeding up to a run during the dance — elements found in both the green corn dance and the African-American ring shout. In a letter written in 1835 to one of his relatives in New York, John Howard Payne wrote about witnessing the green corn festival:

> The dance was very unlike anything I ever saw before. The dancers never crossed their feet, but gave two taps each with the heel and toe of one foot, then of the other, making a step forward as each foot was tapped on the earth ... the dance was quickened, at a signal, till it became nearly a measured run, and the cries of the dancers were varied to suit the motion, when, suddenly, all together uttered a long, shrill whoop, and stopped short....[14]

Black slaves sometimes attended Native American ceremonies. One black slave, Preston Kyles, explained:

> When I wuz a boy, dere wuz lotsa Indians livin' about sic miles from the plantation on which I wuz a slave. De Indians allus held a big dance ever' few months, an' all de niggers would try to attend. On one ob dese ostent'tious occasions about fifty of us niggers conceived de idea of goin', without getting permits frum de master. As soon as it gets dark, we quietly slips outen de quarters, one by one, so as not to disturb de guards. Arrivin' at de dance, we jined in de festivities wid a will.[15]

One aspect of Native American dancing that correlated directly with African dance was the belief that it was of utmost importance to finish a dance gracefully and properly. A perfect ending, executed with finesse, demonstrated true collaboration between dancer and drummer. Spectators watching a dance performance looked forward to seeing if the dancer could accomplish the end gesture flawlessly. If they did not, they opened themselves up to mocking and taunting.[16] This ability to end a dance correctly was of paramount importance in one Native American dance in particular, the Cherokee stomp dance.

The Cherokee Stomp Dance

The Cherokee stomp dance was a series of dances which made up a ceremony of thanksgiving, healing, and social support.[17] Every element within the ceremony was specifically ordered to direct the participant's focus to God. It was believed that the beauty of the stomp dance lay in its perfect order which signified the perfect cosmic order ordained by the deity.

The stomp ceremony was performed by both men and women, with the stomping part of the dance performed by the men, while the women provided additional rhythmic accompaniment. The women traditionally wore rattles attached to their legs made out of turtle shells filled with pebbles.[18] These women were called "shell shakers" or sometimes "shaklers."[19] The male leader of the dance also carried a rattle made out of a pebble-filled turtle shell.

The dance was done on sacred ceremonial grounds called "stomp grounds," or sometimes, "square grounds" or "tribal towns" which were carefully prepared before the ceremony so that the space under the fire was perfectly round and the fire was placed exactly in the center. Outsiders and non–Cherokee were forbidden to desecrate this sacred space by walking on it before the ceremony, and pregnant or menstruating women were not allowed to enter the stomp area because it was believed they would weigh down the procession. The dancing always took place around a fire made up of four logs which were placed so

that they pointed in the cardinal directions.[20]

The ceremony followed a strictly prescribed order.[21] The dancing began when the dance leader entered and circled the fire counterclockwise with six male dancers following.[22] In between each male dancer, a woman shell shaker was placed. All other participants in the ceremony followed behind. The performers walked with heads bowed, continuing to circle the fire wrapping around each previous circle in a serpentine fashion. Upon the leader's cue, the men began running with a flat-footed step. The female dancers wearing the leg rattles then joined in, doing touch-steps or stamp-steps. The remainder of the dancers, both male and female, then joined the others; as the stomp dance continued, the rhythms and the steps varied. The men ran or walked, stomped or hopped. The "shaklers" had three basic steps: a two-step which coincided with the single stomp beat of the men, a hitch-step which was a quick double step on each foot, and a step-tap. At the end of certain passages, the women executed jumps and hit both feet together in the air. All stomp steps were done flat-footed and in a crouched position. Emphasis in the dance was placed on doing the steps rhythmically and following the directions called out by the leader.

The stomp dance was set in a call-and-response format in which a leader signaled rhythm changes that were then taken over by the other performers.[23] Within this set framework the dancer improvised and expressed individual artistry. The two aspects of freedom and constraint were emphasized.

It is commonly believed by scholars and dance historians that many elements of tap dancing can be directly traced to the movements of the Cherokee stomp dance. Certain rhythms and stylistic elements of the stomp dance are especially apparent in Appalachian clogging and buck dancing.

Stomp dancing footwork consisted of small steps with shuffling movements, and flat-footed stamping. Toe-heel action and raising of the knees forward was also common. In Cherokee ceremonial dance, the heel beat was characteristically heavy and this is sometimes found in certain styles of Appalachian clogging.

The rhythm of the average drum beat that accompanied most Cherokee dances was similar to that of a human heartbeat; accents were usually placed on every second step, accompanied with a double bounce in the knees. The influence of these elements can be glimpsed in the standard tap time-step which accents the even beats of eight and two, then four and six. The bouncing feel is also apparent in the time-step. There are several Cherokee dance steps, such as the "flat foot," the "flat foot trot," the "skip-back," the "double stomp," and the "double flat-heel" that bear a striking resemblance to certain Appalachian clogging steps. Clog expert Annie Fairchild states that there are at least three clog steps that can be definitely traced directly to Cherokee dance movements: the single, which is a shuffle followed by a step (known in tap dancing terminology as a triple); the stomp, which is simply stamping the whole foot against the floor and transferring the weight onto it; and the Indian, which consists of a chug forward, a chug back, a chug forward and then a step.

As was stated earlier, Native American ritualistic practices such as the stomp dance, were also integrated with African-American practices and a new synthesis containing elements of both was created.[24] The cultural sharing flowed in both directions. A good example of this sharing appeared in the African-American design of "hush harbors," which was directly based upon the architecture of Southeastern Native American "stomp grounds." "Hush harbors" were makeshift churches made out of tree limbs and branches. They were especially popular during the religious revivals of the Great Awakening, and were a common element during camp meetings. Likewise, the practice of ritual bathing, which was an important part of the Southeastern stomp ceremony, can be traced back to African river-cult rituals which were brought to the Cherokees by escaped black slaves who were former river-cult priests.

The Booger Dance

Another Native American dance used among Eastern Cherokee tribes was the booger or mask dance. The ritual consisted of rowdy dancers, called boogers, who donned masks with exaggerated features and barged into a ceremonial gathering, dancing wildly, demanding women and wanting to fight.[25]

The booger dance began with six musicians seated to one side, called "callers," whose job was to summon the boogers. After the "callers" had completed six songs, seven dancers entered disguised in masks and outlandish costumes. They proceeded to hobble around the dance floor and perform tasks, but always in a backwards, topsy-turvy manner. As the "callers" did their seventh song, the boogers danced and tried to frighten the spectators. After this section was completed, the dancers were seated and asked questions. Their replies were always ludicrous or obscene. After this, each booger performed a clownlike solo dance, using any steps they wanted, often including many heavy-footed rhythmical hops.

All the boogers then performed a bear dance, followed by another dance in which they were joined by the audience. During this dance, the boogers teased and taunted relatives, especially the women. The boogers then left and removed their costumes in secret so they would not be recognized when they returned home. The remaining audience members finished the evening with the friendship dance.

The booger dance symbolized the intrusion of crude, uninvited outsiders upon the Cherokee world. The dancers' masks were often heavy caricatures which parodied white Americans, Europeans, or other non–Cherokees.[26] This ritualization of the white man's invasion into their world allowed the Cherokees to deal with their anxieties in a context that showed the intruders as ridiculous and laughable and therefore less threatening.[27]

Depiction of Native Americans on the Stage

In 1829, gold was discovered on Cherokee land in Dahlonega, Georgia, and whites began to invade the territory to stake out claims, forcing the Native Americans to sign leases, beating up those who refused. The Cherokees did their best to adapt as farmers, carpenters, masons and the like. They developed a written language and established a formal Indian government. They also welcomed missionaries and converted to Christianity in an effort to win the goodwill of the surrounding white society. President Andrew Jackson, however, in a desire to get valuable Cherokee land, issued a removal bill, using the formation of their independent government as a justification. Cherokee land was put up for sale, Native Americans were forcibly evicted, and their homes burned. Thus began the Cherokee migration to Oklahoma in 1838–9 in what became known as the Trail of Tears.[28]

Native American dance ritual was feared by whites and suppressed by the American government because it was a unifying force among tribal communities. Even as late as 1904, the Regulations of the Indian Office in Article Four branded Native American dance as an "Indian offence." The penalty for disobeying this law was withholding of rations or imprisonment. Only men over the age

Playbill showing how Native American dances were put on the stage. From "Washburn's Last Sensation, the Moral Show of the Age" presented at Edward's Hall, Southbridge, Massachusetts (October 14, 1875). *Courtesy of the Library of Congress, Rare Book and Special Collections Division.*

of 40 years were exempt so they could perform in Wild West shows run by whites.[29]

Native Americans were first portrayed on the minstrel stage before the Civil War and were traditionally played with ambivalence. They were alternately romanticized as noble, independent peoples or seen as barbaric pagans who blocked the settlement of land destined for whites. As the Indian Wars of the 1870s raged, skits became more and more anti–Indian, and natives were show as belligerent, vicious savages and as dangerous drunkards. Minstrel shows began "underscoring the message that whites should not mix with or trust Indians."[30] As with the portrayals of African-Americans, minstrel farces showed heavily stereotyped caricatures of Native Americans, and in them Native American dances were performed in a comic and overblown manner.

22

American Country Dance

Acceptance of Dancing in Different Regions of the U.S.

In colonial America there were differing attitudes about the moral value of dancing. The Pilgrims occasionally held community dances, although in general, Puritans were opposed to dancing. The Puritan William Prynne wrote,

> Dancing serves no necessary use! No profitable laudable or pious end at all.... The way to heaven is too steep, too narrow for men to dance and keep revel rout. No way is large or smooth enough for capering roisters, for skipping, jumping, dancing dames but that broad, beaten pleasant road that leads to Hell.[1]

Puritan values often collided with folk customs and throughout the early history of the United States, the diehard extremists and the less pious battled about the morality, vulgarity, and validity of secular dancing. The Puritans who first settled in New England came to America seeking religious freedom. Their lives were ordered upon theocratic principles. These religiously conservative settlers were reticent to accept dance as a suitable pastime. "Mixt" or "gynaecandrical" (couple) dancing was especially frowned upon because Puritans believed it led to sexual miscon-

duct and therefore went against the Seventh Commandment, "Thou shalt not commit adultery."[2]

In the 1700s, as urban areas expanded and more and more people immigrated to the United States seeking economic rather than religious freedom, opinions towards dancing gradually shifted.[3] New educational theories began to support the use of dance as a valid method of learning grace and composure. Dancing in New England became more openly accepted although many continued to view it as sinful.[4]

In the Southern states emphasis was upon aristocratic rather than theocratic principles. Settlers generally came to the area for economic reasons. In addition, the widespread distances between Southern plantations made churchgoing more difficult. Therefore, the church did not exercise as strong an influence on social affairs as in the North, and the status of dance was more secure. Furthermore, members of the upper class had both wealth and leisure time, and so they tended towards more aristocratic forms of amusement. Dance especially enjoyed a prominent role in the social life of old Virginia.[5]

In Virginia, dance was viewed as a worthy form of recreation for the elite as well as the servant and slave classes. It was deemed a necessary ingredient in the education of every gentleman and was used at

"The Country Dance." An engraving after William Hogarth. From the book *Dancing* by Lilly Grove (1901).

such respected institutions as William and Mary College to teach gentle manners and deportment.

> Dance served an even more important role than that of social amusement. It was believed to be one of the accomplishments proper for a gentleman, and not having a knowledge of dance showed a lack of proper education.[6]

In Colonial Virginia, as elsewhere throughout the American colonies, black slave musicians were often called upon to accompany white dances. There are records that mention an 18th century slave named Sy (or Simeon) Gilliat, who "was reputed to be the fiddler at the Governor's Palace in Williamsburg during Baron Botetourt's regime. Gilliat was unquestionably the most popular society fiddler in Richmond for two generations"[7] Mr. Gilliat always played for the annual Race Ball which was held after a week of horse racing. The dances at the Race Ball traditionally began with a stately minuet, but then Gilliat fiddled some peppier tunes.

> The music of "Sy Gilliat's fiddle and the flute or clarionet of his black comrade, London Briggs," was quite "fast and furious," and the dancers cut "all sorts of capers" to it, dancing not only reels, but

contradances, congos, hornpipes, and Jigs.[8]

One of the earliest records of the influence of African-American musical style upon white settlers was a dance described in Colonial Virginia, by Nicholas Cresswell in 1774.

> 37 ladies dressed and powdered to life. All of them fond of dancing…. Betwixt the country dances they have what they call everlasting Jigs. A couple gets up and begins to cut a Jig (to some Negro tune). Others come and cut them out, and these dances always last as long as the Fiddler can play.[9]

Because of the conspicuous role of dance in Virginia, dancing masters were often in demand there and by the end of the 17th century, many had made their way to the area.[10]

Black slave musicians often played for these white dancing masters. In New York, a slave named Caesar "…drove the coach that took the young ladies to the dancing school, played for the dancing, and then served as a waiter during refreshment time."[11]

As in New England, though, dancing was strictly prohibited on the Sabbath in Virginia and offenders were always severely

A slave fiddler playing for a colonial dance. An engraving by Howard Helmick from the article "Old Maryland Homes and Ways" in *Century Magazine* (1894).

punished. One scandal that took place in the 1690s involved the daughter of a Reverend Teakle. While her father was out of town, Margaret Teakle had been talked into giving a ball on a Saturday night by her friend Elizabeth Parker. The reverend returned to find that dancing had not only gone on throughout the night, but had continued until 11 o'clock Sunday morning. What was even worse, it had occurred during the time when church services were normally held. Outraged, Reverend Teakle took Elizabeth Parker and her husband to court and initiated legal proceedings against them.

Dancing in the Appalachian Region

The Appalachian region played a unique and important role in the develop-

ment of American folk and tap dancing for a variety of reasons. First, the populations in these areas were exposed to Native American and African-American influences. Although few Native American dances were ever accepted intact by whites, elements of American Indian dance customs were introduced into country dances circuitously. Because African-Americans did accept Native American dances readily and were commonly used as musicians to accompany white dances, or seen as entertainers by white audiences, some of these Indian stylistic elements were assimilated into mainstream dance.

The exchange of African-American and white dance styles has already been discussed at length in other chapters of this book. This interplay was especially prevalent in the mountain areas of Appalachia, where whites and blacks frequently intermingled dance customs. The resulting potpourri of dance steps resulted in the wilder and noisier forms of African-American jigging gaining prominence over the lighter and more controlled forms of Irish jigging. This heavily African-American-influenced step dancing came to be known as clogging and was commonly used not only in solo dancing, but as ornamentation during group dances as well.

In addition the Eastern mountain regions of America were mostly settled by immigrants who came from rural areas of Europe, such as the highland areas of Britain, Scotland and Ireland. When they moved to Appalachia, these settlers were isolated from the influences of urban culture which depended upon professional dancing masters for their dance figures.

The various national groups tended to stick together, clinging to their own cultural identity and folk traditions. Appalachian dances, therefore, retained more authentic, uncorrupted versions of the rural dances from these immigrants' native homelands. Isolation tended to preserve older country dances in their freer, more original boisterous forms, unaffected by the influence of drawing room manners. One such country dance which probably came from the regions around the north of England and the lowlands of Scotland was the running set, also called the Kentucky running set.

The Kentucky Running Set

The running set survived in the Appalachian Mountains virtually intact into the 20th century.[12] The dance was not performed to music because of the belief that the fiddle was an instrument of the devil, but was often done to the accompaniment of patting. The basic step of the Kentucky running set was a rapid, smooth, gliding walk that made it appear as if the dancer was skating over the floor. The arms were held loosely and in later forms, the dance was ornamented with disjointed clogging actions of the legs and feet.

A caller called out directions to the dance which usually consisted of an introduction and about 14 different figures. These figures included such moves as "wind up the ball of yarn," "shoot the owl," "chase the squirrel," "wild-goose chase," "box the gnat," and "birdie in the cage." Each figure was made up of different patterns and actions. For example, during "birdie in the cage," the dancers ran quickly in a circle to the left, circling one woman who spun in the middle in the opposite direction. When the caller shouted "Bird hop out, crow (or owl) hop in," the woman jumped out of the center of the circle, rejoining it running to the left, and was replaced by her male partner who jumped in. In "chase the squirrel" one of the woman dancers led her partner between another couple, then abandoned her partner and was pursued by the man in the second couple.

Traditionally, the running set was followed with a play-party dance game called "Tucker." During this game, one man went to the center of the circle and all the others danced around him in couples. During the course of the game, the man in the center then tried to capture one of the females and take her away from her dancing partner. When he did, the dispossessed man then went to the center and the process was repeated.

As in the plantation tradition of set de flo', the dance area, called the "set" or the "general set," was enclosed. The phrase "to run a set" meant to do the dance. The Kentucky running set was one of the first examples of a dance that used calling, and therefore was a forerunner of the Western square dance. The running set is still danced today in parts of the South.

The Melungeons

The Appalachian region also had an influence on American social dance because of the connection of Appalachian dances to the Gypsies and, through them, to Indian kathak dance.

In the Appalachian Mountains and along the Atlantic coastal regions of the Southern United States there was a group of people of mixed racial heritage called the Melungeons.[13] There has been much speculation about the heritage of these dark-skinned people with exotic features, and most scholars claim that they are of Gypsy origin.[14]

Throughout Europe, the Gypsies experienced discrimination and were frequently enslaved. After the discovery of the Americas, Europe viewed the newly discovered lands as a dumping ground for their "undesirables." France sent Gypsies to Louisiana, and Germany banished them to

Pennsylvania.[15] Sweden sent them to the Delaware region. As early as the 17th century, Britain was transporting Gypsies to work as slaves in the West Indies and to work as indentured servants on the tobacco plantations in the Tidewater region of Virginia.[16] The Gypsies in this region are of particular interest because after the terms of their indentures were up, they moved into the Appalachian Mountains and formed enclaves of tightly knit Gypsy communities. Although these Gypsies rarely married outside their own culture, the disproportionate number of male Gypsies transported to the United States from Europe meant a high probability that some of these men took Native American wives. Records attest to this in Louisiana in the late 1700s.

Even if intermarriage between these cultures was rare, there is no denying the significant interaction that did take place between the Gypsies, the Native Americans, and the runaway African-American slaves in the region. Many areas of assimilation exist between these three cultures. Most scholars agree that there was a deep influence of Gypsy music upon the music of Appalachia and some speculate that elements of Gypsy music heavily influenced black soul music. It is safe to assume that this hybridization of Gypsy, Native American and African-American cultures had a similar dramatic effect upon dance.

French Influence

During the War for Independence the American colonies formed an alliance with France to fight the British. After the Revolutionary War, these ties with France escalated and with it, exposure to French influences in the dance increased. French dancing masters swarmed to the United States both during and after the American Revolution bringing with them the sophistication and manners of the French court.

A dancing master teaching a young colonial girl to dance. "The Dancing Lesson." An engraving after F. Heilbuth from the book *Dancing* by Lilly Grove (1901).

After the French Revolution, many French dancing masters who had been connected with the aristocracy, came to the United States seeking refuge. They brought the traditional French style court dances with them. However, a new breed of artists who distanced themselves from the tumbled monarchy and associated themselves with the common folk also came to the States. This latter group of dancing masters imported styles of country dancing that were further removed from aristocratic elements.

The most important change the French brought with them was to introduce the quadrille, or dance in the shape of a square.[17] The quadrille utilized four couples and was the forerunner of the American square dance. Although the French did not invent the square dance, the huge influx of French dances around this time caused important and vital changes in the style of American folk dancing.[18]

The Quadrille.—Figure 1 : Le Pantalon
(From Heath's 'Northern Looking-Glass,' 1825)

The Quadrille.—Figure 2 : L'Été
(From Heath's 'Northern Looking-Glass,' 1825)

The Quadrille.—Figure 3 : La Poule
(From Heath's 'Northern Looking-Glass,' 1825)

The Quadrille.—Figure 4 : La Trénise
(From Heath's 'Northern Looking-Glass,' 1825)

Top left and right: "The Quadrille" (1901). *Below:* The Virginia reel or the "Sir Roger de Coverley" as done in 1820. Both from the book *Dancing* by Lilly Grove (1901).

Around the turn of the century the trend in New England was towards urbanization, and the popularity of French quadrilles rose. Before the Revolution, British contra or line dances had been in vogue in the colonies. By the middle of the 19th century because of the French influence, the Virginia reel was one of the only surviving contra dances outside the New England area.

In the North, certain immigrant populations maintained some allegiance to the folk traditions from their homelands, but in general, during this period in American history, social dancing evolved into more delicate, sophisticated, and formal configurations. The people in the Southern Appalachian

Mountains, however, remained virtually untouched by the influence of French manners, and dances tended to be athletic and energetic. In urban areas where dancing masters exercised control, improvisation while dancing was considered taboo. The rules set by the dancing master had to be strictly followed. In rural areas of the South, however, doing one's own steps was not only accepted. but also respected.

Dance on the Western Frontier

As Americans in the Eastern United States were refining dances for the ballroom, dancing in the West remained rooted in earthy and untamed rural forms. The favorite dance among settlers on the frontier was the cotillion which was based on the French quadrille but contained an important difference.[19] The figures of the quadrille had to be memorized, but the movements in the cotillion were spontaneously called out in the middle of the dance. A caller, often also the fiddler, made up dances on the spot to fit whatever tune

"The Cotillion." An engraving after F. Collett from the book *Dancing* by Lilly Grove (1901).

was being played. They then shouted out directions to the dance as the spirit moved them, which led to the invention of new steps and figures and a greater sense of stylistic freedom within the structure of the dance. Square dance callers differed greatly from professional dancing masters who taught memorized figures such as in the quadrille and were interested in manners, deportment, and gentility. Instead, callers shifted the focus away from rigid technique and sequences learned by rote to a freer, more spontaneous, and constantly evolving type of dancing. As the popularity of callers spread throughout the Western regions, dancing masters felt increasingly threatened, frequently attacking the calls as a vulgar verbalization of dance figures. Despite these protests, calling grew in popularity, the greatest factor in the decline in the number of dancing masters in the United States.

It was in the West that square dancing fully developed. Here the square formation of the quadrille along with figures from New England contra dances blended with the freedom of the Kentucky running set and its spontaneous calls. As these elements merged in the form of the cotillion, American square dancing took shape.

Because of the great distances between neighbors out West, invitations were sent in advance when dance parties were being held. These social gatherings were called junkets. Because these rural dances were often held in a barn or a large kitchen from which the furniture had been removed, they were also called barn dances, kitchen junkets, or kitchen rackets. They were also known as hoedowns, heel-burners, and in the South, they were sometimes called twistifications.

Western dances were wild and rowdy gatherings, embellished with noisy percussive footwork such as in the pigeon wing and buck dancing. One type of dance that was a favorite among frontier men and women was the plank dance.

"You stand face to face with your partner on a plank and keep on dancing," a countryman explained to one visiting northerner. "Put the plank up on two barrel heads, so it'll kind of spring.... They dance as fast as they can and the folks all stand around and holler, 'Keep it up, John!' 'Go it, Nance!' 'Old Virginny never tire!' and such kind of observation, and clop and stamp...."[20]

As more and more immigrants moved west, they brought with them styles of the popular social dances from their own native cultures. In the 1830s the polka and the waltz became all the rage in Europe, and their popularity quickly spread to the ballrooms and dancing schools in the Eastern United States and then to the West. The waltz sparked a great deal of outrage, shocking more conservative observers with its closed, face-to-face dance position. Because partners held each other closely while waltzing, the dance was considered by many to be immoral. As it infiltrated frontier dances, several religious groups expressed moral indignation. The Episcopal Church proposed banning all square dancing because it promoted sinful contact between the sexes.

People were also threatened by a particular dance move that was becoming more and more popular. The swing had started innocently enough; the man and woman joined left hands, braced their other hands on the opposite shoulder of their partner and spun together. As the waltz came into vogue, this position changed to spinning in what we know as the typical closed dance position and many considered it not only outrageous, but downright immoral. Ministers warned women against "the abomination of permitting a man who was neither your lover nor your husband to encircle you with his arms, and slightly press the contour of your waist."[21]

The Play-Party

One outgrowth of the moral struggle about the indecency of dancing was the American play-party, a country social gathering which included dancelike movements, marching, and the swinging of partners to the accompaniment of singing only, a phenomenon that resulted from rural cultural isolation and from the church's ban on dancing and playing the fiddle.[22] Mr. W. L. Wilkerson, a farmer from Oklahoma who participated in play-parties, explained them thus:

The church's attitude was against dancing.... The active church members didn't go to dances. If a boy or a girl belonging to any church danced, the saying went around that they had danced themselves out of the church, and that was made a moment of history.... I can't understand why it was but in my boyhood days—I don't know how to express it—but the fiddle was the instrument of Satan. The Devil was in the fiddle—that's the saying exactly.... I don't believe there was any connection between church prejudice and the popularity of the dance. I think circumstances under which we lived caused the dance to flourish, and the conditions under which we lived caused the degeneration. We were all farmers and we had to make our own entertainment....

It was not only self-made but vigorous.[23]

The acceptance of play-party dances on the frontier varied from community to community. Some saw them as far enough removed from actual dancing that they were a wholesome outlet for youthful energy. Others of a more pious nature thought any kind of movement resembling dance should be avoided at all costs. Nevertheless, despite warnings against the evils of dancing, the dance games were always popular with teenagers. One young man named Paul Howard spoke about the thrill of attending a play-party:

> Those who have "got religion" look on them [play-parties] with horror as devices of the devil to lure young folk into sin and everlasting torment. This attitude tends to lend an element of mystery and adventure to them, and the children of religious folk dare not let their parents know that they sang "Old Joe Clark" or that they were at the dance last Friday night.[24]

Strangely enough, play-parties were most popular after religious revivals and many of the tamer games were used at church gatherings. The play-party game, "Jump, Jim Crow," for example, was a favorite at church socials and was performed to the singing of the song popularized by Thomas Dartmouth Rice. It was a fairly simple dance, consisting of hopping on one foot and doing do-si-dos. Songs such as Rice's ditty and other American folk songs or songs from the minstrel stage, such Dan Emmett's "Old Dan Tucker," were often used to accompany the play-party dances.

These play-party dance games were also called party plays, swinging plays, or jig plays. Sometimes they were called gin-arounds, and the dancers were referred to as "ginners" because they marched slowly and methodically around and around like a horse in a gin. Boisterous dance games were called bounce-arounds or frolics. Especially at frolics, the play-party was often just a regular dance in disguise. A man named Lawrence McKiver described how he danced at a play-party frolic.

> I cut the buck a while, another little boy see if he could beat me and be going on around just like that. Then we come back and we do the Charleston. One we think the best get the biggest piece of candy.[25]

Although play-parties were open to the entire community and always organized as a family affair, the dancers were mainly teenagers, single adults, and young married couples.

> … [W]ith the precedent of the singing game before them and the lack of instruments and other facilities for dancing as a motive, the young people hit upon the idea, and once tried and approved, it gained headway, and in competition with the dance had to take over more and more features of the dance, being kept alive as an independent form and prevented from passing over entirely into the square dance as much by the definite advantages it developed as by church restrictions on dancing.[26]

The main effect of square dancing and the American play-party upon tap dancing was its emphasis upon improvisation. The spontaneous freedom fostered by callers and the constant blending of many different cultural styles from various immigrant pioneer groups created an atmosphere that allowed new dance forms such as American tap dance to flourish. Many different ethnic styles of dance were dispersed throughout the country as more and more people moved westward. As these disparate cultures settled into communities out West, all of the various stylistic elements blended into one uniquely American style. As entertainers traveled across the United States in search of new audiences, they were influenced by American Western tastes which found their way into pre-existing percussive dance forms. Likewise, these same entertainers exposed frontier audiences to early forms of tap that had already taken shape in the East. As these Western audiences saw and heard the infectious rhythms of the jig, clog, and buck dancers, they in turn began adding some of the fancy footwork into square dance figures.

23

Conclusions

The historical and sociological factors that led to the development of tap dancing are as intricate and complex as the rhythms made by a tap dancer's feet. By examining the context in which tap was created and the wide variety of societal and cultural contributions that went into making up this unique art form, we can more deeply appreciate these intricacies and complexities.

The process of analyzing the development of a particular dance form involves many factors and can include many contexts. Within the study of dance history and dance anthropology, several sociological, historical, and cultural elements come into play, as do physical and emotional factors. At the most basic levels, the development of dance gestures can initially be traced to three major factors — climate, geography, and economic conditions.

Climate

Climatic conditions often dictated the rhythm of steps and also the movement qualities of indigenous dances. In countries where the temperature is hot, it has been found that dances are more likely to be fluid and flowing, and body positions are seldom held. There is often a rocking between the feet or hips, and rhythms tend to be more intricate. Fewer clothes are worn and therefore body movements are freer. African and Indian dances are examples of this.

In areas where the temperature changes abruptly during the day, such as in Spain, there are also abrupt changes in a dancer's movements. Dances alternate between flowing steps and sudden stamping and rapid footwork. Rhythms change rapidly and are irregular.

In countries where the climate consists of hot summers and bitterly cold winters, the dance movements match these changes with long phrases of contrasting steps and rhythms. The colder the country, the more vigorous the movements. In countries such as England, Ireland and Germany, where the seasonal changes occur more gradually, the rhythms in dances tend to be more regular and the movements more equalized. Dancers keep movements and gestures more closely centralized around the main axis of the body. This evenness of movements has the tendency to create light, easy steps that feature footwork and produce interesting floor patterns. Celtic dancing is a perfect example of this. In Irish solo step dances, every movement is balanced. If the dancer moves to the right, there is an equal movement to the left. Every movement forwards has a corresponding movement backwards.

The directions in which a dance moves either symbolizes important events in that culture's history or mimics of the movement the sun. The Celts migrated westward to the Mediterranean before moving northward into the British isles. Their celebratory dances mimicked this migration by moving clockwise. In contrast, Slavic dances move counterclockwise, symbolizing the migration of their ancestors eastward to the Russian steppes. African dances also travel counterclockwise, because in lands south of the equator, the sun appears to move from east to west.

Geography

Geographic situations also determine the type of dances that develop within a culture. In agricultural plains, the body tends to be drawn downward towards the earth. Desert dwellers utilize many weight-changes, shifting from foot to foot as if the ground is hot. In plains and deserts, large numbers of dancers perform together at the same time, keeping in a tight group, all doing the same steps. Circle dances are also common in plains and deserts, like those found in Africa and among the Native Americans.

Nomadic peoples, such as the Gypsies, often utilize fast-traveling movements. Running steps, leaps and jumps predominate and a wide variety of steps are used. Group dances in these cultures also commonly feature breakout solos in the middle of group numbers.

In countryside which has gently sloping hills, such as in England, chain dances are more common and the movement of the body tends to go up and down. Fewer patterns are used in the dance. Peoples that live in the steppes commonly travel by horseback and this is reflected in an erect stance and galloping, trotting, jumping and rearing types of movements.

Mountain folks, because they live in a confined space on hard ground, use confined steps that feature a stepping type of footwork, punctuated with leaps. The feeling of mountain dancing is generally light, and group dances if done at all are made up of smaller numbers of performers. Irish dancing is included in this category.

Geographic factors also help to either preserve dance traditions or disseminate them. The people of the Appalachian Mountains are a good example of how isolation kept such dances as the Kentucky running set preserved in its original form.

Economic Factors

There are many examples of how economic factors influence the development of dance. In the wealthy court dances of Europe, forms of dance were used to legitimize the social order and the stratification of power. These rigidly codified forms stressed poise and manners and depended upon the services of the dancing master to be learned. In rural areas, peasant dance was freer and more boisterous, relying heavily upon improvisation within the folk tradition.

The development of footwork among African-American slaves was affected by the harsh life these people suffered. The African predilection for improvisation was fostered by the constant need of the slaves to find alternative ways to express themselves within an atmosphere of hostility and deprivation. Dance anthropologists point out that dance which is marked by many changes in rhythm frequently indicate cultures that have a need to adapt quickly, or be alert to danger or the unexpected.

Economic influences upon the nature of dance forms are visible everyday work movements. Dance gestures can be traced to such tasks as the threshing of corn or the weaving of cloth. Floor patterns can represent the intertwining of threads in weaving and foot movements, the process of separating flax fibers before they are spun into linen, or the movement of the shuttle back and forth on the loom. Among the Owo Yoruba tribe in Africa, one stamping dance grew out of the movement of men packing the earth into place with their feet after placing the body in a grave.

Many movements grow out of military exercises. The plantation stick dance which evolved out of the capoeira is a perfect example. The use of sticks in the Morris dance can be traced to military maneuvers. Kathak was also originally used by the military sect as part of their training rituals.

Economic factors determine the architecture, dress, and furniture used by a society and these in turn affect the style of dance through posture and gesture. In Nigeria the people sit on low stools and therefore develop strong leg tendons and flexible knee joints. Their dances often include deep knee bends. The longways form of dance became popular in Tudor England when the wealthy began to remodel their houses and moved country circle dances indoors from outside rural settings. As dances were shifted into a confined space, the architecture of the room determined the shape and figures of the dance.

Costume

Dress and costume used in native dances is dictated by each of the above factors — climate, geography and economy. Obviously in warmer climates, fewer clothes are worn and the movement is freer, although in ritualistic settings, in the African cultures for example, costumes could range from little adornment to outfits that were so fantastical as to transform the human body into a different shape. Therefore costume could either restrict the movement of the dance or facilitate it.

One of the most dominant traits in African costume was its percussive qualities. Adornments such as leg rattles, bells, beads and other sound devices that would make rhythms not only added to the beauty of the costume but also served to provide accompaniment. The costume served both a visual as well as an auditory purpose. Sound makers attached to the body served two purposes: to make music and to enhance the movement.

Masks were also commonly used in Africa, as they were in Native American dances such as the booger dance. The use of masks reflected the spirit of the community and allowed performers to express deep feelings and fears publicly. The mask allowed dancers to be something other than themselves as they were transformed into the spirit of the mask.

To "dance the mask" reveals and defines thoughts and feelings about life which the community shares and has always shared.[1]

Blackface makeup was used by Morris dancers and minstrel entertainers in a similar way; to disguise the performers and therefore free them up to express political and socioeconomic concerns and values and generate archetypal symbols in ritualistic ways.

In colder climates heavy clothing and wooden shoes led to stamping steps. Full skirts led to turns and whirling movements, and the use of leather shorts, or lederhosen, in Germany contributed to the development of the thigh-slapping of the schühplattler.

Footwear is also determined by climate and geographic location and plays an important part in the style of dance and the steps used. Bare feet give the dancer greater freedom, so full body movements are used. Wooden shoes and clogs with leather uppers create stiffer movement and tend to stress the footwork as the body is held more rigid.

Dance gestures typically evolve from the articulation of gesture in a societal context to expression in a more individual sense. Marshall and Jean Stearns in their outstanding book *Jazz Dance,* write that

> Religious dances become secular, group dances become solo, rural dances become more urban, and the literal style of the dance is lost in individual expression.[2]

This process is certainly apparent in the development of tap. The religious dance, the ring shout, was transformed into the walk-around of the minstrel stage. In the jook joints, group dances which had been popular within the rural setting of the plantation were refined and stylized into solo dances which were then disseminated throughout the country and became the basis for many of the social dances that were ultimately incorporated into tap.

Survival Potential for New Dance Forms

In her book *The Anthropology of Dance,* Anya Peterson Royce lists eight characteristics which give a dance form survival potential.[3] They are:

1. Flexibility in the sense of serving more than one function.
2. Flexibility in the sense of not being tied to any one institution.
3. Flexibility in the sense of not being limited to a small elite either in terms of performance or observance.
4. A number of links to other aspects of culture.
5. A structure that allows for improvisation and modification.
6. Attributes that make it entertaining or potentially marketable.

Some of the many dances that influenced tap. "La Belle Assemblée; or, Sketches of Characteristic Dancing." Engraving after G. Cruikshank in *A History of Dancing: From the Earliest Ages to Our Own Times* by Gaston Vuillier (1898).

7. Potential for marking identity in situations of contact.

8. The ability to change from being a recreational dance to one for formal occasions and vice versa.

Each of these eight characteristics is clearly apparent within the creation of American tap dance and perhaps explains why this art form continues to evolve and endure.

1. Flexibility in the sense of serving more than one function:

Percussive dance rhythms have served a variety of purposes, the most obvious of which was to use the body as a musical instrument to accompany the dance. This purpose is visible in many progenitors of American tap. Obvious examples range from the use of bells worn around the ankles in Indian kathak to the use of terrapin leg rattles by stomp dance shaklers. Other clear examples include the use of the body in the American play-party and of course the widespread practice of patting juba.

A second common purpose of percussive dance was communication. Tap dance clearly demonstrates this purpose throughout the many stages of its development. Irish step dancers telegraphed messages to their fellow Catholics by tapping their feet while standing guard outside the Mass. African-American slaves, who had their talking drums taken away after the Stono Rebellion, used body slaps and foot taps to communicate with each other.

Early tap was also used to make political statements. The early forms of tap dance such as the cakewalk were used in this way, in accordance with the African tradition of employing mockery and derision to preserve social order.

The dance was also used as a form of religious expression. The telling of sacred dance stories in ancient India, Celtic ring dances, African tribal dances, the Cherokee

stomp dance, voodoo rituals, Shaker dances, and the ring shout, are all examples of how tap has always been firmly rooted in spiritual traditions.

In a similar way, tap dancing was used as a psychological outlet. This was especially true for African-American workers who used dance as a release from the boredom and cruelty of slavery. In many ways, new forms of repression led to more creative forms of resistance, often expressed in the form of dancing.

The most obvious purpose of tap was to entertain. William Kemp did his "Nine Daies Wonder" jig to entertain Elizabethan crowds, just as Thomas Dartmouth Rice and the host of other minstrel performers did their dances to amuse 19th century audiences. Slaves who danced for eels at the Catherine Market in New York City, and slaves who danced for their masters at the big house, all tapped to entertain. The refinement of tap throughout the early years of vaudeville was largely due to a desire to entertain an audience.

2. Flexibility in the sense of not being tied to any one institution:

The early precursors of tap were never strictly associated with any one particular institution. On the contrary, percussive dancing has been a part of a wide range of disparate social and economic groups. Gypsies, slaves, professional entertainers, church worshipers, mill workers, aristocrats — many types of people from many cultures throughout the world have used percussive footwork to express themselves.

3. Flexibility in the sense of not being limited to a small elite either in terms of performance or observance:

Slaves and slave owners, peasants and aristocrats, natives and immigrants, nomadic cultures and those who remained virtually isolated from outside influences, religious groups and prostitutes, professional choreographers and amateurs: all had some effect upon the development of tap. The broad spectrum of minstrel and vaudeville performers and their many varied backgrounds attest to the wide diversity of peoples who contributed to tap, and the audiences of early forms of tap were as varied as the people who performed the dance. William Henry Lane danced for slum dwellers in the barrooms of the Five Points district of New York and also tapped for Queen Victoria.

Because tap dancing was not based solely in the rigid forms of court dance, but also contained elements of folk dancing and improvisational ornamentations, it became a hodgepodge of everything from African syncopations to Irish footwork; the result was a dance that was truly accessible to all people, performers and audience members alike.

4. A number of links to other aspects of culture:

The history of American tap is inextricably bound up with the culture of American slavery. From the first dancing of the slaves on the deck of the slave ship to the stereotypical caricature of the minstrel man's shuffle, slavery was at the root of tap dance. Tap dance can be directly traced to the banning of African drums as a result of the slave rebellion at Stono in 1739. The emancipation of the slaves led to mass migrations to the urban centers of the North where African-American plantation dances were mixed with the dances of the European immigrants who lived in areas like Five Points in New York.

Religion also played a significant part in the history of this art form. One example is the ring shout which developed out of the church's edicts against dancing. This led to the creation of footwork that accented beats without crossing the feet, an important development in tap.

The creation of tap dance in the United States was influenced by recurring social contact between different cultures and the eventual assimilation of different

cultural elements into the American consciousness. A constant stream of immigrants each contributed their traditions to the dance. The Irish brought step dancing. The English brought clog dancing. German immigrants brought the waltz which led to tap dances done in 3/4 time.

The changing face of American theatrical tastes also helped bring about the birth of tap. The quest for a truly American form of theatre led to the minstrel show, and the need for family entertainment resulted in vaudeville. Both of these venues were vital as far as the development of tap was concerned.

5. A structure that allows for improvisation and modification:

The nomadic Gypsies were masters at modifying their dances as they moved from country to country. The Irish dancing masters who created steps that were suitable for their students or steps that matched the only music available, also used improvisation in their dancing. Even the American square dance caller advanced freedom and innovation in the art form.

The most obvious influence which created a structure based on improvisation was African dance; its improvisational elements have remained the hallmark of American tap. The ability to adapt and to survive adverse conditions was at the heart of the African-American slave experience. Black dance provided social solidarity in a hostile environment. This noble trait was translated into the flexibility and creativeness of their dances and became a vital part of tap.

6. Attributes that make it entertaining or potentially marketable:

Percussive dance has always been entertaining. The early art of tap dancing continually evolved and early tap dancers continually reached a wider audience. The Irish dancing master on top of a soaped barrel and the English dancer clogging on a small square on top of a pedestal, both captured their audiences with their skill and daring. Tourists flocked to watch the dances at Congo Square in New Orleans or to attend a quadroon ball. John Durang with his hornpipe, "Daddy" Rice with Jump Jim Crow, the Virginia Minstrels, and countless minstrel and vaudeville performers all realized that tap dancing was both entertaining and marketable.

7. Potential for marking identity in situations of contact:

As a percussive dance, tap is meant to be heard as well as seen. When feet contact the floor and tap sounds are made, the form of the dance is instantly recognizable.

8. The ability to change from being a recreational dance to one for formal occasions and vice versa:

Certain elements of tap grew out of formal sacred dance rituals which gradually evolved into secularized dances. Other elements came from codified dance forms of the court and the aristocracy that were instilled with new rhythms and structures and modified to suit the demands of the peasant class. Curt Sachs in his book *World History of the Dance* states that

> When the dance in a too highly refined society becomes anemic [it turns first to] the peasantry of the country. [If it cannot find nourishment there, it turns to] foreign peoples, who are more primitive in their way of life and superior in physical mobility and expressiveness.[4]

Tap was continually rejuvenated and refreshed with elements absorbed from the rich cultures of the Africans, Native Americans, or peasant peoples of Europe.

In turn, rural dances were consistently urbanized and formalized. As with the country dances set down in John Playford's *Dancing Master*, what started out as informal entertainment often became structured and codified.

The pigeon wing was a plantation dance that was initially performed for the simple entertainment and pleasure of the performer and perhaps other slaves or white slave owners. This dance evolved into a display piece on the minstrel stage and continued to evolve into the flash movements of vaudeville dancers.

The art of tap dancing contains each of the characteristics set down by Anya Peterson Royce, and the many sociological and cultural influences that created tap have guaranteed its survival. Furthermore, by tracing the development of tap dancing, one can trace the cultural changes within the societies that created the art. Royce states:

> Much about change in dance form and culture is applicable to culture change in general ... dance is a readily observable microcosm of what is happening in a larger social and cultural context.[5]

The Development of Tap Steps

Tap steps evolved in many ways. Sometimes traditional movements were simply recombined in a new way and new steps were created by reworking or reorienting older existing forms. Sometimes existing steps were intensified, exaggerated, or emphasized to such an extent that they became totally new. This especially happened when the dance was moved from urban environments into theatrical settings.

Steps were also varied as different cultures interacted with each other which often resulted in oversimplifications and stereotyping. Interestingly enough these overblown stereotypes were often then taken over by the same group they were originally applied to and incorporated into that group's identity. This was clearly done when plantation dances were used by minstrel performers and later taken over by black entertainers.

Tap steps and terminology were traditionally handed down from dancer to dancer; in addition, dancers developed their own styles as steps were taught, borrowed, or stolen. Even after dancing schools started offering classes in tap, most dancers created their own steps and developed their own style, often watching each other and doing what they called "stealing steps." Stealing steps was not like learning from a teacher today in which the goal is to do the step exactly as taught by the teacher. Instead, it was to get the idea of the step or the feel of the rhythm, and use one's imagination to create a new step. Jimmy Cagney once explained,

> All we ever did was steal from each other, modify steps to suit ourselves and in that way develop our individual styles.[6]

There was an unwritten law that one never really stole someone's step. The cardinal rule was, "Thou Shalt Not Copy Another's Steps — Exactly."[7] There were serious consequences if one did try to plagiarize another dancer's steps. Tap dancer Baby Laurence explained how dancers used to line up to get front row seats at the various tap acts.

> They watched you like hawks and if you used any of their pet steps, they just stood right up in the theater and told everybody about it at the top of their voices.[8]

One of the greatest rhythm tappers of all times, John Bubbles, was notorious for the sly way he could extract a step from a competitor. Watching another dancer at the Hoofers Club, he bided his time until he saw something he could use. "Oh, oh," he said," you lost a beat back there — now try that step again." The dancer would start over only to be stopped again and again until Bubbles had learned the step.

Then Bubbles announced, "You know that reminds me of a step I used to do," and he proceeded to demonstrate a variation or two of that dancer's original step.[9]

Most dancers realized that "stealing steps" from other dancers was the best and quickest way to expand their own repertoire. Because there were no formal tap dance schools, observation of others was the only way to learn anything new. Dancer Eddie Rector said, "Shucks, if you could copyright a step nobody could lift a foot."[10]

Tap Terminology

In 1919, when Ned Wayburn formed the first tap dance school in New York City, steps and combinations took on a more formal structure which could be taught within a classroom setting. As tap dancing gained prominence on the stage, it also gained acceptance in the classroom. The first codified set of terms was put down on paper in the 1930s by physical education teachers who wanted to include rhythm movements in their curriculums.[11]

> Clog and tap dancing attained considerable success in schools and colleges during the 1920s and early 1930s. These dance forms were descended from traditional steps found in the jig of the Elizabethan period, the shuffling and foot-tapping steps of Latin countries and the British Isles, and Negro plantation dances. In its earlier development, the term "clog dance" was used, based on the original use of shoes with wooden soles, which created rather crude and heavy rhythmic patterns. Tap dancing, which made use of leather soles with aluminum heels and toe taps, and of modern, popular music, with faster and more syncopated tempo and rhythms, gradually replaced clog on the musical stage and, ultimately, in dance education.[12]

In 1940, author Anne Schley Duggan, who wrote on tap dancing extensively in this period, elaborated on the use of tap and clog in the educational environment:

> Clog is to tap dancing, therefore, what natural is to modern dance — an immediate predecessor to designate this type of rhythmic work in educational institutions. The term *clog* persisted in education long after it had been replaced by *tap* in professional circles. This was due in part to the school's hesitancy to sponsor activity associated with the theater. The name persists now partly due to habit and partly due to the fact that much published material was brought out during the period when *clog*, not *tap* dance, was the correct term for school teachers....[13]

Tap terminology became fairly standardized between the 1930s and 1950s, although many variations continued to exist. Even today, new terms are continually being coined. Most modern tap dancers agree upon the basic vocabulary even though there is not a general consensus about the names of all steps.

Tap steps get their names from a variety of sources, some of which are:

1. The way they sound:

Examples are the chug, the flap, the quack, the rattle, and the spank, among others. More complex and modern examples are bolero shuffles which mimic the rhythm of Ravel's *Bolero,* and the Addams Family, which imitates the rhythms of the television show theme song of the same name.

2. The way the movement looks or what it resembles:

Examples are bells, in which the feet click to the side as if a bell was ringing; grapevines, the execution of which shows the twistings of a vine; falling off the log, which is demonstrated by the off-balance,

falling feel of the step; and wings, which mimic the flapping wings of a bird.[14] Trenches were so named because they resembled World War I soldiers climbing out of the trenches, as was over the top, which imitated the movement of a doughboy sliding over the top of the trench. The buck dance is a reference to the boisterous movements of buccaneers and later was connected to the bucking of a male deer. Legend has it that the name tack annie came about when a woman was being arrested in Harlem; as she struggled with the police, swaying her body from side to side, the neighborhood children cried, "They're 'tackin' [attacking] Annie." The side to side movement was then imitated in tap dances and labeled as the tack annie.

3. The person who created it or popularized them:

The maxiford was named for dancer, Maxie Ford; the patricola, for Tom Patricola; the kabbibble, for Abe Kabbibble; the Bandy twist, for Jim Bandy; and the Lindy was named for Charles Lindbergh.

4. Where they were created or introduced to the general public:

Examples include the Charleston, the Cincinnati, shuffle off to Buffalo, and the Lancashire clog. The Irish also falls into this category.

5. The purpose the steps serve:

The most obvious example of how the purpose of a step determines its labeling is the time-step, which was originally used to set the tempo or time of a dance. Kenneth Burchill in his book *Step Dancing* explains it thus:

> When a theatrical, particularly a variety artist, is playing at a different theatre each week, he frequently has trouble with the tempo of the music, for even the best of conductors can hardly be expected to secure the right tempo for a very complicated dance which he has never before seen, and which is probably full of cross rhythms and "off beats."

And thus it became necessary to make the first step of a dance a step with clearly-defined rhythm and a readily recognizable one. Hence, the step that set the time was, naturally enough, called "Time Step."[15]

In a similar way, the break, which is used as a break in the rhythm, could also be classified as a tap term named for its function.

6. The number of sounds utilized:

Numbers were often used as the names of steps. For example, a step which made only one sound used to be called a one, a brush-step (or flap), or a brush-brush (or shuffle); which consisted of two sounds were commonly called twos. A three was a shuffle-step and made three sounds. There were also fours, fives, sevens, and so forth. Time-steps were also labeled as singles, doubles, and triples according to the number of sounds utilized.

7. As a memory device:

Mnemonic devices have often been used to teach the rhythm of tap steps, which has frequently resulted in the same phrases becoming the actual term. The best example of this is the phrase "Thanks for the buggy ride," which was used to teach students a single offbeat (stomp) time-step. Time-steps then became known as thanks for the buggy rides, or more simply buggy rides. Other examples include reverse cramproll turns being called happy to tap turns, and the many variations of shave and a haircut used to punctuate the end of dances.

Later Developments

During the first decade of the 20th century the upper body began to be more utilized as tap assimilated the gestures and movements of various social dances. The Charleston and the shimmy especially were regularly incorporated into tap routines during this period. Steps like shuffle off to Buffalo and falling off a log, which had begun as simple jazz steps that did not accent the sound of the feet, were taken over by tappers and sounds were added. Rhythm buck developed around 1910 with the introduction of ragtime which added further syncopation to the simpler rhythm of the basic buck step.

During this time, flash and acrobatic movements started to be more common in tap numbers for two reasons. First, dancers were looking for a way to spice up their routines and grab an audience's attention. Second, when dancers started performing to the accompaniment of bands and orchestras, tappers needed steps that depended upon visual impact so that when the music and the routine reached the climax, the integrity of the piece was still intact when the sound of the taps was drowned out.

With the increasing demand for dancing entertainment in vaudeville and with the advent of the movie musical, with stars such as Fred Astaire, Eleanor Powell, Ann Miller, Gene Kelly, and Shirley Temple, tap reached its zenith. From the 1920s through the 1930s, tap became the most popular form of American entertainment.

Two factors contributed to the decline of tap in the 1950s and 1960s: rock and roll, and the choreography that Agnes de Mille did for the Broadway show, *Oklahoma,* which featured ballet dancing within a theatrical context.[16] Ballet killed tap as the popular dance style for musical comedy and stayed in vogue until Bob Fosse did *Pajama Game* and, with his "Steam Heat" number, made jazz the current fad. Jazz idioms culminated in *West Side Story* and tap was virtually forgotten. The sudden shift in tastes on Broadway, along with the advent of bebop, the move from big bands to small combos, and the coming of rock and roll, all contributed to the decreasing popularity of tap.

Simultaneously in the movies, as the

'50s approached, production costs and the introduction of television killed the Hollywood musical in its original form. Studios could no longer afford to keep musical performers under contract and, as a result, grooming and training programs were terminated. The output of major musicals dropped to about one or two every year which resulted in the virtual absence of tap on the big screen. In addition, a tax levied against dancing nightclubs and the gradual disappearance of variety shows in general made tap fade into the woodwork.

Then in January 1971, 62-year-old Ruby Keeler brought her traditional buck style of dancing back to Broadway in the revival of *No, No, Nanette.* The show packed houses for months. Tap dancing was back, and its appeal was stronger than ever. In Hollywood, movie producers were eager to latch onto the trend, and in 1974, MGM released *That's Entertainment*, presenting clips that spanned the Golden Era of movie musical tap. It was a box-office smash. Dance studios filled up again with students eager to learn tap dancing. Around this same time, young, talented dancers such as Brenda Bufalino sought out the old masters of tap, bringing them out of retirement to teach the art form.

In the 1980s tap was back on Broadway in full force with shows such as *My One and Only, The Tap Dance Kid, 42nd Street,* and *Sophisticated Ladies* with Gregory Hines. Hines also appeared on-screen; his movies *Tap, White Knights,* and *Cotton Club* helped to make tap more popular than ever. Other films such as *Pennies from Heaven* also prominently featured tap

dancing. In the 1990s the trend continued with Broadway shows like *Me and My Girl, Crazy for You, Bring in Da Noise, Bring in Da Funk, Stomp,* and *Tap Dogs,* and in the new millennium, tap is still prominently featured in the revival of *42nd Street* and in Susan Strohman's inventive choreography for *The Producers.* The popularity of these musicals attests to the fact that tap has not lost any of its appeal with audiences.

Performing groups such as the American Tap Dance Orchestra, Manhattan Tap, Rhapsody in Taps, and the Jazz Tap Ensemble, just to name a few, have helped to perpetuate the development of the art form, experimenting with new styles and varieties of rhythm in tap as well as reclaiming some of the older ones. Technical advances with sound equipment and computers have also pushed tap in new directions. Perhaps more importantly, tappers such as Savion Glover have been responsible for infusing a raw, powerful, street energy into tap that has helped spread its appeal to a whole new generation.

Tap dance is truly and definitely an American art form.[17] Like America itself, this dance is composed of many disparate elements from many different cultures. The roots of tap may be planted firmly in American soil, but the seeds of this dance form were brought here from many different lands. This is what makes tap dancing so rich and colorful — it lives beyond boundaries, race, creed, and economics. It is music in the feet and it is as impossible to resist as our own humanity because the roots of tap are our own deep roots.

Notes

1. Irish Influences

1. Pat Murphy, *Toss the Feathers: Irish Set Dancing* (Dublin: Mercier Press, 1995), pp. 17–18.

2. A rising fifth in music occurs when the thematic material played in a certain key is taken up an interval of five steps in a tonic dominant progression.

3. Other variations include "gig," "gigue," "giga," "gigua," and "geige."

4. Sachs also links the word to the Frankish *giga* and the Norse *gigja*. Anne Schley Duggan states that the etymology of "jig" can be traced to a word meaning "to revolve," or "a top," both indicating the whirling and spinning of the dancer. Lilly Grove in her book *Dancing*, traces the word to the German *geige*, which was an early fiddle used to accompany dances.

5. W.G. Raffé, *Dictionary of the Dance* (New York: Barnes, 1964) p. 247.

6. The cinque-pace or cinq-pas was derived from fencing positions. The five steps consisted of:

   a. *droite*, a straight move forward or back
   b. *ouvert*, opening sideways
   c. *ronde*, sweeping the foot on the floor
   d. *glissé*, sliding the foot as in a glissade
   e. *tournée*, turning.

Other moves were added later including jumps and beats. The dance ended with *la salute*, a bow similar to the révérence.

7. The popular longways dance in which two lines of dancers face each other did not get its name from being performed in two long lines. Rather, the name is derived from the old Welsh word *llongsaer* and the Gaelic word *longsaor*, both of which mean shipbuilder. The dance actually grew out of a church ritual in which dancers moved around the outline of a ship in a dance called the "ship of salvation."

8. All of the quotes attributed to William Kemp are from his book *Kemps Nine Daies Wonder* (London: Printed by Nicholas Ling, 1600).

9. John Playford (the Elder) was born in Norwich, England, in 1623. He made his living as a publisher of music and dance books. Playford began collecting tunes for country dances and instructions about how to perform them and published them in his book, *The Dancing Master, or Plaine and Easie Rules for the Dancing of*
Country Dances, with the Tune to Each Dance in 1651. The first manual contained 105 dances. The book's popularity led to 17 subsequent editions. After the first edition, Playford shortened the title to *The Dancing Master* and added new dances. By the 18th edition the book contained more than 1,400 dances. Playford died in London in 1687. The importance and influence of Playford's manual in the development of social dancing cannot be stressed enough. The effect of codifying and naming rural dances not only made them marketable to a wide audience, but also spurred a whole flurry of dance manuals that helped to further disseminate various dances.

10. Dancing masters who came to the American colonies were also influenced by John Playford's *Dancing Master*. A form of the Virginia reel is found in Playford's manual under the name "Sir Roger de Coverley." A dance called the Kentucky running set, which was done in the Appalachian Mountains, was also very similar to an English country dance found in Playford's book. In the *International Encyclopedia of Dance*, vol. 3, p. 238, under the heading "Great Britain: English Traditional Dance," it states, "...the running set was a very early form that had been taken to America, probably by immigrants from rural England, and it predated the dances found in Playford's London repertory."

11. "Ireland: Traditional Dance," *International Encyclopedia of Dance*, Vol. 3 (New York: Oxford University Press, 1998) p. 516.

12. Lilly Grove, *Dancing* (London: Longmans, Green, and Co., 1901) p. 207.

13. This quote was taken from the web article "A Brief Overview of Irish Dance."

14. In England, between 1850 and 1910, cockneys had an expression "to cut capers on a trencher." A trencher was a small wooden platter used for serving food and therefore the phrase meant one could dance in a small space. Annie Fairchild, in her book *Appalachian Clogging: What It Is and How to Do It.* (Ithaca, NY: self-published, 1983) p. 1, relates the following story:

> An Irish friend of mine told me how her grandmother would invite guests to dance on her best china platter, turned upside down on the floor, to demonstrate the lightness of their dancing.

15. In the web article *Irish Step Dancing: A Brief History*, by Don Haurin and Ann Richens, the authors speak of one dancing master who advertised himself as "an artificial rhythmical walker" and "instructor of youth in the Terpsichorean art." This type of advertisement was typical for the more elite class of Irish dancing masters who associated themselves with French manners and training.

16. Murphy, p. 29, quoting Shelton Mackenzie's *Bits of Blarney*.

17. The Irish first came to New York in 1643. Then in a wave of immigration following the American Revolution, they left their homeland because there was a simultaneous explosion in the population and a decline in crop prices. The greatest surge came as a result of the famine or "Great Hunger" as it was called which had resulted from a fungus which blighted the potato harvest between 1845 and 1851. Over 52,000 Irish immigrants landed in New York between June and December 1847 and by 1860, 25 percent of the New York population was Irish.

18. "Jig," *International Encyclopedia of Dance,* Vol. 3 (New York: Oxford University Press, 1998) p. 607.

19. "Ireland: Traditional Dance," *International Encyclopedia of Dance,* Vol. 3 (New York: Oxford University Press, 1998) p. 517.

20. Grove, pp. 205–206.

21. Joan Lawson, *European Folk Dance* (London: Sir Isaac Pittman & Sons, 1953) p. 174, mentions one rarely seen jig called, the "Tune of Occupation," in which the hand is held raised with a clenched fist. The title of the dance is an obvious reference to the English occupation of Ireland, and explains the threatening gesture.

22. Murphy, p. 34.

23. Lawson, p. 143.

24. After an hour or more of playing, Irish pipers often played a tune called "Gather Up the Money" so that dancers would drop coins into the hole he had dug and "pay the piper." The tune today is known as "The Blackberry Blossom." In Victorian England this tradition was continued in the penny hop, a country peasant dance in which each dancer contributed one penny to the fiddler. In Scotland, a similar practice was called the penny wedding.

25. Anne Schley Duggan, *The Complete Tap Dance Book* (Washington D.C: University Press of America, 1977) p. ix, quoting Troy and Margaret Kinney's book *The Dance,* p. 162.

2. English Influences

1. A less likely story suggests that "clog" is a corruption of the word "clod," and referred to the practice of African slaves rhythmically kicking newly plowed clods of earth as they worked. The theory is that this became known as "clod dancing" in the United States.

2. "Hard jig" is still done today. The toe end of the sole of the shoe is built up and sometimes filled with metal nails hammered in to help accentuate the sound of the dancing.

3. "Clogging: Historical Overview," *International Encyclopedia of Dance,* vol. 2 (New York: Oxford University Press, 1998) p. 179.

4. As the popularity of clogging spread throughout England, informal competitions were regularly held on street corners and in pubs. Formal clogging contests were also held, with such prizes as money, medals, cups, and belts awarded to the top dancers. Clogging became so popular in Lancashire, it was taught with other sports like wrestling and boxing at the local gymnasium. Famous minstrel clog dancer, Barney Fagan, stated that the Lancashire clog was first introduced in America in the 1830s by British and Irish sailors. He said that the traditional Lancashire clog was made up of 20 steps and the "shuffle-off." As the dance mutated in the United States, different styles of the dance developed such as the American clog and the American Lancashire clog. Fagan wrote:

> The Lancashire dance, beautiful in its jingly rhythmic excellence, danced on a spot or marble slab 15" square, after years of outstanding favoritism finally gave way to the ingenuity of Americans who created a style of space-covering picturesque, and smartly executed clog dance, of which there were many wonderful exponents.

(The above quote by Barney Fagan is found in Rhett Krause's article, "Step Dancing on the Boston Stage: 1841–1869." In *Country Dance and Song,* no. 22, pp. 1–19, June 1992, p. 4.)

5. Lilly Grove, *Dancing* (London: Longmans, Green, and Co., 1907) p. 11.

6. W.G. Raffé, in the *Dictionary of the Dance* (New York: Barnes, 1964) p. 228, suggests that the hornpipe was originally part of a ritual festival honoring Herne, the Saxon god of the harvest. The hand on the stomach movements that were common in the dance were symbolic of having eaten a good meal. He infers that the word *herne* is the source of the name for the dance and is also equated with the word corn and cornucopia which again relates to harvest themes.

7. "Hornpipe," *International Encyclopedia of Dance,* vol. 3 (New York: Oxford University Press, 1998) pp. 375–376. In the *Dictionary of the Dance,* W.G. Raffé gives additional information about the derivation of the hornpipe when he tells of a rural festival dance done at ancient harvest celebrations in England called the "Herne-Pipe." It was danced to the accompaniment of the pipe and was performed in honor of the god of the harvest, Herne. Lilly Grove, in her book *Dancing* (London: Longmans, Green, and Co., 1907) p. 220, says that hornpipe steps "are modelled on a gipsy dance of Russia called the Barina."

8. The hornpipe was popularized by a performer by the name of T. P. Cooke. Mr. Cooke was also responsible for collecting many hornpipe steps.

9. References to egg-dances can be found in the writings of Chaucer and are also mentioned in the Elizabethan comedy, *The Longer Thou Livest, the More Fool Thou Art.* In that play, one character comments, "Upon my one foote I can hoppe and daunce it trimley about an egge" (Grove, p. 129.) Goethe also wrote of the egg-dance in *Wilhelm Meister:*

> Lightly, nimbly, quickly and with hairsbreadth accuracy, she carried on the dance. She skipped

so sharply and surely along between the eggs, and trod so closely down beside them, that you would have thought every instant she must trample one of them in pieces, or kick the rest away in her rapid turns. By no means! She touched no one of them, though winding herself through their mazes with all kinds of steps, wide and narrow, nay even with leaps, and at last kneeling.

(Translation taken from Mystical World Wide Web—*Folklore of Eggs*.)

10. Lilly Grove, *Dancing* (London: Longmans, Green, and Co.,1907) p. 129.

11. There were many forms of the egg-dance. The simplest forms involved hopping on one foot while trying to coax an egg into a cup or remove a cup covering an egg. Other versions included trying to get eggs into a basket. In 1498 at the wedding celebration of Margaret of Austria and Philip the Handsome, two couples danced among 100 eggs with the promise that if they did not break any, they would receive permission to marry as well. After three attempts, they were successful. At one time, egg-dances were used by the Danish Royal Ballet to sharpen up a dancer's footwork.

12. Morris dances grew out of English sword dances. These weapon dances were based upon ancient sacrificial rites and can be traced to the Romans, who adopted them after their conquest of the Greeks, and brought them to England when they occupied the British Isles. These Greco-Roman forms blended with ancient fertility rites that were already part of Celtic rituals. The dances were not only used as military training exercises, but were also associated with the priests of the Roman god of war, Mars, and with their fertility rites involving the sowing of seeds. The English sword dance mimes decapitation and resurrection during various figures and appears to have symbolized the death and rebirth of the seasons. The rites also refer back to animal and human sacrifices which were used to insure a good growth of crops. These weapon/ fertility dances appeared simultaneously in England, Germany, France, Spain, and Sweden, each with regional variations. They were later the understructure for dances which mimed the conflict between the Christians and the Moors. These particular forms were preserved and perpetuated in England in the distinctive Morris dance (Duggan, *Folk Dances of the British Isles*, pp. 34–35).

13. Other names for the dance include the *Morisco*, the *Moresca*, the *Morisk*, the French *Mourisque*, *Moresque*, the German *Moriskentanz* and *Maruschka-Tanz*, and the Spanish *Mauresque* or *Moresque*.

14. "Morris Dance," *International Encyclopedia of Dance*, vol. 4 (New York: Oxford University Press, 1998) p. 473, and "Moresca" *International Encyclopedia of Dance*, vol. 4 (New York: Oxford University Press, 1998) pp. 460–461.

15. Morris dances were most frequently performed in spring, especially during Lent or Easter, or on May Day. The symbolic battle came to represent winter and darkness being overcome by spring. This pagan spring ritual of the battle between good and evil, summer and winter, and death and resurrection was then connected with the battle between the Moors and the Christians.

16. Thomas Reginald St. Johnson, *A History of*

Dancing (London: Marshall, Hamilton, Kent & Co., 1906) pp. 47–48.

17. There was a category of dance in Spain called *danzas de cascabeles* in which little bells were sewn onto the costume to provide accompaniment to the dances. Grove mentions in her book *Dancing*, on page 218, that English Gypsies adopted the custom of wearing bells on their dancing costumes as early as the 16th century. She quotes someone named Dekker: "Their apparell is od and phantasticke ... hanging [on] their bodies, like morris-dancers, with bels, and other toyses, to intice the country people to flocke about them, and to wonnder at their fooleries...." It was a common folk belief that noise could drive away evil spirits. Bells, clashing sticks, and other noise makers were used for this purpose.

18. Real weapons were sometimes used in Morris dances. At other times, real weapons were replaced with sticks or castanets. In England, it became common to substitute handkerchiefs for the weapons. There is speculation that the Morris dance is closely related to the Matachin, a mock combat sword dance that was popular in the 16th century. These narrative battle dances also utilized clownish performers who attached bells around the knees. The Matachin made its way to the Western Hemisphere with the Spanish conquerors, and such characters as Montezuma and Cortés were included because the dance related the story of the Aztecs' conversion to Christianity. Matachins are still performed in Mexico and the Southwestern United States.

19. In addition to the use of blackface, the typical costume of clog dancers who performed in American minstrel shows was also based upon Lancashire Morris traditions. It typically consisted of a fancy white shirt, knee pants that were decorated down the sides, and a wide sash worn at the waist. Sometimes the dancer's shoes were painted gold or silver or embellished with other decoration.

20. The Morris Brothers Minstrels in Boston presented the "Cocoa Nut Dance" (also called the "Cocoa Congo Dance") in 1860, 1862, and 1863. Rhett Krauss suggests a possible connection between this minstrel dance and the Lancashire Morris dance of Bacup and the Bacup Britannia Coconut Dancers, who he says may have been inspired by English minstrel shows.

21. In "Great Britain: English Traditional Dance," *International Encyclopedia of Dance*, vol. 3, p. 242, it is suggested that perhaps the blacking of the face was a response to the popularity of minstrel shows in Victorian England. During this period of British history, Morris dancers sometimes replaced the sticks, which were traditionally used to make rhythms, with tambourines. References to the Morris Dance being connected to the mining profession in England were found online at the official web site of the Britannia Coconut Dancers.

22. When William Kemp performed his famous Morris-jig dance during his "Nine Daies Wonder," he was met at his destination in Norwich and led into the city by "wifflers," who were officers appointed by the Mayor to keep the crowd back.

23. Anne Schley Duggan, Jeanette Schlottman, and Abbie Rutledge, *Folk Dances of the British Isles* (New York: Barnes, 1948) p. 37.

24. "Jack-in-the-Green" became a popular folk

hero throughout England, and especially in London where he became associated with chimney sweeps. The characters of Robin Hood, Maid Marian, Friar Tuck, Will Scarlet, Little John, and Robin's other Merry Men were commonly represented in Morris dancing. The character of Maid Marian was connected to the cult Mary Gypsy or St. Mary of Egypt. St. Mary of Egypt had lived in Alexandria, Egypt as a prostitute until age 29 when she took a pilgrimage to Jerusalem, selling her body to sailors along the way to pay for her passage. In Jerusalem, invisible forces prevented her from entering the Church of the Holy Sepulchre. She begged for forgiveness and promised to repent and was then able to enter the church where she saw the wood of the true cross. She was baptized in the Jordan River, and led by a vision of the Virgin Mary, she journeyed into the desert where she lived as a hermit until she died in A.D. 530. Crusaders returned to England with tales of the holy woman and medieval England became so involved in Mary worship that England became known as Merry England, "merry" being a corruption of "Mary." The character of Mary Gypsy was connected to the ancient sea-goddess, Marian, a "merry-maid," or mermaid whose symbol was the scallop sea shell. Many crusaders sewed scallop shells to their clothes in honor of her. Eventually Mary Gypsy was converted into the "May Bride," the partner of Merlin. Merlin in turn was transformed into Robin Hood, a character frequently associated with the Morris dance. It is highly possible that the term "Morrismen" was actually derived from the words "Mary's men."

3. African Influences

1. Lynn Fauley Emery, *Black Dance: From 1619 to Today* (Princeton, NJ: Princeton Univ. Press, 1988) p. 2.

2. Thomas Reginald St. Johnson, *A History of Dancing.* (London: Marshall, Hamilton, Kent & Co., 1906) p. 63.

3. Lee Warren, *The Dance of Africa: an Introduction* (Englewood Cliffs, NJ: Prentice-Hall, 1972) p. 28.

4. Jacqui Malone, *Steppin' On the Blues: The Visible Rhythms of African American Dance* (Chicago: University of Illinois Press, 1996) p. 12.

5. The aspects of African dance that are listed in this chapter were gathered from various sources. Numbers one through seven are discussed in Marshall and Jean Stearns' book *Jazz Dance: The Story of American Vernacular Dance*, pp. 14–15. (The Stearns combine number six and number seven: propulsive rhythm and swing.) Numbers eight and nine, polyrhythmic body movements and the aspect of mockery, derision and parody, are found on pp. 17–18 and pp. 32–36 in *Steppin' On the Blues: The Visible Rhythms of African American Dance*, by Jacqui Malone. (Malone also discusses numbers four and six in these pages, and number eleven on pp. 18–19.) Number ten, and number five, are discussed by Edward Thorpe, in *Black Dance*, p. 13. Number eleven, and further discussion on number seven, are found in the chapter "Tap Dance: Manifestation of the African Aesthetic," by Cheryl Willis in the book *African Dance: An Artistic, Historical, and Philosophical Inquiry*

pp. 147–150. All of the books listed above were valuable resources in researching African and African-American dance, as were Lynn Fauley Emery's book, *Black Dance: From 1619 to Today,* and Katrina Hazzard-Gordon's book, *Jookin': The Rise of Social Dance Formations in African-American Culture.*

6. Malone, p. 9, quoting a Kongo proverb.

7. Roger D. Abrahams, *Singing the Master: The Emergence of African American Culture in the Plantation South* (New York: Pantheon Books, 1992) p. 98.

8. Coolness was considered the most important expression of a person's character in African culture. For the Yoruba in southwestern Nigeria, a composed, cool appearance expressed by a rhythmically controlled body and a calm face, reflected a prudent, collected mind and demonstrated an individual's inner character. In West African dance, status was determined by the type of dance that one performed. A restrained dance style denoted prestige. Gerald Jonas, in his book *Dancing: The Power of Dance Around the World* (New York, Harry Abrams, 1992) p. 167, wrote,

> To exhibit cool by moving properly signifies power (both temporal and spiritual) and the well-being such power brings.

9. Cheryl Willis, "Tap Dance: Manifestation of the African Aesthetic," in *African Dance: An Artistic, Historical, and Philosophical Inquiry*, ed. Kariamu Weish Asante, pp. 145–159 (Trenton, NJ: Africa World Press, 1996) p. 152.

10. Marian Hannah Winter, "Juba and American Minstrelsy" In *Chronicles of the American Dance* (New York: Henry Holt, 1948) p. 39.

11. In the article "Our Third Root; On African Presence in American Population" in *Annual Editions: African American History 2000/2001*, pp. 9–10, Luz María Martínez Montiel describes the vast numbers of people that died as a result of the slave trade. She states:

> According to Du Bois, the number of men and women seized from the African continent approximates 15 million, while De la Roncière puts it at 20 million; if however, to these numbers are added those who died during the voyage (35 percent), in the slave pens on the African coast (25 percent), or on the journey from the interior of the continent to the ports (50 percent), as well as the victims of the manhunt (50 percent), a more precise idea of the number sacrificed can be had.

12. Many Africans committed suicide believing they would be reborn again back in Africa. To prevent further suicides, slave traders and slave owners began beheading suicide victims, thinking that it would discourage others who would not want to be reborn mutilated. What the Christian slave owners, who believed in bodily resurrection, did not realize, was that Africans believed that it was the soul that returned. In some parts of Africa, burial practices included the removal of the head of the deceased which was then kept for annual commemoration ceremonies.

13. Howard Zinn, *A People's History of the United States, 1492–Present* (New York: Harper Collins, 1999) p. 29.

14. Dena J. Epstein, in her book *Sinful Tunes and*

Spirituals: Black Folk Music to the Civil War (Chicago: University of Illinois Press, 1977) p. 11, wrote;

> [By 1801,] the practice of "dancing the slaves" on shipboard was so widely known that it became one of the clichés of didactic literature. "The Sorrows of Yamba," a poem, was included in a collection of sermons, tracts, and dialogues "recommended to all masters and mistresses to be used in their families." It described life in Africa and the horrors of the slave ship as a prelude to the supreme indignity:
>
> > At the savage Captain's beck
> > Now like brutes they make us prance;
> > Smack the cat about the deck,
> > And in scorn they bid us dance.

A strange verse to find among sermons dealing with the duty of obeying one's master! Its sympathy with the slaves indicates that it might have been written during the second half of the 18th century, probably in England, when the Enlightenment was in full sway, and the stereotype of the brutish, happy slave had not yet been standardized.

15. Emery, p. 8.
16. Emery, pp. 6–7.
17. Katrina Hazzard-Gordon, *Jookin': The Rise of Social Dance Formations in African-American Culture* (Philadelphia: Temple University Press, 1990) p. 8.
18. Emery, p. 10.

4. Dance in the West Indies

1. The information about Columbus and the Native American slave trade was drawn from two primary sources; *Lies My Teacher Told Me,* by James W. Loewen, pp. 29–65, and *A People's History of the United States, 1492–Present,* by Howard Zinn, pp. 1–22.
2. Howard Zinn, *A People's History of the United States, 1492–Present* (New York: Harper Collins, 1999) p. 7.
3. James W. Loewen, *Lies My Teacher Told Me* (New York: The New Press, 1995) p. 53
4. Lynn Fauley Emery, *Black Dance: From 1619 to Today* (Princeton, NJ: Princeton Univ. Press, 1988) p. 16.
5. Ring dances were common in African ritual. Roger D. Abrahams, in his book *Singing the Master: The Emergence of African American Culture in the Plantation South* (New York: Pantheon Books, 1992) p. 104, makes an interesting observation: he says that dancing inside of a ring surrounded by others who encouraged the person in the center with clapping, singing and patting, was "the ultimate opportunity for personal reassurance, for feeling the warmth and support of a tight-locked and indestructible circle within which [each] could act out … feelings without any fear of rejection or shame."
6. Dena J. Epstein, *Sinful Tunes and Spirituals: Black Folk Music to the Civil War* (Chicago: University of Illinois Press, 1977) pp. 30–31.
7. Emery, p. 21.
8. Emery, p. 26.
9. The word "juba" was probably derived from the African word *giouba,* the name of the original dance form. In *Step It Down,* Bessie Jones and Bessie Lomax Hawes give an alternative explanation, stating that the word was derived from "jibba" which was a modification of the word "giblets." The remains and leftover ends of food, called the "giblets," were mixed together with milk in a mush, and the name was given to the dance and patting game because they were similarly composed of a mixture of various elements. In Charles Earle Funk's book, *Heavens to Betsy!,* there is an explanation of the colloquial phrase, "to dance juba." Drawing from the interpretation of Dr. Mitford M. Mathews originally given in *American Speech,* Funk suggests that juba was a common name given to African-American girls who were born on a Monday. Tradition stated that girls born on this day were inclined to mischievous behavior so they had to be regularly punished. The movements which were later taken over by minstrels and called the juba, were an imitation of the involuntary motions that resulted from these girls being hit with a switch. It is doubtful that this is the real explanation for the development of patting juba and the juba dance in the United States. The word "juba" was not only used to describe a dance, but was often also used to describe the dancer. William Henry Lane, for example, was nicknamed "Master Juba." His story is discussed fully in chapter 15.
10. The juba as it was done in Africa and later in the United States was almost always performed as a circle dance. In Haiti, it was done as a set dance with two lines facing each other. Performed like this, the dance was also called the Martinique. This version of the juba was clearly influenced by European elements. In the Stearns book, *Jazz Dance,* p. 28, the authors quote Lisa Lekis, *Folk Dances of Latin America* (New York: Scarecrow Press, 1958), p. 226, as saying that the dance in Cuba was done "using steps and figures of the court of Versailles combined with the hip movements of the Congo."
11. Emery, p. 29.
12. Albert Raboteau, *Slave Religion: The "Invisible Institution" in the Antebellum South* (Oxford: Oxford University Press, 1978) p. 13.
13. After the mass immigration of blacks from the West Indies to New Orleans following the slave insurrection of 1803, dances appeared on the mainland which featured a character called the King of the Wake which had striking similarities to John Canoe. The King of the Wake was the forerunner of the Mardi Gras figure, the King of the Zulus. Because the carnival celebrations of Mardi Gras were segregated, an organization called the Zulu Social Aid and Pleasure Club created separate festivities for the local blacks. The King of the Zulus was the leader of these festivities and was named after the founding organization. The climax of the black Mardi Gras carnival was the Zulu ball. Other characters that are similar to John Canoe are the elected kings of Negro Election Day and Pinkster celebrations, discussed in Chapter Eight.
14. Harvest festival dances helped to further cross-pollinate white and black cultural influences when African slaves began to imitate white dances. In *Black Dance,* p. 47, Lynn Fauley Emery has a passage from the book *Jamaican Folk-lore,* by Martha Beckwith, which

tells of the cakewalk being done at a harvest festival in the West Indies. The book quotes Martin Briggs of Barbados, who stated,

> At crop-gathering time the people [of Barbados] danced in couples, men and women dressed in "Sunday best," in figures the steps of which resembled a "cake-walk."

The imitation of white dances in the West Indies was also fostered by the people of mixed blood. Not accepted by either whites or blacks, these people, called mulattos, took pride in removing themselves from African influences by doing the waltzes, quadrilles and minuets of the white races. Because mulattos were given more privileges than blacks, the tendency was for blacks to imitate the mulattos. This imitation caused black dances to drift further away from their African roots. The move away from purer forms of African dance was also fostered by the growth of the Methodist Church in the islands, which condemned dancing and caused many African forms of dance to either disappear or move underground into secret rituals.

15. The Haitian Voodoo god, Damballa, was taken directly from the African pantheon of gods, but he was depicted in drawings and other artwork as St. Patrick leading the snakes out of Ireland. The representation of African deities as Catholic figures initially provided the slaves a way of secretly worshiping their own gods under the guise of venerating the saints. According to Albert Raboteau, *Slave Religion: The "Invisible Institution" in the Antebellum South.* (Oxford: Oxford University Press, 1978) p. 22,

> African religions have traditionally been amenable to accepting "foreign" gods of neighbors and enemies. It has not been unusual for one people to integrate gods of another into their own cult life especially when social changes, such as migration or conquest, require mythic and ritualistic legitimation.

16. Marshall Stearns, *The Story of Jazz* (New York: Oxford University Press, 1956) p. 48, quotes anthropologist Zora Neal Hurston, who attended a Voodoo ceremony in New Orleans:

> The heel-patting was a perfect drum rhythm, while the hand-clapping had various stimulating breaks, and the fury of the rhythm kept the dancers going until they became possessed.

17. As in Voodoo, the gods of Shango were also depicted as Catholic saints. The identification of certain saints with African deities was based upon the corresponding attributes shared by them. For example, Shango, for whom the cult was named, was the god of thunder, lightning, and sunlight. He was often depicted as St. Barbara, the saint who protected Catholics from lightning and thunder. The emblem of Shango was an ax. When the Shango cult was eventually brought to the United States, there developed an interesting folk tradition among the slaves of chopping the ground or swinging an ax through the air when a storm threatened, so that the storm would be cut in half.

18. Emery, p. 62.

19. The Baptist sect grew in the Caribbean islands with the influx of black slaves who were brought from North America by their Loyalist masters who emigrated there during the American Revolution.

20. Even though it is doubtful that there is any connection between the two groups, there are nevertheless, interesting similarities between the rituals of the Spiritual Baptists in Trinidad and the dance services of the American Shakers. The Spiritual Baptists called their dancing "laboring in the spirit." Shakers also called their dances "laboring." Revival meetings consisted of counterclockwise movement around an altar with stamping movements done to trample evil spirits underfoot. As the body was bent forward, the breath was exhaled, and this was followed by a sharp intake of breath as the body became erect again. This movement was called "trumping" (also "jumping" or "spiritual dancing") and the quick in and out of the breath induced dizziness which in turn signaled the onset of possession. These movements are not only quite similar to Shaker dances, but also closely tied to movements of the ring shout that was done in the United States.

5. Dance in New Orleans

1. The first Africans were brought to New Orleans in 1709. By the Louisiana Purchase in 1803, 38 percent of the total population consisted of enslaved blacks. Free African-Americans made up about 20 percent of the residents of New Orleans.

2. François Dominique Toussaint L'Ouverture was a self-educated Haitian slave who was freed shortly before 1791 and became the organizational head of a rebellion to liberate the slaves. Sparked by the French revolution, mulattos on the island of Haiti rebelled against not being given representation in the French National Assembly. The resulting revolt destroyed the entire structure of Haitian society. In 1792 during the Napoleonic Wars, the British invaded Haiti and occupied the coastal cities, but L'Ouverture, forming an alliance with the remnants of the French government, led a black army against the British and forced their withdrawal from the island. In 1795, Spain ceded its territories on the island to France, and in 1801, L'Ouverture conquered and governed the island, abolished slavery and claimed control over all Hispaniola. Frustrated with L'Ouverture's defection from France and his blockage of French colonial ambitions in the Caribbean, Napoleon sent his brother-in-law, General Charles LeClerc, with a large army to remove him from power. The people resisted and LeClerc was unable to conquer the interior, but a peace treaty was eventually signed. L'Ouverture was seized by trickery and sent to France where he died in the dungeon at Fort-de-Joux. The revolt in Haiti continued and the rebels received aid from American President Thomas Jefferson, who was afraid that Napoleon would use the island as a base to invade Louisiana. The French, who were also ravaged by yellow fever, were forced to withdraw from the island, and Haiti gained its independence in 1804. All whites on the island were either killed or forced to flee, many taking their slaves with them. More than 8,000 immigrants came to New Orleans from Santo Domingo, and in 1809, 34 ships brought more than 5,500 who had

fled from Cuba. Only about one third were white the rest were slaves. This influx of black immigrants from the West Indies brought with it Caribbean dances that were disseminated throughout New Orleans and the surrounding plantations and influenced the development of black dance in the United States.

3. Edward Thorpe, *Black Dance* (Woodstock, New York: Overlook, 1990) p. 12.

4. Lynne Fauley Emery, *Black Dance: From 1619 to Today* (Princeton, NJ: Princeton Univ. Press, 1988) p. 148.

5. There was one incident in which a white man wanted to marry a black women but was not allowed to because of the *Code Noir*. In desperation, the two lovers cut themselves and the white man transferred some of his lover's blood into his body, claiming that he now had black blood in his veins.

Besides prohibiting cohabitation between blacks and whites, the *Code Noir* stated that the condition of slavery was passed on through a mother to her offspring. It also forbade blacks from owning property and holding office. In addition, slaves were prevented from obtaining manumission papers from their masters without consent from the *Conseil Supérier*, the colony's governing body. However, the relative scarcity of white women in New Orleans insured a rather lax enforcement of these regulations. Relationships between white men and black and mixed-blooded women were common. Children of these unions were often set free, and eventually a caste system developed with whites at the top, free blacks in the middle, and slaves at the bottom. One interesting ordinance that grew out of the *Code Noir* and that came about during the Spanish rule of New Orleans stated that women of color were not allowed to flaunt themselves by dressing like whites. Therefore the use of mantillas, elaborate coiffures, caps and feathers was forbidden. Instead, women of color were ordered to wear kerchiefs or *tignons* which signified their lesser status. The women responded by choosing kerchiefs made out of brilliantly colored material, which they twisted into elaborate turbans, attracting even more attention.

6. A system of classification was created by the French to determine a person's racial makeup. The purity of one's blood had to be proven through eight generations. It was mathematically determined that each individual was therefore composed of the 128 units, one unit for each of their 128 ancestors within those eight generations. The race of each of these ancestors determined whether or not a person was colored. This racial caste system extended throughout the black community as well as the white community and those with lighter–toned skin were deemed superior to those with darker skin. Various proportions of black blood determined one's hierarchy within the caste system and each different proportion was assigned a name.

One incident that took place before the Civil War involved one family who accused another of having some black blood. This resulted in a lawsuit. The family that appealed lost their case and was determined in court to be of African heritage. A lampoon of the scandalous court case was written by a quadroon named Joe Beaumont (1820–72). Beaumont's song in turn spurred a Creole folk song called "Tou-cou-tou," which spoke of a maid of dark skin who couldn't find soap strong enough to bleach her skin so she could attend the quadroon balls.

7. The word *placage* in French means a "placing." (A more modern definition is "veneering" or "patchwork.") A *placée* was a woman who was "placed" or "situated." A common nickname for *placées* was *sirènes*, or "sirens."

8. Katrina Hazzard-Gordon, *Jookin': The Rise of Social Dance Formations in African-American Culture* (Philadelphia: Temple University Press, 1990) pp. 60–61.

9. Lyle Saxon, *Fabulous New Orleans* (New Orleans: Robert L. Crager & Co., 1958) p. 182, quoting Harriet Martineau, *Society in America*, 1837. The tragic quadroon became a common character in novels, short stories, and melodramas in the 19th-century.

10. The word "Creole" had various meanings in New Orleans. It generally meant persons who were born in the United States but whose parents were of European origin. The word Creole can be traced to the Spanish *Criollo*, a label used to distinguish those who were born in the New World as opposed to the *Peninsulares*, or those born on the Iberian Peninsula in Spain. Although both *Criollos* and *Peninsulares* were the progeny of two Spanish parents, the *Peninsulares* having been in the mother country, were considered to be of higher status. After the Spanish took over New Orleans, they similarly applied the word to the French. Here, since Spanish blood was in a higher caste than pure French blood, the word began to be used for those who were of mixed Spanish and French blood and was no longer used to speak of those of just Spanish descent. The word was first associated with *gens de couleur* when it was used by Creoles themselves as an adjective to refer to their property. The Catholic Church was the first to use the word as a noun to refer to biracial people, in regard to compliance with the *Code Noir* and the requirement that all slaves be baptized as Catholic. When the United States took possession of New Orleans, English-speaking Americans were confused by the subtle intricacies of French grammar and began to refer to anyone who lived in the French Creole parts of the city as Creole.

128 parts white	0 parts black	White
127 parts white	1 part black	Sang Melée
120 parts white	8 parts black	Mameloque
112 parts white	16 parts black	Metif or Octoroon
96 parts white	32 parts black	Quadroon or Quarteron
64 parts white	64 parts black	Mulatto
48 parts white	80 parts black	Marabou
32 parts white	96 parts black	Griffe
16 parts white	112 parts black	Sacatra
0 parts white	128 parts black	Negro

(The progeny of a Native American and a black was called an *os rouge*.)

11. Although dueling was illegal, it was commonplace in old New Orleans during the height of the quadroon balls. Duels were often fought between the aristocratic Creole men themselves, or between a visiting guest and a native Creole, when he objected to the flirtations made towards his favorite quadroon by another young man. Many duels were fought in the garden of St. Louis Cathedral which was near the *Salle d'Orleans,* or at the Oaks, an area that was just beyond the city limits on the plantation of Louis Allard. Dueling became so fashionable that fencing academies sprang up throughout the city.

12. The Sisters of the Holy Family (or Holy Family Sisters) was founded by a free-born octoroon named Henriette Delille (sometimes spelled Delisle). Born the daughter of a white father and a quadroon mother in 1813, Delille was trained as a girl in the etiquette and deportment required of a *femme de couleur.* She attended quadroon balls as was expected of a woman of her station, but met a French nun named Sister St. Marthe who influenced her to give her life to the church, so Delille began dedicating her life to the poor of her own race. She refused to attend any more quadroon balls and her family was outraged. Her mother suffered a nervous breakdown when Delille refused to marry an aristocratic white man. In November 1836, Delille started an interracial religious community, selling her inheritance to fund a school for the education of blacks in New Orleans, which at that period in history was illegal. She also worked for the legalization of marriages between black slaves. In 1837 (or 1838) the church gave its permission for a religious community to be founded under the leadership of Delille, and in 1842, she and two other women formed a group called the Sisters of the Presentation, eventually changing the name to the Sisters of the Holy Family. In 1852 the women took formal vows, but were so controversial, that they were not allowed to wear habits until 1872. The sisters were frequently called "the little colored sisters." The Salle d'Orleans was purchased with money that was given to the order by Thomy Lafon, a man of color who began selling confections to waterfront laborers and through investments grew quite wealthy. After Delille's death in 1862, the religious order continued to flourish. By the turn of the century, the community had a novitiate, eight other schools, orphanages, homes for the aged, and three other convents. The order is still in existence and runs the oldest continuous Catholic home for the aged in the United States. They have missions in Louisiana, Texas, California, Washington, D.C. and Belize. In 1989, Henriette Delille became the first American born woman of African descent to be considered for canonization by the Catholic Church.

13. The wall of the chapel which was housed in the old ballroom was directly next to the wall of the Orleans Theatre. The devotions of the sisters were often interrupted by the sounds of the circuses which were held next door. The Orleans Theatre eventually burned, but the convent miraculously escaped the fire. The mother superior then bought the lot and built an orphan asylum on the land where the theatre used to stand.

14. Voodoo was also known in slave religion as hoodoo, the name for a whole variety of folk superstitions and magical beliefs. It was also sometimes called root work or conjure, and was not only practiced in New Orleans, but was also widespread among the slave culture throughout the United States. On St. John's Eve on June 23 and the feast of the nativity of St. John the Baptist on June 24, Voodoo festivities took place on the shores of Lake Ponchartrain. These midsummer celebrations included wild dancing and were supposedly initiated by the great Voodoo queen Marie Laveau, who chose the saint's birthday because of her mixed Catholic and Voodoo beliefs. The celebrations combined African ritual and Catholic rites, and included recitations of the Apostles' Creed, prayers to the Virgin Mary in French, and nude bathing and wild rhythmic dancing.

15. Thorpe, p. 35.

16. Herbert Asbury, in his book *The French Quarter: An Informal History of the New Orleans Underworld* (New York: Garden City Publishing, 1938) pp. 240–241, writes,

> On October 15, 1817, the Municipal Council adopted an ordinance directing that "assemblies of slaves for the purpose of dancing or other merriment, shall take place only on Sundays, and solely in such open or public places as shall be appointed by the mayor." Congo Square was designated by the Mayor as the only place to which the slaves might resort, and thereafter all such gatherings were held under strict police supervision. The dancing stopped at sunset, and all slaves were driven out of the square and sent home. Under these and other regulations, the custom of permitting slave dancing in Congo Square continued for more than 20 years, when it was abolished, for which [reason] the old city records do not make clear. It was resumed in 1845, when this ordinance was adopted:
> Whereas, numerous citizens have requested the Council of Municipality No. One, to grant permission to slaves to assemble on Sundays on Circus Square, for purpose of dancing.
> Whereas, when such merriment takes place before sunset and is not offensive to public decency, it can be tolerated; provided, it being under police inspection.
> Resolved that from the 1st of May to the 31st of August of each year, the slaves, provided with written consent of their master, be permitted to assemble on Sundays on the Circus Square for the purpose of dancing from 4 to 6½ o'clock, P.M.
> Resolved that it shall be the duty of the commissaries of police of the 3rd and 5th wards, of the commanding officer at Post Trèmé and five men of the day police, to watch that no police ordinance be violated during the time allowed to Negroes to dance on Circus Square.

17. Congo Square was located approximately where Beauregard Square now stands in Louis Armstrong Park. The area was originally sacred ground for the Oumas Indians and was used specifically for corn festival ceremonies. Later the park became officially known as Circus Square because M. Cayetano's circus was set up there whenever it came to town. After slave dances began in the park, it was popularly known as *Place des Nègres,* Congo Plains or Congo Square. After the Civil War, the park was officially christened Beauregard Square

after General P. G. T. Beauregard of the Confederate Army.

18. G. W. Cable, "Creole Slave Dances: The Dance in the Place Congo," in *The Century; a popular quarterly*, vol. 31, issue 4, p. 522, February 1886. The large numbers of slaves who participated in the dances at Congo Square is also described by Marshall Stearns in *The Story of Jazz* (New York: Oxford University Press, 1956) p. 51, who quotes Herbert Asbury writing in *The French Quarter* (New York: Alfred A. Knopf, 1936) p. 243:

> ... the entire square was an almost solid mass of black bodies stamping and swaying to the rhythmic beat of the bones on the cask, the frenzied chanting of the women, and the clanging pieces of metal which dangled from the ankles of the men.

19. Two sizes of drums were used in Congo Square: a larger one, hollowed out of a single piece of wood and covered at one end with a stretched goat- or sheepskin, and a smaller one made out of one or two joints of a large bamboo. The smaller drum was called the bamboula, also the name of a dance which is discussed in the Chapter Four on dance in the West Indies. "Beaters" would sit beside the larger of the drums and play counterrhythms by hitting sticks against the wooden sides of the instrument as the drummer played. At times, the drums would be augmented by other percussionists pounding on the tops of barrels with cow bones. Other instruments included jawbones that were rasped, bones, and the quills, a type of panpipe made out of cut reeds. The other ubiquitous instrument was the banjo. The crowd also participated by patting juba. In his article "Creole Slave Dances: The Dance in the Place Congo," G. W. Cable wrote, "The quick contagion is caught by a few in the crowd, who take it up with spirited smitings of the bare sole upon the ground, and of open hands upon the thighs."

20. Lynne Fauley Emery, in her book *Black Dance: From 1619 to Today*, p. 160, states that composer Louis Gottschalk was inspired by the sights and sounds he heard at Congo Square and used them in some of his earlier works.

21. Emery, p. 159.

22. Herbert Asbury, in his book *The French Quarter: An Informal History of the New Orleans Underworld* (New York: Garden City Publishing, 1938) p. 244, quotes German trader, J. G. Flugel, who witnessed slave dances in Congo Square in February 1817:

> Their posture and movements somewhat resembled those of monkeys. One might by a little imagination take them for a group of baboons. Yet as these poor wretches are entirely ignorant of anything like civilization (for their masters withhold everything from them that in the least might add to the cultivation of their minds) one must not be surprised at their actions. The recreation is at least natural and they are free in comparison with those poor wretches, slaves of their passions. I saw today among the crowd Gildemeister of Bremen, clerk or partner of Teetzmann. He told me that three of the negroes in the group closest to us were formerly kings or chiefs in Congo. I perceive in them a more gen-

teel address. They are richly ornamented and dance extremely well.

23. G. W. Cable, "Creole Slave Dances: The Dance in the Place Congo," in *The Century; a popular quarterly*, vol. XXXI, issue 4 (February 1886) p. 520.

24. Cable, p. 522. In the book *The Music of Black Americans* (New York: W. W. Norton & Co., 1977) p. 138, Eileen Southern states that chants would be repeated over and over again for as long as five or six hours, regularly resulting in ecstatic trances among the dancers who fell in a faint onto the ground.

25. The most famous dancer at Congo Square was a black slave named Squier, who was owned by General William de Buys. Squier's specialty was the bamboula and he was said to be the first dancer in Congo Square to attach bells to his ankles instead of bits of metal. General de Buys was known as an indulgent master because he gave Squier a rifle, taught him to shoot, and allowed the slave to hunt on his own. Squier became an expert marksman and practiced shooting with both hands because he had a premonition that he would lose one of his arms. Tempted by the freedom he experienced while hunting, Squier tried to escape bondage several times, but was always returned to de Buys. In 1834, while trying to escape, he was shot by patrollers and his right arm had to be amputated. He was then given the name Bras Coupé. After his wound healed, Bras Coupé (Squiers) fled again and hid in the swamps, where he organized other escaped slaves into a band of outlaws. The group went on frequent forays into the city where they robbed and murdered, and eventually Bras Coupé gained the reputation among whites as being New Orleans' most feared bandit. Among blacks his exploits assumed legendary proportions. Slaves believed he had superhuman powers; that he was fireproof, invulnerable to wounding: could paralyze people with a look; and that he could dematerialize at will. On July 18, 1837, Bras Coupé was hiding out in the hut of Francisco Garcia, a fisherman, when he was betrayed and murdered as he slept. Garcia brought the slain outlaw to Mayor Dennis Prieur, who then ordered that Bras Coupé's body be placed in the *Place d'Armes* for two days. Several thousand black slaves were then forced to march past and look at it as a warning.

26. One other common dance event among the French-speaking Creole settlements of Louisiana was the fais-do-do. These were country dance parties that were held among the settlers. Invitations were passed from neighbor to neighbor and the custom was to bring the babies along and sing them to sleep before the dancing got under way. "Fais-do-do" meant to go to sleep or to go bye-bye. The dances at these parties consisted of quadrilles and cotillions but usually contained African-American steps which were interpolated into the French figures. This practice was also common in New England where the dances were called "junkets."

6. Dance on the Plantation

1. Because of the large slave population in South Carolina and the horrors of the slave system, the area was ripe for rebellion. Trying to foment discontent in

the English colonies because of the war between England and Spain, Governor Montiano of Florida issued a proclamation offering refuge, freedom, and free land to any black slave who deserted to St. Augustine. Earlier, in 1726, the Governor had established a military colony of black fugitive slaves just north of St. Augustine called Fort Mossa, or Negro Fort as it was commonly known. This settlement became a beacon for African-Americans wishing to escape bondage. Although the punishment for trying to escape and join the Spanish was branding and cutting the hamstring of the leg, many slaves attempted to flee South Carolina anyway. When word of the war between England and Spain was spread throughout the black population by the Yamasee Indians, who promised to guide blacks to Florida, the slaves were eager to side with Spanish interests and revolt against their English masters. In the late summer of 1739, whites in the Charleston area suffered from a yellow fever contagion that killed people at a rate of a least a half-dozen every day. Although the cool weather of October killed mosquitoes and caused the epidemic to subside, the resulting confusion from the disease was probably a factor in the timing of the revolt. It was further triggered by the passing of the Security Act in Charleston, which required whites to carry firearms to church on Sundays. The law was to go into effect at the end of September, 1739. Knowing that Sunday was the best day to catch their white owners unarmed and unaware, the slaves decided to have their insurrection before the enactment of this law.

2. From "An Account of the Negroe Insurrection in South Carolina," written October 9, 1739, by General Oglethorpe to the accountant Mr. Harman Verelst. Available in several current sources.

3. According to Edward Eggleston's article "Social Conditions in the Colonies" in *The Century; a popular quarterly*, vol. 28, issue 6, October 1884, the fight between the rebellious slaves and the militia ironically took place on a plantation known as the "Battlefield."

4. Holiday dances were used by white slave owners as a means to release tension among their workers and thus curtail insurrectionary activity by momentarily freeing the slaves from the desperate drudgery of their work tasks. Nevertheless, the celebrations also provided a perfect opportunity for slaves to gather, exchange information, and plan revolts. In the United States, revolts were often planned to take place during holidays such as Christmas, Easter, or the Fourth of July. These occasions gave the slaves an opportunity to gather without suspicion under the guise of celebrating the holiday. "One analysis revealed that 35 percent of rebellions in the British Caribbean were either planned for or took place in late December. The high pitch of emotions at these dances could serve as a pretext for touching off a previously planned revolt. The links between dance and rebellion give these occasions a striking resemblance to war dances, or dances in which preparation for battle was the central theme" (Katrina Hazzard-Gordon, *Jookin'*, p. 34).

5. The earlier uprising took place in South Carolina in 1730. An account is given in Katrina Hazzard-Gordon's book *Jookin'*, p. 183, which was originally extracted form *A Refutation of the Calumnies Circulated Against the Southern and Eastern States* by Edwin C. Holland (1822).

One, that the negroes in each family in the dead of night, were to murder all their masters and the white men of every family, in the neighborhood in which there were no Negroes. There was so much distrust and want of confidence, however, among them that they resolved to adopt the other proposition, which was, they should assemble in the neighborhood of the town, under the pretense of a "Dancing Bout" and when the proper preparations were made, to rush into the heart of the city, take possession of all arms and ammunition they could find, and murder all the white men, and then turn their forces to the different plantations.

6. The legislation enacted in Charleston in 1740 was called the Statutes at Large for the State of South Carolina. In addition to banning drums, the laws forbade blacks from growing their own food, earning money, learning to read, or traveling without written permission from the master.

7. In his book, *On the Real Side*, p. 56, Mel Watkins states

In all probability, dance — along with music and singing — was also an activity that initially allowed the slaves to communicate furtively with one another. Forbidden directly to voice any protest about their condition or even to speak in their native languages, slaves used music and dancing not only to establish a symbolic or kinesthetic connection to their homeland and one another, but also to convey feelings and thoughts to other slaves.

8. Many slaves were literate in Arabic and a large proportion of those Africans that were brought to America in chains came from the intellectual elite. Statistics reported by both the British and French colonial governments listed at least 3,000 schools for the study of the Koran in Guinea and 25,000 such schools in northern Nigeria. The institution of slavery was especially distressing to these Muslim Africans because according to Islamic law, no Muslim could be considered a slave.

9. Jacqui Malone, *Steppin' On the Blues: The Visible Rhythms of African American Dance* (Chicago: University of Illinois Press, 1996) p. 37–38.

10. White colonial Americans based most of their social dances upon instructions found in French and English dancing manuals such as John Playford's *Dancing Master*, and favored such dances as Playford's "Sir Roger de Coverley," which was better know as the Virginia reel. Minuets and other court dances were also common. Families that could afford it frequently hired a dancing master to instruct their children in the art of manners, deportment, and dance. After the French Revolution, many dance instructors from France sought refuge in the States and brought with them the French style of dancing.

11. Lynn Fauley Emery, *Black Dance: From 1619 to Today* (Princeton, NJ: Princeton University Press, 1988) p. 102, quoting the Virginia Writers' Project, *Negro in Virginia*, p. 35.

12. Emery, p. 101, quoting the Federal Writers' Project, *Slave Narratives*, IV, part 3, p. 1.

13. White slave owners also hired out their slaves as entertainers and there are even accounts of blacks being used as dancing masters.

14. Emery, p. 90, quoting the Virginia Writers' Project, *Negro in Virginia*, p. 92.

15. Beth Tolman, Beth Page and Ralph Page state in *The Country Dance Book: The Best of the Square and Contra Dances and All About Them* (Brattleboro, VT: Stephen Greene Press, 1976) p. 102: "Some people claim that the pigeon's wing is of Irish origin, but the point is debatable."

16. In *Jazz Dance: The Story of American Vernacular Dance* (New York: Da Capo, 1994) pp. 25–26, Marshall and Jean Stearns describe a version of the buzzard lope, discovered in Georgia, that was performed to the accompaniment of patting. One performer lay on the ground to represent the dead cow, and another dancer acted as the buzzard. The dance was done to the following lyric which spelled out instructions for the dancer.

> March aroun'!
> Jump across!
> Get the eye!
> So glad!
> Get the guts!
> Go to eatin'!
> All right – cow mos' gone!
> Dog comin'!
> Scare the dog!
> Look aroun' for mo' meat!
> All right – Belly full!
> Goin' to tell the res'.

17. Emery, p. 92, quoting Tom Fletcher, *The Tom Fletcher Story–100 Years of the Negro in Show Business*, p. 19.

18. Douglas Gilbert in his book *Lost Chords*, p. 245, says that white song-and-dance team Dave Genaro and his wife, Ray Bailey, originated the cakewalk. This is doubtful, since the cakewalk was regularly featured in all-male minstrel shows and by the 1890s was often used to liven up such straight plays as *Uncle Tom's Cabin*. Nonetheless, Genero and Bailey were considered the foremost exponents of the dance. In 1898, the dance was presented in the all-black musical *Clorindy, or the Origin of the Cakewalk*. The dance was also featured in 1899 in *The Creole Show* and performed by Dora Dean and Charles Johnson, who took it back to its roots by performing as a male-female couple, thus breaking the dance away from its constrictive minstrel-show format. This African-American team was wellknown for their cakewalk and truly popularized it on the professional stage.

19. In the West Indies, the word "cakewalk" was used to describe a custom practiced in association with the marriage ritual. The best dancers in the village took turns balancing a wedding cake upon their heads and went from house to house to collect donations for the couple that was getting married. This custom is reminiscent of water-balancing dances.

20. Douglas Gilbert, *Lost Chords: The Diverting Story of American Popular Songs* (Garden City, NY: Doubleday, 1942) p. 246.

21. Gilbert, p. 246.

22. Richard Kislan, *Hoofing on Broadway: A History of Show Dancing* (New York: Prentice Hall, 1987) pp. 19–20.

23. John W. Blassingame, *The Slave Community: Plantation Life in the Antebellum South* (New York: Oxford University Press, 1972) p. 55, quoting Solomon Northup, *Twenty Years a Slave* (London, 1953) p. 219.

24. Eileen Southern, *The Music of Black Americans* (New York: W. W. Norton & Co., 1977) p. 168, quoting W. C. Handy, *Father of the Blues* (New York, 1941) p. 5.

25. David C. Barrow, Jr., "A Georgia Corn-Shucking" in *The Century Magazine; a popular quarterly*. Vol. 24, issue 6, pp. 873–878, October 1882, p. 878.

26. Southern, p. 168.

27. The use of disguised messages, especially through wordplay, was known as signifying, and was a common practice among the slaves in the face of societal oppression. The concealment of messages commenting upon the hardships of slavery or the cruelty or ignorance of whites was commonly used in songs, and in folk tales such as the Br'er Rabbit stories. Signifying was also done with the mocking movements of such dances as the cakewalk.

28. Roger D. Abrahams, *Singing the Master: The Emergence of African American Culture in the Plantation South* (New York: Pantheon Books, 1992) p. 94, quoting Gladys-Marie Fry, *Night Riders in Black Folk History* (Knoxville: U. of Tennessee Press, 1975) p. 85.

29. Langston Hughes and Milton Meltzer, *Black Magic: A Pictorial History of Black Entertainers in America* (New York: Bonanza Books, 1967) p. 18.

30. In *The Century; a popular quarterly*. vol. 25, issue 3, p. 480, January 1883, there is an article called "Uncle Remus's Christmas Dance-Songs," which lists a few songs by "Uncle Remus" author, Joel Chandler Harris. The first song is called "Rabbit-tum-a-hash," and the first verse is

> RABBIT foot quick, Rabbit foot light,
> Tum-a-hash, turn-a-heap!
> Hop, skip, jump! Oh, mon, he's a sight!
> Kaze he res all de day en run all de night,
> Turn-a-hash, turn-a-heap,
> Oh, Rabbit-tum-a-hash!

The song includes the following instructions:

> The songs are sung with what Uncle Remus would call the knee-racket; that is to say, they are patting songs.

Another reference to patting and the rabbit hash is found in the book *Step It Down: Games, Plays, Songs, and Stories from the Afro-American Heritage*, by Bessie Jones and Bess Lomax Hawes (New York: Harper & Row, 1972) p. 25, in which the authors describe a patting game called "Green Sally Up" which contains a reference to rabbit hash. At the end of the lyric the phrase "Oh the rabbit in the hash" is done to the accompaniment of clapping and slapping and is repeated over and over as the tempo accelerates.

31. Douglas Gilbert, *American Vaudeville: Its Life and Times* (New York: Whittlesey House, 1940) p. 171.

32. In the book *Step It Down: Games, Plays, Songs, and Stories from the Afro-American Heritage*, by Bessie Jones and Bess Lomax Hawes (New York: Harper & Row, 1972) pp. 37–40, there is a description of the juba

dance game which has Charleston steps in it. The basic Charleston step is referred to as "jump for joy" and utilizes the traditional Charleston footwork, except it is more restrained, with the feet being kept close to the ground and the flicking up of the feet to the side eliminated.

33. The word "capoeira" is derived from the Brazilian word *capão* which refers to a small male bird similar to a partridge that fiercely attacks its rivals. A *capoeira* is actually a basket that contains chickens and roosters and such birds. The martial art form was developed to its highest degree in Palmares, Brazil, which became a refuge for escaped slaves. The blacks of Palmares used their military skills honed by capoeira to resist well-armed, experienced white soldiers who frequently tried to return the ex-slaves to captivity. The soldiers were most often unsuccessful in their attempts, but the few blacks who were recaptured and returned to plantations taught capoeira fighting skills to other blacks who were there.

34. Sticks and canes were commonly used props in many dances in Egypt, Libya and the Sudan. In North Africa and the Middle East, sword dances were performed, but sticks were substituted for the swords. In the book *The Music of Black Americans*, by Eileen Southern (New York: W. W. Norton & Co., 1977) p. 19, an African stick dance, observed by a Major Denham in 1826, was described thus:

> The dance was performed by men armed with sticks, who springing alternately from one foot to another, while dancing around in a ring, frequently flourished their sticks in the air, or clashed them together with a loud sound. Sometimes a dancer jumped out of the circle, and springing around on his heel for several minutes, made his stick whirl above his head at the same time with equal rapidity; he would then rejoin the dance.

Brooms were also used in dances. In Dahomean rituals of the god, Obaluaiye, brooms and lances are used in healing rites to combat smallpox. Robert Farris Thompson in his book, *Flash of the Spirit: African & Afro-American Art & Philosophy* (New York: Random House, 1984), p. 65, writes of one such ritual: "The broom is 'danced' with gestures that are smooth and orchestrated...."

35. Other plantation dances included wringin' and twistin', the forerunner of the twist, snake hips, Elvis Presley's hip swivels, popular dances like the jerk, poplocking, and breakdancing. Another dance was called going to the east and going to the west. The main attraction of this dance was that it involved a man kissing his partner without wrapping his arms around her.

36. As the word "jig" came to be associated with all forms of black movement, it also came to be used as an generic epithet for African-Americans.

37. The ability to stay within the boundaries that were set was also called being able to "walk chalk," or sometimes to "walk jawbone." This same image has come down to us today in the phrase "walk the line."

38. In Africa, nearly everything was transported by carrying it on the head and there were religious rituals in which clay pots or containers holding fire were balanced on the head while dancing. In North Africa, feats of balancing were often used to exhibit skill while

dancing. Brass trays were piled high with glasses, tier upon tier, and balanced on the heads of male dancers as they performed. Roger D. Abrahams in his book, *Singing the Master: The Emergence of African American Culture in the Plantation South* (New York: Pantheon Books, 1992) pp. 99–100, writes:

> Much of European social dancing involves asserting, testing, and maintaining one's balance, through adroitness in executing steps. The placement of the arms and the hands complements the foot movements. Raising the hands above the head or placing them on the hips calls attention to the footwork that is being carried out, and tests of agility or balance which are being put into action.... While slave dancing tested balance, the site of order was at the head and not the torso. This is most evident in chalk-line and cakewalk dances.

39. Emery, p. 91, quoting James W. Smith, Federal Writers' Project, *Slave Narratives*, XVI, part 4, p. 34.

40. Corn husking festivities were the model for a wide range of plantation and frontier activities. Commonly known as "bees" and "frolics," these included work, song, dance, and food. There were also quilting bees and frolics associated with barn-raisings. Corn shuckings were also called husking bees. The form of harvest celebrations was also similar to other holiday get-togethers like Christmas and Fourth of July frolics. John Williamson Palmer, in his article "Old Maryland Homes and Ways," in *The Century*, December 1894, described one such Christmas dance.

> Then the cabin floor was cleared for the dance jig and breakdown, pigeon-wing and juba, the later a characteristic survival of the aboriginal barbarism, delivered with vigorous shouts and cries and shuffling feet to a rhythmic accompaniment of hand-clapping and patting of knees, in melodious deference to the jigging of a fiddle by the light of flaming pine-knots.

41. The captains, or "gin-r'ls" as they were called, were also in charge of dividing the corn pile. They did this by placing a fence rail across the top of the pile after much wrangling and argument about how equally it was divided. The gin-r'ls then stood on top of the corn when the work began and shouted directions to their teams. Cheating was not uncommon and workers might try to shift the position of the rail or throw extra ears of corn on the other side. The workers also tried to knock the opponents' leader off the cornpile to cause a panic among the other team. Corn gin-r'ls were expected to have a good voice and be adept at improvising verses to inspire their followers.

42. Roger D. Abrahams suggests that the word "breakdown" may have come from the corn-shucking ritual. "Breaking down the corn" was the phrase used to describe the process of stripping the ear of corn. He points out that the first uses of the word "breakdown" as a form of dance were used in association with accounts of slave holidays and probably referred to the dances at the end of the corn shuckings.

43. In the African bardic traditions, the poet who improvised served the community as a commentator,

setting moral standards for the society in general. By pointing out the misdeeds of those who had erred as well as singing the praises of heroes and kings, the poet reaffirmed the guidelines and criteria of acceptable behavior. In a certain sense, the caller in the call-and-response dances served the same purpose.

44. Quote taken from "A Georgia Corn-Shucking," by David C. Barrow, Jr., in *The Century Magazine; a popular quarterly*, vol. 24, issue 6, pp. 873–878, October 1882, pp. 877–878.

45. Abrahams, p. 228, quoting Charles Lanman, *He-He Noo: Or Records of a Tourist* (Philadelphia: 1850).

46. Abrahams, p. 93, quoting Nancy Mills, in Perdue et al., *Weevils in the Wheat*, p. 318.

47. Abrahams, p. 93 (paraphrased), quoting John Wyeth, *With Sabre and Scapel* (New York: Harper, 1914) pp. 60–61.

48. Minstrel songwriters often used corn shucking, working in the corn fields, or eating corn as subjects in their lyrics. Corn-shucking dances were also performed in minstrel shows. One such dance, presented by Christy's Minstrels, was called down in Carolina. Many minstrel companies toured the South during the corn-shucking season and were probably exposed to the African-American songs and dances that accompanied the harvest festivities.

49. Plantation dances were often accompanied by fiddle music, but when accompanying authentic African dances, black fiddle players would only use three or four notes in monotonous, repetitive figures. The bow would be bounced on the strings percussively in complicated rhythmic patterns. It is believed that these patterns were actually encoded messages that were "drummed" out after drums were officially banned. Likewise, "beaters" would pat covert messages when striking instruments with straws or knitting needles. White audiences were unaware of these secret communications, only associating loud horn or drum music with danger.

50. Hazzard-Gordon, p. 122.

51. Malone, p. 38.

52. As the attitude towards African-Americans became increasingly hostile in the United States, a strange phenomenon took place — black society increasingly imitated white society. In their dancing, the movements which started with original African elements evolved and became more and more stylized, refined, and formal. A caste system developed between the house slaves, who considered themselves on a higher level, and the field hands, who considered themselves on a lower level. The house slaves would imitate the dances of white "genteel" society and therefore most of their dances were based on European quadrilles and cotillions. Lynn Fauley Emer, in her book, *Black Dance: From 1619 to Today* (Princeton, NJ: Princeton University Press, 1988) p. 100, quotes, Isaac Stier, a former slave, who described such dances done on the plantation where he lived in Mississippi:

> Us danced plenty, too. Some o' de men Clogged an' pigeoned, but when us had dances dey was real cotillions, lak de white folks had.

53. Depending upon the good nature of the master, slaves could receive permission to hold Saturday night dances of their own on the plantations where they worked or sometimes obtain passes to visit other plantations to attend dances and frolics there. A written pass was always required from the master because patrollers policed the roads and any black found away from the plantation without a pass was beaten. The widespread practice of these Saturday night dances called "stompin' the blues" was as a potent counterstatement against horrific oppression and was used by slaves to relieve tension and express their own outrage at being enslaved.

7. Slave Religion and the Ring Shout

1. Albert Raboteau, *Slave Religion: The "Invisible Institution" in the Antebellum South* (Oxford: Oxford University Press, 1978) p. 96, quoting Gomes Eannes De Azurara (15th century) *Chronicle*, 1:50–51.

2. Eileen Southern, *The Music of Black Americans* (New York: W. W. Norton & Co., 1977) p. 39, quotes the Reverend Hugh Jones (1724): "As for baptizing Indians and Negroes, several of the people disapprove of it; because they say it often makes them proud, and not as good servants."

3. The Methodist Church originally declared that if a slave owner converted, they must free their slaves immediately. This tenet was soon discarded, though, and in 1804, the church agreed to let its members own and sell slaves. By the early 1880s the Baptist Church had also stopped interfering with the issue of slavery. The belief that baptism might lead to manumission was not only held by slave owners, but by slaves. In the early 1700s, Francis La Jau, the missionary to Goose Creek, South Carolina, made slaves sign a document that stated they were not seeking baptism in order to be freed, before he would baptize them.

4. Noel Rae, ed., *Witnessing America; The Library of Congress Book of Firsthand Accounts of Life in America 1600–1900* (New York: Penguin, 1996) p. 375, quoting the Virginia law found in *The Annals of America*, vol. 1, published by Encyclopaedia Britannica, Inc.

5. A slave catechism was created to reinforce the slave system, rationalize the treatment of blacks, and remind slaves of their duties. The following excerpt appeared in the *Southern Episcopalian*, published in Charleston, South Carolina in April 1854. (Noel Rae, p. 375.)

Q.: Who gave you a master and mistress?

A.: God gave them to me.

Q.: Who says you must obey them?

A.: God says I must.

Q.: What book tells you these things?

A.: The Bible.

6. African-American membership in the Methodist Church grew from 3,800 to nearly 32,000 in the years between 1786 and 1809. The Baptist Church had black membership swell from 18,000 to 40,000 between 1793 and 1813. The Baptist Church was the most popular among blacks, partly because of its informal organization which designated that any gathering of four people constituted a congregation, but also because it stressed total immersion during baptism. This

appealed to many African-Americans who saw this custom as corresponding with similar rites from river cults in Africa.

7. Raboteau, p. 149.

8. Black preachers were granted special privileges even though they remained slaves. Some were excused from manual labor and others were granted permission to travel freely between neighboring plantations.

9. Noel Rae, p. 393, quoting Peter Cartwright's "Autobiography," 1856.

Apparently jerking and other types of physical manifestations were a later development during the revival period. Marshall Stearns in his book *The Story of Jazz* (New York: Oxford University Press, 1956) p. 87, quotes G. G. Johnson, *Ante-Bellum North Carolina* (Chapel Hill: The University of North Carolina Press, 1937), p. 399.

> The jerking exercise, or the jerks, as it was commonly called, together with the dancing and barking exercises, did not appear at the beginning of the great Revival. The Reverend Eli Caruthers refers to these phenomena as '*fungi,* which grew out of the revival in its state of decay.' At first, the jerks were manifested by an involuntary twitching of the arms; later this twitching spread over all the body. It was perhaps the most contagious of all the exercises. Sometimes the mere mention of it was enough to set most of a congregation to jerking.... Whenever a woman was taken with the jerks at a camp meeting her friends formed a circle about her, for the exercise was so violent that she could scarcely maintain a correct posture. Men would go bumping about over benches, into trees, bruising and cutting themselves, if friends did not catch and hold them. Some were ashamed of having the jerks, but most persons agreed that it was impossible to resist them.

10. Raboteau, p. 67, quoting John Watson's *Methodist Error or Friendly Advice to Those Methodists.*

11. Southern, p. 88, quoting Robert W. Todd, *Methodism of the Peninsula* (Philadelphia: Methodist Episcopal Book Rooms, 1886) p. 183.

12. Raboteau, p. 167, quoting Carey Davenport of Walker County Texas as her story was told in *The American Slave: A Composite Autobiography,* 19 vols. George P. Rawick, ed. (Westport, CT: Greenwood, 1972) vol.4, *Texas*, pt. 1, p. 281.

13. Self-control and the ability to keep silent were traits highly esteemed in African culture. Among the Yoruba, the importance of this code of silence was represented in their art, exemplified by sculptures that were carved with sealed lips. In Cuba, this same idea took the form of a ritual drum called the *sese* which was never played as a symbol of the importance of silence. This practice was carried on by American slaves who rarely revealed information about their fellow slaves, even when brutally questioned by their masters. As with religion, slaves were often secretive about getting together to dance. They sometimes used the code name "Jenny" when referring to a dance party or other social event (or sometimes to talk about a specific dancer or dance). Therefore, they might refer to "settin' the flo'" with Jenny."

14. Quote from Mark Galli's web article "Christian History" in *Christianity Today International/Christian History Magazine.*

15. One major slave revolt that was initiated by Christianized African-Americans was the Vesey Conspiracy which took place in Charleston, South Carolina in 1822. Denmark Vesey, an ex-slave who had purchased his freedom with lottery winnings, won supporters for the insurrection by quoting verses in the Bible. Vesey preached to members of the African Methodist Episcopal Church of Charleston and led them to believe that God had commanded them to rebel. He was supported by Gullah Jack, one member of the church who combined Christianity with sorcery. The slaves believed that Gullah Jack was invulnerable and couldn't be captured, shot or killed because of his magical powers. They also believed that he endowed others who were with him with the same immunity from death. The conspirators were purported to have gathered up to 6,600 supporters around the Charleston area and the plan was to take ships and sail to Haiti after the insurrection. The plot was discovered when a domestic slave leaked information to his master, who in turn warned the mayor. The city guard was put on alert and the leaders of the conspiracy were captured and put on trial. In 1831, the Vesey Conspiracy was followed by the bloodiest insurrection in U. S. history which occurred in Southampton, Virginia. It was planned by a black Baptist preacher, Nat Turner, who believed that he was divinely appointed to lead the slaves out of bondage. Although not officially ordained, Turner was recognized as a religious leader and allowed to preach to his fellow slaves. He was also permitted to travel freely between plantations to speak at Sabbath meetings. This freedom of movement allowed him to become familiar with the geography of the area and also to organize slaves on surrounding plantations. Nicknamed the "Prophet," Turner commanded a band of 60 followers in a violent uprising which killed 55 whites. The rebellion ultimately failed and led to the enactment of even more stringent laws curtailing slave rights. It also brought about the demise of the organized abolition movement in Virginia. Both of these incidents convinced whites that religion could be a dangerous thing in the hands of blacks.

16. Hoping to get around the "no-dancing on the Sabbath rule," ingenious slaves sometimes stuffed rags into the chinks between the logs of the cabin where they met to dance on Saturday nights. If the sun could not get in through the cracks in the wall, they reasoned, it would not be Sunday and therefore they would not desecrate the Sabbath by continuing to dance.

17. The ring shout was used in many services but especially during church "Watch Meetings." "Watch Meetings" were gatherings that grew out of the African-American custom in which worshipers watched the old year go out and the new year come in.

18. Cosmograms were drawn to represent the cosmos. Most often the symbol consisted of a circle surrounding a cross. The horizontal bar of the cross represented the division between the living and the dead. The vertical bar of the cross represented the connection between God and the underworld. By circumscribing the circle, the dancer symbolically moved

through life to death and then into rebirth. The pattern also mirrored the rising and setting of the sun.

19. Art Rosenbaum, *Shout Because You're Free: The African American Ring Shout Tradition in Coastal Georgia* (Athens: The University of Georgia Press, 1998) p. 41, quoting James Weldon Johnson, *The Book of American Negro Spirituals* (New York: Viking Press, 1925) pp. 32–33.

20. Rosenbaum, p. 5, writes,

> White camp-meeting songs also utilized call-and-response and white sects, such as the Shakers, worshipped in moving circles, but exposure of blacks to these white practices does not negate the African origins of the shout, though it might suggest a reinforcement or modification of African-derived practices.

21. The term "shout" was specifically used by slaves to describe the dance movements rather than the song or the polyrhythmic percussive accompaniment. Sometimes the dancers were called "fist and heel worshipers."

22. Beating sticks were used as a substitute for the drums, which had been banned after the Stono uprising. The increase in tempo signaled by the stick let the dancers know when to begin the various shout steps. The polyrhythms created by the stick in tandem with the clapping and the feet, were commonly done in a syncopated 3+3+2 rhythm similar to that found in ragtime, jazz and swing music.

23. In addition to the traditional religious shout footwork, there developed a nonreligious shout step that was used in ring plays and games. It consisted of a backward chug which was executed while swinging the other foot forward. As the weight was shifted from foot to foot in a step, chug, step, chug, step, chug, step, chug, the body was hardly moved forward at all. This secular shout step is described in *Step It Down: Games, Plays, Songs, and Stories from the Afro-American Heritage* (New York: Harper & Row, 1972,) by Bessie Jones, and Bessie Lomax Hawes, pp. 45–46.

24. Marshall and Jean Stearns, *Jazz Dance: The Story of American Vernacular Dance* (New York: Da Capo, 1994) p. 30, quoting the *Nation* (30 May 1867).

25. Many of the upper-body movements that were done in the shout were taken from traditional plantation dances. Movements in one of the most common shouts, "Move, Daniel" (also preserved in the ring-play game "Daniel"), included the eagle wing, which consisted of the exact same movements as the buzzard lope. Other plantation steps that mimicked animals included fly, in which the arms were stretched fully at the sides imitating the soaring of a bird, and fly the other way, the same movement but executed with the arms circling backwards. Other common shout steps included the rock, which was done by bending side to side at the waist, and the kneebone bend. This was done with a slight jump forward onto both feet and upon landing bending the knees sharply. It is important to remember that spirituals developed as communal songs which were meant to be accompanied with dancing, and clapping. Most were originally not sung, but shouted, that is they were performed as the ring dance. Therefore, the words of the spiritual were acted out with mimed movement.

Although not all spirituals were shouted, every one did usually include some rhythmic movement of the body, whether it was the tapping of the foot, patting of the hands, or just swaying. The words of spirituals were often intentionally ambiguous and contained veiled social commentary and hidden messages. Religious language about slavery, flight, and deliverance had double meanings which slaves used to communicate with each other in the presence of whites.

26. Lynn Fauley Emery, *Black Dance: From 1619 to Today* (Princeton, NJ: Princeton University Press, 1988) p. 122, quoting Parrish, *Slave Songs of the Georgia Sea Islands*, p. 85. (Also quoted in Raboteau, p. 71.)

27. In the Kongo culture, crossing the legs was believed to negate the spiritual state. The Shango cult in the West Indies also held the belief "that anything crossed, including the legs, would keep the gods away." Thorpe, p. 30.

28. James Haskins, *Black Dance in America: A History Through Its People* (New York: Thomas Crowell, 1990) p. 8.

29. Katrina Hazzard-Gordon, *Jookin': The Rise of Social Dance Formations in African-American Culture* (Philadelphia: Temple University Press, 1990) p. 70, quoting the Federal Writers Project, WPA *Texas Narratives*, vol. 16 of *Slave Narratives*, pt. 4 (Westport, CT: Greenwood Press, 1972) p. 198.

30. Emery, p. 125, quoting Benjamin A. Botkin, *A Treasury of Southern Folklore* (New York: Crown Publishers, 1949) p. 658.

31. Plantation corn-shucking dances also have many elements found in the ring shout. One particular movement in the ring shout, the eagle wing in which bent arms were flapped wings, was the same as the buzzard lope.

8. Dispersion of African-American Dances

1. Marshall and Jean Stearns, *Jazz Dance: The Story of American Vernacular Dance* (New York: Da Capo, 1994) p. 29, quoting from Mark Twain's *Life on the Mississippi* (1883). Apparently this passage was also part of the 1876 draft of *Huckleberry Finn*.

2. Philip Graham, *Showboats: The History of an American Institution* (Austin: University of Texas Press, 1951) p. 24.

3. Lynn Fauley Emery, *Black Dance: From 1619 to Today* (Princeton, NJ: Princeton Univ. Press, 1988) p. 147.

4. Stearns, p. 23, quoting Lafcadio Hearn, "Levee Life," *Cincinnati Commercial*, March 17, 1876.

5. Emery, p. 145, quoting Lafcadio Hearn, "Levee Life," *Cincinnati Commercial*, March 17 1876.

6. In the first few decades of the 19th century, there was a movement among some northern slave owners to sell their slaves down South so they would not loose too much money when the emancipation finally came. This in turn led to the horrible practice of "blackbirding," in which gangs roamed the ghettos of New York and other big Northern cities to kidnap free African-Americans for sale to southern slave traders. How much these northern blacks may have influenced the dances on southern plantations is conjecture.

7. By the first decade of the 19th century, the Five Points district was one of the most densely populated areas in New York City. It housed at least 31 percent of the city's immigrant population, mostly Irish and German, and at least 12 percent of the city's African-American population. It was considered one of the most depraved and dangerous urban spots in America. Built over a marshy landfill on what used to be Collect Pond, the slums of Five Points, sometimes called the "Swamp," were overcrowded, filthy and a breeding ground for disease. In 1832 there was an outbreak of cholera in New York; one-third of the cases occurred in the Five Points district. The most famous site in the area was a building called the "Old Brewery." When the building was too dilapidated to use for its original purpose, it was converted into a tenement. It housed 1,200 people, who were crammed together in miserable squalor, the tenants being equally divided between Irish and African-Americans. It was estimated that for 15 straight years there was at least one murder per night in the "Old Brewery." The building was located on "Cutthroat Lane." The streets next to the building were named "Murderer's Alley" and "Den of Thieves." In December 1852, the building was bought by the Ladies Home Missionary Society, who planned to demolished it. Before the building was torn down, the society gave tours through the squalid building to raise awareness among the middle-class of the desperate plight of the poor in the city. When the "Old Brewery" finally came down, the wreckers were seen carrying out sacks full of human bones from the murdered who had been secretly buried in the cellars. The building was replaced with a chapel, school, bathing facilities and dwellings for the poor.

8. W. T. Lhamon Jr., *Raising Cain: Blackface Performance from Jim Crow to Hip Hop* (Cambridge, MA: Harvard University Press, 1998) p. 1, quoting Thomas F. De Voe, *The Market Book* (1862). Besides dancing at Catherine Market, there was also regular dancing at the Bear Market which was located in Maiden Lane.

9. Whistling was a common part of blackface representations. Both George Washington Dixon and Thomas D. Rice included whistling in their performances. London critics commented particularly about Rice's "strange whistle" that lent his depiction of Jim Crow an "extraordinary reality."

10. Emery, p. 141, quoting *The Negro in New York, An Informal Social History*, Roi Ottley and William J. Weatherby, eds. (New York: New York Public Library, 1967) p. 26.

11. Jacqui Malone, *Steppin' on the Blues: The Visible Rhythms of African American Dance* (Chicago: University of Illinois Press, 1996) p. 48.

12. Emery, pp. 140–141, quoting *The Negro in New York, An Informal Social History*, Roi Ottley and William J. Weatherby, eds. (New York: New York Public Library, 1967) pp. 25–26.

13. Eileen Southern, *The Music of Black Americans* (New York: W. W. Norton & Co., 1977) p. 19, quoting Orville Platt, "Negro Governors," *The New Haven Historical Society Quarterly* 6, (1900) pp. 324, 331.

14. Baton twirling can be traced to African military practices from the northern Congo. It was brought to Haiti by black slaves, and eventually made its way to Mississippi.

15. Malone, p. 46.

16. The most famous Pinkster king was "King Charles" (ca. 1699–1824), better known as "Charley of Pinkster Hill." He was the instigating spirit of the dance celebrations and held the privileged responsibility of calling out the dances to be performed. As the day progressed the dances traditionally got wilder and wilder and new dancers had to join in as others who were fatigued had to drop out. The celebrations started on a Monday and were repeated each day until Sunday when the celebrants finally rested. "King Charley" lived to be well over one hundred. In his old age, his costume consisted of the scarlet coat of a British brigadier, buckskin pants, a tricornered hat, and black shoes with big silver buckles. Legend surrounded "King Charley." It was believed that he had been purchased as a slave when he was an infant in Angola and that he was of African royal heritage.

17. Katrina Hazzard-Gordon, "Dancing Under the Lash: Sociocultural Disruption, Continuity, and Synthesis," in *African Dance: An Artistic, Historical, and Philosophical Inquiry*, ed. Kariamu Weish Asante, pp. 101–130 (Trenton, NJ: Africa World Press, 1996) p. 118.

18. Emery, p. 141, quoting James Fenimore Cooper, *Satanstoe; or, The Littlepage Manuscripts; A Tale of the Colony*, two vols. (New York: Burgess, Stringer and Co., 1845) vol. 1, p. 65.

19. Emery, p. 141, quoting James Fenimore Cooper, *Satanstoe; or, The Littlepage Manuscripts; A Tale of the Colony*, two vols. (New York: Burgess, Stringer and Co., 1845) vol. 1, p. 70.

20. Southern, p. 56, quoting John Fanning Watson, *Annals of Philadelphia*, 2nd ed. rev. (Philadelphia: 1850) vol. 2, p. 265.

21. Female African-American singers were regularly featured in jooks. A good jook singer was broad in the hips with a belly that shook when she sang. The sound had to be loud and powerful and produced right from the bottom of her gut. If she could do this, she was said "to jook."

22. Katrina Hazzard-Gordon, *Jookin': The Rise of Social Dance Formations in African-American Culture* (Philadelphia: Temple University Press, 1990) pp. 81–82.

23. Ragtime also developed in brothels, especially in New Orleans' infamous Storyville district. Storyville was created in January 1898 when an ordinance was introduced that limited brothels, saloons and other businesses of vice to a five-block area of the city. The law was introduced by Alderman Sidney Story and much to the horror of the conservative politician, newspapers quickly dubbed the area Storyville. During its peak years Storyville contained 2,000 prostitutes and 30 piano players, including King Oliver, Clarence Williams, and Jelly Roll Morton, by many considered to be the father of jazz. Storyville was closed down during World War I when the federal government issued an order prohibiting prostitution within a five-mile radius of military sites. Legal protests against the closing went all the way to the Supreme Court but were not successful.

9. Early Theatrical Developments

1. Two years earlier in 1794, Madame Gardie had starred in *La Forêt Noire,* the first serious ballet to be

presented in the United States. The ballet premiered at the New Chestnut Theater in Philadelphia in 1794 and featured specialty numbers, character dances, and a hornpipe. John Durang danced the male leading role in this production when it premiered in New York in 1795. Later Durang danced opposite Gardie in several ballets. Madame Gardie was born in Santo Domingo. While there she had a son with a man named Maurison, but the two separated and the dancer then married a French nobleman named Gardie. The Frenchman took his new wife home to France but his aristocratic family refused to accept their son's marriage to a person of the lower class. A defiant Madame Gardie returned to the stage. One night while dancing in Paris, the audience demanded that she sing *Le Marseillaise*. When Madame Gardie refused, an angry mob drove her from the theatre and she was forced to flee the country with her husband and son. The trio moved to America, but Madame Gardie's husband developed severe depression and in August 1798, when the family was having money problems, it was decided that he would return to France while Madame Gardie returned to her home in Santo Domingo with her seven-year-old son. The husband, unable to bear the separation, went into his wife's bedroom on the night before his departure and stabbed her and her son to death and then committed suicide. The murder-suicide took place in New York City in the same building (on the corner of Broad and Pearl Streets) in which George Washington had given his farewell address to his troops at the close of the Revolutionary War.

2. Richard Kislan, *Hoofing on Broadway: A History of Show Dancing* (New York: Prentice Hall, 1987) p. 9, lists the date of Durang's first performance as Friday in the pantomime based on *Robinson Crusoe* as December 5, 1792.

3. John Durang, *The Memoir of John Durang, American Actor, 1785–1816*, ed. by Alan S. Downer (Pittsburgh: University of Pittsburgh Press, 1966) p. 11.

4. Lillian Moore, "John Durang — The First American Dancer," in *Chronicles of the American Dance*, ed. by Paul Magriel (New York: Henry Holt, 1948) p. 21.

5. John Bill Ricketts was America's first circus proprietor. He originally had a riding school in Philadelphia and was well-respected for his exceptional skill with horses. In England, Ricketts had performed in equestrian circuses and brought this knowledge into play when he created the same type of format in the United States. Like Durang, he was known to dance the hornpipe on the saddle of his horse as it galloped at full speed. Under Ricketts' tutelage, Durang himself became an expert rider. One of Durang's tricks was to stand on two horses simultaneously while tied in a sack as he changed into women's clothes. He also rode two horses while Ricketts stood balanced on his shoulders and a third man posed on top of Ricketts.

6. After Ricketts lost his circus in Philadelphia, his luck went steadily downhill. After unsuccessful attempts to start other circuses in the States, he finally gave up and decided to move to the West Indies. On the way there, his ship was attacked by pirates. Fortunately the same man who had been responsible for the fire in Philadelphia, hid Ricketts' sword and pistol in some horse manure. When the beleaguered ship finally reached land, Ricketts was able to sell them and raise enough money to start a small circus. But his company ran into problems when two of its members died from yellow fever and a third was arrested for deserting a native girl he had married. Giving up, Ricketts sold his horses and decided to sail to England. On the ocean trip, the ship was lost and Rickets drowned.

7. Robert C. Toll, *Blacking Up: The Minstrel Show in Nineteenth-Century America* (New York: Oxford University Press, 1974) pp. 3–4.

8. The Astor Place Opera House riot occurred in 1849. It was fueled by a running feud between the supporters of American actor, Edwin Forrest, who were class-conscious common folk, and prominent, uppercrust New Yorkers, like Herman Melville and Washington Irving, who supported British tragedian, Charles Macready. Forrest had lambasted Macready for anti–Americanism, and accused him of trying to sabotage his 1845 tour of England and of running him, Forrest, off of the English stage. In 1848, when both men opened simultaneously in Philadelphia theatres, Macready had to struggle through his opening night, protesting his innocence in the London affair, amid jeers, hisses and rotten eggs which the angry audience tossed at him. Macready cut short his run in Philadelphia but continued his tour of the U.S. meeting even stronger, pro–Forrest audiences. In Cincinnati, one protester threw half a dead sheep carcass on stage at the actor. Macready decided to return to New York to end the tour with a production of *Macbeth*, but Forrest was also appearing there and the conflict came to a head. Posters were plastered around the town which read, "WORKING MEN, SHALL AMERICANS OR ENGLISH RULE IN THIS CITY?" On the evening of Macready's performance at the Astor Place Opera House, four troops of soldiers and 325 policemen surrounded the theatre to preserve order. When the actor first appeared on stage, he received a 15-minute ovation from his supporters, but this was followed by an equally rowdy response from his opponents. The leaders were arrested but their anti–Macready followers picked up the struggle and drove the actor from the stage. The violence spread and outside the theatre the mob started throwing bricks and stones and tried to storm the door. When the police tried to stop them, a full-scale riot broke out, and the soldiers opened fire into the crowd. This fight for control over the content of American theatre pieces eventually fragmented popular entertainments into high- and low-class forms, which energized the development of show business in the United States by expanding the potential audience base and legitimizing new types of characters, styles, themes, and forms of entertainment. This incident is explored at length in Robert Toll's book, *On With the Show: The First Century of Show Business in America*, pp. 19–23.

9. Toll, pp. 1–10.

10. There are many wonderful books on the subject of American blackface minstrelsy and I used several as sources for my research. If the reader is interested in learning more about this subject I recommend Wittke's classic book *Tambo and Bones: A History of the American Minstrel Stage*. Much of the information about

individual performers was gleaned from this entertaining book. I also found much information in the 1911 edition of Edward LeRoy Rice's book, *Monarchs of Minstrelsy: From "Daddy" Rice to Date*. This book lists hundreds of minstrels by name and gives brief biographies of each. It was an extremely valuable resource for me. *Dan Emmett and the Rise of Early Negro Minstrelsy* by Hans Nathan is a classic and I highly recommend it for anyone wanting to read about minstrelsy. Robert C. Toll's *Blacking Up: The Minstrel Show in Nineteenth-Century America*, is easy to read and full of information, as is his other book, *On with the Show: The First Century of Show Business in America*. The first book I read on the subject was *Demons of Disorder: Early Blackface Minstrels and Their World*, by Dale Cockrell, a wonderfully written exploration of blackface minstrelsy. *Love and Theft: Blackface Minstrelsy and the American Working Class* by Eric Lott can be difficult reading, but offers insight into the political and social structures and racial and sex/gender issues that influenced blackface. *"Gentlemen Be Seated": A Parade of the American Minstrels,* by Dailey Paskman, leans more towards a photographic survey than a written exposition. *Inside the Minstrel Mask: Readings in Nineteenth-Century Blackface Minstrelsy* is a collection of articles, edited by Annemarie Bean, James V. Hatch, and Brooks McNamara. *Raising Cain: Blackface Performance from Jim Crow to Hip Hop* by W. T. Lhamon, Jr., was very interesting and helpful to me in the writing of this book. Other books which have sections on minstrel shows include *On the Real Side: Laughing, Lying, and Signifying — The Underground Tradition of African-American Humor that Transformed American Culture, from Slavery to Richard Pryor* by Mel Watkins, *Lost Chords: The Diverting Story of American Popular Songs* by Douglas Gilbert, *Chronicles of the American Dance*, edited by Paul Magriel, which features an exceptional article by Marian Hannah Winter about Juba and others, and of course Marshall and Jean Stearns' book *Jazz Dance: The Story of American Vernacular Dance*, which is a must for dance enthusiasts. I have done my best to credit these fine authors throughout the text of my book. Often the information is repeated from book to book and therefore goes specifically uncredited. I urge the reader who is interested in further exploring the fascinating world of the American minstrel show to look for any of the many fine books I have mentioned above and in others in the bibliography.

11. This description of how to apply blackface makeup is found in the article "Negro Minstrels," by Charles Townsend in the book *Inside the Minstrel Mask: Readings in Nineteenth-Century Blackface Minstrelsy* (Hanover: Wesleyan University Press, 1996) p. 124. The use of blackface can be traced back to African and Native American rituals when sacred clown characters crossed over into areas that were taboo in order to facilitate healing. One of these areas dealt with menstrual blood which was symbolized by brown water or mud smeared upon the face.

12. Marshall Stearns, *The Story of Jazz* (New York: Oxford University Press, 1956) p. 119, states

"Zip Coon," better known as "Turkey in the Straw," has been traced back to a Mississippi

river-boat breakdown, or dance, called "Natchez under the Hill."

13. Carl Wittke *Tambo and Bones: A History of the American Minstrel Stage* (Durham, N.C.: Duke University Press, 1930) p. 17.

14. Two other blackface performers, George Nichols and Bob Farrell, also claimed to have authored the song, "Zip Coon," and to have been the first to introduce it to the public. Nichols, a circus clown for Purdy Brown's Theatre and Circus of the South and West, also claimed to have first introduced "Jim Crow" years before Thomas Rice. He said he learned it from a black banjo player named Picayune Butler, and used to dance a "rough jug [jig]" to the song. In *Curiosities of the American Stage*, page 122, author Laurence Hutton says "that Robert Farrell, 'a circus actor,' was the original 'Zip Coon,' and that the first colored gentleman to wear 'The Long-tailed Blue,' was Barney Burns, who broke his neck on a vaulting board in Cincinnati in 1838."

15. The name Zip came from the African-American name Scipio and was associated with brothel life.

16. William Torber Leonard, *Masquerade in Black* (Metuchen, N.J.: The Scarecrow Press, 1986) p. 210.

17. Dale Cockrell, *Demons of Disorder: Early Blackface Minstrels and Their World* (New York: Cambridge University Press, 1997) p. 138, quoting the *Lowell Courier*, July 19, 1842.

10. "Daddy" Rice

1. Thomas Darmouth Rice's father was probably John Rice, a ship's rigger, who at the time of his son's birth, lived at 60 Catherine Street near the docks.

2. This description of Rice was made by English actor Joe ("Sam") Cowell, who was working with him at the Park Theatre in the production of "Bomabastes Furioso" starring Hilson and Barnes when Rice was fired. Cowell said, "this man [Rice], whose name did not even appear in the bills, was the only actor on the stage whom the audience seemed to notice." This information was taken from Laurence Hutton's article "The Negro on the Stage" in *Harper's Magazine*, p. 138, June 1889.

3. Sources differ as to the location of Rice's first performance. Some say it was in Cincinnati or Pittsburgh, although Hans Nathan mentions a playbill for September 22, 1830, in Louisville, Ky., that has a listing for the number "'Jim Crow' by Mr. Rice," which seems to suggest that the first dance did indeed take place in Louisville. In his book *Tambo and Bones*, Carl Wittke states that Rice first performed in Louisville, then toured to Cincinnati, Pittsburgh, Philadelphia, Boston, and finally the Bowery Theatre in New York, where he received 20 curtain calls. Edward Rice, in *Monarchs of Minstrelsy* states that Rice first heard the song in Cincinnati, then planned an act around it, and later presented the act in Pittsburgh at the old theatre on Fifth Street in the autumn of 1830. *In Raising Cain,* W. T. Lhamon, Jr., says that Rice performed a version of his dance at age 20 on February 17, 1829, in Pensacola, Florida.

4. In his book *Raising Cain: Blackface Performance from Jim Crow to Hip Hop* (Cambridge MA: Harvard University Press, 1998), W. T. Lhamon, Jr., states emphatically that the traditional accounts of the origins of Jim Crow are not true. He says on p. 153:

> The stories [about the origins of Rice's Jim Crow] are false in fact and spirit. There was no hostler, no such baggage handler. What's more, the way these stories tell it is simply not the way cultural gestures come into being. These apocryphal tales indicate, instead, how distant our stories are from the way people produce culture and how starved they are for legitimate detail.

Lhamon's book fully and convincingly explores the reasons why he believes these legends are fictitious. He proposes that Rice was first exposed to black dance as a youngster while living in the Seventh Ward near the Catherine Market. Rice's interest in African-American gestures, music, folklore and traditions was further augmented when he toured the South as a young actor.

5. Most African-American folk tales tell stories of a trickster and his foolish, impish behavior. These stories were told not only to entertain, but also to educate — they taught such valuable lessons as the ability to improvise, to react quickly, to accommodate to adverse surroundings and situations, and to be covert. The tricks performed by the trickster character were not done in order to benefit the perpetrator but rather so that the perpetrator could experience the simple joy of the challenge. There is an interesting parallel between the character of Jim Crow and the voodu trickster god, Legba (pronounced Lahbah). In Haitian culture, Legba was the intermediary between the *loa* and the human worshiper. He was often depicted as a poor, old, crippled man. Erik Davis in his web article, "Trickster at the Crossroads" wrote, "Moving along the seam between two different worldviews, he confuses communication, reveals the ambiguity of knowledge, and plays with perspective." Legba was often syncretized with various Catholic saints such as St. Anthony, St. Lazarus and St. Peter. In Africa, there was a dance performed in honor of Legba which included scratching. This movement later became very common in many African-American vernacular dances such as the itch and find the flea. The scratching gestures were also later incorporated into the breakaway section of the Lindy and in the 1950s and 1960s in an improvised section of the mambo. Perhaps T. D. Rice's Jim Crow dance included such scratching movements.

6. The step became known as "rockin' the heel."

7. Noah Ludlow, *Dramatic Life as I Found It* (New York: Benjamin Bloom, 1966; first published St. Louis, 1880) p. 392.

8. An apocryphal account of Rice's first performance, set in Pittsburgh in 1830, appeared in the article "Stephan C. Foster and Negro Minstrelsy" in *The Atlantic Monthly* vol. 29, issue 121, November 1867 pp. 608–161. It tells of how Rice confiscated the clothes of an African-American porter named Cuff, who supplemented his income carrying luggage by catching pennies in his open mouth.

> There was a negro in attendance at Griffith's Hotel, on Wood Street, named Cuff, — an exquisite specimen of his sort, — who won a pre-

carious subsistence by letting his open mouth as a mark for boys to pitch pennies into, at three paces, and by carrying the trunks of passengers from the steamboats to the hotels. Cuff was precisely the subject for Rice's purpose. Slight persuasion induced him to accompany the actor to the theatre, where he was led through the private entrance, and quietly ensconced behind the scenes.... Rice, having shaded his own countenance to the "contraband hue, ordered Cuff to disrobe, and proceeded to invest himself in the cast-off apparel. When the arrangements were complete, the bell rang. Rice was habited in an old coat forlornly dilapidated, with a pair of shoes composed equally of patches and places for patches on his feet, and wearing a coarse straw hat in a melancholy condition of rent and collapse over a dense black wig of matted moss. [Onstage] the extraordinary apparition produce an instant effect.... The effect was electric. Such a thunder of applause was never heard before within the shell of that old theatre....

> Now it happened that Cuff, who meanwhile was crouching in dishabille under concealment of a projecting flat behind the performer, by some means received intelligence, at this point, of the near approach of a steamer to the Monongahela Wharf....

> After a minute or two of fidgety waiting for the song to end, Cuff's patience could endure no longer, and, cautiously hazarding a glimpse of his profile beyond the edge of the flat, he called in a hurried whisper: "Massa Rice, must have my clo'se! Massa Griffif wants me, — steamboat's comin'!"

> The appeal was fruitless. Massa Rice did not hear it ... driven to desperation, and forgetful in the emergency of every sense of propriety, Cuff, in ludicrous undress as he was, started from his place, rushed upon the stage, and, laying his hand upon the performer's shoulder, called out excitedly: "Massa Rice, Massa Rice, gi' me nigga's hat, — nigga's coat, — nigga's shoes, — gi' me nigga's t'ings! Massa Griffif wants 'im, — STEAMBOAT'S COMIN'!!"

> The incident was the touch, in the mirthful experience of that night, that passed endurance....

> Next day found the song of Jim Crow, in one style of delivery or another, on everybody's tongue. Clerks hummed it serving customers at shop counters, artisans thundered it at the toil to the time-beat of sledge and of tilt-hammer, boys whistled it on the streets, ladies warbled it in parlors, and house-maids repeated it to the clink of crockery in kitchens.

9. Marshall Stearns, *The Story of Jazz* (New York: Oxford University Press, 1956) pp. 111–112, quoting Edmon S. Conner's account from the *New York Times*, June 5, 1881. A fuller account of Conner's tale is as follows:

> Back of the theatre was a livery stable kept by a man named Crow. The actors would look into the stable yard from the theatre, and were particularly amused by an old decrepit negro, who used to do odd jobs for Crow. As was then usual

with slaves, they called themselves after their owner, so that old Daddy had assumed the name of Jim Crow. He was very much deformed, the right shoulder being drawn up high, the left leg stiff and crooked at the knee, giving him a painful, but at the same time laughable limp. He used to croon a queer old tune with the words of his own, and at the end of each verse would give a little jump and when he came down he set his 'heel-a-rockin'.' He called it 'jumpin' Jim Crow.... Rice watched him closely, and saw that here was a character unknown to the stage. He wrote several verses, changed the air somewhat, quickened it a good deal, made up exactly like Daddy, and sang it to a Louisville audience. They were wild with delight, and on the first night he was recalled twenty times.

10. The phenomenal success of Rice's portrayal of Jim Crow cannot be overstated. Noah Ludlow (*Dramatic Life as I Found It*, p. 393) quotes a Mr. Ireland, who stated in *Records of the New York Stage,*

> His [Rice's] popularity was unbounded, and he probably drew more money to the Bowery treasury than any other American performer in the same period of time.

Eric Lott (*Love and Theft*, p. 3) quotes the *New York Tribune* from 1855 in his book:

> It was at this epoch that Mr. T. D. Rice made his debut in a dramatic sketch entitled "Jim Crow," and from that moment everybody was "doing just so," and continued "doing just so" for months, and even years afterward. Never was there such an excitement in the musical or dramatic world; nothing was talked of, nothing written of, and nothing dreamed of, but "Jim Crow." The most sober citizens began to "wheel about, and turn about, and jump Jim Crow." It seemed as though the entire population had been bitten by the tarantula; in the parlor, in the kitchen, in the shop and in the street, Jim Crow monopolized public attention. It must have been a species of insanity, though of a gentle and pleasing kind....

11. A. H. Saxon, *P.T. Barnum: The Legend and the Man* (New York: Columbia University Press, 1989) p. 76.

12. While in England, Rice purchased a copy of *Othello Travestie* by Maurice Dowling. He adapted the material for his own use, inserting blackface plantation elements and topical issues. He entitled this burlesque *Otello* and when he presented it in the United States, it set the trend for American minstrel entertainers to utilize English, French and Italian operatic material as well as African-American elements.

13. Dale Cockrell, *Demons of Disorder: Early Blackface Minstrels and Their World* (New York: Cambridge University Press, 1997) p. 66.

14. Cockrell, p. 66.

15. Lott, p. 57, quoting the *Knickerbocker*, 1845.

16. Cockrell, p. 75.

17. Hans Nathan, *Dan Emmett and the Rise of Early Negro Minstrelsy* (Norman: University of Oklahoma Press, 1962) p. 52.

18. In *Raising Cain*, p. 217, W. T. Lhamon Jr. writes, "Jim Crow's bent knee was an African-Ameri-

can posture teaching nimble motion. His bent knee fostered coexistence and survival rather than rigid relations and extermination."

19. The song was "De New York Nigga" and is mentioned in *Raising Cain*, by W. T. Lhamon Jr. p. 48.

20. On p. 181 of *Raising Cain: Blackface Performance from Jim Crow to Hip Hop* (Cambridge MA: Harvard University Press, 1998), W. T. Lhamon, Jr., states

> No single man authored Jim Crow; no single stable hand made up or taught the song. Instead there was a widespread African-American folk dance   impersonating — delineating — crows, based in agricultural ritual and, some say, "magical in nature."

In African and African-American folklore, the crow was synonymous with the black vulture. W. T. Lhamon, Jr., on p. 119 of *Raising Cain* quotes John K. Terres, *Audubon Society Encyclopedia of North American Birds* (New York: Knopf, 1980) p 958:

> Particularly along the seaboard of the southeastern states, a vernacular name for the Black Vulture has been the Jim Crow.

The relationship between crows, vultures and buzzards is seen again in *African American Folktales: Stories from Black Traditions in the New World*, ed. by Roger D. Abrahams (New York Pantheon, 1985) p. 63. In the story "The John Crows Lose Their Hair" it states: "In a time before time, there lived a man who hated the John Crows (which is what we call those buzzards) because they were so greedy...."

Jim Crow dances were probably similar in nature to the buzzard lope, one of the most popular and widespread dances throughout the plantation culture and were related to gestures that accompanied tales about the Ibo "king buzzard." This probability is substantiated by an African-American dance game that has been preserved in the same Gullah community of the Georgia Sea Islands where the ring shout is still performed. Although the arm movements are not those of the traditional buzzard lope, the lyric of the song again points to the buzzard. The dance is called "Knock Jim Crow," and is explained in *Step It Down: Games, Plays, Songs, and Stories from the Afro-American Heritage* by Bessie Jones and Bessie Lomax Hawes (New York: Harper & Row, 1972) pp. 55–56.

The movements of the dance game accompany the following lyric:

Where you going buzzard?
Where you going crow?
I'm going down to new ground to knock Jim Crow.
Up to my kneecap,
Down to my toe,
And every time I jump up,
I knock Jim Crow.
I knock, I knock Jim Crow.
I knock, I knock Jim Crow.
I knock, I knock Jim Crow.
Repeat...

The dance to "Knock Jim Crow" is as follows:
    a. Step right and raise left leg in goose-step and

simultaneously clap (on the offbeat) under the raised leg, reverse and repeat, doing a total of 8 steps.

　　b. Raise right knee and slap it with right hand, reverse

　　c. Point right index finger to ground, reverse

　　d. Then repeat first step, accelerating until exhausted.

It is interesting to note that at the end of the dance, the movements are repeated and deliberately sped up. This was a common trait during "cutting contests" among early black dancers.

　　21. There are fascinating similarities between the Jim Crow gesture of the raised finger and the hand on the hip, and a gesture commonly used in African art to depict the thunder god, Shango. This ancient gesture consists of Shango pointing one hand to the sky while the other points to his reproductive organs. In viewing representations of this god and representations of T. D. Rice (and also the drawing of the man dancing for eels at Catherine Market) I was startled at how much these various depictions resembled one another.

　　22. Marshall and Jean Stearns in their comprehensive book, *Jazz Dance: The Story of American Vernacular Dance* (New York: Da Capo, 1994) p. 41, explain the movement of truckin' (or trucking):

> In Trucking, the shoulders are often hunched up, one above the other, the hips sway in Congo fashion, and the feet execute a variety of shuffles while the index finger on one hand wiggles shoulder-high at the sky. The movement tends to be more or less straight ahead. Trucking is a highly individual dance with as many fine versions as there are people. Everybody had his own style, although the dance is usually based on short steps forward, turning the heel in after each step. Thereafter, almost anything goes.

　　23. Rice and his own brother, George, presented Jim Crow simultaneously when they were both performing in New York in 1837.

　　24. All quotes from *The Life of Jim Crow* were extracted from *Raising Cain* by W. T. Lhamon, Jr., pp. 197–205.

　　25. In 1896, the Supreme Court, in the case of *Plessy vs. Ferguson,* upheld a Louisiana statute that mandated racial segregation on railroad cars, stating that the Fourteenth Amendment of the Constitution called for political but not social equality. This decision quickly led to the creation of many discriminatory regulations throughout the South in which whites and blacks were treated as "separate but equal." These laws came to be known as the Jim Crow laws. Besides segregating blacks in schools, restaurants, boarding houses, and public institutions, one of the major impacts of these regulations was that they restricted the African-American's right to vote by creating poll taxes and literacy requirements. Jim Crow laws were in effect until 1954, and legal sanctions against African-Americans were not totally eliminated until the civil rights movement in the 1960s and the passage of the Civil Rights Act of 1964, the Voting Rights Act of 1965, and the Fair Housing Act of 1968.

　　26. George Washington Dixon is said to have popularized this character and claimed, although many dispute it, to have authored the song, "Long Tail Blue." Clown Dan Rice was also famous for wearing a costume similar to that worn by Uncle Sam.

　　27. Part of a theatrical dynasty, Joseph Jefferson III went on to become an extremely successful actor on the American stage. During one tour to Springfield, Illinois, Joseph Jefferson III and his troupe were unable to perform because of an exorbitant tax levied on theatrical presentations, launched against the local theatre by the church fathers during a religious revival. A young lawyer was hired to represent the actors and through his "humorous" arguments, was able to get the tax lifted so the show could go on. The young lawyer representing Jefferson and his fellow actors was Abraham Lincoln. Ironically, one of Jefferson's most popular roles was the character of Asa Trenchard, which he created for the play *Our American Cousin,* the same play Lincoln was watching when he was assassinated, although Joseph Jefferson III was not in the cast that night at the Ford's Theatre.

　　28. Quote from Joseph Jefferson, "The Autobiography of Joseph Jefferson" In *The Century; a popular quarterly,* Vol. 39, issue 1, November 1889, pp. 4–6.

　　29. Carl Wittke, *Tambo and Bones: A History of the American Minstrel Stage* (Durham, N.C.: Duke University Press, 1930) p. 31, quoting a New York editor who saw Rice perform in the summer of 1840. The full quote, originally taken from George C. D. Odell's book *Annals of the New York Stage* (New York: 1927), reads:

> Entering the theatre, we found it crammed from pit to dome, and the best representative of our American Negro that we ever saw was stretching every mouth in the house to its utmost tension. Such a natural gait!– such a laugh!– and such a twitching-up of the arm and shoulder! It was the Negro, par excellence. Long live James Crow, Esquire!

　　30. Cecelia Conway, in her book *African Banjo Echoes in Appalachia,* p. 92, quotes William Winter's *The Wallet of Time: Containing Reminiscences of the American Theater* (1913) vol. II, p. 615:

> [Rice was a] convivial man, and not less eccentric than convivial. It pleased him to wear gold pieces — soveriegns and the like — as buttons on his garments, and not infrequently the boon companions, into whose hands he fell, would stupefy him with liquor then rob him of those ornaments.

　　31. Other sources place the date of Rice's death as September 8, 1860.

11. The King of Diamonds and Master Juba

　　1. Hans Nathan, *Dan Emmett and the Rise of Early Negro Minstrelsy* (Norman: University of Oklahoma Press, 1962) p. 62, quoting an announcement of the Vauxhall gardens in the *Morning Herald* (New York, July 18, 1840.)

　　2. Diamond was born in 1823, and after being discovered by Barnum, was managed by him for a while. Because Diamond was under age, Barnum contracted

the young dancer's services through his guardian, Joseph W. Harrison. In his biography *Life of Hon. Phineas T. Barnum* (Philadelphia, 1891), pp. 103–104, Joel Benton writes:

> Barnum had formed the acquaintance of a very clever young dancer named John Diamond, and soon after leaving the paste-blacking enterprise, he [Barnum] gathered together a company of singers, etc., which, with the dancer, Diamond, he placed in the hands of an agent, not caring to have his name appear in the transaction. He hired Vauxhall Garden Saloon in New York and gave a variety of performances. This, however, proved unprofitable, and was abandoned after a few months.

Benton goes on to relate how a reluctant Barnum then took Diamond to New Orleans on January 2, 1841, and eventually arranged a dance contest.

> A dancing match between Diamond and a negro from Kentucky put nearly $500 into Barnum's pocket, and they continued to prosper until Diamond, after extorting as much money as possible from his manager, finally ran away.

3. Marian Hannah Winter in the article "Juba and American Minstrelsy" in *Chronicles of the American Dance*, Paul Magriel, ed. (New York: Henry Holt, 1948) pp. 45–46, mentions some of the dances that Diamond performed, then quotes an uncredited source:

> ... all of which he will come in those Unheard of, Outlandish and Inimitable Licks, what is Death to all de Long Island darkies, and which secures him the title of King of Diamonds.

Winter's article is probably the most thorough source of information about William Henry Lane.

4. Nathan, p. 62.

5. Winter, p. 47.

6. Noah M. Ludlow, *Dramatic Life as I Found It* (New York: Benjamin Bloom, 1966; first published St. Louis, 1880) p. 533.

7. Nathan, p. 61. The playbill was from the New Theatre, Mobile, Alabama on February 24, 1841.

8. Nathan, p. 61.

9. Winter, p. 47.

10. Joel Benton, *Life of Hon. Phineas T. Barnum* (Philadelphia: Edgewood Publishing, 1891) p. 104.

11. A.H. Saxon, *P.T. Barnum: The Legend and the Man* (New York: Columbia University Press, 1989) p. 82.

12. Eric Lott, *Love and Theft: Blackface Minstrelsy and the American Working Class* (New York: Oxford University Press, 1993) pp. 112–113.

13. Paradise Square in the Five Points District was in lower Manhattan at the intersection of Baxter, Worth and Park Streets.

14. Winter, p. 42.

15. Winter, p. 43, quoting from 1845 handbill now found in the Harvard Theatre Collection.

16. Winter, pp. 43–45, quoting from 1845 handbill now found in the Harvard Theatre Collection.

17. Winter, pp. 42–43.

18. Douglas Gilbert, *Lost Chords: The Diverting Story of American Popular Songs* (Garden City, NY: Doubleday, 1942) p. 217.

19. Dale Cockrell, *Demons of Disorder: Early Blackface Minstrels and Their World* (New York: Cambridge University Press, 1997) p. 138, quoting the *New York Sporting Whip*, January 28, 1843.

20. Charles Day, "Fun in Black" in *Inside the Minstrel Mask: Readings in Nineteenth-Century Blackface Minstrelsy*, Annemarie Bean, James V. Hatch, and Brooks McNamara, eds. (Hanover: Wesleyan University Press, 1996.) p. 49.

21. Rhett Krause, in his article "Step Dancing on the Boston Stage: 1841–1869," in *Country Dance and Song*, no. 22, pp. 1–19 (June 1992) p. 8, wrote:

> Diamond had already defeated Lane at a jig dance tournament held in the early 1840's at the Boylston Gardens, Boston. Lane and Diamond met again in New York City in 1844 in perhaps the most famous competition of all, with Lane decisively winning the $500 prize. Lane returned to Boston in triumph the next year, billed as "King of All the Dancers," performing there for two weeks, with additional competitions against the jig dancer Frank Diamond (no relation to John).

22. Charles Dickens, *American Notes and Pictures from Italy* (London, Chapman and Hall, 1874) p. 104.

23. Winter, pp. 49–50, quoting an anonymous London critic.

24. Winter, p. 50.

25. Winter, p. 50, quoting an anonymous clipping entitled *Juba the American Dancer* (circa 1848).

26. In *Jazz Dance: The Story of American Vernacular Dance* (New York: Da Capo, 1994) p. 47, Marshall and Jean Stearns list two dancers that were greatly influenced by Lane: a white dancer named Richard M. Carroll (1831–1899), and Ralph Keeler, who wrote in his article "Three Years as a Negro Minstrel" (*Atlantic Monthly*, Vol. 24, issue 141, p. 72, July 1869) that he learned to dance by studying the "complicated shuffles of Juba." The lives and careers of both are discussed more fully in Chapter 13.

27. Winter, p. 42.

28. Winter, p. 39.

12. The Virginia Minstrels

1. Mel Watkins, *On the Real Side: Laughing, Lying, and Signifying — The Underground Tradition of African-American Humor that Transformed American Culture, from Slavery to Richard Pryor* (New York: Simon & Schuster, 1994) p. 87.

2. Hans Nathan in *Dan Emmett and the Rise of Early Negro Minstrelsy*, p. 107, writes at length about this part of Emmett' life. Emmett excelled at drumming and went on to write the first drummer's manual to be used by the United States Army. In *Way Up North in Dixie*, Howard and Judith Sacks suggest that Emmett's exposure to black music was mainly due to a close friendship with the Snowdens, an African-American family of musicians who lived near him in Mt. Vernon, Ohio.

3. Robert Sheerin, "'Dixie' and Its Author," in *The Century; a popular quarterly*, vol. 50, issue 6, Oct 1895, p. 958.

4. Nathan, p. 113.

5. Joel Walker Sweeney was considered the best banjo player around. He could play the instrument both left-handed and right-handed. He was originally taught to play the banjo by the slaves on his family's plantation in Virginia. A flamboyant man, Sweeney used to light his cigars with $20 bills.

6. Nathan, p. 115.

7. Laurence Hutton, in his book *Curiosities of the American Stage*, pp. 124–122, says that Bill Whitlock claimed credit for the idea of forming the Virginia Minstrels. In a quote from his autobiography, a part of which was published in the *New York Clipper*, he told his daughter, Mrs. Edwin Adams,

> The origin (organization) of the minstrels I claim to be my own idea, and it cannot be blotted out…. One day I asked Dan Emmett, who was in New York at the time, to practise the fiddle and the banjo with me at his boarding house in Catherine Street. We went down there, and when we had practised Frank Brower called in by accident. He listened to our music, charmed to his soul. I told him to join with the bones, which he did. Presently Dick Pelham came in, also by accident, and looked amazed. I asked him to procure a tambourine, and make one of the party, and he went out and got one. After practising for a while we went to the old resort of the circus crowd — the 'Branch,' in the Bowery — with our instruments, and in Bartlett's billiard-room performed for the first time as the Virginia Minstrels. A programme was made out, and the first time we appeared upon the stage before an audience was for the benefit of Pelham at Chatham Theatre. The house was crammed and jammed with our friends; and Dick, of course, put ducats in his purse.

Benefits were usually held at the end of the run of a show. A particular performer got all the proceeds.

8. The group chose the name Virginia Minstrels based upon the success of a group called the Tyrolese Minstrel Family which had just successfully toured America. At times the foursome called themselves the Virginia Serenaders.

9. Nathan, p. 117, quoting *the New York Clipper*, May 19, 1877.

10. There is some debate about the exact date of the first performance by the Virginia Minstrels. Some sources claim it was in December 1842, others in early 1843. Apparently the act was first performed at either Bartlett's Billiard Parlor in the Bowery or in the Branch Hotel for an audience of theatrical cronies and friends. According to accounts given by Emmett, during the first performance the crowd jeered at them, unfamiliar with the new combination of instruments, but despite the shaky beginning, the audience was eventually won over and at the end of the night, the room roared with applause. Later the show was presented to the general public in February 1843, somewhere around the 6th of the month at the Chatham Theatre and at the Bowery Theatre on the 17th. William Torbert Leonard, in his

book *Masquerade in Black* (Metuchen, N.J.: The Scarecrow Press, 1986) p. 226, lists January 31, 1843, as the date the group tested their material at the Chatham Theatre in New York, and February 6, 1843, as the official debut at the Bowery Amphitheatre.

11. The classic minstrel characters "Tambo" and "Bones" were named for the instruments the two dancing endmen traditionally played.

12. Nathan, p. 133, quoting sayings that were recorded by Daniel Emmett and probably used by Pelham and Brower.

13. The first public performance of the Virginia Minstrels consisted of sketches and songs. One song that was performed was "Old Dan Tucker," one of Emmett's most popular songs. He composed it when he was 15 years old and first performed it at a Fourth of July celebration in his home town of Mt. Vernon, Ohio. He named the song for himself and his dog, whose name was Tucker.

14. Carl Wittke, *Tambo and Bones: A History of the American Minstrel Stage* (Durham, N.C.: Duke University Press, 1930) p. 45.

15. Cockrell, pp. 152–154.

16. Robert C. Toll, *Blacking Up: The Minstrel Show in Nineteenth-Century America* (New York: Oxford University Press, 1974) p. 30, quoting a program from a Dublin, Ireland, performance of the Virginia Minstrels, 1844.

17. Richard Kislan, *Hoofing on Broadway: A History of Show Dancing*, (New York: Prentice Hall, 1987) pp. 17–18.

18. Nathan, p. 136. Richard Kislan in his book, *Hoofing on Broadway: A History of Show Dancing* (New York: Prentice Hall, 1987) p. 17, states that one of the dances that the Virginia Minstrels did while touring Scotland was called the "Corn Husking Jig."

19. After Pelham left the group in England he was replaced by banjo player Joe Sweeney. The new group then toured Scotland and Ireland. Whitlock was the first to return to the U.S., where he joined P.T. Barnum's minstrel band. Brower and Sweeney worked for Cooke's Circus for a while, and Emmett reteamed again with Pelham and performed in London for an eight-week engagement at Astley's Theatre. Brower and Emmett then returned to the U.S. to form another group.

20. In her book *Black Dance: From 1619 to Today*, pp. 192–193, Lynne Fauley Emery quotes Charles Sherlock's article "From Breakdown to Ragtime," which appeared on page 635 of *Cosmopolitan* in Oct. 1901:

> [The walk around] was intended to be written in march time, and to its spirited strains the whole company would circumnavigate the stage, in a dance step that was little more than a jerky elevation of the legs below the knees, much like the 'buck and wing' dances of the present day. It was as long ago as this — the walk-around being in highest estate with Bryant's Minstrels in the sixties — that the patting of dance-time with the outspread palms upon the knees was invented. To this manual accompaniment the breakdowns were often done.

21. Douglas Gilbert, *Lost Chords: The Diverting Story of American Popular Songs* (Garden City, NY: Doubleday, 1942) pp. 13–14.

22. Hans Nathan in *Dan Emmett and the Rise of Early Negro Minstrelsy*, pp. 262–266, puts forth several conjectures about the etymology of the word "Dixie." One is that the word is a reference to a slaveholder, named Dixey, who sold his slaves down South. Another suggests it could be a corruption of the word "Dixon" referred to in the Mason-Dixon Line. Nathan also explores the possibility that the word is derived from the French word *dix*, which was the name of the $10 bill in Louisiana. These $10 bills were the most popular bank notes in New Orleans and uneducated boatmen, stevedores and tradesmen referred to them as "dixies." The lower South eventually took on that name.

23. Wittke sets the date of the first presentation of "Dixie" on September 12, 1859.

24. In their fascinating book, *Way Up North in Dixie*, Howard L. Sacks and Judith Rose Sacks suggest that the source for the song was an African-American family named Snowden who Daniel Emmett knew in his hometown of Mt. Vernon, Ohio. John Lair in his book, *Songs Lincoln Loved* (New York: Duell, Sloan and Pearce, 1954) p. 39, says that author-composer Will S. Hayes was the original composer of the melody and that he wrote it "as a marching song in a parade held in Louisville during a time when Emmett was appearing at a local theater and had an opportunity to pick up the catchy tune, remember it, and later appropriate it."

25. The song "Dixie" was first introduced in the South by Mrs. John Wood in a production in New Orleans. She was accompanied by 40 women dressed as Zouaves, in French artillery outfits, marching to a military drill. The number was a sensation and after the outbreak of the Civil war, the song was arranged for the Louisiana regiments and thus found its way into the Confederacy.

26. Emmett had sold the song "Dixie" for only $500 dollars and therefore never was able to financially capitalize on its enormous success.

27. Nathan, p. 71, quoting Frances Anne Kemble, *Journal of a Residence on a Georgia Plantation in 1838–1839* (New York, 1863) p. 96.

28. Nathan, p. 71.

13. The Development of the Minstrel Show

1. The interlocutor is an outgrowth of the circus ringmaster. Just as the end-men directed their jokes at the interlocutor, the circus clown traditionally kidded the ringmaster who controlled the running of the show.

2. Lynne Fauley Emery, *Black Dance: From 1619 to Today* (Princeton, NJ: Princeton University Press, 1988) p. 191, quoting Arthur Todd's article "Four Centuries of American Dance: Negro American Theatre Dance, 1840–1900" which appeared in *Dance Magazine*, XXIV (November, 1950) p. 21.

3. Stephen Foster himself performed in blackface when he was as young as nine years old. In his teens, he saw Thomas "Daddy" Rice perform and tried to sell Rice his songs, although he was unsuccessful.

4. Besides the pigeon wing, the buck, and the other plantation dances already discussed elsewhere in

this book, minstrels used many other common movements. One popular minstrel step included kicking the lower leg in a circular motion while the knees remained close together in a movement resembling the Charleston. Slides were also frequently used, especially in a dance called cutting the long J bow, in which one leg was slid forward on the back heel of the flexed foot. Hopping backwards, sometimes called backaction springs, and running on the heels, called tracking upon the heel, were also common. Walking the jawbone probably involved rapid tapping of the foot, similar to nerve taps so that the sound imitated the noise made by a stick being drawn over the teeth of a jawbone. Kneeling and rising were other motions regularly employed by minstrel dancers.

5. Marian Hannah Winter, "Juba and American Minstrelsy" In *Chronicles of the American Dance*, ed. by Paul Magriel, pp. 39–63. (New York: Henry Holt, 1948) p. 53.

6. Edward LeRoy Rice in *Monarchs of Minstrelsy* states that Mitchell died in Victoria, B.C.

7. Myron Matlaw, ed., *American Popular Entertainment: Papers and Proceedings of the Conference on the History of American Popular Entertainment* (Westport, CT: Greenwood Press, 1977) p. 235.

8. Marshall and Jean Stearns, *Jazz Dance: The Story of American Vernacular Dance* (New York: Da Capo, 1994) p. 53.

9. Ralph O. Keeler, "Three Years as a Negro Minstrel," in *The Atlantic Monthly*, Vol. 24, issue 141, pp. 71–86, July 1869, p. 71.

10. Keeler, p. 72.

11. In his article "Three Years a Negro Minstrel" p. 74, Keeler also tells how he auditioned for one minstrel troupe by dancing juba. His dance was accompanied by the troupe's comedian, who patted for him while he danced.

12. Keeler, p. 72.

13. Philip Graham, *Showboats: The History of an American Institution* (Austin: University of Texas Press, 1951) p. 32.

14. Keeler, p. 73.

15. W.T. Lhamon suggests that the Virginia essence was something like running in place and grew into dances like Michael Jackson's moonwalk and M. C. Hammer's running man.

16. Carl Wittke, *Tambo and Bones: A History of the American Minstrel Stage* (Durham, N.C.: Duke University Press, 1930) p. 223.

17. Stearns, p. 51, quoting an interview with Billy Maxey, 1960–61.

18. Stearns, p. 52, quoting Harland Dixon.

19. Marshall and Jean Stearns state that Primrose was supposed to have been the great Bill Robinson's idol.

20. Douglas Gilbert, *American Vaudeville: Its Life and Times* (New York: Whittlesey House, 1940) p. 130.

21. There were many popular child stars. Master Peanut clogged in Boston at the early age of six. Many child stars were genuinely the age they advertised, although several claimed in their press releases to be many years younger than they really were. As they grew older, most continued to be presented as younger than their real age.

22. Constance Rourke, *Troupers of the Gold Coast or The Rise of Lotta Crabtree* (New York: Harcourt, Brace, 1928) p. 135.

23. Rourke, p. 137.

24. Rourke, pp. 192–193.

25. Richard Kislan, *Hoofing on Broadway: A History of Show Dancing* (New York: Prentice Hall, 1987) p. 21.

26. The word "hoofer" was not commonly used when referring to a tap dancer until the 1920s.

27. Rhett Krause, "Step Dancing on the Boston Stage: 1841–1869," in *Country Dance and Song*, no. 22, pp. 1–19 (June 1992) p. 11. One typical advertisement used by Queen read:

Clog dancing taught. J. Queen would respectfully inform the public that he will receive a few pupils in clog dancing. Clogs furnished. Pupils qualified for the stage. Persons desirous of learning legitimate clog dancing will please address J. Queen, Morris brothers' Opera House.

When Queen began teaching with Carroll, they called their enterprise "Carroll and Queen's Clog, Jig, Reel, Comic, and Burlesque Dancing School." Rates were: banjo and clog lessons with clogs included—$8; jig lessons—$6; and song and dance—$3.

28. Douglas Gilbert *American Vaudeville: Its Life and Times* (New York: Whittlesey House, 1940) p. 24.

29. McIntyre's first partner was a man by the name of Butler. While the team was performing in San Antonio, Butler had to leave town suddenly because he was being shot at. Rumors floated around that he was either run out of town by natives because he wore a top hat, or more likely, because he was caught in bed with the wrong woman. Heath happened to be in the same show and replaced Butler as McIntyre's partner.

30. Joe Laurie, Jr., *Vaudeville: From the Honkytonks to the Palace* (New York: Henry Holt & Co., 1953) p. 140. On the same page, Laurie relates a story about sitting with Heath in a hotel lobby while Heath was chewing tobacco. Laurie had his foot near the cuspidor. Laurie wrote,

I was afraid to pull my foot away for fear he would think I was underestimating his aim (Remember, I was a kid and he was a big star.) He certainly had me nervous for an hour, but he proved just as big a star at spittin' tobacco as he was on stage; he never missed the cuspidor once.

31. Krauss, p. 11.

32. Gilbert, *Lost Chords*, p. 19.

14. Black Minstrelsy and Musical Theatre

1. Marian Hannah Winter, in her article, "Juba and American Minstrelsy," in *Chronicles of the American Dance*, ed. by Paul Magriel, pp. 39–63 (New York: Henry Holt, 1948) p. 60, writes:

In the last minstrel troupe of real darkies which went over the country the end men insisted on corking up as black as possible over their naturally dark skin, because, as they said, the public had gotten used to seeing the Negro minstrel as he is depicted by the whites and when the genuine article came along the public was a little disappointed to find that he was not so black as he was painted.

2. Kersands often danced his buck and wing to Stephen Foster's "Swanee River." His son, who was billed as the Infant Kersands, was also considered to be a top-notch dancer.

3. Mel Watkins, *On the Real Side: Laughing, Lying, and Signifying— The Underground Tradition of African-American Humor that Transformed American Culture, from Slavery to Richard Pryor* (New York: Simon & Schuster, 1994) p. 113.

4. Marshall and Jean Stearns, *Jazz Dance: The Story of American Vernacular Dance* (New York: Da Capo, 1994) p. 51, quoting Arthur Marshall.

5. Watkins, p. 114.

6. Watkins, p. 113.

7. Henry T. Sampson, *Blacks in Black Face: A Source Book on Early Black Minstrel Shows* (Metuchen, NJ: The Scarecrow Press, 1980) pp. 390–391. Another part of Sam Lucas's article relates a story about Kersands as a boy.

I often sit and think of the funny stories he used to tell me of himself and the old folks at home when he was a boy. Among them, one of his duties was to fill and light his grandmother's pipe, which task had to be performed many times a day. Billy, by way of diversion and occasion, placed a little charge of gunpowder in the bowl of the pipe, piled the tobacco upon it, lighted it and passed it to his grandmother. The mild explosion which ensued gave her a great shock and him amusement.

8. Stearns, p. 120, quoting Edward B. Marks, *They All Sang* (New York: Viking press, 1935) p. 91.

9. An interesting bit of trivia is that Harriet Beecher Stowe's sister, Catherine Beecher, was an early promoter of women's education in the United States and believed movement was a vital part of female schooling. She combined music and exercise into a form that greatly resembled dancing, although she hesitated to call it by that name. She stated that her method was "a far more efficient means than dancing, for improving the form and manners, without any of its evils." Catherine Beecher wrote two books about physical education, *Course of Calisthenics for Young Ladies* in 1832, and *A Manual of Physiology and Calisthenics for Schools and Families* in 1856.

10. *The South Before the War* was conceived by minstrel performer Billy Mclain who was instrumental in creating jobs for thousands of African-American performers. In 1895, he produced the outdoor summer extravaganza, *Black America*. The success of the show helped to make white theatre owners aware of the vast talent available in the black community.

11. Thomas L. Riis, *Just Before Jazz: Black Musical Theatre in New York, 1890–1915* (Washington, D.C.: Smithsonian Institution Press, 1989) p. 23.

12. Stearns, p. 76.

13. Stearns, p. 76.

14. Stearns, p. 76.

15. Lynn Fauley Emery, *Black Dance: From 1619 to Today* (Princeton, NJ: Princeton Univ. Press, 1988) p. 208.

16. The white managers who previously had a monopoly tried to sabotage the tour of *A Trip to Coontown*, threatening that any performer who did the show would be blackballed for life, and that any theatre that presented the show would be boycotted and would never be able to book another black show. This threat was effective in preventing the show from playing in any of the major theatres and limited the tour to the worst theatres in small out-of-the-way towns. The show finally found a long run and good success in Canada. When word of the show's success in Canada made its way back to the United States, one theatre defied the ban and booked the company in New York, opening the show during Holy Week, supposedly the worst time of the year for theatre. Despite this, crowds flocked to see the show.

17. After the show's run in New York, Williams and Walker did replace Hogan for an unsuccessful tour.

18. Will Marion Cook, "Clorindy, The Origin of the Cakewalk," in *The International Library of Negro Life and History — Anthology of the American Negro in the Theatre; A Critical Approach,* ed. by Lindsay Patterson (New York: Publishers Company, 1968) p. 52.

19. Cook, p. 54

20. Cook, p. 54. The composer recalled that on opening night he was so thrilled with the audience's response, he drank a glass of water (believing it was wine), and got completely drunk.

21. Cook wrote the music for other successful musicals. One was *The Southerners*. This show had an integrated cast, a rare phenomenon on Broadway at the time. One of the stars of the show was the famous minstrel dancer, Eddie Leonard.

22. Edward Thorpe, *Black Dance* (Woodstock, New York: Overlook, 1990) p. 57.

23. Henry Louis Gates, Jr., and Cornel West, *The African-American Century: How Black Americans Have Shaped Our Country* (New York: The Free Press, 2000) p. 41.

24. Gates and West, pp. 40–41.

25. Bert Williams wrote a song in tribute to the cakewalk dancer, Dora Dean, entitled, "Miss Dora Dean." The chorus for the song was:

Oh have you seen Miss Dora Dean,
She is the sweetest gal you ever seen.
Some day I'm going to make this Gal my Queen.
On next Sunday morning, I'm going to marry
Miss Dora Dean.

It was the presentation of this song that introduced Williams and Walker to the New York stage.

26. Stearns, p. 122, quoting Walter Crumbley.

27. Charles W. Stein, ed., *American Vaudeville as Seen by Its Contemporaries* (New York: Knopf, 1984) p. 242, quoting Bert Williams.

28. Anthony Slide, *The Vaudevillians: A Dictionary of Vaudeville Performers* (New Rochelle, NY: Arlington House, 1981) p. 169.

15. Other Forms of Entertainment

1. Thomas Dartmouth Rice later became a part of Ludlow's troupe. He first performed his Jim Crow dance with this company.

2. Medicine boats were notoriously disreputable. One in particular supposedly played to African-American audiences and sold a lotion that was guaranteed to turn black skin white.

3. William Chapman's son, Samuel, who had died from a fall from a horse before the family purchased the showboat, had been married to Elizabeth Jefferson, the daughter of actor Joseph Jefferson II, and sister to Joseph Jefferson III, the boy who danced Jim Crow with Thomas Dartmouth Rice.

4. Phillip Graham, *Showboats: The History of an American Institution* (Austin: University of Texas Press, 1951) p. 13

5. A young couple who had run away from home and wished to be married in the boat's museum were readily welcomed and wed among the stuffed animals and other curiosities. When the girl's angry brother arrived and created a scene, the manager of the showboat was overjoyed at receiving all the free publicity.

6. Marshall and Jean Stearns, *Jazz Dance: The Story of American Vernacular Dance* (New York: Da Capo, 1994) p. 63, quoting Dewey "Pigmeat" Markham from interviews held in New York: 1959–63.

7. Stearns, p. 66.

8. Peter Leslie, *A Hard Act to Follow: A Music Hall Review* (New York: Paddington Press, 1978) p. 33.

9. By the middle of the 19th century, gangs of Irish thugs, such as the "Plug Uglies," the "Dead Rabbits," the "Hudson Dusters," the "Atlantic Guards," and the "Bowery Boys," roamed the Five Points district and the Bowery, terrorizing the neighborhood. Made up of boys, the gangs often achieved the size of small armies. The "Hudson Dusters" for example had over 1,500 members at its height. The battles between rival gangs sometimes reached enormous proportions. One fight between the "Dead Rabbits," aided by the "Plug Uglies," against the "Bowery Boys" and the "Atlantic Guards" escalated to such a point that it took two regiments of militia and 150 police to quell the violence. One of the most interesting gangs was the "Baxter Street Dudes." The group was started by a boy named Baby-Face Willy, who convinced the boys in the gang to start their own theatre with scenery and props they had stolen from legitimate theatres in the Bowery. They called their playhouse the "Grand Duke Theatre" and they opened it in the basement of a beer joint. They wrote their own songs and skits and performed in them as well. The shows became a successful attraction among the street kids and also for the social elite that were "slumming." When rival gangs tried to stop shows by throwing stones at the building, the performers left the stage, went out onto the streets and fought to defend their turf. The shows were eventually closed down by the police when the boys didn't pay the amusement tax levied by the city.

10. Edward Van Every, *Sins of New York: As Exposed by the Police Gazette* (New York: Frederick A. Stokes Co., 1930) p. 289, quoting the *Police Gazette*.

11. Although vaudeville was traditionally family

entertainment, some of the seedier establishments were not so family-oriented. Cheap vaudeville houses sometimes held amateur nights that promised female performers the opportunity of getting an agent. These were usually just a ruse to procure the girls' services as prostitutes.

12. Robert W. Snyder, *The Voice of the City: Vaudeville and Popular Culture in New York* (New York: Oxford University Press, 1989) p. 4.

16. Vaudeville

1. Ransome may have gotten the term from the "Vaudeville Theatre" in San Antonio, Texas, established as early as 1882. Peter Leslie, *A Hard Act to Follow: A Music Hall Review* (New York: Paddington Press, 1978) p. 27, says that the first use of the word was in 1871 when "Sargent's Great Vaudeville Company" opened in Louisville, Kentucky, at Weisiger's Hall.

2. Pastor himself hated the term "vaudeville," considering it too sissy. B.F. Keith was the one who really propagated the use of the word.

3. Douglas Gilbert, *American Vaudeville: Its Life and Times* (New York: Whittlesey House, 1940) p. 10.

4. Robert W. Snyder in *The Voice of the City: Vaudeville and Popular Culture in New York*, says Pastor was born in 1834.

5. In his *Pirates of Penzance* burlesque, Pastor introduced singer Lillian Russell to the stage. He styled her a ballad singer whom he had brought over from England "at great trouble and expense." She was actually from Clinton, Ohio and when hired by Pastor, had been living in Brooklyn.

6. Benjamin Franklin Keith (1846–1914), one of the most successful producers of vaudeville fare, also geared his shows to a family audience, and the Keith Circuit became known as the "Sunday School Circuit." Warnings were posted backstage in all Keith vaudeville houses with rules listed for what was acceptable and what wasn't. One such notice from 1899 read:

> You are hereby warned that your act must be free from all vulgarity and suggestiveness in words, action, and costume, while playing in any of Mr. _____'s houses, and all vulgar, double-meaning and profane words and songs must be cut out of your act before the first performance. If you are in doubt as to what is right and wrong, submit it to the resident manager at rehearsal. Such words as liar, slob, son-of-a-gun, devil, sucker, damn, and all such words, unfit for the ears of ladies and children, also any reference to questionable streets, resorts, localities, and bar-rooms are prohibited under fine of instant discharge.

This notice is found in several books on vaudeville such as *The Voice of the City: Vaudeville and Popular Culture in New York* by Robert W. Synder (New York: Oxford University Press, 1989) p. 29, and *American Vaudeville as Seen by Its Contemporaries,* Charles W. Stein, ed. (New York: Knopf. 1984) p. 24.

7. Charles and Louise Samuels, *Once Upon a Stage: The Merry World of Vaudeville* (New York: Dodd, Mead & Co., 1974) p. 19, quoting Tony Pastor.

8. Most audiences assumed that wooden-soled shoe dancing was more difficult, although this wasn't necessarily so. Nevertheless, the number of clog and buck dancers in vaudeville rocketed, especially between 1900 and 1907. When metal taps were introduced around 1915, hard-soled shoe dancing and soft-soled-shoe dancing began to merge.

9. I hazard a guess that the old Mother Goose rhyme, "Jack be nimble, Jack be quick" is a reference to the old English folk dance called "leap-candle." The candle-rush or leap-rush was originally danced only by girls. It was commonly performed during the ceremony of Candlemas held on February 2nd or February 14th.

10. Charles W. Stein, editor, *American Vaudeville as Seen by Its Contemporaries* (New York: Knopf 1984) p. 246, quoting Eddie Leonard.

11. According to Douglas Gilbert in his book *Lost Chords: The Diverting Story of American Popular Songs* (Garden City, NY: Doubleday, 1942) pp. 117–118, Francis Wilson went on to become a successful comedian on the legitimate stage after the death of his partner, Jimmy Mackin. In 1919, Wilson was one of the driving forces behind the formation of the theatrical union Actors Equity, and became the group's first president.

12. In the tradition of tap challenges, there were many sand jig contests. Judges were placed under the stage and listened to performers' feet sliding through the sand, giving or taking away points depending upon the accuracy of the rhythms.

13. Eddie Foy's life contained many interesting events. He started dancing while selling newspapers as a boy to help support his family after his father had been injured in the head during the Civil War and had gone insane. It was during this period in his life that Foy first learned how to dance from the shoeshine boys and newsboys. The family later moved to Chicago when Eddie's mother went to work as the nurse companion to Mary Todd Lincoln in Springfield, Illinois. As a young performer, Foy toured the West. He was in Dodge City, Kansas, when he made a few disparaging remarks about cowboys while on stage. That night a group of cowboys dragged Foy from his hotel room and took him out to a tree to hang him. Despite the situation, he remained cocky and kept making jokes, and the lynch mob was eventually swayed by his pluck and courage. They decided not to hang him and instead, just ducked him in the water trough. Another time while performing in Dodge City, there was a shootout when Bat Masterson and Doc Holliday ran two drunken Texans out of the saloon where Foy was dancing. When Foy went backstage, he discovered bullet holes in the newly purchased suit he had just hung there. He was also once temporarily deputized by the famous Masterson.

14. Marshall and Jean Stearns, *Jazz Dance: The Story of American Vernacular Dance* (New York: Da Capo, 1994) p. 210, quoting Harland Dixon.

15. Joe Laurie, Jr., in *Vaudeville: From the Honkytonks to the Palace* (New York: Henry Holt & Co., 1953), states that Lew Randall was thought by some to be the first professional buck and wing dancer in vaudeville, and that the first buck dancing in burlesque was supposedly done by Johnny Jess.

16. Stearns, p. 53.

17. Samuels, p. 4.

18. Anthony Slide, *The Vaudevillians: A Dictionary of Vaudeville Performers* (New Rochelle, NY: Arlington House, 1981) p. 128.

19. Slide, p. 128.

20. Slide, p. 128.

21. Samuels, p. 212.

22. George White (1890–1968) danced for pennies in New York clubs until 1912, when he went to Paris and saw the French *revue à grand spectacle*. He returned to the U.S. and decided to mount his own opulent extravaganzas, called *George White's Scandals*. He also produced conventional musicals, including one very important show which opened in October 1923 called *Runnin' Wild*. This show featured a group of chorus boys called the "Dancing Redcaps," who did the Charleston accompanied by patting juba. Legend has it that the dance had been originally taught to the cast by a trio of African-American youngsters that Flourney Miller had seen dancing on a street corner. The choreographer, Lida Webb, then created the show-stopping number for the male chorus and in this way, the Charleston was introduced to the general public. Apparently George White did not like the Charleston and originally wanted to cut it from *Runnin' Wild*, but wisely left it in. When the show opened in New York City, it created a sensation. Throughout his career as a producer, White had a reputation of being a bit pretentious and of always trying to tone down any African-American styles of dancing in his shows. In the Great Depression, he stopped his series of *Scandals* and tried to put his revues into films and nightclubs but had only limited success. George White was an excessively wasteful man, and often had to file for bankruptcy throughout his life. He was once jailed for causing a fatal auto accident.

23. Samuels, pp. 214–215.

24. Stearns, p. 207.

25. Samuels, p. 217.

26. One person that Dixon imitated was jig dancer Jimmy Monahan. Dixon incorporated elements from Monahan's jig dancing while he balanced a glass of beer on his head as part of the act. Dixon also utilized elements from Lew Dockstader's distinctive strut walk and the twisting walk of a dancer named Billy Rock. He even incorporated hand gestures made famous by the vaudevillian orator, Henry E. Dixey. Dixon also imitated dances of different nationalities, such as Irish, Dutch, Russian, and Chinese, and was a master at impersonating characters such as tramps, city slickers, and the like.

27. Samuels, p. 217.

28. Stearns, p. 210.

29. Stearns, p. 210.

30. Stearns, p. 200, quoting Alexander Woollcott from an unidentified newspaper clipping, May 18, 1923.

31. Stearns, p. 200, quoting an anonymous critic, May 18, 1923.

32. Stearns, p. 202.

33. Stearns, p. 203.

34. Two tap steps were popularized by Toots Davis — through the trenches, which is known today simply as trenches, and over the top, which involved one foot jumping over the other leg.

35. In 1913, a show opened at the Lafayette Theatre in Harlem in New York called *My Friend from Kentucky*, but it was better known by the name of the company, the *Darktown Follies*. It was one of the most important black shows of the teens and featured many dances including ballin' the jack, the tango, the cakewalk and a new dance that was introduced for the first time on stage called the Texas tommy, forerunner of the Lindy. The highlight of the show was a circle dance which was the finale of the second act, called "At the Ball." Based on the African ring shout, it featured such African-American dances as the mooch, the slide, and the Texas tommy wiggle. At the end of the circle was a dancer named Ethel Williams who danced ballin' the jack. As the curtain closed, Williams let her hand trail behind her so only her wiggling fingers were seen continuing the dance. Jacqui Malone, in her fine book, *Steppin' On the Blues: The Visible Rhythms of African American Dance* (Chicago: University of Illinois Press, 1996) p. 74, relates how Williams told the story:

> We had some wonderful dancers, a featured dance called the Texas Tommy, and a fine cakewalk for the finale, but the most fun was a circle dance at the end of the second act. Everybody did a sort of sliding walk in rhythm with their hands on the hips of the person in front of them and I'd be doing anything but that — I'd 'Ball the Jack' on the end of the line every way you could think of — and when the curtain came down, I'd put my hand out from behind the curtain and 'Ball the Jack' with my fingers.

The audience went wild and the New York critics were likewise in awe, claiming that the entire number had been spontaneously improvised. The success of *Darktown Follies* soon attracted white audiences to Harlem to see the exciting and energetic new show. One man who saw it was Florenz Ziegfeld, who was so impressed with the "At the Ball" number that he bought it and added it to his *Follies of 1914*. It became "one of the greatest hits the Ziegfeld Follies ever had" (Malone, p. 74). Ethel Williams was brought in by Ziegfeld to coach the dancers in his production, but neither she nor any of the other original African-American dancers were hired by him to perform it at the New Amsterdam Theatre downtown.

36. According to his daughter Essie, the Reverend Whitman was a first cousin to Walt Whitman. Although he initially taught his daughters to dance, he insisted it was just for exercise and disowned them when the girls went into show business.

37. Jacqui Malone, *Steppin' On the Blues: The Visible Rhythms of African American Dance* (Chicago: University of Illinois Press, 1996) p. 62, quoting tap dancer Jeni LeGon.

38. Stearns, p. 90.

39. In 1927, Leonard Reed and Willie Bryant created a dance they called the goofus which they originally performed at a fairly brisk tempo as a farm number to end their act. This dance was stolen by others who saw Reed and Bryant perform it in vaudeville and took it to New York where it was put in as a girls' chorus number at the "Shim Sham Club." Slowed down and softened up, the dance quickly became a standard and was thereafter known as the shim sham shimmy, the

shimmy being a reference to the shaking of the shoulders of the Shim Sham Club dancing girls.

40. Stearns, p. 89.

41. Stearns, p. 175, quoting Dewey "Pigmeat"
Markham.

42. The Hoofers Club was located in the back
room of a gambling joint located next door to the
Lafayette Theatre on the corner of Seventh Avenue and
131st Street in New York City. From the late 1920s to
the 1940s, tap dancers met there for friendly competitions and demonstrations. Another tradition associated
with the Hoofers Club was to pat the "Tree of Hope"
which stood outside the stage entrance to the Lafayette
Theatre. Tap dancers touched the tree and said a prayer
that they would get work.

43. The big-name dancers always improvised
while tapping at the Hoofers Club, so that other dancers
had a harder time picking up their moves, although
King Rastus Brown was well-known for his generosity
in sharing his steps with younger dancers. (Comedian
Bob Hope was taught by King Rastus Brown.) Hoofers
were very protective of their material and Brown loudly
criticized Bill Robinson for having stolen his famous
stair dance from him, even though Brown had taken
it from someone else, probably Al Leach. Stearns,
Jazz Dance, p. 185, tells a story of a time when
Eddie Rector was once doing a stair dance in Paris
when Robinson cabled him and told him "to stop it or
die."

44. I have chosen not to cover fully the life of Bill
Robinson because the bulk of his career falls after the
date set as the limit for this book and also because there
has been so much material written about this great tap
dancer already. Nevertheless, I would like to give a few
facts about this amazing man. Bill "Bojangles" Robinson was born in Richmond, VA December 14, 1878
(some sources list the date as May 25, 1878). He was
christened Luther, a name he never liked, so when he
got older, he asked his brother Bill to switch names with
him. When his brother refused, he beat him up and the
exchange was made. At the age of six, Robinson began
dancing in beer gardens and by the age of eight was
touring with various companies. He made appearances
on the black theater circuit until the age of 50 when he
finally danced for white audiences on Broadway in
Blackbirds of 1928. That performance instantly turned
him into a star. During the 1920s, Robinson was a regular at the Palace, billed as the "Dark Cloud of Joy."
He was traditionally put in the number-two spot on the
bill, but often that had to be changed so that he went
on last, because no one wanted to go on after him. Publicity surrounded Bill Robinson — his successful gambling exploits, his generosity with those in need, his
ability to run backwards, his love of ice cream, his coin-
ing of the word "copacetic." His most famous dance
was the stair dance, which he said he invented, although
most experts dispute that claim. Bill Robinson's contribution to tap dancing lay in the way he kept the rhythm
swinging while he danced up on the balls of his feet.
Previously, jig and clog dancers had danced with their
heels off the ground but did not swing the rhythm, and
buck dancers, such as King Rastus Brown, who did
swing the rhythm, danced flat-footed.

45. Stearns, p. 175, quoting Willie Covan.

17. English Music Hall

1. In May 1869, a theatre opened in Paris that
had been modeled after the Alhambra music hall in London. It was called the Folies-Bergère which became
famous for its scantily clad beautiful women, spectacular shows and the cancan.

2. Interestingly enough, the music hall stage was
sometimes used in the same way that medicine shows
were, to try to get audience members to buy remedies.
Lyrics to certain music hall songs humorously promoted
quack medicines and sometimes the printed song sheets
contained advertisements for the same medicinal products that had been satirized in the performance.

3. Mary Clarke and Clement Crisp, *The History
of Dance* (New York: Crown, 1981) pp. 233–234.

4. It was during the second U.S. tour with
Karno's comedy troupe that Chaplin was discovered and
signed by Mack Sennet's Keystone Studios.

5. It is said that Dan Leno's ghost haunts the
Drury Lane to this day. His apparition was first noticed
during auditions for a production of *The King and I*.

6. Little Tich also had six fingers on each hand
and six toes on each foot.

7. Clive Unger-Hamilton, general editor of the
book *The Entertainers* (New York: St. Martin's Press,
1980) p. 158, included the following passage:

> Tich himself hated his boots and eventually
> dropped them from his act. He despised such
> easy applause, but was proud of his forty years
> of unbroken success and remained aloof, culti-
> vating in private life an almost aristocratic dis-
> dain, and enjoying the friendship of such figures
> as Toulouse Lautrec.

8. Little Tich was famous for his several drag
characterizations. He did one parody of the famous
modern dancer Loie Fuller which he entitled "Miss Tur-
pentine." During the routine, Tich swirled the voluminous folds of material of his costume and then
suddenly paused, looked irritated, and hiked up his
gown to scratch his leg.

9. Laurence Senelick, "Music Hall: British Traditions" in *International Encyclopedia of Dance*, vol. 4,
ed. by Selma Jeanne Cohen, pp. 520–523 (New York:
Oxford University Press, 1998) p. 520.

10. A fancy dancer was a skirt dancer who danced
on her toes.

11. Skirt dancing originally started in the Orient
and was later used by the Gypsies in their dances. They
performed scarf and shawl dances, sometimes holding
one end of the scarf in their mouth to create a sort of
veil. Oriental veil dancing later found its way to the
American stage with cootch dancers such as Little Egypt
who introduced her scandalous dance at the 1893
Chicago World's Fair.

12. Thomas Reginald St. Johnson, *A History of
Dancing* (London: Marshall, Hamilton, Kent & Co.,
1906) p. 131.

13. St. Johnson, p. 126.

14. One of Fuller's friend's was Marie Curie.
Fuller wrote to Curie and got some radium and tried to
make a phosphorescent paint which she wanted to apply
to the butterfly wings of her costume to make them

glow. She eventually did make such a paint in 1904 from the residue of pitchblende, and created what she called her "Radium Dance." Fuller also became an expert electrician, devoting her life to the study of electricity and often relating it to her dances.

15. From 1914 to 1931, Ruth St. Denis was married to dancer Ted Shawn. Together they formed a dance school and performing company both of which they called Denishawn. Denishawn was the first serious school of dance in the United States with a curriculum and set of standards; it featured classes in everything from ballet to world dance. The training focused on finding and nurturing the specific talents of each individual rather than focusing on only technique. Many important innovators in the world of modern dance were initially trained at the Denishawn school, including Martha Graham, Doris Humphrey and Charles Weidman. The performing company of Denishawn toured extensively and introduced exotic choreography to many provincial Americans who never would have had a chance to see serious dance. The troupe was also the first American company of dancers to tour the Orient and while there, St. Denis and Shawn did extensive research into the dances of India and Asia generally. They learned and recorded many of these ethnic dances, and thus saved them from extinction.

18. Women on the Stage

1. Robert C. Toll, *On with the Show: The First Century of Show Business in America* (New York: Oxford University Press, 1976) p. 210.

2. Menken ended her affair with Swinburne when he refused to help with the publication of her poetry. He told her "My darling, a woman with beautiful legs need not bother about poetry" (Toll, p. 213).

3. Composer, Jerome Kern, was a collector of Menken memorabilia and is purported to have based the character of Julie, the mulatto actress in *Showboat*, upon her.

4. Toll, p. 213. Menken was also called "Cleopatra in Crinoline," and "The Royal Bengal Tiger."

5. Menken was briefly married to the Irish-American prizefighter, the U.S. titleholder in 1860, John Camel Heenan. During the American tour of *Mazeppa*, while performing in Virginia City, Menken made the claim that she could box as well as any man. A match was set up and Menken knocked out a miner in the second round.

6. The cause of Menken's death is unclear. Some sources say that she died of tuberculosis. Others claim it was a result of injuries sustained while performing *Mazeppa* in London.

7. Toll, p. 214.

8. The chorus girls in *The Black Crook* were much plumper than showgirls of today. The average dancer weighed about 150 pounds with a 40- to 45-inch bust and 25- to 28-inch thighs. The more lithe and svelte figure came into vogue in the 1890s. The average norm for the Floradora Girls who first appeared in 1901 was about 130 pounds with a 25-inch waist and 43-inch hips.

In the last quarter of the 1800s, chorines had a very tough life. They were poorly paid and many of them had to work as waitresses or in factories by day to supplement the meager salaries they got for performing at night. In addition, most were socially ostracized. Theater managers often advertised the girls as Parisians and had them assume fake French names. Since the French were notorious for their amorousness, the dancers were automatically assumed to be wicked and were shunned by "decent" society.

9. A Reverend Charles B. Smythe preached to an audience of 3,000 people for an entire afternoon about the sinfulness of *The Black Crook*.

10. Toll, pp. 214–215.

11. Bonfanti and her troupe also toured the South and West for a while as did other ballet troupes. Traditionally these troupes carried with them only a few dancers, hiring others in the towns where they performed. Since the women had to appear onstage in tights, most upstanding women who professed to have good morals refused to even consider dancing with the companies, so the troupes often resorted to recruiting in bordellos. In Omaha, one brothel owner had his girls sit in rocking chairs in front of the whorehouse in ballet skirts to publicize the show.

12. According to Peter Leslie, *A Hard Act to Follow: A Music Hall Review* (New York: Paddington Press, 1978) p. 28, Thompson and her Blondes were first presented by Barnum at Wood's Museum and Menagerie (later named Daly's Theatre) on 34th Street. K.F. Gänzl, in the web extract form of his book, *Encyclopaedia of the Musical Theatre*, says that her first appearance in New York was under the management of Samual Coville and Alexander Henderson at Wood's Theatre. Alexander Henderson was Thompson's second husband and he did come to the United States with her and later accompanied her on tours throughout the country.

13. In the web article about Thompson extracted from K.F. Gänzl's *Encyclopaedia of the Musical Theatre*, Mr. Gänzl writes that "Berlin went mad for her 'saylorboys dance.'"

14. According to Agnes de Mille's book *America Dances* (New York: MacMillan, 1980) p. 31, another spectacular entitled, *The Forty Thieves, or, Stealing Oil in Family Jars*, featured "a formation of forty females [who] put cigarettes in their mouths, lifted one foot, struck matches on their heels, and lit their forty cigarettes."

15. Toll, p. 219.

16. Toll, p. 218.

17. Toll, p. 218.

18. Toll, p. 219.

19. Peter Leslie, *A Hard Act to Follow: A Music Hall Review* (New York: Paddington Press, 1978) p. 29.

20. Toll, p. 221.

21. Robert C. Toll in his book *On with the Show: The First Century of Show Business in America* (New York: Oxford University Press, 1976) p. 222, tells a story about how Leavitt and ten of the blondes were arrested in San Francisco by a policeman who said the show was "the most indecent [performance] he had ever witnessed." At the trial, Leavitt offered all of the members of the jury tickets to the show to prove that the policeman was wrong. After the 12 attended the show, they "promptly handed down a guilty verdict."

22. Tiller's system usually included training for at least ten years.

23. Ziegfeld's first job in show business was in 1883 when as a boy he saw Buffalo Bill Cody's *Wild West Show* in Chicago and accepted the nightly audience challenge to compete in a shooting match with Annie Oakley. The audience responded so favorably to the shooting contest that night that Cody offered the youth a regular job with the show. The job lasted only a few weeks, though, until Ziegfeld's father tracked him down and demanded that his son return home. Despite his father's disdain for show business, young Florenz continued to do small vaudeville shows on the sly. When he was 22, he had his first "chorus line." It comprised several ducks that jumped around the stage. He first presented the act in a tent show in Chicago and called it the "Dancing Ducks of Denmark." The show was shut down when officials from the Society for the Prevention of Cruelty to Animals discovered gas jets underneath the metal stage that Ziegfeld was using to heat the ducks' dancing floor.

24. Clive Unger-Hamilton, general editor, *The Entertainers* (New York: St. Martin's Press, 1980) p. 161.

25. John Bubbles was an important innovator in the world of tap dancing. In 1922 he created what he called rhythm tap, a casual but complex, highly syncopated style of tapping performed at half the tempo of most of the dances of its day. Bubbles added unusual accents by dropping his heels, all the while keeping a relaxed traveling pace. This dropping of the heels was a crowning achievement for it allowed extraordinary rhythmical complexity to be added to the dance.

26. Only 4'11" in heels and weighing only 100 pounds, Ann Pennington, nicknamed Tiny, was credited with popularizing the black bottom after she did the dance in George White's *1926 Scandals*. Pennington became one of America's most celebrated, sought-after and well-loved dancers.

27. This information was taken from Richard Kislan's book *Hoofing on Broadway: A History of Show Dancing* (New York: Prentice Hall, 1987) pp. 47–48.

28. Marshall and Jean Stearns, *Jazz Dance: The Story of American Vernacular Dance* (New York: Da Capo, 1994) p. 223.

29. Richard Kislan, *Hoofing on Broadway: A History of Show Dancing* (New York: Prentice Hall, 1987) p. 48.

30. Wayburn divided his stage dancers into categories according to height and function. The tall girls were called "showgirls." They were required to be exceptionally beautiful, sing well and look stunning in a costume. The short girls were called "ponies." They did the most dancing. Those in between were called either "chickens" or "peaches."

31. Barbara Stratyner, *Ned Wayburn and the Dance Routine: From Vaudeville to the Ziegfeld Follies* (Studies in Dance History, No. 13) (Madison, WI: Society of Dance History Scholars, 1996) p. 26.

32. Aubrey Haines, "Where the Tap Dance Came From...," in *Dance Digest*, pp. 92–95, March 1958, p. 94.

19. Indian, Gypsy, and Spanish Influences

1. Gerald Jonas, *Dancing: The Power of Dance Around the World* (New York, Harry Abrams, 1992) p. 60.

2. Jonas, p. 60, quoting Dr. Kapila Vatsysyan.

3. Projesh Banerji, *Dance of India*, fifth edition (Allahabad, India: Kitabistan, 1956) p. 10.

4. When the British came to India in the 1600s they also influenced the development of ancient kathak dances, in the use of certain thematic material and in theories of performance. Patronage of Indian arts by the English middle class in the 19th century colonial period meant the dance was also influenced by the British morality of the day.

5. Foot rhythms were regulated by basic syllables called *that*. The footwork in kathak dancing was called *tatkar*.

6. Jon Borthwick Higgins, "The Music of Bharata Natyam," *vol. I,* 1973, quoting Singha.

7. Gaston Vuillier, *A History of Dancing: From the Earliest Ages to Our Own Times* (New York: Appleton & Co. 1898) p. 276.

8. Nebojsa Bato Tomasevic, and Dr Rajko Djuric, *Gypsies of the World* (London: Flint River Press, 1988) p. 13.

9. Gypsies call themselves Roma, Romany, or Romani. The Gypsy language is also called Romany and is closely related to the Indo-Iranian languages. The word Rom is derived from the Sanskrit *domba*, or *doma*, which was a male musician of the low caste. Gypsies have a caste system which can probably be traced back to the Indian idea of "clean" and "unclean."

10. Lilly Grove in her book *Dancing* (London: Longmans, Green, and Co., 1907) p. 219, tells of a Gypsy wedding dance in which the man swings a cudgel. Perhaps there is a relationship between this dance and the early use of the shillelagh, in the Irish jig.

11. Belly dancing or *danse du ventre* was probably brought to North Africa by the ancient Phoenecians. The Gypsies in their travels also absorbed the sensual elements of various dances of the Phoenician, Berber and Arabic traditions while in Egypt and elsewhere and eventually brought them to Spain. In addition, Spanish adventurers made extensive explorations of Africa and eventually the city of Seville became the largest black slave market on the Iberian Peninsula. Many African families lived in Spain. Experts believe that African music did have some effect upon Spanish music and dance.

12. Others say that the word "flamenco" was a bastardization of the Arabic words for peasant, *felag*, and fugitive, *mengu*, and referred to the Gypsies.

13. There is conjecture that the emphasis of inducing a trance state shows the influence of Jewish dance, elements of which were incorporated into Gypsy culture as they traveled through countries with Jewish populations.

14. Ninothcka Bennahum, "Flamenco Dance," in *International Encyclopedia of Dance*, vol. 3, ed. by Selma Jeanne Cohen, pp. 6–11 (New York: Oxford University Press, 1998) p. 6.

15. Castanets consist of two shell-shaped pieces of wood which are held in each hand in pairs. Each pair is struck together to provide rhythmic accompaniment to the dance. The discs held in the right hand are higher in pitch than those of the left and are referred to as the female or *hembra* castanets. *Hembra* castanets are rolled and trilled. Those held in the left mark the rhythm with single strokes and are called the male or *macho* castanets. Castanets probably originated around 3000 years ago in ancient Egypt and were used as throwing weapons similar to boomerangs. In ancient Greece, they were commonly used in the worship of the goddess Diana. In Rome, dances were accompanied by discs called *crotalia*, which were often made of bronze. Handheld percussive instruments have existed in many cultures and it is unclear when castanets made their way to Spain. The Greeks controlled Spain by 550 B.C. and there are records of their bringing their dances to the country along with castanets. When Spain became part of the Roman Empire between 201 B.C. and A.D. 406, Roman *crotalia* were also commonly used there.

16. The zapateado is closely related to the Bavarian schülplattler.

20. German and Shaker Influences

1. The Germans were also the first to bring gymnastics to the United States.

2. Anne Schley Duggan, Jeanette Schlottman, and Abbie Rutledge, *Folk Dances of European Countries* (New York: Barnes, 1948) p. 74.

3. Suzanne Youngerman, "Shaker Dance," in *International Encyclopedia of Dance*, Vol. 5, ed. by Selma Jeanne Cohen (New York: Oxford University Press, 1998) p. 576.

4. In New England, the children of slaves were sometimes traded to the Shakers for food by their masters. In this way several African-Americans became members of Shaker communities.

5. Edward D. Andrews, *The Gift to Be Simple: Songs, Dances and Rituals of the American Shakers* (New York: Dover, 1940) p. 156. Mr. Andrews attributes these quotes to Horace Greeley and George Combe.

6. Melville lived near two Shaker communities in Massachusetts and based his fanatical character Gabriel, in *Moby Dick*, upon the Shakers.

7. Flo Morse, *The Shakers and the World's People* (Hanover: University Press of New England,1980) p. 164.

8. Morse, p. 153.

9. Edward D. Andrews lists many songs and dances in his fine book, *The Gift to Be Simple: Songs, Dances and Rituals of the American Shakers*. On page 72, Andrews records one Indian song called "A Little Pappoose Song" which has the following lyric:

> Te ho te haw te hotti-ty hoot
> Me be Mother's goody Pappoose
> Me ting, me dant, te I didy um
> Cause me to whity's here can come
> Hi-de di-de ti diddle O
> Round e round and round me go
> Me leap me jump e up & down
> On good whity shiny ground,

On p. 76, Andrews recounts an African-American song:

> What makes you look so sober, what makes you feel so sad,
> Is it because you're weary or are you almost mad,
> If not then cast off sadness and wear the pleasant smile,
> And with we African spirits be simple as a child.

(Punctuation and spelling are given here as they were originally written in Andrews' book.)

10. Noel Rae, ed. *Witnessing America; The Library of Congress Book of Firsthand Accounts of Life in America 1600-1900*. (New York: Penguin, 1996) p. 373, quoting an anonymous account appearing in *History of American Socialisms*, by Henry Noyes, 1870.

11. Rae, p. 374.

12. William J. Mahar, *Behind the Burnt Cork Mask: Early Blackface Minstrecsy and Antebellum American Popular Culture* (Urbana and Chicago: University of Illinois Press, 1999) pp. 29–30.

13. One such song was "The Black Shaker's Song," better known as "Fi, Hi, Hi," written by "Eph" Horn in 1851. The song was accompanied by a polka and performed by the Fellows Ethiopian Troupe.

14. Andrews, pp. 158–159.

15. Andrews, p. 157.

21. Native American Influences

1. Reginald and Gladys Laubin, *Indian Dances of North America: Their Importance to Indian Life* (Norman: University of Oklahoma Press, 1976) pp. 44–45, quoting Henry R. Schoolcraft, *The Indian in His Wigwam* (Philadelphia, 1848), p. 195.

2. Laubin, p. 3.

3. Laubin, p. 13.

4. Laubin, p. 14.

5. In Northeastern United States, 90–96 percent of the Native American people died within three years of being exposed to European diseases in 1617. A smallpox epidemic especially affected the Cherokee people, who believed that they had been abandoned by their gods. Several converted to Christianity or committed suicide as a result. Richard Zacks, in his book *An Underground Education* (New York: Doubleday, 1997) p. 357, states that Puritan settlers believed that God had sent the disease as a sign that white men were ordained to rule. He quotes Governor John Winthrop, who wrote in 1634, "…But for the natives in these parts, God has so pursued them, for 300 miles space the greatest part of them are swept away by the smallpox which still continues among them. So God hath thereby cleared our title to this place…." Zacks goes on to say "King James I of England thanked God for sending 'this wonderful plague among the savages.'"

Africans were not as susceptible to European diseases. Many carried the sickle-cell trait in their blood, which has been discovered to have had a positive influence in warding off certain diseases. For this reason, African slaves were hardier than Native American slaves.

6. The information about the Native American

slave trade and the mingling of indigenous peoples with African-Americans was drawn from three primary sources: an on online article by Patrick Neal Minges, entitled "All My Slaves, whether Negroes, Indians, Mustees, or Mulattoes: Towards a Thick Description of 'Slave Religion,'" 1999, and the books, *Lies My Teacher Told Me*, by James W. Loewen, pp. 67–129, and *A People's History of the United States, 1492–Present*, by Howard Zinn, pp. 125–148.

7. African male slaves outnumbered African female slaves three to one, whereas there were three to five times more Native American female slaves than men. African males were often paired with Native American females by the slave owners. Because Native Americans are matrilineally based, this promoted a prominent role for women in American slave culture. This blending of Native American and African cultures had actually begun much earlier, in 1526, when the Spaniards abandoned an attempt to settle South Carolina. They had brought with them African slaves who escaped and sought refuge with the Native Americans who lived in the area. Later, the blending of the two cultures was fostered in other ways. For example, because few white missionaries spoke native languages, African-Americans, known as "linksters," were often used as intermediaries between these missionaries and the Indians. One well-known person of mixed African and Native American parentage was Crispus Attucks, the first patriot to be killed in the American War of Independence.

Another aspect of history that is often ignored is the interculturation between whites and Native Americans which began early in the colonization process. Many Native American day laborers and slaves lived among white settlers. There are accounts of Native American women participating in colonial cotillions. Furthermore, many whites fled to the wilderness to live with the Indians, hoping to escape autocratic English laws. James W. Loewen, in *Lies My Teacher Told Me*, p. 101, quotes Benjamin Franklin as having said, "No European who has tasted Savage Life can afterwards bear to live in our societies." Defections among the Pilgrims were so feared by authorities that they made it a crime for men to have long hair, thinking this caused them to become "Indianized." In another attempt to influence settlers to resist the temptation to live among the natives, colonial writers developed a new genre of literature which related the horrors of being captured by Indians. Despite this, many colonists continued to seek life with Native Americans. White traders especially found that their business flourished through unions with native women. In *Native Roots: How the Indians Enriched America* (New York: Crown, 1991), p. 277, Jack Weatherford writes, "She [the native woman] gave him [the trader] status within the kinship organization of the tribe, and her relatives gave him a network of trading partners and helpers."

8. By the latter part of the 18th century, colonial whites tried to foster a policy of discord between Native Americans and African-Americans. By doing so, whites hoped that these two populations, which greatly outnumbered them, would keep each other in check, so to speak. African-Americans were called upon to fight against Native American uprisings and Native Americans were often offered bounties if they assisted in the hunting of escaped slaves. Laws were also passed that prohibited intermarriage. Nevertheless these two cultures continued to mix.

9. Just as the "underground railroad" system assisted slaves on their journeys North, a similar system developed that helped slaves escape into the wilderness and to the South.

10. Many Native American tribes did practice slavery, but unlike white slaveowners, they treated their slaves almost like family. In his web article "Beneath the Underdog: Race Religion and the 'Trail of Tears,'" Patrick Minges quotes the House Reports, No. 30, 39th Congress, 1st Session, Washington, D.C. 1867, Pt. IV, Vol. II, pp. 162:

> The Indian masters treated their slave[s] with great liberality and upon terms approaching perfect equality, with the exception that the owner of the slave generally does more work that the slave himself.

Slaves were allowed to own land, travel freely and marry as they pleased, including members of their owner's family. Slaves were also welcomed at Native American dances and rituals and encouraged to demonstrate and teach their own African-based dances to their Native American owners. Henry Bibb, in his autobiography *Narrative of the Life and Adventures of Henry Bibb, an American Slave* (New York: 1850) pp. 152–153, wrote:

> The Indians allow their slaves enough to eat and wear. They have no overseers to whip or drive them. If a slave offends his master, he sometimes, in a heat of passion, undertakes to chastise him; but it is as often the case as otherwise, that the slave gets the better of the fight, and even flogs his master, for which there is no law to punish him; but when the fight is over that is the last of it. So far as religious instruction is concerned, they have it on terms of equality, the bond and the free; they have no respect of persons, they have neither slave laws nor negro pews. Neither do they separate husbands and wives, nor parents and children.

Native Americans were well aware of the difference in the way they treated their slaves in comparison with white slave owners, and among the Seminole, it was expressly forbidden to sell an African-American slave to a white person. Minges states that the Second Seminole War was a direct result of the attempt by some merchants to sell Oseola's African wife back into slavery.

11. It is unclear when the first people of African descent came to the New World. Many archaeologists and anthropologists believe that African explorers journeyed to the Americas before the voyages of Columbus. There is some evidence that Afro-Phoenician explorers visited the New World and landed in Central America as early as 1000 B.C. to A.D. 300 and that people from West Africa came to the Caribbean between 1311 and 1460. Mandinkan Muslim explorers traveled to the Americas as early as five centuries before Columbus. Anthropologists have discovered ruins of mosques that have inscribed verses from the Koran on them in Cuba, Mexico, Texas and Nevada. There are even writings

found at Four Corners, Arizona, which suggest they may
have brought elephants with them. There is solid evidence that these travelers from Northern and Western
Africa came to the continent and established schools of
higher learning located in a widely diverse area ranging
from Indiana to New Mexico. Some scholars state that
the these Muslim visitors were the ancestors of the Iro-
quois, Algonquin and other Native American tribes.
The names of many Native American tribes, including
the Cherokee, the Mohawk, the Apache, the Cree, the
Zuni and numerous others have Arab and Islamic origins.

Celtic explorers also journeyed to the New World
before Columbus. Irish legends tell of St. Brendan
(Brandan, Brenainn), a monk in the late fifth and early
sixth centuries, who made many voyages and purport-
edly crossed the Atlantic to North America. Prince
Madoc of Wales was said to have made the journey in
1170, and interestingly enough, there are documented
accounts of colonial people finding Native Americans
who could speak Welsh. Another explorer from the
British Isles who predates Columbus may have included
Prince Henry Sinclair, the Earl of Orkney, who sailed
to the West in A.D. 1395 How much these explorers
influenced the development of native culture is a mystery. There were many similarities, for example, between
certain European Christian practices, and religious rituals among native tribes that suggest some kind of cultural impact. How much these early African and Celtic
explorers may have influenced dance practices among
Native Americans is in the realm of pure speculation.
There is certainly evidence of an intermingling of dance
styles occurring much later, after the advent of the
Atlantic slave trade.

12. The green corn ceremony began with the
drinking of an emetic, a sacred black-colored drink con-
cocted from the leaves of the ilex vine which induced
vomiting. The first dances usually included the crazy
dance and the drunken dance which were followed on
the second day by dances such as the feather dance. An
important part of the busk included the mutilation of
the body during the dance ceremonies. Children from
ages four to 12 as well as teenaged boys presented their
calves and thighs to be stabbed with sharp instruments.
As they bled, the blood was scooped up and flung
against the walls of the ceremonial chamber, and this
was believed to insure a good future for the tribe. To
survive the gashing without flinching gave the participant glory. Even a shudder caused the chiefs to stab
harder and deeper. Participants were not caused pain as
a punishment, but rather to teach them to endure pain
and hardship and to learn the responsibilities of adult-
hood. The busk, or green corn dance ceremony symbolized a time for renewal, open-mindedness and
forgiveness. Any problems within the tribes were
inspected, solutions attempted, and amnesty was available for those who had committed crimes. The ceremony was also a popular time to enter into marriage
contracts. Near the end of the ceremony, fire was taken
from the central sacred ceremonial fire to individual
hearths to symbolize starting again. The ceremony
ended with the sacred ball game, *pelote*. The culmina-
tion of the busk was a solemn meal in which the new
corn was shared.

13. Patrick Neal Minges, in the web article *All My
Slaves* quoting Lucinda Davis from Works Progress
Administration: Oklahoma Writers Project, *Slave Nar-
ratives* (Washington, D.C.: U.S. Government Printing
Office, 1932) p. 220.

14. John Howard Payne, "The Green-Corn
Dance," in *Continental monthly: devoted to literature and
national policy*, vol. 1, issue 1, pp. 17–29, January 1862,
p. 22.

15. Quote originally from Work Projects Administration: Arkansas Writers Project, Interview with Preston Kyles (Washington, D.C.: U.S. Government
Printing Office, 1932) p. 220. Extracted from the web
article "Religion and Resistance."

16. The dance ended when the caller ran out of
stanzas to sing. If ended successfully by the dancers,
there would be cries in Cherokee of "wa-do, wa-do,"
which meant "thank-you" and "well-done."

17. There was a prescribed order of prestomp
activities as well. The ceremony began with the lighting and feeding of the fire, in which deer organs were
placed in the flames as an offering. This was followed
by a pipe ceremony, and then a sacred ballgame. Supper would be eaten and then the actual stomp dances
would begin. After the final dance, there was the taking of medicines.

18. Anya Peterson Royce, *The Anthropology of
Dance* (Bloominton: Indiana University Press, 1977) p.
113, tells of an English man named Nicholas Cresswell,
who visited Native Americans during the middle of the
18th century and witnessed a dance. Cresswell wrote:

> The women have Morris bells or Thimbles with
> holes in the bottom and strung upon a leather
> thong tied around their ankles, knees and waists.

19. In 1775, an Indian trader, James Adair, published a book entitled, *The History of the American Indians* in which he mentioned the stomp dance, and
described the movement of the shaklers. He wrote,
"Each strikes the ground with the right and left feet
alternately, very quick, but well timed." In his book,
Adair speculated that the Cherokees were descended
from the Ten Lost Tribes of Israel and he referred to the
Indians as "red Hebrews." He tried to prove that the
dances of the American Indians were derived from religious dances of the Israelites. His theory was that as
time passed, the dances had been lengthened and had
begun to deteriorate from their original form, but still
retained their religious connotations and other recognizable elements. This information was extracted from
Reginald and Gladys Laubin's book, *Indian Dances
of North America: Their Importance to Indian Life*
(Norman: University of Oklahoma Press, 1976) pp.
18–19.

20. The numbers four and seven were both important within Cherokee culture. The number four represented completeness and connection to heaven. Four
logs were placed on the fire. Four repetitions of the call-
and-response were used in most songs, and during the
pipe ceremony, the smokers paused at the four cardinal
points. The number seven represented the highest level
attainable. It was believed that there were seven heavens. There were seven clans and seven clan representatives. Seven stanzas were used in both the friendship

dance and the old folks dance, dances which were always part of the stomp ceremony.

21. The first dance of the stomp ceremony was always the friendship dance. This dance was a favorite among the Cherokees and was also performed outside the realm of the stomp ceremony. It featured clapping, and was related to the bear who was believed to clap his paws when pleased. When not used in the context of the stomp ceremony, the main purpose of the friendship dance was as a mixer, so that young Native Americans could meet a potential spouse from among their various relatives. The dance was filled with joking and flirtations and young braves would scratch, poke, and gently slap the girls to tease them. The friendship dance was also performed to cheer people up, such as when a family member had died.

22. Cherokee dance was always performed counterclockwise with the left shoulder facing the center of the circle. It was believed that moving in this direction brought greater benefit from the gods.

23. The calls shouted out by the leader were not always translatable in the usual sense. They often consisted of sacred words that were believed to have been give to the ancient Cherokees by God. It was thought that only God could know their meaning.

24. In the web article "Le Cakewalk" it states that the cakewalk originated in Florida with African-Americans who imitated the gait of Seminole Indian dancing couples.

25. Dancers in this ritual were called boogers, bogeys, or buggers. The word "bogey" refers to the apparition of any number of frightening and annoying beings. It is probably of Scandinavian origin and was adopted into Middle English, where it first referred to a "scarecrow," and later to more threatening supernatural beings such as ghosts or goblins. In the United States around 1820, a colloquial expression became popular in which the devil was referred to as "Old Bogey," and around 1860, the slang for a landlord was "the bogeyman." This is the origin of the phrase, "the bogeyman is gonna get you!" It is unclear when the Native Americans adopted the word.

26. Ritual masks were an important part of many Cherokee dances. Each different mask had its own power which the dancer strived to reveal through their movements.

27. Cherokee medicine men had a tradition of treating illnesses by frightening the patient. For example, if someone had a backache the medicine man threatened to throw a knife at the patient. More broadly, this tradition related to the whole society's being healed when frightened by the boogers.

28. A census done in 1835 right before the forced displacement of the Cherokee people showed that at least 10–15 percent of the Five Civilized Tribes were made up of African-Americans. This number was probably much greater in that the census did not take into account free blacks or people of mixed African-American and Indian blood. The nine-month trek to Oklahoma along the Trail of Tears resulted in the death of 4,600 to 8,000 Cherokees. It is estimated that one quarter to one third of these were African-American.

29. When one older Native American dancer from the Blackfoot tribe who had danced in Wild West Shows was asked about his steps, and why certain ones did not look traditional, he responded, "I do all kinda dancin', black bottom, jitterbug, big apple, ever'thin'" (Laubin, p. 42).

30. Robert C. Toll, *Blacking Up: The Minstrel Show in Nineteenth-Century America* (New York: Oxford University Press, 1974) p. 166.

22. American Country Dance

1. Richard Nevel, *A Time to Dance: American Country Dancing from Hornpipes to Hot Hash* (New York: St. Martin's Press, 1977) p. 29, quoting William Prynne's *Histriomatrix*.

2. In addition to objecting to mixed dancing, the Puritans objected to maypole dancing because of its pagan origins. Dancing which was tied to drinking or feasting was also frowned upon. Certain tamer forms of dance were sometimes accepted by the Puritans if they were used to teach manners to children. Group dances that utilized formations were also accepted. Joseph E. Marks III, in his book *America Learns to Dance: A Historical Study of Dance Education in America Before 1900* (New York: Exposition Press, 1957) pp. 20–21, tells of how in 1684, ministers in Boston issued a tract (probably written by Increase Mather, son of Cotton Mather, the famous preacher) entitled *An Arrow Against the Profane and Promiscuous Dancing, drawn out of the quiver of the Scriptures. By the Ministers of Christ at Boston in New-England*. The ministers stated that mixed dancing of any kind was sinful but did admit that dance could be used to teach children "due poyse and Composure of Body," if they were sent to the proper kind of teacher, "a grave person who will teach them decency of behaviour, and each sex by themselves." Mather also reminded ministers that they were not even allowed to be a spectator at an event where dancing took place.

3. By the middle of the 18th century in New England, it became increasingly popular to send young ladies and gentlemen to schools to be educated in the art of dancing. Joseph E. Marks III in his book *America Learns to Dance* (New York: Exposition Press, 1957) pp. 44–45, relates a story from the *Boston Evening Post*, December 10, 1744, in which a wife tries to convince her husband that their daughter should go to dancing school. She says:

My dear, you will breed this girl a very fool,
Why don't you send her to dancing-school?
See how she holds her head and treads her toes,
Like a meer Bumpkin, when she stands or goes
Is so shame-fac'd, tho' enter'd in her teens
That she looks downwards, like a sow in beans.
Prithee, my dear, consider and bestow
Good breeding on her for a year or two.

Marks goes on to write that the husband insisted that his daughter "...should first be schooled in the household arts then she 'shall jig her cupper at the dancing school.' The wife then points out that their less fortunate neighbors could afford to send their daughter to dancing school, and with such an argument won the debate."

4. Many antidance tracts were written which gave a litany of excuses why dancing should be avoided at all costs. Besides decrying it on moral grounds, they denounced it because of the frivolous expense incurred in preparing for a ball — buying ball gowns or jewelry and so on. Other detractors warned about the health hazards of dancing. These included using up the oxygen in the room, becoming overly excited, or going into the cold night air when overheated.

5. Both Thomas Jefferson and George Washington loved dancing and frequently attended balls in old Virginia. Washington's favorite dance was one that was taken from John Playford's *Dancing Master* called the "Sir Roger de Coverley," sometimes known as the American jig. Today the dance is better known as the Virginia reel.

6. Joseph E. Marks III, *America Learns to Dance* (New York: Exposition Press, 1957) p. 25.

7. Dena J. Epstein, *Sinful Tunes and Spirituals: Black Folk Music to the Civil War* (Chicago: University of Illinois Press, 1977) p. 115. Epstein also gives an obituary for Simeon Gilliat (p. 116) found in the Richmond *Patriot*, October 16, 1820:

> [Gilliat was] ... a man of color, very celebrated as a Fiddler, and much caressed by polished society who will long deplore the loss.

8. Eileen Southern, *The Music of Black Americans* (New York: W. W. Norton & Co., 1977) p. 135, quoting Mordecai, *Richmond* reprint in RBAM, p. 135–136.

9. Southern, p. 44, quoting *The Journal of Nicholas Cresswell, 1774–1777*, ed. by Lincoln MacVeagh (New York: 1924) pp. 52–53.

10. Many dancing masters plied their trade in larger cities in the North such as New York, Boston and Philadelphia. With the growing number of professional dancing masters, older dance forms like the circle and square dances fell out of popularity and contra dances took their place. One explanation for this is that column dances allowed the teachers to include as many dancers as they wanted and thus increase their profits.

11. Southern, p. 43.

12. The running set was rediscovered and first notated by the renowned dance folklorist Cecil Sharp, who recorded the dance in 1917 after he saw it in the Appalachian Mountains. Sharp was especially interested in the dance because it lacked the "courtesy movements," such as honors and bows which were always found in other country dances. This demonstrated that the dance was more authentic and had survived in an original country dance form from prior to the influence of John Playford's *Dancing Master*.

13. The Spanish word for Muslim is *Mudajjan*, a word that is related to Melungeon. There has been conjecture that the derivation of the word "Melungeon" springs from two Turkish words: *melun* which means "cursed" and *can* which means "life." Put together the words, pronounced Melungeon, would translate as "one whose life is cursed." Other names for the Melungeons include WIN, which stands for White-Indian-Negro, Carmel Indians, Mustees, Nanacokes, Jersey Whites, Moors, Tri-Racial Isolates and Brass Ankles. I was unable to find out why the Melungeons were called Brass Ankles. It is tempting to try to connect the word to the common practice of Indian kathak and, later, Gypsy dancers tying bells around their ankles when they danced. One bit of trivia: it is believed that the mother of Abraham Lincoln, Nancy Hanks, was Melungeon.

14. Another theory about the Melungeon people is that they were descended from converted Muslims and Jews, called *Conversos,* who were brought to the United States when the Spanish established a colony at Santa Elena, South Carolina, in 1566, a settlement which preceded the founding of Jamestown by the English by 40 years.

To understand why Spanish ships were bringing Jews and Muslims to the New World it is important to remember the historical context. These events took place during the time of the Spanish Inquisition when over 500,000 Jews and Muslims fled Spain to escape religious persecution. Even the *Conversos,* who professed Christianity, were forced to flee the religious witch-hunt. Many went to North Africa where a group of them banded together and sought revenge against Spain as the Barbary Coast pirates. These Jewish and Muslim pirates participated in many fierce sea battles with the Spanish and those that were captured by Spain were frequently punished by being sentenced to lives as galley slaves on Spanish ships that sailed across the Atlantic. The settlement of Santa Elena was established by Catholic Spaniards who brought with them these Jewish and Muslim slaves. The settlement was abandoned in 1587 after an attack by the English. The settlers, including the Muslims and Jews, fled into the mountains of North Carolina, eventually intermarrying with the Native Americans who lived there.

A year before the fall of Santa Elena, in 1586, the English navigator, Sir Francis Drake, attacked Spanish and Portuguese holdings along the coast of Brazil and records show that after his victory, he liberated at least 300 Moorish and Turkish galley slaves, as well as some Africans and a few South American Indians. Drake had the intention of taking these men to Cuba to be used as a force against the Spanish but bad weather forced his ship up the Eastern seaboard of the United States to Roanoke, Virginia. While there, the English settlers begged to be taken back to England so Drake left at least 200 of the galley slaves behind. These people ultimately moved inland, intermarried with the native Americans, mostly Powhatan, and eventually encountered a remnant of the Muslims and Jews who had fled during the fall of Santa Elena. These two groups formed a community. Historical accounts relate stories of a people who lived among the Powhatan tribes and called themselves Turks or Portuguese or sometimes Mecca Indians. There has been some conjecture that these people became the Melungeon. A sidelight that demonstrates the connection between Muslim culture and Native American culture is the description of Heaven in the 17th century Powhatan religion which is identical almost down to the last letter with the description of Heaven found in the Muslim Koran.

15. The German slave trade in Gypsies arose because Gypsies were expressly forbidden to immigrate to the United States as free people. Therefore, they sold themselves into servitude in order to book passage to the New World and escape persecution in Germany.

Many families were broken up as they sold themselves into slavery. Some worked to repay their passage; others simply ran away. Those who were able to reunite with their families took to the road out of habit and most moved southward through Philadelphia to the Appalachian region. These German Gypsies were known as the Black Germans or the Black Deutsche. Americans, hearing the word Deutsche, incorrectly interpreted it as Dutch. Today many Melugeons claim Black Dutch ancestry. German Gypsies were also called Chicanere, a low German corruption of the word *Zigeuner*, perhaps meaning "go away, thief," although this word had no relation to the word for mischief, "chicanery." In his article, *Origins of the Mulungeon Appalachian Sub-culture: A More Plausible Explanation for the Origin of the Mulungeons,* Henry Robert Burke, also tells of Chicanere (or Chikener) girls who as early as 1875, smoked pipes, wore short skirts, bobbed their hair and "...were fond of a wild dance, perhaps the ancestor of the present 'Charleston.'" There is speculation that these Gypsy girls may have had some influence in the radical modernization of fashion that occurred during the Roaring Twenties.

Evidence of the Gypsies influence upon Pennsylvania Dutch culture can be witnessed in the use of barn hex signs which were an outgrowth of Gypsy superstitious rituals. Interest in Gypsy superstitions led a man named Johann Georg Hohman to write a book called *The Long Lost Friend: A Collection of Mysterious Arts and Remedies for Men As Well As Animals,* originally published in 1820 in Pennsylvania. Hohman collected his information from the Gypsies and his book became the second-most popular book in the United States after the *Bible.* Hohman's book has stayed in continuous printing until the present day, and was influential not only in Pennsylvania Dutch culture, but was also in the development of Voodoo because it was purchased from German Jewish peddlers by African-Americans in the South. The book was especially popular in the Appalachians.

16. Another wave of Gypsy immigrants came from Britain to the U.S. in the mid–1800s and after the abolishment of serfdom in Romania in 1864, large groups of Eastern European Gypsies came to America.

17. There were three basic figures used in country dancing: the circle, sometimes called the big set; the double column, also called the contra, longways or reel; and the square, also called the quadrille. The circle was the most primitive and prevalent of the three figures. In the United States, the popularity of these figures varied from region to region. Double column or contra dances were most popular in the Northeast while circle dances were most favored in the Southeast and in the mountains of Appalachia. Square dances were the most popular in the West.

Double column or contra dances featured active and inactive couples. In other words, the couple who usually started at the end of the column was the couple who did the most movement as they progressed through various patterns, eventually reaching the opposite end of the column. They were called the active couple. The length of their movement depended upon the length of the tune, although it usually comprised 32 measures of music. The inactive couple kept moving up one position at a time until one by one they too reached the first position and became the active couple.

Circle dances had active and inactive couples but usually they were called odd or even couples. As in the contra dances, the dance was structured with progressive elements and the pattern usually took place during 32 bars of music. The difference was that there was no definite beginning or ending to the progression.

Square dances varied from this in that there were no active or inactive couples. Although a head couple was designated, all the couples danced at once.

The word quadrille was originally used to described a group of knights performing figures at a tournament. The term also later referred to a card game popular in the 18th century, before it came to be used as the name of the dance.

18. The French influence in square dancing can easily be seen in one of the most common dance moves, the do-si-do. The term comes from the French *dos-à-dos* which means back-to-back.

19. The word "cotillion" is derived from the Old French word *cotillon* which meant "petticoat."

20. Richard Kraus, *History of Dance in Art and Education* (Englewood Cliffs, NJ: Prentice-Hall, 1969) p. 108.

21. Kraus, p. 109.

22. Cecil Sharp stated that he believed that the ancient source of singing games was well-worship.

23. B. A. Botkin, *The American Play-party Song* (New York: Frederick Ungar Publishing, 1937) p. 21, quoting Mr. W. L. Wilkerson.

24. Botkin, p. 22, quoting Paul Howard.

25. Art Rosenbaum, *Shout Because You're Free: The African American Ring Shout Tradition in Coastal Georgia* (Athens: The University of Georgia Press, 1998) p. 93.

26. Botkin, p. 18.

23. Conclusions

1. Lee Warren, *The Dance of Africa: an Introduction* (Englewood Cliffs, N.Y.: Prentice-Hall, 1972) p. 33.

2. Marshall and Jean Stearns, *Jazz Dance: The Story of American Vernacular Dance* (New York: Da Capo, 1994) pp. 31–32.

3. Anya Peterson Royce, *The Anthropology of Dance* (Bloominton: Indiana University Press, 1977) p. 110.

4. Stearns, p. 32; Sachs, p. 350.

5. Royce, p. 110.

6. Robert W. Snyder, *The Voice of the City: Vaudeville and Popular Culture in New York* (New York: Oxford University Press, 1989) p. 60, quoting several previous sources, including *Cagney by Cagney,* by James Cagney, p. 27.

7. Stearns, p. 338.

8. Stearns, p. 338, quoting Baby Laurence.

9. Stearns, p. 214.

10. Stearns, p. 338.

11. Mary Jane Hungerford, in her book *Creative Tap Dancing* (New York: Prentice-Hall, 1939) p. 108, wrote,

The chief neuro-muscualr value of clog and tap dancing comes from developing balance and coordination. Gestures and hand-clapping combined with a variety of foot patterns, are most common types of coordination which clog and tap involve. In addition, this type of activity makes a tremendous contribution to the development of a fluent motor response to rhythm.

12. Richard Kraus, *History of Dance in Art and Education* (Englewood Cliffs, NJ: Prentice-Hall, 1969) pp. 133–134.

13. Kraus, p. 134, quoting Anne Schley Duggan, "The Evolution of Tap Dancing," *Educational Dance*, February 1940, p. 2.

14. Wings were originally done by throwing one foot out to the side while the other foot executed a hop. Dancers began to expand upon this movement around 1900 and by 1920, the three tap wing was fairly common. During the 1930s dancers began to experiment with even more complicated maneuvers such as the pump, the saw, the fly, rolling, stumbling Russian, and double back. The six tap wing was invented by Frank Condos in 1922.

15. Kenneth Burchill, *Step Dancing: A Course of Twenty Lessons for the Beginner* (London: Sir Isaac Pitman & Sons, 1938) p. 41.

16. The first real blow that ballet dealt to tap dancing on Broadway occurred in 1936 when George Balanchine choreographed the "Slaughter on Tenth Avenue" number for the musical *On Your Toes*.

17. Nicola Daval, Carol Vaughn and Linda Christensen under the auspices of an organization called the Tap America Project (TAP) worked to create an official holiday to celebrate the art of tap dancing. House Joint Resolution 131 was introduced by John Conyers, Jr. (D-MI) and Senate Joint Resolution 53 was introduced by Alfonse D'Amato (R-NY) to designate May 25th, the birth date of Bill "Bojangles" Robinson, "National Tap Dance Day." The resolution read:

Whereas the multifaceted art form of tap dancing is a manifestation of the cultural heritage of our Nation, reflecting the fusion of African and European cultures into an exemplification of the American spirit, that should be, through documentation, and archival and performance support, transmitted to succeeding generations;

Whereas tap dancing has had an historic and continuing influence on other genres of American art, including music, vaudeville, Broadway musical theater, and film, as well as other dance forms;

Whereas tap dancing is a joyful and powerful aesthetic force providing a source of enjoyment and an outlet for creativity and self-expression for Americans on both the professional and amateur level;

Whereas it is in the best interest of the people of our Nation to preserve, promote, and celebrate this uniquely American art form;

Whereas Bill "Bojangles" Robinson made an outstanding contribution to the art of tap dancing on both stage and film through the unification of diverse stylistic and racial elements; and

Whereas May 25, as the anniversary of the birth of Bill "Bojangles" Robinson is an appropriate day on which to refocus the attention of the Nation on American tap dancing:

Now therefore, be it resolved by the Senate and House of Representatives of the United States of America in Congress assembled, that May 25, 1989 is designated "National Tap Dance Day." The President is authorized and requested to issue a proclamation calling upon the people of the United States to observe such a day with appropriate ceremonies and activities.

The resolution was signed into law on November 7, 1989, by President George Bush.

Bibliography

Publications

Abrahams, Roger D., editor. *African American Folktales: Stories from Black Traditions in the New World*. New York: Pantheon, 1985.

_____. *Singing the Master: The Emergence of African American Culture in the Plantation South*. New York: Pantheon Books, 1992.

Ajello, Elvira. *The Solo Irish Jig*. London: C. W. Beaumont, 1932.

Ali, Aisha, Mardi Rollow, and Leona Wood. "North Africa," in *International Encyclopedia of Dance* vol. 4, ed. by Selma Jeanne Cohen, pp. 662–666. New York: Oxford University Press, 1998.

Almanac of Famous People, 6th ed. Gale Research, 1998. "Eddie Leonard."

Almeida, Bira. *Capoeira: A Brazilian Art Form — History, Philosophy, and Practice*. Berkeley, CA: North Atlantic Books, 1986.

Ames, Jerry, and Jim Siegleman. *The Book of Tap*. New York: McKay, 1977.

Andrews, Edward D. "The Dance in Shaker Ritual," in *Chronicles of the American Dance*, ed. by Paul Magriel, 3–14. New York: Henry Holt, 1948.

_____. *The Gift to Be Simple: Songs, Dances and Rituals of the American Shakers*. New York: Dover, 1940.

Anstey, F. "London Music Halls," in *Harper's New Monthly Magazine*, vol. 82, issue 488, January 1891.

Appiah, Kwame Anthony, and Henry Louis Gates. *Africana: The Encyclopedia of the African and African American Experience*. Perseus Books Group, 1999.

Armstrong, Lucile. *A Window on Folk Dance*. Huddersfield, England: Springfield Books, 1985.

Asante, Kariamu Weish, editor. *African Dance: An Artistic, Historical, and Philosophical Inquiry*. Trenton, NJ: Africa World Press, 1996.

Asbury, Herbert. *The French Quarter: An Informal History of the New Orleans Underworld*. New York: Garden City Publishing, 1938.

The Atlantic Monthly, "The Bowery at Night," vol. 20, issue 121, pp. 602–608, November 1867.

Audy, Robert. *Tap Dancing*. New York: Vintage Books, 1976.

Ayto, John. *Dictionary of Word Origins*. New York: Arcade, 1990.

Banerji, Projesh. *Dance of India*, fifth edition. Allahabad, India: Kitabistan, 1956.

Banting, John. "The Dancing of Harlem," in *Negro: An Anthology*, ed. by Nancy Cunard, pp. 203–204. New York: Frederick Ungar Publishing, 1970.

Barrow, David C., Jr. "A Georgia Corn-Shucking," in *The Century Magazine; a popular quarterly*, vol. 24, issue 6, pp. 873–878, October 1882.

Baskervill, Charles Read. *The Elizabethan Jig: and Related Song Drama*. Chicago: University of Chicago Press, 1929.

Bean, Annemarie, James V. Hatch, and Brooks McNamara, editors. *Inside the Minstrel Mask: Readings in Nineteenth-Century Blackface Minstrelsy*. Hanover: Wesleyan University Press, 1996.

Bennahum, Ninothcka. "Flamenco Dance," in *International Encyclopedia of Dance*, vol. 3, ed. by Selma Jeanne Cohen, pp. 6–11. New York: Oxford University Press, 1998.

Benton, Joel. *Life of Hon. Phineas T. Barnum*. Philadelphia: Edgewood, 1891.

Bernstein, Ira G. *American Clogging Steps and Notation*. Malverne, New York: 1984.

Bibb, Henry. *Narrative of the Life and Adventures of Henry Bibb, an American Slave*. New York: published by author, 1850 (reprinted Miami: Mnemosyne Publishing, 1969).

Bishop, Susan. *Tapsteps*. England: Chapel Press, 1993.

Blassingame, John W. *Black New Orleans: 1860–1880*. Chicago: University of Chicago Press, 1973.

_____. *The Slave Community: Plantation Life in the Antebellum South*, New York: Oxford University Press, 1972.

Botkin, B. A. *The American Play-party Song*. New York: Frederick Ungar Publishing, 1937.

Brainard, Ingred. "Moresca," in *International Encyclopedia of Dance*, vol. 4, ed. by Selma Jeanne Cohen, pp. 460–463. New York: Oxford University Press, 1998.

Breuer, Katharina. *Dances of Austria*. New York: Chanticleer Press, 1948.

Brooks, Lynn. "Spain: Dance Traditions before 1700," in *International Encyclopedia of Dance*, vol. 5, ed.

by Selma Jeanne Cohen, p. 667–670. New York: Oxford University Press, 1998.

Bryant, Billy. *Children of Ol' Man River: The Life and Times of a Showboat Trouper*. Chicago: Lakeside Press, 1988.

Buckland, Theresa Jill. "Great Britain: English Traditional Dance," in *International Encyclopedia of Dance*, vol. 3, ed. by Selma Jeanne Cohen, pp. 238–243. New York: Oxford University Press, 1998.

Buckman, Peter. *Let's Dance*. New York: Paddington Press, 1978.

Burchill, Kenneth. *Step Dancing: A Course of Twenty Lessons for the Beginner*. London: Sir Isaac Pitman & Sons, 1938.

Burroughs, Marie. *The Marie Burroughs Art Portfolio of Stage Celebrities: A Collection of Photographs of the Leaders of Dramatic and Lyric Art*. Chicago: A. N. Marquis & Co., 1894.

Busby, Roy. *British Music Hall: An Illustrated Who's Who from 1850 to the Present Day*. London: Paul Elek, 1976.

Buttree, Julia M. *The Rhythm of the Redman: In Song, Dance and Decoration*. New York: A. S. Barnes, 1930.

Cable, G. W. "Creole Slave Dances: The Dance in the Place Congo," in *The Century; a popular quarterly*, vol. 31, issue 4, pp. 517–531, February 1886.

_____. *The Creoles of Louisiana*. New York: Scribner's Sons, 1901.

Cahn, William. *The Laugh Makers: A Pictorial History of American Comedians*. New York: G.P. Putnam's Sons, 1957.

Cambell, Edward D. C., Jr., with Kym S. Rice, editors. *Before Freedom Came: African-American Life in the Antebellum South*. Richmond: The Museum of the Confederacy, 1991.

Caney, Steven. *Teach Yourself Tap Dancing*. New York: Workman Publishing, 1991

Carleton, George W. *The Suppressed Book About Slavery*. New York: 1864.

Cass, Joan. *Dancing Through History*. Englewood Cliffs, NJ: Prentiss Hall, 1993.

Charbonnel, Raoul, Francis Casadesus, and Jules Maugué. *La Danse: Comment On Dansait, Comment On Danse*. Paris: Garnier Frères, 1899.

Chujoy, Anatole, and P. W. Manchester. *The Dance Encyclopedia*. New York: Simon and Schuster, 1967.

Chunestudy, William R. *The Stomp Dance in the Keetoowah Society of the Western Cherokees: Ceremony and Context*. Claremont, CA: A Claremont Graduate School Paper, 1994.

Clarke, Mary, and Clement Crisp. *The History of Dance*. New York: Crown, 1981.

Cockrell, Dale. *Demons of Disorder: Early Blackface Minstrels and Their World*. New York: Cambridge University Press, 1997.

Cohen, Selma Jeanne, founding editor. *International Encyclopedia of Dance*. New York: Oxford University Press, 1998.

Conlan, Roberta, managing editor. *Tribes of the Southern Woodlands*. Alexandria, VA: Time-Life Books, 1994.

Conway, Cecelia. *African Banjo Echoes in Appalachia: A Study of Folk Traditions*. Knoxville: University of Tennessee Press, 1995.

Cook, Will Marion. "Clorindy, The Origin of the Cakewalk," in the *International Library of Negro Life and History — Anthology of the American Negro in the Theatre; A Critical Approach*, ed. by Lindsay Patterson. New York: Publishers Company, 1968.

Craig, Hardin and David Bevington. *The Complete Works of Shakespeare*. Glenview, IL: Scott, Foresman and Co., 1973.

Csida, Joseph, and June Bundy Csida. *American Entertainment; A Unique History of Popular Show Business*. New York: Billboard Publications, 1978.

Dalsemer, Robert G. "Clogging in Appalachian Dance Traditions," in *International Encyclopedia of Dance*, vol. 2, ed. by Selma Jeanne Cohen, pp. 180–181. New York: Oxford University Press, 1998.

D'Aquino, Iria. "Capoeira," in *International Encyclopedia of Dance*, vol. 2, ed. by Selma Jeanne Cohen, pp. 58–59. New York: Oxford University Press, 1998.

Dary, David. *Seeking Pleasure in the Old West*. New York: Alfred A. Knopf, 1995.

Day, Charles. "Fun in Black," in *Inside the Minstrel Mask: Readings in Nineteenth-Century Blackface Minstrelsy*, ed. by Annemarie Bean, James V. Hatch, and Brooks McNamara, pp. 46–50. Hanover: Wesleyan University Press, 1996.

De Mille, Agnes. *America Dances*. New York: Macmillan, 1980.

Dempsey, David, with Raymond Baldwin. *The Triumphs and Trials of Lotta Crabtree*. New York: William Morrow, 1968.

Devi, Ragini. *Dances of India*. Calcutta: Susil Gupta, 1962.

Devi, Ritha. "Kathak," in *International Encyclopedia of Dance*, vol. 3, ed. by Selma Jeanne Cohen, pp. 658–660. New York: Oxford University Press, 1998.

Dickens, Charles. *American Notes and Pictures from Italy*. London, Chapman and Hall, 1874.

Dictionary of American Biography, Base Set. "Daniel Decatur Emmett," "Ralph Olmstead Keeler," "Thomas Darmouth Rice." American Council of Learned Societies, 1928–1936.

Dictionary of American Biography, Supplement 7. "Pat Rooney." American Council of Learned Societies, 1981.

Dictionary of American Biography, Supplement 10. "Charles Spenser Chaplin." Charles Scribner's Sons, 1995.

Drewel, Henry John. "Costume in African Traditions," in *International Encyclopedia of Dance*, vol. 2, ed. by Selma Jeanne Cohen, pp. 209–213. New York: Oxford University Press, 1998.

Duggan, Anne Schley. *The Complete Tap Dance Book*. Washington D.C: University Press of America, 1977.

_____. *The Teaching of Folk Dance*. New York: Barnes, 1948.

_____. Jeanette Schlottman, and Abbie Rutledge. *Folk*

Dances of European Countries. New York: Barnes, 1948.

_____, _____, and _____. *Folk Dances of the British Isles.* New York: Barnes, 1948.

_____, _____, and _____. *Folk Dances of the United States and Mexico.* New York: Barnes, 1948.

Duke, Jerry C. *Clog Dance in the Appalachians.* San Francisco: Duke, 1984.

_____. "Clogging: Historical Overview," in *International Encyclopedia of Dance,* vol. 2, ed. by Selma Jeanne Cohen, pp. 178–180. New York: Oxford University Press, 1998.

Dunin, Elsie Ivancich. "Gypsy Dance," in *International Encyclopedia of Dance,* vol. 3, ed. by Selma Jeanne Cohen, pp. 330–331. New York: Oxford University Press, 1998.

Durang, John. *The Memoir of John Durang, American Actor, 1785–1816,* ed. by Alan S. Downer. Pittsburgh: University of Pittsburgh Press, 1966.

Eastman, Mary Henderson. *Aunt Phillis's Cabin; or, Southern Life As It Is.* Philadelphia: Lippincott, Grambo & Co., 1862.

Ed, James. *Jig, Clog, and Breakdown Dancing Made Easy, with Sketches of Noted Jig Dancers.* New York: 1873.

Eggleston, Edward. "Social Conditions in the Colonies," in *The Century; a popular quarterly,* vol. 28, issue 6, October 1884.

Emerson, Ken. *Doo-dah! Stephan Foster and the Rise of American Popular Culture.* New York: Simon & Schuster, 1997.

Emery, Lynn Fauley. *Black Dance: From 1619 to Today.* Princeton, NJ: Princeton University Press, 1988.

Encyclopedia of World Biography, 2nd ed., 17 vols. "Charles Spenser Chaplin." Gale Research: 1998.

Epstein, Dena J. *Sinful Tunes and Spirituals: Black Folk Music to the Civil War.* Chicago: University of Illinois Press, 1977.

Fairchild, Annie. *Appalachian Clogging: What It Is and How to Do It.* Ithaca, NY: self-published, 1983.

Ferrero, Edward. *The Art of Dancing, Historically Illustrated.* New York: self published, 1859.

Filmer, Paul. "Methodologies in the Study of Dance; Sociology," in *International Encyclopedia of Dance,* vol. 4, ed. by Selma Jeanne Cohen, pp. 360–362. New York: Oxford University Press, 1998.

Fletcher, Beale. *How to Improve Your Tap Dancing.* New York: Barnes, 1957.

Flynn, Arthur. *Irish Dance.* Gretna, Louisiana: Pelican, 1998.

Foley, Catherine. "Ireland: Traditional Dance," in *International Encyclopedia of Dance,* vol. 3, ed. by Selma Jeanne Cohen, pp. 345–348. New York: Oxford University Press, 1998.

Fonteyn, Margot. *The Magic of Dance.* New York: Alfred A. Knopf, 1979.

Forrest, John. "Matachins: Matachines Dances in the Southwestern United States," in *International Encyclopedia of Dance,* vol. 4, ed. by Selma Jeanne Cohen, pp. 329–330. New York: Oxford University Press, 1998.

_____. "Morris Dance" In *International Encyclopedia of Dance,* vol. 4, ed. by Selma Jeanne Cohen, pp. 473–475. New York: Oxford University Press, 1998.

Frank, Henry. "Vodun," in *International Encyclopedia of Dance,* vol. 6, ed. by Selma Jeanne Cohen, pp. 667–670. New York: Oxford University Press, 1998.

Frank, Rusty E. *Tap!: The Greatest Tap Dance Stars and Their Stories.* New York: Morrow, 1990.

Frost, Helen. *Clog and Character Dances.* New York: Barnes, 1931.

_____. *The Clog Dance Book.* New York: Barnes, 1928.

_____. *Tap, Caper and Clog.* New York: Barnes, 1931.

Funk, Charles Earle. *Heavens to Betsy! And Other Curious Sayings.* New York: Harper & Row, 1983.

Gates, Henry Louis, Jr., and Cornel West. *The African-American Century: How Black Americans Have Shaped Our Country.* New York: The Free Press, 2000.

Genovese, Eugene D. *Roll, Jordan, Roll: The World the Slaves Made.* New York: Pantheon Books, 1974.

Gilbert, Douglas. *American Vaudeville: Its Life and Times.* New York: Whittlesey House, 1940.

_____. *Lost Chords: The Diverting Story of American Popular Songs.* Garden City, NY: Doubleday, 1942.

Goldman, Martin S. *Nat Turner and the Southampton Revolt of 1831.* New York: Franklin Watts, 1992.

Gottschild, Brenda Dixon. "Cakewalk," in *International Encyclopedia of Dance,* vol. 2, ed. by Selma Jeanne Cohen, pp. 25–26. New York: Oxford University Press, 1998.

_____. "United States of America: African-American Dance Traditions," in *International Encyclopedia of Dance,* vol. 6, ed. by Selma Jeanne Cohen, pp. 253–261. New York: Oxford University Press, 1998.

Graham, Philip. *Showboats: The History of an American Institution.* Austin: University of Texas Press, 1951.

Grau, Andrée. *Dance.* New York: Alfred A. Knopf, 1998.

_____. "Central and East Africa," in *International Encyclopedia of Dance,* vol. 2, ed. by Selma Jeanne Cohen, pp. 86–93. New York: Oxford University Press, 1998.

Grove, Lilly. *Dancing.* London: Longmans, Green, and Co., 1907.

Haines, Aubrey. "Where the Tap Dance Came From …," in *Dance Digest,* pp. 92–95, March 1958.

Halasz, Nicholas. *The Rattling Chains: Slave Unrest and Revolt in the Antebellum South.* New York: David McKay, 1966.

Hamptom, Barbara L. "Music for Dance: African Music," in *International Encyclopedia of Dance,* vol. 4, ed. by Selma Jeanne Cohen, pp. 483–487. New York: Oxford University Press, 1998.

Hanna, Judith Lynne. "Methodologies in the Study of Dance; Cultural Context," in *International Encyclopedia of Dance,* vol. 4, ed. by Selma Jeanne Cohen, pp. 362–366. New York: Oxford University Press, 1998.

_____. "West Africa," in *International Encyclopedia of Dance,* vol. 6, ed. by Selma Jeanne Cohen, pp. 381–385. New York: Oxford University Press, 1998.

Hanvik, Jan Michael. "Caribbean Region," In *International Encyclopedia of Dance,* vol. 2, ed. by Selma Jeanne Cohen, pp. 61–67. New York: Oxford University Press, 1998.

Hardy, Camille. "United States of America: Musical Theater," in *International Encyclopedia of Dance*, vol. 6, ed. by Selma Jeanne Cohen, pp. 267–290. New York: Oxford University Press, 1998.

_____. "Wayburn, Ned," in *International Encyclopedia of Dance*. vol. 6, ed. by Selma Jeanne Cohen, pp. 370–371. New York: Oxford University Press, 1998.

Hare, Maud Cuney. "Folk Music of the Creoles: Discussion About the Spirit and Song of a Created Race," in *Negro: An Anthology*, ed. by Nancy Cunard, pp. 242–246. New York: Frederick Ungar Publishing, 1970.

Harper, Peggy. "Sub-Saharan Africa: An Overview," in *International Encyclopedia of Dance*, vol. 6, ed. by Selma Jeanne Cohen, pp. 12–22. New York: Oxford University Press, 1998.

Harris, Joel Chandler. "Uncle Remus's Christmas Dance-Songs," in *The Century; a popular quarterly* vol. 25, issue 3, p. 480, January 1883.

Harris, William H., and Judith S. Levey. *The New Columbia Encyclopedia*. New York: Columbia University Press, 1975.

Haskel, Arnold L. *The Wonderful World of Dance*. Garden City, NY: Doubleday and Co., 1969.

Haskins, James. *Black Dance in America: A History Through Its People*. New York: Thomas Crowell, 1990.

Hazzard-Gordon, Katrina. "Dancing Under the Lash: Sociocultural Disruption, Continuity, and Synthesis," in *African Dance: An Artistic, Historical, and Philosophical Inquiry*, ed. by Kariamu Weish Asante, pp. 101–130. Trenton, NJ: Africa World Press, 1996.

_____. *Jookin': The Rise of Social Dance Formations in African-American Culture*. Philadelphia: Temple University Press, 1990.

_____. "United States of America: African-American Social Dance," in *International Encyclopedia of Dance*, vol. 6, ed. by Selma Jeanne Cohen, pp. 261–263. New York: Oxford University Press, 1998.

Hendrickson, Carol. "The Evolution of Irish Step Dance: From Early Irish History to Modern American Tap Dance," in *Viltis*, vol. 46, no. 6, pp. 10–11, March-April 1984.

Heth, Charlotte, general editor. *Native American Dance: Ceremonies and Social Traditions*. Washington, D.C.: Smithsonian, 1992.

_____. "Native American Dance: Southeastern Woodlands," in *International Encyclopedia of Dance*, vol. 4, ed. by Selma Jeanne Cohen, pp. 558–560. New York: Oxford University Press, 1998.

Holand, Hjalmar. *Explorations in America Before Columbus*. New York: Twayne Publishers, 1956.

Hughes, Langston, and Milton Meltzer. *Black Magic: A Pictorial History of Black Entertainers in America*. New York: Bonanza Books, 1967.

Hungerford, Mary Jane. *Creative Tap Dancing*. New York: Prentice-Hall, 1939.

Hurston, Zora Neale. "Characteristics of Negro Expression," in *Negro: An Anthology*, ed. by Nancy Cunard, pp. 34–35. New York: Frederick Ungar Publishing, 1970.

_____. "Shouting," in *Negro: An Anthology*, ed. by Nancy Cunard, pp. 24–31. New York: Frederick Ungar Publishing, 1970.

Hutton, Laurence. *Curiosities of the American Stage*. New York: Harper & Brothers, 1891.

_____. "The Negro on the Stage," in *Harper's Magazine*, vol. 79, issue 469, pp. 131–147, June, 1889.

Illustrated London News. "The Tide of Emigration to the United States and to the British Colonies," July 6, 1850.

Jackson, Phyllis Wynn. *Golden Footlights: The Merrymaking Career of Lotta Crabtree*. Holiday House, 1949.

Jaffé, Nigel Allenby. *Folk Dances of Europe*. North Yorkshire, England: Folk Dance Enterprises, 1990.

Jefferson, Joseph. "The Autobiography of Joseph Jefferson," in *The Century; a popular quarterly*, vol. 39, issue 1, pp. 3–25, November 1889.

Johnson, Anne E. *Jazz Tap: From African Drums to American Feet*. New York: Rosen Publishing Group, Inc., 1999.

Johnson, Charles, Patricia Smith; and the WGBH Series Research Team. *Africans in America; America's Journey Through Slavery*. San Diego: Harcourt Brace, 1998.

Johnson, Edward A. "A Brief Outline of Negro History in the U. S. Until Abolition," in *Negro: An Anthology*, ed. by Nancy Cunard, pp. 4–9. New York: Frederick Ungar Publishing, 1970.

Jonas, Gerald. *Dancing: The Power of Dance Around the World*. New York, Harry Abrams, 1992.

Jones, Bessie, and Bessie Lomax Hawes. *Step It Down: Games, Plays, Songs, and Stories from the Afro-American Heritage*. New York: Harper & Row, 1972.

Jones, Clifford Reis. "India: History of Indian Dance," in *International Encyclopedia of Dance*, vol. 3, ed. by Selma Jeanne Cohen, pp. 451–461. New York: Oxford University Press, 1998.

Kane, Harnett T. *Queen New Orleans*. New York: Wm. Morrow & Co., 1949.

Keeler, Ralph O. "Three Years as a Negro Minstrel," in *The Atlantic Monthly*, vol. 24, issue 141, pp. 71–86, July 1869.

Kelley, Charles. *American Tap Dancing Dictionary*. Dance Educators of America, 1990.

Kemp, William. *Kemps Nine Daies Wonder: Performed in a Daunce from London to Norwich London:* Printed by Nicholas Ling, 1600.

Kennedy, Douglas. *England's Dances: Folk Dances Today and Yesterday*. London: G. Bell & Sons, Ltd., 1950

King, Grace. *New Orleans: The Place and the People*. New York: Macmillan, 1926.

Kislan, Richard. *Hoofing on Broadway: A History of Show Dancing*. New York: Prentice-Hall, 1987.

Knowles, Mark. *The Tap Dance Dictionary*. Jefferson, NC: McFarland, 1998.

Koon, Helene Wickham. *Gold Rush Performers: A Biographical Dictionary of Actors, Singers, Dancers, Musicians, Circus Performers, and Minstrel Players in America's Far West, 1848–1869*. Jefferson, NC: McFarland, 1994.

Kraus, Richard. *History of Dance in Art and Education*. Englewood Cliffs, NJ: Prentice-Hall, 1969.

Krause, Rhett. "Step Dancing on the Boston Stage: 1841–1869," in *Country Dance and Song,* no. 22, pp. 1–19, June 1992.

Kurath, Gertrude Prokosch. "Native American Dance: An Overview," in *International Encyclopedia of Dance,* vol. 4, ed. by Selma Jeanne Cohen, pp. 549–556. New York: Oxford University Press, 1998.

Lair, John. *Songs Lincoln Loved,* New York: Duell, Sloan and Pearce, 1954.

Lamp, Frederick. "Aesthetics: African Dance Aesthetics," in *International Encyclopedia of Dance,* vol. 1, ed. by Selma Jeanne Cohen, pp. 13–15. New York: Oxford University Press, 1998.

Lamya' al-Faruqi, Lois. "Aesthetics: Islamic Dance Aesthetics," in *International Encyclopedia of Dance,* vol. 1, ed. by Selma Jeanne Cohen, pp. 18–19. New York: Oxford University Press, 1998.

Laubin, Reginald and Gladys. *Indian Dances of North America: Their Importance to Indian Life.* Norman: University of Oklahoma Press, 1976.

Laurie, Joe, Jr. *Vaudeville: From the Honky-tonks to the Palace.* New York: Henry Holt & Co., 1953.

Lawson, Joan. *European Folk Dance.* London: Sir Isaac Pittman & Sons, 1953.

Leonard, William Torbert. *Masquerade in Black.* Metuchen, NJ: The Scarecrow Press, 1986.

Leslie, Peter. *A Hard Act to Follow: A Music Hall Review.* New York: Paddington Press, 1978.

Lhamon, W. T., Jr. *Raising Cain: Blackface Performance from Jim Crow to Hip Hop.* Cambridge MA: Harvard University Press, 1998.

Loewen, James W. *Lies My Teacher Told Me.* New York: The New Press, 1995.

Lott, Eric. *Love and Theft: Blackface Minstrelsy and the American Working Class.* New York: Oxford University Press, 1993.

Ludlow, Noah M. *Dramatic Life as I Found It.* New York: Benjamin Bloom, 1966 (first published St. Louis, 1880).

MacMinn, George R. *The Theater of the Golden Era in California.* Caldwell, Idaho: Caxton Printers, 1941.

Magriel, Paul, editor. *Chronicles of the American Dance.* New York: Holt, 1948.

Mahar, William J. *Behind the Burnt Cork Mask: Early Blackface Minstrelsy and Antebellum American Popular Culture.* Urbana and Chicago: University of Illinois Press, 1999.

Mails, Thomas E. *The Cherokee People: The Story of the Cherokees from Earliest Origins to Contemporary Times.* New York: Marlow and Company, 1996.

Malinsky, Barbara Ferreri. "John Durang," in *International Encyclopedia of Dance,* vol. 2, ed. by Selma Jeanne Cohen, pp. 466–468. New York: Oxford University Press, 1998.

Malone, Jacqui. *Steppin' On the Blues: The Visible Rhythms of African American Dance.* Chicago: University of Illinois Press, 1996.

Marks, Joseph E., III. *America Learns to Dance: A Historical Study of Dance Education in America Before 1900.* New York: Exposition Press, 1957.

Massey, Reginald, and Jamilla Massey. *The Dances of India: A General Survey and Dancer's Guide.* London: Tricolor Books, 1989.

_____ and _____. *Indian Dances: Their History and Growth.* New York: George Braziller, 1967.

Matlaw, Myron, editor. *American Popular Entertainment: Papers and Proceedings of the Conference on the History of American Popular Entertainment.* Westport, CT: Greenwood Press, 1977.

Matteo. "Castanets," in *International Encyclopedia of Dance,* vol. 2, ed. by Selma Jeanne Cohen, p. 78. New York: Oxford University Press, 1998.

McGlone, William R., and Phillip M. Leonard. *Ancient Celtic America.* Fresno: Panarama West Books, 1986.

McNamara, Brooks. *Step Right Up.* Garden City, NY: Doubleday, 1976.

Meri, La. *Dance as an Art Form: Its History and Development.* New York: A.S. Barnes and Co., 1933.

Montiel, Luz María Martínez. "Our Third Root: On African Presence in American Population," in *Annual Editions: African American History 2000/2001,* ed. by Rodney D. Coates, pp. 9–15. Guilford, CT: Dushkin/McGraw-Hill, 2000.

Moore, Lillian. "John Durang—The First American Dancer," in *Chronicles of the American Dance,* ed. by Paul Magriel, pp. 15–37. New York: Henry Holt, 1948.

Morrison, James E. "Jig," in *International Encyclopedia of Dance,* vol. 3, ed. by Selma Jeanne Cohen, pp. 607–608. New York: Oxford University Press, 1998.

Morse, Flo. *The Shakers and the World's People.* Hanover: University Press of New England, 1980.

Murphy, Pat. *Toss the Feathers: Irish Set Dancing.* Dublin: Mercier Press, 1995.

Nathan, Hans. *Dan Emmett and the Rise of Early Negro Minstrelsy.* Norman: University of Oklahoma Press, 1962.

Nevel, Richard. *A Time to Dance: American Country Dancing from Hornpipes to Hot Hash.* New York: St. Martin's Press, 1977.

Newman, Richard, and Marcia Sawyer. *Everybody Say Freedom: Everything You Need to Know About African-American History.* New York: Penguin, 1996.

O'Keefe, J.G., and Art O'Brien. *A Handbook of Irish Dances; With an Essay on Their Origin and History.* Dublin: M.H. Gill & Son, Ltd., 1954.

Page, Thomas Nelson. *Social Life in Old Virginia Before the War.* New York: Charles Scribner's Sons, 1897.

Palmer, John Williamson. "Old Maryland Homes and Ways," in *The Century; a popular quarterly,* vol. 49, issue 2, December 1894.

Parker, Derek, and Julia Parker. *The Natural History of the Chorus Girl.* Indianapolis: Bobbs-Merrill, 1975.

Paskman, Dailey. *"Gentlemen Be Seated": A Parade of the American Minstrels.* New York: Clarkson N. Potter, Inc., 1976.

Patterson, Lindsay, editor. *International Library of Negro Life and History: Anthology of the American Negro in the Theatre.* New York: The Publishers Company, Inc., 1967.

Payne, John Howard. "The Green-Corn Dance," in *Continental monthly: devoted to literature and national policy,* vol. 1, issue 1, pp. 17–29, January 1862.

Percival. James G. "The Shakers," in *The North American Review*, vol. 16, issue 38, pp. 76–102, January 1823.

Petermann, Kurt. "Germany: Traditional and Social Dance," in *International Encyclopedia of Dance*, vol. 3, ed. by Selma Jeanne Cohen, pp. 138–143. New York: Oxford University Press, 1998.

Pforsich, Janis. "Hornpipe," in *International Encyclopedia of Dance*, vol. 3, ed. by Selma Jeanne Cohen, pp. 375–379. New York: Oxford University Press, 1998.

Pilling, Julian Olivier. "Step Dancing: Step Dancing in Great Britain and Ireland," in *International Encyclopedia of Dance*, vol. 5, ed. by Selma Jeanne Cohen, pp. 694–696. New York: Oxford University Press, 1998.

Playford, John. *The Dancing Master, or Directions for Dancing Country Dances, with the Tunes to Each Dance, for the Treble Violin*, 10th ed. London: Printed by J. Heptinstall, for H. Playford, 1698.

Ploski, Harry A., editor. *Reference Library of Black America*. New York: Bellwether Publishing Company, 1971.

Pohl, Frederick. *Atlantic Crossings Before Columbus*. New York: W. W. Norton and Company, 1861.

Popwell, Sheila. *The Clogging Book of Appalachian Square Dance Figures*. Huron, OH: Burdick Ent., 1983.

Raboteau, Albert. *Slave Religion: The "Invisible Institution" in the Antebellum South*. Oxford: Oxford University Press, 1978.

Rae, Noel, editor. *Witnessing America: The Library of Congress Book of Firsthand Accounts of Life in America 1600 1900*. New York: Penguin, 1996.

Raffé, W.G. *Dictionary of the Dance*. New York: Barnes, 1964.

Reynolds, William C. "European Traditional Dance," in *International Encyclopedia of Dance*, vol. 2, ed. by Selma Jeanne Cohen, pp. 536–561. New York: Oxford University Press, 1998.

Rice, Edward LeRoy. *Monarchs of Minstrelsy: From "Daddy" Rice to Date*. New York: Kenny Publishing, 1911.

Riis, Thomas L. *Just Before Jazz: Black Musical Theatre in New York, 1890–1915*. Washington: Smithsonian Institution Press, 1989.

_____. *More Than Just Minstrel Shows: The Rise of Black Musical Theatre at the Turn of the Century*. Brooklyn: Institute for Studies in American Music, 1992.

Roan, Carol. *Clues to American Dance*. Washington, D.C.: Starrhill Press, 1993.

Rosenbaum, Art. *Shout Because You're Free: The African American Ring Shout Tradition in Coastal Georgia*. Athens, GA: The University of Georgia Press, 1998.

Rourke, Constance. *Troupers of the Gold Coast or The Rise of Lotta Crabtree*. New York: Harcourt, Brace, 1928.

Royce, Anya Peterson. *The Anthropology of Dance*. Bloomington: Indiana University Press, 1977.

Ruyter, Nancy Lee Chalfa. *Reformers and Visionaries: The Americanization of the Art of Dance*. New York: Dance Horizons, 1979.

Sachs, Curt. *World History of Dance*. New York: W.W. Norton, 1937.

St. Johnson, Thomas Reginald. *A History of Dancing*. London: Marshall, Hamilton, Kent & Co., 1906.

Sampson, Henry T. *Blacks in Blackface: A Source Book on Early Black Musical Shows*. Metuchen, NJ: The Scarecrow Press, 1980.

Samuels, Charles, and Louise Samuels. *Once Upon a Stage: The Merry World of Vaudeville*. New York: Dodd, Mead & Co., 1974.

Saxon, A.H. *P.T. Barnum: The Legend and the Man*. New York: Columbia University Press, 1989.

Saxon, Lyle. *Fabulous New Orleans*. New Orleans: Robert L. Crager & Co., 1958.

Schneider, Gretchen. "United States of America: An Overview," in *International Encyclopedia of Dance*, vol. 6, ed. by Selma Jeanne Cohen, pp. 230–253. New York: Oxford University Press, 1998.

Seeger, Mike. *Talking Feet: Buck, Flatfoot and Tap — Solo Southern Dance of the Appalachian, Piedmont and Blue Ridge Mountain Regions*. Berkeley: North Atlantic Books, 1992.

Segal, Ronald. *The Black Diaspora: Five Centuries of the Black Experience Outside Africa*. New York: Farrar, Straus, and Giroux, 1995.

Senelick, Laurence. "Music Hall: British Traditions," in *International Encyclopedia of Dance*, vol. 4, ed. by Selma Jeanne Cohen, pp. 520–523. New York: Oxford University Press, 1998.

_____. "Vaudeville," in *International Encyclopedia of Dance*, vol. 6, ed. by Selma Jeanne Cohen, pp. 315–320. New York: Oxford University Press, 1998.

Sheerin, Robert. "'Dixie' and Its Author," in *The Century; a popular quarterly*, vol. 50, issue 6, pp. 958–960, Oct. 1895.

Shimmer, Genevieve. "Playford, John," in *International Encyclopedia of Dance*, vol. 5, ed. by Selma Jeanne Cohen, pp. 199–200. New York: Oxford University Press, 1998.

Shomer, Louis. *Tip Top Tapping*. New York: Padell, 1937.

Slide, Anthony. *The Vaudevillians: A Dictionary of Vaudeville Performers*. New Rochelle, NY: Arlington House, 1981.

Snipe, Tracy D. "African Dance: Bridges to Humanity," in *African Dance: An Artistic, Historical, and Philosophical Inquiry*, ed. by Kariamu Weish Asante, pp. 63–77. Trenton, NJ: Africa World Press, 1996.

Snyder, Robert W. *The Voice of the City: Vaudeville and Popular Culture in New York*. New York: Oxford University Press, 1989.

Sommer, Sally R. "Feet Talk to Me!" in *Dance Magazine*, pp. 56–60, September, 1988.

_____. "Tap Dance," in *International Encyclopedia of Dance*, vol. 6, ed. by Selma Jeanne Cohen, pp. 95–104. New York: Oxford University Press, 1998.

Sorell, Walter. *The Dance through the Ages*. New York, Grosset & Dunlap, 1967.

Southern, Eileen. *The Music of Black Americans*, New York: W. W. Norton & Co., 1977.

Speaight, George. *A History of the Circus*. London: The Tantivy Press, 1980.

Stage Dance Council, The. *The Sailor's Hornpipe*. London: The Dancing Times Ltd., 1961.

Stearns, Marshall. *The Story of Jazz*. New York: Oxford University Press, 1956.

_____, and Jean Stearns. *Jazz Dance: The Story of American Vernacular Dance*. New York: Da Capo, 1994.

Stein, Charles W., editor. *American Vaudeville as Seen by Its Contemporaries*. New York: Knopf, 1984.

"Stephen C. Foster and Negro Minstrelsy," in *The Atlantic Monthly*, vol. 29, issue 121, pp. 608–61, November 1867.

Stratyner, Barbara. *Ned Wayburn and the Dance Routine: From Vaudeville to the Ziegfeld Follies*. (Studies in Dance History, No. 13.) Madison, WI: Society of Dance History Scholars, 1996.

Sutton, Julia, with Elizabeth Kurtz. "Matachins: Historical Overview," in *International Encyclopedia of Dance*, vol. 4, ed. by Selma Jeanne Cohen, pp. 325–328. New York: Oxford University Press, 1998.

Thompson, Robert Farris. *Flash of the Spirit: African and Afro-American Art and Philosophy*. New York: Random House, 1984.

Thompson, U. S. "Florence Mills," in *Negro: An Anthology*, ed. by Nancy Cunard, p. 201. New York: Frederick Ungar Publishing, 1970.

Thompson-Drewel, Margaret. "Mask and Makeup: African Traditions," in *International Encyclopedia of Dance*, vol. 4, ed. by Selma Jeanne Cohen, pp. 286–294. New York: Oxford University Press, 1998.

_____. "Yoruba Dance," in *International Encyclopedia of Dance*, vol. 6, ed. by Selma Jeanne Cohen, pp. 422–424. New York: Oxford University Press, 1998.

Thorpe, Edward. *Black Dance*. Woodstock, NY: Overlook, 1990.

Toll, Robert C.. *Blacking Up: The Minstrel Show in Nineteenth-Century America*. New York: Oxford University Press, 1974.

_____. *On with the Show: The First Century of Show Business in America*. New York: Oxford University Press, 1976.

Tolman, Beth, and Ralph Page. *The Country Dance Book: The Best of the Square and Contra Dances and All About Them*. Brattleboro, VT: The Stephen Greene Press, 1976.

Tomasevic, Nebojsa Bato, and Dr Rajko Djuric. *Gypsies of the World*. London: Flint River Press, 1988.

Townsend, Charles. "Negro Minstrels," in *Inside the Minstrel Mask: Readings in Nineteenth-Century Blackface Minstrelsy*, ed. by Annemarie Bean, James V. Hatch, and Brooks McNamara, pp. 121–125. Hanover: Wesleyan University Press, 1996.

Towsen, John H. *Clowns*. New York: Hawthorne Books, 1976.

Tucker, Henry. *Clog Dancing Made Easy*. New York: Robert DeWitt Publisher, 1874.

Tutterow, Gayle. *The Tap Talk Dictionary*. Largo, Florida: 1992.

Twain, Mark. *Autobiography*, ed. by Albert Bigelow Paine. New York: Harper & Bros., 1924.

_____. *Life on the Mississippi*. Boston: James R. Osgood & Co., 1883.

Unger-Hamilton, Clive, general editor. *The Entertainers*. New York: St. Martin's Press, 1980.

Van Every, Edward. *Sins of New York: As Exposed by the Police Gazette*. New York: Frederick A. Stokes Co., 1930.

Vatsyayan, Kapila. *Indian Classical Dance*. New Delhi: Government of India, Patiala House, 1976.

Vuillier, Gaston. *A History of Dancing: From the Earliest Ages to Our Own Times*. New York: Appleton & Co., 1898.

Wade, Rosalind. *Tap Dancing in 12 Easy Lessons*. Philadelphia: David McKay Co., (no date).

Warren, Lee. *The Dance of Africa: an Introduction*. Englewood Cliffs, N.Y.: Prentice-Hall, 1972.

Watkins, Mel. *On the Real Side: Laughing, Lying, and Signifying— The Underground Tradition of African-American Humor that Transformed American Culture, from Slavery to Richard Pryor*. New York: Simon & Schuster, 1994.

Wayburn, Ned. *The Art of Stage Dancing*. New York: Ned Wayburn Studios of Stage Dancing, 1925.

Weatherford, Jack. *Native Roots: How the Indians Enriched America*. New York: Crown, 1991.

Willis, Cheryl. "Tap Dance: Manifestation of the African Aesthetic," in *African Dance: An Artistic, Historical, and Philosophical Inquiry*, ed. by Kariamu Weish Asante, pp. 145–159. Trenton, NJ: Africa World Press, 1996.

Wilson, Olly. "The Association of Movement and Music as a Manifestation of a Black Conceptual Approach to Music making," in *More Than Dancing: Essays on Afro-American Music and Musicians*, ed. by Irene Jackson, pp. 9–23. Westport, CT: Greenwood Press, 1985.

Winter, Marian Hannah. "Juba and American Minstrelsy," in *Chronicles of the American Dance*, ed. by Paul Magriel, pp. 39–63. New York: Henry Holt, 1948.

Winter, William. *Other Days: Being Chronicles and Memories of the Stage*. New York: Moffat, Yard, 1908.

Wish, Harvey. "American Slave Insurrections Before 1861," in *Annual Editions: African American History 2000/2001*, ed. by Rodney D. Coates, pp. 63–67. Guilford, CT: Dushkin/McGraw-Hill, 2000.

Wittke, Carl. *Tambo and Bones: A History of the American Minstrel Stage*. Durham, NC: Duke University Press, 1930.

Woll, Allen. *Black Musical Theatre: From Coontown to Dreamgirls*. New York: Da Capo Press, 1989.

Wood, Peter H. *Black Majority: Negroes in Colonial South Carolina from 1670 through the Stono Rebellion*. New York: W.W. Norton & Co., 1974.

Woodward, Grace Steele. *The Cherokees*. Norman, OK: University of Oklahoma Press, 1963.

Youngerman, Suzanne. "Shaker Dance," in *International Encyclopedia of Dance*, vol. 5, ed. by Selma Jeanne Cohen, pp. 575–577. New York: Oxford University Press, 1998.

Zacks, Richard. *An Underground Education*. New York: Doubleday, 1997.

Ziegfeld, Richard, and Paulette Ziegfeld. *The Ziegfeld Touch: The Life and Times of Florenz Ziegfeld, Jr.* New York: Harry N. Abrams, 1993.

Zinn, Howard. *A People's History of the United States, 1492–Present*. New York: Harper Collins, 1999.

Web Sites

"Africans, French and Spanish Slavery, and the Origins of the Tignon."
www.gnofn.org/~hggh.GFP3.html

"Another Black Catholic Woman of Faith: Sister Henriette Delille."
holyangels.com/SISTER-HENRIETTE-DELILLE-1.HTM

Bakewell, Sarah. "Medicine and the music hall."
www.wellcome.ac.uk/en/1/awtpubnwswnoi23pol6.htnl

"A Black History of Jamaica, New York."
www.innerexplorations.com/home/black.htm

"A Brief Overview of Irish Dance"
www.nhptv.org/kn/vs/artlabd4.htm

Britannia Coconut Dancers official web site
pages.co.uk/coconutters/

Burke, Henry Robert. "Origins of the Melungeon Appalachian Sub-culture: A More Plausible Explanation for the Origin of the Mulungeons," 1999.
www.coax.net/people/lwf/hrb_mel.htm

Conner, Lynne, with additional text by Gillis, Susan. "Ruth St. Denis, Burlesque and the Female Dancer."
www.edanz.com/modern/ruth.htm

Corr, Paul. "Tap America Project [TAP]," Tap Dance Homepage.
www.tapdance.org/tap/people/tapproj.htm

Davis, Erik. "Trickster at the Crossroads." First appeared in *Gnosis*, Spring 1991.
www.eleggua.com/Legba.html

Devin, Marilyn. "Clogging: What Is It?" First appeared in *Folk Dance Scene*.
members.aol.com/mdevin/clogtext.html

"Dixie."
www.fortunecity.com/tinpan/parton/2/dixie.html

Doherty, Jan. "Louisiana Black Women: An Ignored History."
www.loyno.edu/~journal/1895-6/doherty.htm

Donovan, F.R. "Wild Kids." Taken from his book *Wild Kids*, Harrisburg, PA: Stackpole Books, 1967.
www.bookrags.com/books/bloal/PART5.htm

East London Advertiser: Latest News. "Down Memory Lane: East End's Music Hall of Fame."
www.leevalley.co.uk/ela/sportz.html

Encyclopedia Britannica, "Storyville."
www.britannica.com/bcom/eb/article/2/0,5716,71662,00.html

"Five Points Neighborhood."
fargo.itp.tsoa.nyu.edu/~nance/titanic/fivepoints3.html

Forrest, Linda Carol. "What is Clogging?" Reprinted from *Square Dancing*. 1984.
clogmaster.tripod.com/clog.html

Foster, Barbara. "Adah Isaacs Menken: An American Original."
www.nassaulibrary.org/hewlett/olamj01.html

"Gaelic Gotham: A History of the Irish in New York." From the Museum of the City of New York web site.
wwwmcny.org/irish.htm

Galli, Mark. "Christian History, Spring 1999," in *Christianity Today International/Christian History Magazine*, 1999.
www.christianitytoday.com/ch/62h/62h010.html

Gänzl, K.F. "Lydia Thompson." Extracted from the *Encyclopaedia of the Musical Theatre*.
home.att.net/~mforder/THEATREhtm.

"Ghosts in the Theatre." Article in "Rubin's Corner" 1998, *Mersinger Theatrical Services*.
www.1501broadway.com/library/1098.txt

Gioia, Ted. "The Prehistory of Jazz: The Africanization of American Music," 1997.
www.allaboutjazz.com/journalists/Gioia4.htm

"Gospel Music," Africana.com
www.african.com/tt_653.htm

Griggs, Linda D. "Wayfaring Stranger: The Black Dutch, German Gypsies, or Chicanere, and Their Relations to the Melungeon." Reprinted from the *Patrin Web Journal*, 2000.
www.geocities.com/Paris/5121/melungeon.htm

Haurin, Don, and Ann Richens. "Irish Step Dancing: A Brief History."
www.7.50megs.com/aerobin/irdance/irhist.html

"Henriette Delille."
mo.essortment.com/henriettedelill_rqbj.htm

Higgins, Jon Borthwick. "A Brief History of Classical Dance From South India." Excerpt from Ph.D. thesis "The Music of Bharata Natyam," vol. I, 1973, pp. 3–9.
www-acc.scu.edu/~ajuner/bharatapage.html

Hindle, Theresa. "History of Clogs & Clog Dancing in Great Britain Especially around Hyndburn, East Lancashire."
www.cougaro1.co.uk/History/

"History of Storyville."
www.thestoryvilledistrict.com/

Irving, Gordon. "Little Titch."
www.bigginhill.co.uk/littletitch.htm

Jenkins, George. "How the Irish Became White." Based on the book, *How the Irish Became White* by Noel Ignatiev.
home.earthlinl.net/~ekistics10/mcnair/nltr9803.htm

Johnson, Chevel. "Hollywood or Sainthood? Slave descendant's story piques interest to dismay of beatification supporters."
www.s-t.com/daily/o4-99/04-04-99/e0li161.htm

Jung, Ashton. "Creole in Black and White."
www.loyno.edu/~tlkinnon/Creoles.htm

Kennedy, Brent. "The Melungeons: An Untold Story of Ethnic Cleansing in America." Published in *Islamic Horizons magazine*, Nov/Dec issue 1994. Extracted from his book, *The Melungeons: The*

Resurrection of a Proud People (Mercer University Press, 1994).
207.138.41.133/group/islam-1/message/863

"Kentucky Running Set."
www.cam.ac.uk/societies/round/dances/krs/

Kippen, Cameron. "The History of Clogs," 2000.
www.curtin.edu.au/curtin/dept/physio/podiatry/clog.html

"Le Cakewalk."
rockandswing.multimania.com/divers/ckaewalk.htm

"Lotta Crabtree."
www.zpub.com/sf/history/crab.html

MacKinnon, Richard. "Square Dancing: The Historical Geography of an American Folk Custom."
www.heritagedance.com/HISTORY/am_folk.html

"Melungeons in General."
freepages.geneology.rootsweb.com/~gowenrf/msie.htm

"Methodists in the Metropolis."
users.drew.edu/~kknaack/intro.html

Micheletti, Ellen. "All About Romance: The Free Black Men and Women of New Orleans and the Placage System."
www.likesbooks.com/neworleans.html

Minges, Patrick Neal. "All My Slaves, whether Negroes, Indians, Mustees, or Mulattoes: Towards a Thick Description of 'Slave Religion,'" 1999.
users.interport.net/~wovoka/aar99.html

_____. "Beneath the Underdog: Race Religion and the 'Trail of Tears,'" 1994, 1998.
www.users.interport.net/~wovoka/underdg7.html

Mourat, Elizabeth Artemis. "The Veil and Oriental Dance." From her manuscript, "The Illusive Veil."
www.shira.net/veilhistory.htm

"Moving Uptown: Nineteenth-century Views of Manhattan."
www.nypl.org/research/chss/spe/art/print/exhibits/movinguo/labelvi.htm

Mroueh, Youssef. "In America Before Columbus."
users.erols.com/zenithco/index.html

Mystical World Wide Web, "Folklore of Eggs."
www.mystical-www.co.uk/eggs.htm

Neuwirth, Jessica, and Matthew Cochran. "Archeology in the East Wing of the Brice House, Annapolis, Maryland."
www.bsos.umd.edu/anth/bricearch.htm

"Outline of the Louisiana Civil Code: A Note on the Black Code."
www.Law.tulane.edu/library/special/civil/outl.htm

Paine, Albert Bigelow, editor. From Mark Twain's *Autobiography*. New York: Harper & Bros., 1924.
Etext.lib.virginia.edu/railton/omstage/mtauto.html

Pawlicki, Father James. "The Sisters of the Holy Family."
members.aol.com/srdechantl/hfamily/

Rath, Richard Cullen. "Drums and Power: Ways of Creolizing Music in Coastal South Carolina and Georgia, 1730–1790." To appear in *Creolization in the Americas: Cultural Adaptions to the New World*, ed. by Steven Reinhardt and David Buisseret (Arlington, TX: Texas A & M Press).
way.net/creole/drumsandpower.html

"Religion and Resistance"; Chapter One: "Red, Black and White in the Old South."
users.rcn.com/wovoka/Pmchap1-07.htm

Riding, Joyce. "Music and Dance of the Appalachian Mountains of North America," 1997.
freespace.virgin.net/michael.jackson/shredded/appdana.html

Sevilla, Paco, "Flamenco: The Early Years." First appeared in the magazine *Jaleo*, vol. VIII, no. 1.
www.arts.unimelb.edu.au/amu/ucr/student/1996/j.flower/projects/hist.htm

"Slavery/Free Will/Revivalism/Second American Awakening."
www.piney.com/RevivAwk.html

Smith, Ernie. "Crazy Feet." From "Black Traditions in American Dance." The Alvin Ailey American Dance Center/Fordham BFA Program.
web.mit.edu/defrantz/ailey/BlackTrad/syllabus.htm

"Square Dancing: History and Heritage."
www.geocities.com/Nashville/Opry/5154/histeng.htm

"Tap Dance's Irish Roots."
www.iol.ie/~ronalan/tapdnce.html

Tawakul, Mobin. "The Spiritual Struggles of Enslaved African Muslims in the Americas from the 16th Century through Early 19th Century."
www.personal.ewngin.umich.edu/~mtawakul/islamclass.html

Thompson, Robert Farris. "An Aesthetic of the Cool: West African Dance Culture." From "Black Traditions in American Dance," p.85–102. The Alvin Ailey American Dance Center/Fordham BFA Program.
web.mit.edu/defrantz/ailey/BlackTrad/syllabus.htm

Weiss, P. "Henriette Delille: Servant of the Slaves." Information taken from Ann Ball, author of *Modern Saints*, vol. I and II.
members.aol.com/blfrdamien/delille.htm

"What's Flamenco?"
www.flamenco-world.com/what/what.htm

Wilson, Leon F. "The Mathematics of Miscegenation: The Code Noir," 1999.
www.kwaku.org/rm/code_noir.htm

"Women of the West: Adah Isaacs Menken."
www.tu-chemnitz.de/phil/amerikanistik/projekte/west/adah.htm

Index

Numbers in bold refer to illustrations and photographs

Purcella Brothers 140
Puck, Eva and Harry 140

quack (dance step) 208
quadrille (dance) 32, 36, 64, 68, 177, 194–196, **195**, 215–6 *(n. 14)*, 219 *(n. 26)*, 223 *(n. 52)*, 247 *(n. 17)*
quadroon balls 34–36, 37, 206
Quashdiddle, Dinah Rumpfizz 83
Queen, Johnny **112**, 113, 235 *(n. 27)*
"Queen of Tap" (Alice Whitman) 148
Queen Victoria *see* Victoria, Queen of England
quills (musical instrument) 14, 219 *(n. 19)*

rabbit hash (dance) 49, 221 *(n. 30)*
"race improvement" organizations 68
racial classifications 34, 217 *(n. 6)*
racial epithets, derived from dance 84, 222 *(n. 36)*
ragtime 69, 114, 124, 125, 209
Randall, Lew 141, 237 *(n. 15)*
Ransome, John 135
rattle (dance step) 208
rattlesnake jig (dance) 86
Rector, Eddie 147, 207, 239 *(n. 43)*
The Red Crook 159
Reed, Dave (David) 103, **104**, 129
Reed, Leonard 130, 131, 148, 238–9 *(n. 39)*
"Reed Birds" 103
reel (dance) 7, 12, 16, 32, 36, 64, 88, 90, 91, 97, 110, 146, 177, 184, 191, 235 *(n. 27)*, 247 *(n. 17)*; in clog dancing 16
Relf, Harry *see* Little Tich
Remington, Mayme 147
reverse cramproll turns (dance step) 209
Rhapsody in Taps 210
rhumba (dance) 29, 30
rhythm as communication 39, 204; in African dance 23; in Indian dance 169; in Irish dance 13, 204; in nautch dance 169, 204; using instruments 23, 48–9, 204, 223 *(n. 49)*; *see also* covert messages
Rice, Dan 231 *(n. 26)*
Rice, Thomas Dartmouth ("Daddy") 44, 78–85, **78**, **79**, **82**, **84**, **85**, 94, 198, 204, 206, 226 *(n. 9)*, 228 *(n. 14)*, 228 *(n. 1, n. 2, n. 3, n. 4)*, 229 *(n. 5, n. 8, n. 9)*, 230 *(n. 10, n. 12)*, 231 *(n. 21, n. 23, n. 30)*, 234 *(n. 3)*, 236 *(n. 1, n. 3)*
Ricketts, John B. 75, 227 *(n. 5, n. 6)*

The Rifle 78
ring dances, African 26, 101–2, 201, 215 *(n. 5)*; calenda 29; capoeira 49; Celtic 7; chica; 29; juba 30; ring shout 57, 59–62, 97, 103, 185, 203, 205, 224 *(n. 17, n. 31)*, 238 *(n. 35)*; Shaker 177
ring plays 225 *(n. 23)*
ring shout (dance) 57, 59–62, 97, 103, 185, 203, 205, 224 *(n. 17, n. 31)*, 238 *(n. 35)*; origin of name 61–2
rising fifth 7
ritual bathing 187
Ritz Brothers 140
rival dance 139
Robin Hood, in Morris dance 20
Robinson, Bill "Bojangles" 121–2, 141, 142, 147, 149, 234 *(n. 19)*, 239 *(n. 43, n. 44)*, 248 *(n. 17)*
Robinson Crusoe, or Harlequin Friday 73
Rock, Billy 238 *(n. 26)*
Rogers, Will 163
roll (dance step) 121
Romeo and Juliet 9
Rooney, Pat, Jr. 142–143, **143**
Rose and Moon 140
Ross, Alex 102
roughhouse dance 138–9
round dances, jig as 9
Roussel 73
Rowley, Bob *see* Bobolink Bob
Royal, Tommy 152
rubber legs (dance) 146
Runnin' Wild 238 *(n. 22)*
running set *see* Kentucky running set
"running sperichils" 59
running upon the heels (dance step) 74, 86, 234 *(n. 4)*
Russell, Lillian 123, 237 *(n. 5)*
Ryan, Ben 141

Saint-a Louis pass (dance step) 119
St. Denis, Ruth 155, 159, 240 *(n. 15)*
Salle d'Orleans 35, 218 *(n. 11)*
Sambo 125
Sand, George 156
sand dance 118, 121, 139, 142, 149, 152; Egyptian sand dance 142; in nautch dancing 169; sand jig 106, 109, 139, 237 *(n. 12)*; soft shoe sand dance 139
sand jig *see* sand dance
Sands, Richard "Dick" (George R.) 97, 105
Sanford, Jim (James) 89, 103
Santley, Mabel 161
Sapp, Kid 131
Scandinavians, influence upon development of jig 12

schottiche clog 152
schottische (dance) 174
schühplattler 44, 174–5, 202, 242 *(n. 16)*
Scott, Jem 65
Seamon and Somers 110
seasoning of slaves 28, 33
"second John Diamond" (Frank Lynch) 94, 105
Seeley Blossom 148
Segal, Vivienne 163
Seminole corn dance 62
Seminoles 184, 243 *(n. 10)*
set 193
set de flo' (dance) 50–1, 193, 224 *(n. 13)*
settin' the flo' *see* set de flo'
sevens (dance step) 209
Sexton, Bert 112
Seymour, Dainty Katie 154
Shaker dance: floor patterns 177; influenced by African-American and Native American 177; justification for 175; possession in 178; use in minstrel shows 178–180, **179**
Shakers 175–81, 204, 216 *(n. 20)*, 225 *(n. 20)*, 242 *(n. 4, n. 6, n. 9, n. 13)*
Shakespeare, William 8, 9, 73, 113, 128
shaklers 186, 204, 244 *(n. 19)*
Shango 32–3, 216 *(n. 17)*, 231 *(n. 21)*
Sharp, Cecil 246 *(n. 12)*, 247 *(n. 22)*
shave and a haircut (dance step) 209
Shawn, Ted 240 *(n. 15)*
shell shakers *see* shaklers
Sheridan, John F. 115
Sheridan and Mack (John F. and James H.) 115
shillelagh, use in Irish dance 13, 241 *(n. 10)*
shim sham shimmy (dance) 148, 238–9 *(n. 39)*
shimmy (dance) 29, 37, 209, 238–9 *(n. 39)*
shingle 66
"shoe clapping" dances 174
"shoe music" 14, 16
shoes *see* footwear
"Shoo Fly" 103, 108
shout 225 *(n. 20, n. 21)*; etymology of 61–62
shouters, dancers in ring shout 60; Spiritual Baptists 33, 216 *(n. 20)*
shouting 33, 59
Showboat 240 *(n. 3)*
showboats 103, 117, 127–9
"showing your stuff" 66
Shubert Brothers 162
shuffle (dance) 129

792.78   Knowles, Mark,
KNO   1954-

          Tap roots.

$35.00